CONTENT AREA READING

CONTENT AREA READING

Teaching and Learning in an Age of Multiple Literacies

Maureen McLaughlin
East Stroudsburg University of Pennsylvania

Boston • New York • San Francisco
Mexico City • Montreal • Toronto • London • Madrid • Munich • Paris
Hong Kong • Singapore • Tokyo • Cape Town • Sydney

Vice President, Editor-in-Chief:	Aurora Martínez Ramos
Associate Sponsoring Editor:	Shannon Steed
Associate Sponsoring Editor:	Barbara Strickland
Senior Development Editor:	Hope Madden
Editorial Assistants:	Jacqueline Gillen and Amy Foley
Vice President, Marketing and Sales Strategies:	Emily Williams Knight
Vice President, Director of Marketing:	Quinn Perkson
Executive Marketing Manager:	Krista Clark
Production Editor:	Janet Domingo
Editorial Production Service:	Nesbitt Graphics, Inc.
Composition Buyer:	Linda Cox
Manufacturing Buyer:	Megan Cochran
Electronic Composition:	Nesbitt Graphics, Inc.
Interior Design:	Carol Somberg
Photos:	Maureen McLaughlin
Cover Administrator:	Linda Knowles

For related titles and support materials, visit our online catalog at www.pearsonhighered.com.

Between the time website information is gathered and then published, it is not unusual for some sites to have closed. Also, the transcription of URLs can result in typographical errors. The publisher would appreciate notification where these errors occur so that they may be corrected in subsequent editions.

Library of Congress Cataloging-in-Publication Data

McLaughlin, Maureen.
    Content area reading : teaching and learning in an age of multiple literacies / Maureen McLaughlin.
        p. cm.
ISBN 0-205-48661-4
1. Content area reading.   I. Title.
LB1050.455.M48 2010
428.4071–dc22   2009026211

Printed in the United States of America

10 9 8 7 6 5 4 3 2 1 [EDW] 13 12 11 10 09

www.pearsonhighered.com

ISBN-10:   0-205-48661-4
ISBN-13: 978-0-205-48661-8

ABOUT the AUTHOR

Maureen McLaughlin is department chair and professor of reading education at East Stroudsburg University of Pennsylvania. She earned her doctorate at Boston University in reading and language development. Prior to her tenure at the University, Maureen spent fifteen years as a classroom teacher, reading specialist, and department chair in a public school system.

A member of the Board of Directors of the International Reading Association from 2005–2008, Maureen is the author of numerous publications about the teaching of reading, reading comprehension, and content area literacies, including *Critical Literacy: Enhancing Students' Reading Comprehension, Guided Comprehension in Grades 3–8,* and *Guided Comprehension in the Primary Grades.* A frequent speaker at international, national, and state conferences, Maureen is a consultant to school districts and universities throughout the United States and Canada.

For Connor Michael Watkins
I hope you will learn well, think deeply,
and pursue your dreams.

CONTENTS

CHAPTER 3
Standards-Based Teaching and High-Stakes Assessments 27

PART TWO

CHAPTER 4
Comprehending Content Area Text 42

CHAPTER 5
Using Comprehension Strategies to Guide Thinking   62

CHAPTER 6
Using Comprehension Strategies to Extend Thinking   78

CHAPTER 7
Teaching Vocabulary in the Content Areas   93

CHAPTER 8
Organizing for Teaching and Learning   112

CHAPTER 9
Teaching Culturally and Linguistically Diverse Students   138

PART THREE

CHAPTER 10
Writing in the Content Areas   157

CHAPTER 11

Using Technology in the Content Areas 178

CHAPTER 12
Inquiry: Key to Critical and Creative Thinking in the Content Areas   194

CHAPTER 13
Poetry, Drama, Music, and Art: Alternative Representations of Thinking   211

APPENDIX A   271

APPENDIX B 321

APPENDIX C 336

APPENDIX D 356

APPENDIX E 369

APPENDIX F 376

REFERENCES 381

NAME INDEX 391

SUBJECT INDEX 395

PREFACE

I have written this book because I believe that teaching in the content areas is an exciting, innovative, student-centered practice. I believe that, as teachers, we have the knowledge and ability to motivate students to learn. I think that integrating what we know about best practice, student engagement, multiple literacies, reading as a thinking process, and innovative instructional techniques provides a solid foundation for teaching and learning.

This book is a unique addition to the existing list of content area texts because it is a complete, student-centered resource for grades six through twelve. It uses a series of features to help students "make connections" between what they read and how they apply this in the classroom. It transitions theory into practice and features a wide-range of innovative instructional approaches. The teaching ideas are initially taught using explicit instruction to scaffold student learning. Student examples from a variety of disciplines are featured throughout the text, and the book includes a variety of teaching resources that are readily available. The central theme of this text is multiple literacies and their effects on today's teachers and classrooms. In the past, being literate required only that we be able to read and write, but in today's world, we need to be fluent in multiple literacies that require us not only to be able to read and write, but also to understand a variety of disciplines, navigate myriad information sources, examine the author's intent, and comprehend beyond the printed page. Skills of the 21st century are also associated with multiple literacies, particularly information literacy and the use of the Internet. Chapters 2 and 11 integrate 21st century skills in our teaching of Content Area Reading. These skills range from question generation to how to effectively search a topic to using such literacies to research. Among other topics, the book features information about educational standards, comprehension strategies, teaching ideas, and innovative approaches. Resource-filled appendixes are also included.

This is a desktop resource to be used throughout your teaching career. It is a practical guide to teaching for understanding in the content areas at middle and high school levels. It is a complete information source—a book that will emerge dog-eared and well-used over the years.

I should also tell you that I am a certified content area teacher, and whether inservice or preservice, I think of all of us as teachers. This is why I refer to us as "we" throughout the text. We are in this together. We will learn and then we will teach, encouraging our content area students to reach their greatest potentials, as we continue our quest to become the best possible teachers.

ORGANIZATION OF THE BOOK

The book is organized in four sections. In Part One, we begin by learning about our students and innovations in content area teaching. Then we explore multiple literacies (adolescent literacy, discipline-specific literacies, critical literacy, information literacy, media literacy, and multicultural literacy) and how we, as teachers, can help our students to actively participate in them. Next, we learn about educational standards and high-stakes testing. We make connections between state standards and instruction, as we examine teacher-authored lessons. We also discuss high stakes testing and how it impacts teaching and learning.

Helping students learn course content is the focus of Part Two. In Chapters 4, 5, and 6 we contemplate reading comprehension and learn about the repertoire of strategies that readers use to construct meaning. We examine teaching ideas related to each strategy and student examples of each. We also discuss the literacy professionals who support us in our content area teaching. Next, Chapter 7 explores vocabulary, focusing on current best practice and ideas for teaching vocabulary effectively. In Chapter 8 we consider how to organize for learning and teach essential skills, such as generating questions and study skills. This is also the section of the book in which a lesson plan focused on engaging, guiding, and extending student thinking is introduced. In Chapter 9 we learn how to teach culturally and linguistically diverse students in content area classrooms.

In Part Three, we continue to focus on teaching our students how to actively engage in learning. We explore how to help them use writing to learn and to express their ideas in a variety of formats in Chapter 10. Then we focus on integrating technology in the content areas in Chapter 11. In Chapters 12 and 13 we examine inquiry-based learning and how students can use alternative modes, such as poetry, drama, art, and music to represent their thinking. In Chapter 12 we explore inquiry-based learning, a project-oriented teaching method in which students generate questions to gain deeper understanding. Alternative modes of representation, such as poetry, drama, art, and music, are the focus of Chapter 13. These alternative modes permeate all content areas and provide students with unique ways to express their knowledge.

Assessment and professional development are the focuses of Part Four. In Chapter 14 we learn about assessment that is dynamic, authentic, reflective, and standards-based. In the final chapter we explore how to become lifelong learners by experiencing success in our teaching, participating in mentoring programs, and engaging in professional development.

The appendixes feature materials designed to support teaching and learning. The appendixes are organized in six sections and include a variety of reproducible pages related to teaching ideas, skills, writing, checklists and rubrics, alternative modes of representation, and project examples.

SPECIAL FEATURES

Throughout the book, special features focus on issues of importance to content area teachers. The features are designed to extend understanding of key concepts and encourage you to think about the issues in greater depth.

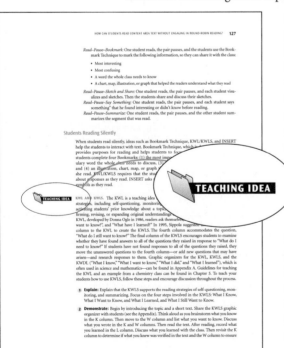

■ **Teaching Idea** icons found throughout chapter margins highlight practical strategies to use across content areas. Teaching Ideas that are specific to fostering student comprehension feature 5-steps of explicit instruction: 1. explain, 2. demonstrate, 3. guide, 4. practice, 5. reflect. After learning how to teach the strategies, you will see applications of each strategy-based Teaching Idea within content-specific classroom examples. Student artifacts, student dialogues, and student writing samples show the real-life application of the Teaching Ideas.

■ Every chapter opens with a **Chapter Overview** highlighting the key questions addressed within each chapter. Chapter Overviews also include a complete list of the Teaching Ideas presented in the chapter.

Chapters are supported by feature streams designed to enhance comprehension by "making connections":

■ **Making Connections to Multiple Literacies** links chapter topics to aspects of different literacies, including adolescent literacy, discipline-specific literacies, critical literacy, information literacy, media literacy, and multicultural literacy.

■ **Making Connections to Struggling Readers** applies chapter topics to issues associated with struggling readers.

■ **Making Connections to English Learners** explores issues related to teaching English language learners.

■ **Making Connections to Writing** links chapter topics to writing opportunities.

■ **Making Connections to Study Skills** associates chapter topics with ideas for teaching study skills to support student learning.

■ **Making Connections** boxes encourage you to actively engage in learning by posing a question and asking you to think about a response and share your ideas with a small group.

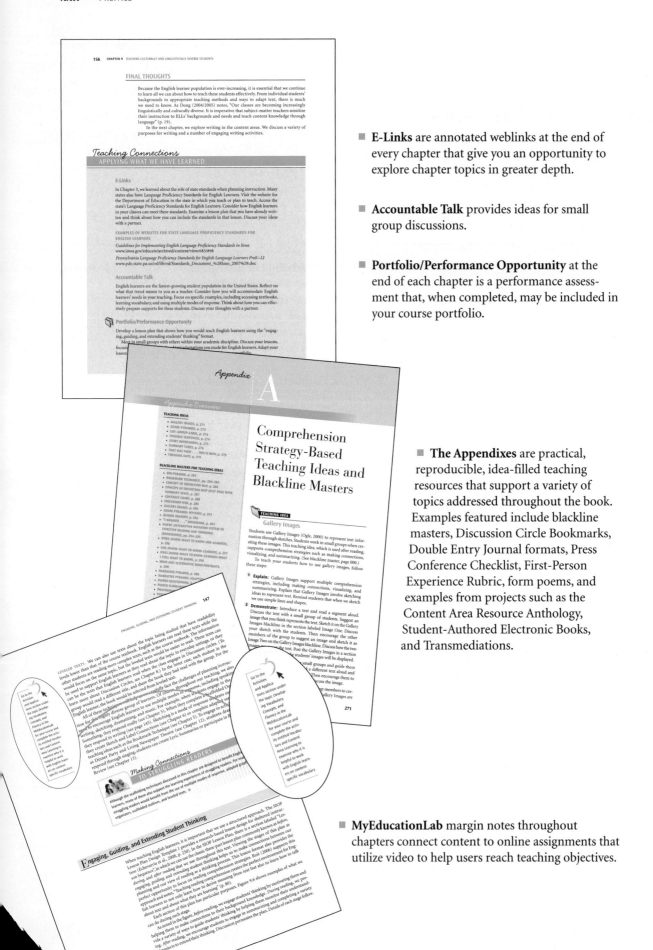

- **E-Links** are annotated weblinks at the end of every chapter that give you an opportunity to explore chapter topics in greater depth.

- **Accountable Talk** provides ideas for small group discussions.

- **Portfolio/Performance Opportunity** at the end of each chapter is a performance assessment that, when completed, may be included in your course portfolio.

- **The Appendixes** are practical, reproducible, idea-filled teaching resources that support a variety of topics addressed throughout the book. Examples featured include blackline masters, Discussion Circle Bookmarks, Double Entry Journal formats, Press Conference Checklist, First-Person Experience Rubric, form poems, and examples from projects such as the Content Area Resource Anthology, Student-Authored Electronic Books, and Transmediations.

- **MyEducationLab** margin notes throughout chapters connect content to online assignments that utilize video to help users reach teaching objectives.

SUPPLEMENTS and LEARNING AIDS

The following supplements provide an outstanding array of resources that facilitate learning about content area reading. For more information, ask your local Pearson Education representative or contact the Pearson Faculty Field Support Department at 1-800-526-0485. For technology support, please contact technical support directly at 1-800-677-6337 or http://247 .pearsoned.com. Many of the supplements can be downloaded from the Instructor Resource Center at www.pearsonhighered.com/irc.

Resources for Instructors

INSTRUCTOR'S MANUAL. The Instructor's Manual includes a wealth of interesting ideas and activities designed to help instructors teach the course. Each chapter includes a chapter-at-a-glance grid, the chapter purpose, underlying concepts, learning objectives, vocabulary and key concepts, and activities and discussion questions for before, during, and after reading. (Available for download from the Instructor Resource Center at www.pearsonhighered.com/irc.)

TEST BANK. The Test Bank has more than 500 questions and includes short answer, multiple choice, and true/false questions. Page references to the main text, suggested answers, and skill types have been added to each question to help instructors create and evaluate student tests. (Available for download from the Instructor Resource Center at www.pearsonhighered.com/irc.)

TESTGEN COMPUTERIZED TEST BANK. The printed Test Bank is also available electronically through Allyn & Bacon's computerized testing system, TestGen. The user-friendly interface enables instructors to view, edit, and add questions, transfer questions to tests, and print tests in a variety of fonts. Search and sort features allow instructors to locate questions quickly and arrange them in any preferred order. (Available for download from the Instructor Resource Center at www.pearsonhighered.com/irc.)

POWERPOINT™ PRESENTATION. Ideal for classroom presentations and student handouts, the PowerPoint™ Presentation created for this text provides dozens of ready-to-use graphic and text images. (Available for download from the Instructor Resource Center at www.pearsonhighered.com/irc.)

Resources for Students

Grounding teacher education in real classrooms— among real teachers and students and among actual examples of students' and teachers' work—is an important, and perhaps even an essential, part of training teachers for the complexities of teaching today's  students in today's classrooms. We have created a website that provides you and your students with the context of real classrooms and artifacts that research on teacher education tell us is so important. Through authentic in-class video footage, interactive skill-building exercises and more, MyEducationLab offers you and your students a uniquely valuable teacher education tool.

In *Content Area Reading: Teaching and Learning in an Age of Multiple Literacies,* look for the MyEducationLab logo and directive within the margins. Follow the directive and the simple navigation instruction to access the multimedia *Activities and Applications* assignments in MyEducationLab that correspond with the chapter topics.

- The Activities and Applications exercises offer opportunities to understand content more deeply and are explicitly connected to chapter topics. These exercises present thought-provoking questions that probe the students' understanding of the concept that is presented in the text through classroom footage or teacher and student artifacts.

The rich, authentic, and interactive elements that support the Activities and Applications you will encounter throughout MyEducationLab include:

- **Videos**: The authentic classroom videos in MyEducationLab show how real teachers handle actual classroom situations.
- **Artifacts**: Authentic student and teacher classroom artifacts offer practice in working with the actual types of materials encountered every day by teachers.
- **Lesson & Portfolio Builder**: With this effective and easy-to-use tool, students can create, update, and share standards-based lesson plans and portfolios.

Visit www.myeducationlab.com for a demonstration of this exciting new online teaching resource.

ACKNOWLEDGMENTS

I offer my sincere appreciation to Aurora Martinez, Executive Editor, at Allyn and Bacon for her amazing expertise and perseverance. I am also deeply indebted to Shannon Steed, Managing Editor, at Allyn and Bacon for the extraordinary knowledge and endless patience she demonstrated throughout the publication process.

Of course, as always, there are a number of colleagues and students who have supported me throughout the writing of this book. I acknowledge them now for their myriad contributions, but most especially for their boundless enthusiasm.

I am particularly grateful to:

Dr. Maryellen Vogt, Professor Emerita, California State University, Long Beach

Dr. Richard Allington, Professor of Education, University of Tennessee

Dr. Stephanie Romano, Alexandria Gibb, and Matthew W. Baker

Susan Matol, Lisa Jaferis, Christine Godiska, Lucia Martins, and Salina Lewandowski

Maria Archer, Bobbie Jo Balmer, Jason Engerman, Zach Hester, Jeanette Male, Justin McCord, and Brandon Salvatore

Joshua C. Miller, Cali Roberts, Telsa Sparks, Crystal Pierce, Liz Rega, Carolyn Meral, Nancy Roman, Jamie Harbaugh, Amanda Popielski, and Joanne Blackledge

Stephen Inghrim, Louis Pacchioli, Ken Gilbride, Javier Martinez, Janice Rodriguez, Kristi Streightiff, and Edit Vergara

Dan O'Brien, Polson School District, Montana

Dave Fitzpatrick, Charlo School District, Montana

Sue Moore, Glenn Blake, and Polly Dupuis

Dr. Maryellen Mross, Principal, Junior High School and Jeffrey Sodl, Principal, High School, Stroudsburg Area School District, Pennsylvania

Janet Domingo, Production Editor

Dee Josephson, project management for Nesbitt Graphics, Inc.

I have received thoughtful input from the following educators who offered comments on the manuscript chapters:

Mary L. Agnew, *University of Maryland Eastern Shore*
Jill A. Aguilar, *California State University, Dominguez Hills*
Brett Elizabeth Blake, *St. John's University*
Leslie W. Crawford, *Georgia College & State University*
Stephenie Hewett, *The Citadel*
Carol Jones, *Pasco-Hernando Community College*
Dr. Dana Key, *The University of Alabama*
Dr. Barry Mitchell, *BYU Hawaii*
Jennifer McCarty Plucker, *Augsburg College and Eastview High School*
Cynthia E. Sharp, *Nevada Department of Education*
Barbara Stanley, *Valdosta State University*
Barbara Jean Van Meter, *Montgomery College*
Erin K. Washburn, *Texas A&M University*

I also extend thanks to the members of the advisory council who offered their expertise and advice on multiple aspects of the text and supplements throughout the development process:

Dee Acklie, *College of Saint Mary*; Randy Allman, *Seminole County Public Schools*; Cheryl Almeida, *Johnson & Wales University*; Samantha Alperin, *Christian Brothers University*; Nedra Atwell, *Western Kentucky University*; JuliAnna Avila, *Georgia Southern University*; Norma S. Blecker, *Richard Stockton College*; Connie Bowman, *University of Dayton*; Jane Brower, *University of Tennessee at Chattanooga*; Kathy Bunch, *Polk County School District*; Jeanne Clidas, *Roberts Wesleyan College*; Ann Corfman, *Urbana University*; Karen Dunnagan, *Spalding University*; Virginia Fender, *University of Texas at Tyler*; Adrian Fernandez, *A Career In Teaching*; Lynne Gelinas, *Brevard Public Schools*; Brenda Gunnell, *Crosby Middle School*; Arlene M. Hall, *Murray State University*; Kirsten Dara Hill, *University of Michigan-Dearborn*; Diann Huber, *iteachTEXAS*; Dennis Jacobsen, *Cal Poly University, Pomona*; Carla G. Jankowski; Brandeis Johnson, *The New Teacher Project*; Larry J. Kelly, *Texas A&M University*; Diana F. Kelly, *Southern University and A & M College*; Misty LaCour, *University of West Florida*; Sharon Lekawski, *Houston ISD ACP*; Sharen Lom, *Alternate Route to Certification*; Vicki A. McGinley, *West Chester University;* Martha L. Meyer, *University of Dayton*; Roxane Moore, *California State University Fullerton*; Laura Neidringhaus, *Garden Grove Elementary*; Roxanne Farwick Owens, *DePaul University*; David D. Paige, *Bellarmine University*; Priya Parmar, *Brooklyn College - CUNY*; James Pelech, *Benedictine University*; Placida McDonald, *Dallas Alternative Certification Program*; Sue A. Poston, *Cardinal Stritch University*; Debbie Powell, *University of North Carolina at Wilmington*; Kalyani Rai, *University of Wisconsin, Milwaukee*; Linda Reetz, *CESA 6*; Patricia Ruff, *Mount Saint Mary College*; Maureen Siera, *St. Martin's University*; Susan Simpson, *Bowling Green State University*; Jayna Snyder, *Surfside Elementary*; Barbara Stanley, *Valdosta State University*; Anna Stave, *SUNY College at Oneonta*; Janice Strop, *Cardinal Stritch University*; Kay Teehan, *Bartow Middle School*; Julie Thomas, *Polk County Public Schools*; Kristen Turner, *Fordham University*; Miriam. A. Ward, *Oklahoma State University*; A. Lee Williams, *Slippery Rock University*; Pamela Zhu, *Campbellsville University.*

1

Chapter Overview

Teaching in the 21st Century

If you are reading this book, you are probably either a preservice or inservice teacher of science, mathematics, social science, language, the arts, physical education, or some other content area. Chances are you have completed many course hours in your area of specialization and you are now very knowledgeable about your field. You know the content. You know how to plan and teach lessons. So you may find yourself wondering, "What could be left to learn?" The answer is an essential element of teaching and learning. You are going to learn how to teach your students to be strategic thinkers—to access texts, to question, and, ultimately, to create personal meeting. This book will build on all that you already know and deepen your understanding of your content area. It will enable you to see how strategic thinking can help your students to read texts and reason through issues.

Our job is to teach our discipline-specific content with the knowledge and expertise of those who fully understand the subject area, including the types of thinking and the literacies it involves. We will use what our students know about reading to help them think through the content areas. We will teach our students how to use multiple literacies, including discipline-specific literacies, information literacy, and critical literacy, to help them fully access and understand the content we teach. When we view reading this way—as a thinking process—it helps us and our students to understand at deeper levels.

Now that we know why we are taking this course and reading this book, you may be wondering, (1) "What are our goals?" (2) "What kind of teachers will we strive to become?" (3) What kinds of students will we teach?" (4) "What will we teach?" (5) "How will constructivism support our teaching?" (6) "What roles will motivation and engagement play in our teaching?" (7) "What kinds of texts will we use?" (8) "What will we learn?" and (9) "How will we begin?" All these questions and more are probably racing through your minds. Let's begin our time together by responding to each of them.

What Are Our Goals?

As content area teachers, our overarching goal is to teach our students to the best of our abilities within the framework of best practice—that is, current research-based theories and beliefs that have been proven to be effective in the classroom. We will also make connections between best practice and the national and state standards that have been developed for our content area. (For a detailed discussion of the role of state standards in our teaching, see Chapter 3.)

Another goal we have is to engage our students in learning. We will embrace motivation and make it a part of everything we do. We will encourage our students to be active learners and teach the most cutting-edge information in ways that will inspire our students. We will scaffold our students' learning experiences so they become strong, independent thinkers. Finally, we will encourage our students to show what they know by using their knowledge and experience to support their performances.

We will expand our perception of context and view curriculum, activity, classroom environment, teaching, talk, text, and society as context (Duke, 2001). We will support researchers' and practitioners' belief that it is impossible to separate teaching and learning from the contexts in which they are taught (Cambourne, 2002).

Of course, reflection, integration, and discussion will permeate our teaching. We don't want to teach our students to robotically regurgitate the information contained in texts. Instead, we will integrate multiple literacies and teach our students to be successful thinkers. They will analyze what they have learned in meaningful ways, and reflect on what they have learned and how they applied their knowledge. Throughout this process, we will encourage our students to question, to ponder, and to make connections to their everyday life experiences.

What Kind of Teachers Will We Strive to Become?

What does the research have to say about effective teachers? What qualities do we need to possess to successfully teach our content area? How do exceptional teachers characterize themselves? What is the theoretical framework from which they teach? In this segment of the chapter, we respond to these questions by examining the qualities of effective teachers and exploring how the constructivist theory of learning underpins their instruction.

Making Connections | **Thinking about Our Teachers**

- Think about your content area teachers. Who was the best content area teacher you ever had? What made learning with him or her memorable? What was it about his or her teaching that motivated you to learn? How did having this teacher influence your decision to teach? Share your thoughts in small-group discussions.

- Who was the worst content area teacher you ever had? What made learning with him or her such a negative experience? What could the teacher have done to make the experience better? How did having this teacher influence your decision to teach? Share your thoughts in small-group discussions.

The research has a great deal to say about the teachers we are striving to be. It describes them as "excellent" and "influential," and notes that teachers are valued participants in the learning process. As the National Commission on Teaching and America's Future (1997) has reported, the single most important strategy for achieving America's educational goals is to recruit, prepare, and support excellent teachers for every school.

Both researchers and professional organizations have described the characteristics of influential teachers (International Reading Association, 2000; Ruddell, 1995, 2004). The following characterizations of such teachers integrate their perceptions.

Influential teachers believe that all students can learn. They base their teaching on the needs of the individual child. They strive to reach all students, including English learners and struggling readers. They know that motivation and multiple kinds of texts are essential elements of teaching and learning. They understand that reading is a social constructivist process that functions best in authentic situations. They teach in print-rich, concept-rich environments.

The teachers we are striving to become have in-depth knowledge of various aspects of learning. They teach for a variety of purposes, using diverse methods, materials, and grouping patterns to focus on students' individual needs, interests, and learning styles. They know the strategies that good learners use and they can teach students how to use them. They create experiences and environments that introduce, nurture, and extend students' literacy abilities to engage with text. Their teaching frameworks include direct explanation, modeling, and scaffolding. They are aware of what is working well and what each student needs to be successful.

These teachers view their teaching as multifaceted, and they view themselves as participants in the learning process. They integrate their knowledge of the learning cycle, learning styles, and multiple intelligences into their teaching.

They understand the relationship between assessment and instruction, and they assess in multiple ways for a variety of purposes. They use instructional strategies that provide formative feedback to monitor the effectiveness of teaching and student performance. They know that assessment informs teaching as well as learning. They know that national policies, state standards, and state assessments contribute to the contexts in which they teach. (For more information about national and state standards, see Chapter 3.)

When asked which features they perceived as important to their teaching, influential teachers cite personal characteristics, understanding of learners' potential, attitudes toward their subject areas, life adjustments, and the quality of their instruction. Their thoughts are featured in Figure 1.1 (Ruddell, 2004, p. 983).

Making Connections | **Thinking about Ourselves as Teachers**

■ Consider issues 1 and 3 from the list of influential teachers' self-perceptions in Figure 1.1, and compare and contrast them with your own preservice/inservice self-perceptions.

■ Focus on what you perceive to be your strengths; then consider areas in which you may need to improve.

■ Share your thoughts with others in small-group discussions.

Whether the characteristics of influential teachers are derived from the perceptions of others or themselves, these teachers emerge as knowledgeable, thoughtful, well organized, creative, and actively engaged in the learning process. These teachers have the respect of students and colleagues. They are worthy models for those of us who strive to be successful teachers.

If we were to observe these teachers while they were engaged in instruction, we would notice that they

■ Develop and use standards-based lesson plans underpinned by a sound instructional framework.

■ Motivate students and demonstrate high expectations for learning.

■ Activate and integrate students' background knowledge and experiences in the construction of meaning.

1. Personal Characteristics
   - Have energy, commitment, and passion
   - Are warm and caring
   - Are flexible
   - Have high expectations of self

2. Understanding of Learner Potential
   - Are sensitive to individual needs, motivations, and aptitudes
   - Understand where students are developmentally
   - Place high demands on learners

3. Attitude Toward Subject
   - Have enthusiasm
   - Create intellectual excitement
   - Consider alternative points of view

4. Life Adjustment
   - Show concern with students as persons
   - Are attentive to academic problems and personal problems

5. Quality of Instruction
   - Make material personally relevant
   - Stress basic communication: clear writing, comprehension of text, critical thinking
   - Develop logical and strategy-oriented instruction: (a) clear statement of problems, (b) use of familiar concrete examples, (c) extension to more abstract examples, (d) analysis of abstract concepts involved, and (e) application of concepts to new contexts
   - Assist in identifying issues that should be considered before conclusions are reached
   - Engage students in the process of intellectual discovery

Source: Ruddell, 2004.

FIGURE 1.1
Influential Teachers' Shared Beliefs about Teaching

- Infuse higher-level thinking and questioning strategies into the learning experience.
- Use inquiry-based learning and a variety of text types and levels to encourage intellectual discovery.
- Encourage students to be active thinkers.
- Involve the learning community in meaning negotiation.
- Demonstrate sensitivity to individual students' needs, motivations, and abilities.
- Use a variety of instructional settings, including whole class, small groups, and pairs.
- Assess in multiple ways for a variety of purposes (McLaughlin & Allen, 2002; Ruddell, 1995, 2004).

The qualities of these teachers are extensive, but their value is clearly evident when observing instruction. In subsequent chapters, we will more fully explore these aspects of instruction and integrate them into our teaching.

What Kinds of Students Will We Teach?

Our students will be different from students of the past. We will teach the students of the 21st century, students who have been born into a digital age. They have never known a world without computers or the Internet. They have always had access to cell phones and text messaging and have always been able to download their favorite music to their computers and iPods. These students have always had access to traditional texts, such as books, magazines, newspapers, and electronic text either created by others or self-generated. These are the students of the 21st century, those whom many refer to as Millennials (Howe, 2005; Howe & Strauss, 2000, 2001; Moorman & Horton, 2007).

Howe and Strauss (2000) note that Millennials are the most educated and most diverse generation in history. They are optimists and team players, and they follow rules more readily and accept authority more easily than their parents did at their age. Further, Moorman and Horton (2007, pp. 264–265) point out:

> Millennials bring to school a unique set of skills, knowledge, and attributes unlike any other in history. . . . Today's adolescents read and write more, have a more realistic and broader view of the world, are more accomplished socially, and process information in fundamentally different ways than previous generations.

According to Howe and Strauss (2000), Millennials have seven distinguishing characteristics: They are special, sheltered, confident, team oriented, achieving, pressured, and conventional. When describing Millennials, Oblinger (2003, p. 38) reports that they

- Gravitate toward group activity.
- Identify with their parents' values and feel close to their parents.
- Spend more time doing homework and less time watching television.
- Believe "it is cool to be smart."
- Are fascinated by new technologies.
- Are racially and ethnically diverse.
- Often (one in five) have at least one immigrant parent.

She further observes that, "Along with differences in attitudes, Millennials exhibit distinct learning styles. For example, their learning preferences tend toward teamwork, experiential activities, structure, and use of technologies. Their strengths include multitasking, goal orientation, positive attitudes, and a collaborative style."

According to Dunn and Dunn (1993), *learning styles* describe the way learners interact with new information. We use our learning styles to focus on, process, internalize, and retain academic information. As seen in Figure 1.2, Dunn and Dunn (1993) characterize learners as visual, auditory, and kinesthetic/tactile. Because we do not all learn in the same way, the same instructional environment, methods, and resources will be effective for some learners and ineffective for others (Burke & Dunn, 2003).

Learning styles are evident in many modes, ranging from biochronological preferences to eating preferences to the different forms of representation we use to express what we know. For example, biochronological preferences include our preferred times for waking, learning, and studying. Interestingly, many students have preferences in this area that do not correspond to the hours during which we teach school. Eating preferences include how often we eat and portions we choose to eat. For example, some people may choose to eat just three meals a day, while others may choose to eat smaller portions five or six times a day.

Learning style preferences that relate to how we express what we know are of particular interest to us as teachers. We may often ask our students to provide either an oral or written

FIGURE 1.2
Types of Learners

Visual learners: Learn through seeing
- These learners need to see the teacher's facial expression and body language.
- They learn best from visual displays, including PowerPoint slide shows, overhead transparencies, illustrations, diagrams, videos, and handouts.

Auditory learners: Learn through listening
- These learners need to interpret voice, pitch, speed, and other aspects of speech. They need to hear information and often benefit from using tape recorders.
- They learn best through lectures, discussions, and listening to others.

Tactile/kinesthetic learners: Learn through doing, touching, and moving
- These learners need to actively explore to learn. They often have difficulty sitting for long periods of time.
- They learn best through hands-on activities such as projects.

response, because those are the response modes that teachers asked us to use. Oral and written responses are good choices, but we also need to offer students alternative modes of response—including sketching, dramatizing, and singing. In addition, we need to ensure that we integrate approaches such as project-based learning in our teaching.

Offering alternative modes of response accommodates students' strength modes of expression. Although offering multiple modes of response is motivational for all students, it is particularly beneficial for more global learners, who are often struggling readers. (For more information about how students can use alternative ways to represent ideas, see Chapter 13.)

Making Connections | Thinking about Learning Styles

■ Think about your learning styles. Do you consider yourself to be a visual learner? An auditory learner? A kinesthetic/tactile learner?

■ Consider your response and think about whether your strength modality was accommodated when you were a student in middle school or high school.

■ Think about how you will accommodate the needs of visual, auditory, and kinesthetic/tactile learners in your teaching.

■ Share your thoughts in small-group discussions.

Finally, Jason Frand (2000) perceives Millennials as having an information-age mindset. He characterizes this mindset as people who believe the following:

■ *Computers aren't technology.* Computers are just a part of life. Millennials believe this because they have never known life without computers.

■ *The Internet is better than television.* Television viewing is declining as time spent online is increasing. One reason for this trend may be the ample opportunities for socializing that the Internet provides.

■ *Reality is no longer real.* What seems to be real may not be. Digital images can be altered and email content may or may not be accurate.

■ *Doing is more important than knowing.* Being able to use knowledge is valued more than accumulating facts.

■ *Learning more closely resembles Nintendo than logic.* Losing is the fastest way to master the game, and losing represents learning.

■ *Multitasking is a way of life.* Students are comfortable doing more than one thing at once. For example, they may listen to music, do homework, and send instant messages simultaneously.

■ *Typing is preferred to handwriting.* Students believe their handwriting is not the best, but they can clearly communicate by using a keyboard.

■ *Staying connected is essential.* Students use multiple devices to maintain contact with family and friends throughout the day.

■ *There is zero tolerance for delays.* Students expect that service will always be available and that responses will be immediate.

■ *The lines between consumer and creator are blurring.* Students cut and paste information, blurring the lines among creator, owner, and consumer.

When reviewing the various characteristics of Millennials, those that relate to learning are of particular importance to us as teachers. We need to infuse those elements into our teaching. We can begin by ensuring that we (1) view technology not as an add-on to our coursework, but rather as a natural component of everyday teaching and learning; (2) make certain that cooperative and collaborative work permeates our courses; (3) accommodate students' needs to process information in different ways; and (4) adapt our teaching techniques to honor the diverse nature of Millennials.

What Will We Teach?

We will teach the standards-based content necessary for our courses and enrich it by integrating our knowledge of multiple literacies. We will begin by incorporating what we learn about the reading process. We will focus on students' background knowledge and teach strategies they can use to think through multiple types of text. Our work will be informed by national and state standards, as well as policy documents such as *Reading Next: A Vision for Action and Research in Middle and High School Literacy* (Biancarosa & Snow, 2006).

We will also teach our students other literacies, including critical literacy and new literacies such as information literacy, media literacy, and multicultural literacy. We will integrate all these literacies in our teaching and help our students learn to think and understand in new and exciting ways.

How Will Constructivism Support Our Teaching?

Teaching and learning are social constructivist processes. Constructivism is a theory about knowledge and learning. From a constructivist perspective, learning is understood as "a self-regulated process of resolving inner cognitive conflicts that often become apparent through concrete experience, collaborative discourse, and reflection" (Brooks & Brooks, 1993, p. vii). Constructivists believe that learners make sense of their world by connecting what they are learning to what they know and have experienced. They construct meaning through these connections when educators pose relevant problems, structure learning around primary concepts, seek and value students' ideas, and assess student learning in context (Brooks & Brooks, 1993).

According to Short and Burke (1996), constructivism frees students of fact-driven curricula and encourages them to focus on larger ideas. It also allows students to reach unique conclusions and reformulate ideas, and encourages them to see the world as a complex place with multiple perspectives. Finally, constructivism emphasizes that students are responsible for their own learning and should attempt to connect the information they learn to the world around them through inquiry.

Cambourne (2002, p. 26) suggests that constructivism has the following core theoretical assumptions:

- *What is learned cannot be separated from the context in which it is learned.* We cannot talk about what is learned separately from how it is learned because experiences do not lead to the same understanding. Our understanding is a function of the content, context, goals, and activity of the learner (Savery & Duffy, 1995).

- *The purposes or goals that the learner brings to the learning situation are central to what is learned.* The goal stimulates learning and determines what the learner attends to, what background knowledge he uses to construct meaning, and what understanding is constructed (Savery & Duffy, 1995).

- *Knowledge and meaning are socially constructed through the processes of negotiation, evaluation, and transformation.* Although the real world exists, there is no one correct set of meanings about it. Social interaction provides a medium for expanding our understanding.

Constructivists believe that students construct knowledge by linking what is new to what is already known. In reading, this concept is reflected in schema-based learning development, which purports that learning takes place when new information is integrated with what is already known. The more experience learners have with a particular topic, the easier it is for them to make connections between what they know and what they are learning (Anderson, 1994).

When we learn things or have experiences, we may store the information as background knowledge in our brains. We don't store everything we have ever experienced or learned, but rather what we deem to be important. For example, if we were asked what we ate for lunch a week ago, most of us wouldn't be able to respond correctly because what we ate for a meal seven days ago wasn't important enough for us to remember. But if we were asked what our favorite food was or who our best teacher was, we would be able to respond because that information was important enough to store in our brains. When we engage in reading as a social constructivist process, we construct meaning by making connections between what we are learning and what we have stored in our brains as background knowledge.

Discussion—a process that has cognitive, social, and affective dimensions—is an essential component of constructivism. It affords us opportunities to engage in higher-order thinking, interact with others, and take ownership of our learning (Almasi, 1996). Draper (2002) notes that it is through discussion that the teacher "comes to understand what the learner is prepared to learn (wants to learn) and how to orchestrate experience and more conversations so that the learner is able to construct meaning, understanding, and knowledge" (p. 522).

Cambourne (2002) suggests that we use the following principles when creating constructivist classrooms:

1. Create a classroom culture that supports and encourages deep engagement with multiple demonstrations of effective reading behavior.
2. Employ teaching activities and strategies that are a judicious mix of the four dimensions of teaching and learning:
   - Explicit—deliberately demonstrating the knowledge and skills students need to be effective readers
   - Systematically planned—instruction based on proactive, rational planning; a blueprint of future teaching
   - Mindful—openness to new information and different points of view
   - Contextualized—learning that makes sense to the learner.
3. Employ structures and processes that create continuous opportunities for the development of intellectual unrest.
4. Develop each learner's metatextual (text function) awareness of the processes and understandings implicit in effective reading behavior.
5. Design and use tasks that will coerce authentic use of the processes and understandings implicit in effective reading behavior (p. 30).

In social constructivist classrooms, we and our students take active roles in the educational process. Rather than require rote memorization and "the right answer," constructivism supports a more student-centered approach that is rich in conversation. In constructivist content area classrooms, students are engaged learners. They have numerous opportunities to use higher-order thinking and they play an active role in the construction of meaning.

Making Connections | **Thinking about Constructivist versus Traditional Classrooms**

■ Consider the characteristics of the constuctivist classroom: student centered, active, engaged participants, social in nature.

■ Think about your teaching and explain how a constructivist classroom would function in your content area.

■ Share your thoughts in small-group discussions.

What Roles Will Motivation and Engagement Play in Our Teaching?

Motivation and engagement are key factors in teaching and learning. We know from our own experience that if we are studying a topic of interest to us, we learn more readily. The same is true for our students. Motivation makes it easier to make connections between what we are learning and what we already know. This supports our constructivist view of learning.

Motivation is multifaceted. It is described in terms of competence and efficacy beliefs, goals for reading, and social purposes of reading (Baker & Wigfield, 1999). Motivated learners believe they can be successful and are willing to try to read more challenging reading material. They also possess intrinsic reasons for reading, such as gaining new knowledge about a topic or enjoying the reading experience. Motivated readers enjoy the social aspects of sharing new meanings gained from their reading with others.

Gambrell (1996) suggests that "classroom cultures that foster motivation are characterized by (1) a teacher who is a good reading model, (2) a book-rich classroom environment, (3) opportunities for choice, (4) familiarity with books, and (5) literacy-related incentives that reflect the value of reading" (p. 20). Gambrell, Palmer, Codling, and Mazzoni (1996) note that highly motivated readers read for a wide variety of reasons, including curiosity, involvement, social interchange, and emotional satisfaction (p. 518). Patrick and Yoon (2004) note that motivation also plays an important role in inquiry. They report that "the type of motivational beliefs that students hold, particularly beliefs about their competence and their reasons for engaging in tasks, appears vital" (p. 327).

The engagement perspective on reading integrates cognitive, motivational, and social aspects of learning (Baker, Afflerbach, & Reinking, 1996; Baker & Wigfield, 1999; Guthrie & Alvermann, 1999). Engaged learners achieve because they want to understand, they possess intrinsic motivations for interacting with text, they use cognitive skills to understand, and they share knowledge by talking with teachers and peers (Guthrie & Wigfield, 1997). Cambourne (1995) suggests that engaged learners have a purpose, seek to understand, believe in their own capability, and take responsibility for learning.

Engaged readers construct understandings based on connections between prior knowledge and new information. As teachers we can nurture students' ability to make connections by encouraging students to read for authentic purposes and respond in meaningful ways, always focusing on comprehension, personal connections, and reader response. Engaged readers coordinate strategies and knowledge (cognition) within a community of learners (social) to fulfill their personal goals (Guthrie, Wigfield, Metsala, & Cox, 1999). Baker and Wigfield (1999) note that "Engaged readers are motivated to read for different purposes, utilize knowledge gained from previous experience to generate new understandings, and participate in meaningful social interactions around reading" (p. 453).

What Texts Will We Use?

One of the biggest differences between teaching in the 21st century and the way in which we were taught is the current focus on multiple types of text. We may recall when the textbook was the only information source used to teach in the content areas. It is still part of our repertoire, but now we use multiple resources.

In today's classrooms, the most familiar content area textbook is the discipline-specific text purchased as part of a publisher's series. Many of these texts are comprehensive and innovative, and they often are complemented by ancillary materials such as kits, videos, and related websites. But the types of text we need to be able to "read" do not end there. "Text" has a variety of other meanings. It may refer to trade books, informational articles, song lyrics, movies, newspapers, television shows, poetry, conversations, everyday life situations, and more. The term is so far reaching because multiple literacies, such as information literacy, critical literacy, and media literacy, permeate every aspect of our lives.

The "reading" of texts also takes on new meaning when situated within multiple literacies. We are accustomed to reading print, but some literacies, such as critical literacy, require us to read beyond the printed word to examine the author's intent and the text's purpose. (For a more detailed discussion of multiple literacies, see Chapter 2.)

Making Connections | **Thinking about Texts We Have Used**

- Think about the texts you used during your high school experience. Focus on a text you felt was particularly effective, and explain your thinking. Focus on a text you felt was particularly ineffective, and explain your thinking.

- Share your thoughts with others in small-group discussion.

Throughout the world, in part because of the widespread availability of the Internet and other media, access to "text" is readily available. From the page to the screen, we are bombarded with increasing amounts and types of texts that require us as readers to digest, synthesize, and respond, often with a sense of urgency and immediacy. Literacy demands are incessant as we learn to read these new texts and formats (Vogt & McLaughlin, 2004).

What Will We Learn?

We will learn many ideas and techniques that will enrich our teaching and, consequently, our students' learning. We will see the "big picture" of multiple literacies in the content areas and come to understand how our teaching is part of it. We will learn a wide variety of strategies to help our students understand what they read and multiple ways to assess what they learn. We will learn how to accommodate struggling readers and how to support English language learners. We will integrate all that we learn into our knowledge base, so we can become the most effective teachers possible.

How Will We Begin?

We will begin with step 1: taking a deep breath and visualizing ourselves teaching. Then we will fully participate in this course and use this textbook as our teaching resource. We will make connections between what we are learning and our personal experiences. We will learn to question in meaningful ways and teach our students how to be inquirers—how to set the course for their own learning. Because we will integrate our content area expertise and our understanding of multiple literacies, we will be able to teach better than we ever thought possible. We will view literacies as thinking processes and use them to unlock the content we are teaching. We will learn, practice, and apply. Then we will teach.

FINAL THOUGHTS

Our journey formally begins in the next chapter, when we examine the topic of multiple literacies. In Chapter 2, we will learn about adolescent literacy and content literacy. Then we will expand our thinking as we explore critical literacy, information literacy, media literacy, and multicultural literacy.

Teaching Connections
APPLYING WHAT WE HAVE LEARNED

E-Link

To learn more about adolescent literacy, visit the International Reading Association (IRA) website at www.reading.org and read the position statement on adolescent literacy. Entitled "Adolescent Literacy: A Position Statement for the Commission on Adolescent Literacy of the International Reading Association," this document includes seven principles for supporting adolescent literacy growth.

After reading the position statement, reflect on the seven principles and consider how they relate to students in your content area. Do you agree or disagree with the principles? Which do you consider to be especially powerful? Are there other principles you would choose to add to the list? Document your thinking in a portfolio reflection.

Accountable Talk

As content area teachers of the 21st century, our work is very different from how our disciplines were taught in the past. Although we still value texts, we have moved beyond the "read the chapter/answer the questions mode" in which content area subjects have long been taught (and sadly still are taught in some classrooms) to teaching from a constructivist perspective. Imagine teaching your first classes. What challenges do you think you will face in teaching from this perspective? What tensions, if any, do you think you and your fellow teachers may experience? How might we address them? Discuss your responses in small-group conversations and help share your group's thoughts in whole-class discussion.

 ### Portfolio/Performance Opportunity

Knowing the kinds of educational experiences our students have had in the past will help us teach them more effectively. We can learn about their past experiences in a variety of ways, including asking them to write their own Literacy Histories. A Literacy History describes a person's reading and writing experiences from earliest memory to present day. To fully understand how the past influences the future, please write your Literacy History (see the prompts in Figure 1.3) and include it as an entry in your portfolio.

FIGURE 1.3 **Literacy History Prompts**

These prompts have been developed to guide you in creating your Literacy History. This is not a definitive list of questions to which you should respond, but rather a sequence of ideas to stimulate your thinking about your literacy development, starting with your earliest literacy memories. Although you may choose to include many of the ideas expressed in the prompts, do not allow them to restrict your thinking. Use this creative freedom as you record your experiences.

Early Memories
1. What are your earliest recollections of reading and writing?
2. Were you read to as a child?
3. Before you were able to read, did you pretend to read books? Can you remember the first time you read a book?
4. As a child, did you read and/or write with your siblings or friends?
5. Can you recall your early writing attempts (e.g., scribbling, labeling drawings)?
6. Was a newspaper delivered to your home? Do you recall seeing others read the newspaper? Did you read the newspaper?
7. Did you subscribe to children's magazines? Did your parents or siblings have magazine subscriptions?
8. Did your parents belong to a book club? Did they maintain a personal library? Did they read for pleasure?
9. Can you recall seeing family members making lists and receiving/sending mail?
10. Did you receive/send mail (i.e., birthday cards, thank-you notes, letters) when you were a child?
11. Can you remember any other indications that reading and writing were valued in the environment in which you grew up?

School Memories
12. What can you recall about your first memories of reading/writing instruction? Materials used? Methods of teaching? Content?
13. What can you recall about reading for pleasure in elementary school?
14. What can you recall about writing for pleasure in elementary school?
15. What can you recall about the first book you chose to read in elementary school?
16. What can you recall about your first writing assignment in elementary school?
17. Did you write a report in elementary school? What do you remember about this experience?
18. Do you remember the purposes for your reading and writing in elementary school? Do you recall any particular type of instruction you received? Can you describe any instructional materials that were used?
19. When you were in school, what would you have described as the three most important things you learned in content area classes?
20. What do you remember about how you were taught in content area subjects?
21. Did you have a library card when you were in elementary school? Did you use it then? In later school years?
22. Did you consider yourself to be a reader when you were in middle school?
23. Were you required to read certain books when you were in high school? How did you feel about that?

Reading for Pleasure and Social Purposes
24. Can you recall the first book you "couldn't put down"?
25. Have you ever read a book that has made a difference in your life?
26. Have you ever read a book that you knew had been challenged or censored? How did you feel about reading it?
27. Can you recall pleasurably sharing books with friends?
28. Did you read a certain type of book (i.e., mysteries, biographies) at a particular age? Why do you think you made such choices?
29. When did you first visit a bookstore? What was it like?
30. What is your all-time favorite children's book? Novel? Nonfiction work?
31. Have you ever seen a book you've read turned into a film?
32. Have there been times in your life when you have viewed reading as a pleasurable activity?
33. What contributions have your reading and writing abilities made to your life?
34. Are you a reader now?
35. Are you a writer now?
36. Do you feel comfortable modeling reading and writing for your students?
37. What are you currently reading? Writing?

Technology
38. How would you describe your first experience using a computer?
39. How do you use the Internet in your academic work?
40. How do you use a computer in your everyday life?
41. Do you communicate through email?
42. Which aspects of technology are you comfortable using in your teaching?

Critical Awareness
43. Have you ever questioned the veracity of an information source? Provide an example.
44. Have you ever questioned an author's intent or a text's purpose? Provide an example.
45. When you are reading and writing, do you consider multiple perspectives? Provide an example.

2

Chapter Overview

Teaching and Learning in an Age of Multiple Literacies

Whatever our discipline—mathematics, science, social science, foreign language, English, or other content area—literacies underpin everything we teach. In the past, being literate required only that we be able to read and write. In today's world, however, we need to be fluent in multiple literacies that require us not only to be able to read and write, but also to understand a variety of disciplines, navigate myriad information sources, examine the author's intent, and comprehend beyond the printed page.

Our ever-changing world has caused us to rethink literacy and the role it plays in our lives. We are living in an information age, one in which world news is readily available and access to friends on the other side of the world takes no longer than contacting the neighbor next door. We can shop, get the latest news, take university courses, or view the latest offerings in real estate in the privacy of our homes. The world is at our fingertips, and our resulting needs demand that we move beyond traditional views of literacy and embrace new perspectives.

In this chapter, we learn about multiple literacies and how we can integrate them into our teaching. We begin by questioning the nature of literacies. Next, we explore content literacies, which relate to the specific disciplines we teach. After that, we discuss adolescent literacy, which addresses the age category into which our students fall. Then we turn our focus to critical literacy. Finally, we learn about new literacies, such as information literacy, media literacy, and multicultural literacy. In each of these sections, we gain knowledge of a particular type of literacy and discover how we can integrate it into teaching.

What Do the Terms *Literacy*, *Multiple Literacies*, and *New Literacies* Mean?

In the past, *literacy* was typically defined as the ability to read and write. It was viewed as *functional literacy* and encompassed those literacy skills that were required for navigating satisfactorily in society. It referred to the ability to read words well enough to complete forms (such as job applications), follow directions (such as how to plug in a toaster or other appliance), or understand simple communications (such as a note from a child's teacher). Adults with a functional level of literacy were considered capable of being successful workers in their communities.

In recent years, the term *literacy* has expanded in meaning. The word itself has changed to *literacies,* reflecting the many different literacies that have emerged over time. These *multiple literacies* are diverse, multidimensional, and learned in different ways. For example, we still support adolescent literacy, but now each discipline also has its own literacy: Mathematics literacy, science literacy, and history literacy are just a few examples. There are technology-related literacies such as information literacy and media literacy. In addition, there is critical literacy, which has been in existence for decades and is now experiencing a wider range of acceptance. This widespread use has led to its inclusion in the list of literacies for the 21st century—the skills needed to flourish in today's society and in the future (Abilock, 2007). There is also multicultural literacy, which facilitates our understanding of our own cultures, as well as others.

New literacies are characterized by change and emerge from developments in technology (Reinking, 1998). We need to learn the new literacies to help our students learn how to use the emerging technologies. The new literacies "include the skills, strategies, and insights necessary to successfully exploit the rapidly changing information and communication technologies that continuously emerge in our world" (Leu, 2002, p. 313). Lonsdale and McCurry (2004) concur, observing that new literacies include the ability to "read" texts, master evolving technologies, manage information, and engage critically with texts. They further note that the boundaries of these literacies are not always clearly defined. For example, the term *information literacy* is often used interchangeably with *cyber, digital, electronic, computer, technological,* and *library literacy.* *Critical literacy* is thought to underpin all other literacies. Discipline-specific literacies, such as science, history, and mathematics literacy, are also viewed as new literacies.

According to Leu, Kinzer, Coiro, and Cammack (2004):

New literacies include the skills, strategies, and dispositions that allow us to use the Internet and other Information Communication Technologies (ICTs) effectively to identify important questions, locate information, critically evaluate the usefulness of that information, synthesize information to answer those questions, and then communicate the answers to others. We encounter new literacies nearly every time we try to read, write, and communicate with the Internet and other ICTs. In fact, when reviewing the following list, we can easily see how students completing a long-term project would need to engage in new literacies.

- Using a search engine to effectively locate information
- Evaluating the accuracy and utility of information located on a webpage relative to one's purpose
- Using a word processor effectively, including using functions such as checking spelling accuracy, inserting graphics, and formatting text
- Participating effectively in bulletin board or listserv discussions to get needed information
- Knowing how to use email to communicate effectively
- Inferring correctly the information that may be found at a hyperlink on a webpage. (p. 1590)

The emergence of new literacies can be linked to social, economic, and political change. Examples of these changes include learning being viewed as a lifelong process; individuals locating, managing, and evaluating a proliferation of information; teaching becoming more learner centered and inquiry based; a globalized economy demanding greater economic competition; intellectual capital replacing physical capital; and workers needing to be geographically mobile, adaptable, and multi-skilled (Lonsdale & McCurry, 2004). Leu (2002) notes that new literacies build on existing literacies and believes we can cautiously characterize these skills and strategies in the following ways:

- Change is a defining element.
- New kinds of strategic knowledge are required.
- Reading from a critical perspective is involved.
- They are socially constructed.
- Interest and motivation underpin them.
- Teachers thoughtfully guide learning within information environments.
- Governments around the world are investing in the new literacies monetarily and academically.

Because technology is changing so quickly and new literacies are constantly emerging, critics of the new literacies have expressed concerns about the need for greater teacher preparation, potentially higher costs, and inappropriate use of technology in the classroom (Leu, 2002). The new literacies are often described as including information literacy, media literacy, and multicultural literacy.

In the sections that follow, we examine content literacies, adolescent literacy, critical literacy, information literacy, media literacy, and multicultural literacy. We share current understandings about each topic and discuss how we can integrate these types of literacy into our teaching.

What Do We Know about Adolescent Literacy and Content Literacies?

We view *adolescent literacy* as,

> a set of socially organized practices which make use of a symbol system and a technology for producing and disseminating it. Literacy is not simply knowing how to read and write a particular script but applying this knowledge for specific purposes in specific contexts of use. The nature of these practices, including, of course, their technological aspects, will determine the kinds of skills associated with literacy (Scribner & Cole, 1981, p. 236). Moje (1996) supports this view and suggests that literacy involves the practices in which the processes of reading, writing, speaking, and listening are embedded. She views these processes "as tools for engaging in and making sense of social practice." (p. 175)

In other words, we and our students need to be able to read, write, speak, and listen to make sense of the world in which we live. One might assume that we would "be literate" by now, but over time literacy has evolved into an ongoing process. *Being literate* has become obsolete. *Becoming literate* is now the more relevant term (Leu & Kinzer, 2000).

Content literacies is a term that refers to how we use literacy in specific disciplines. Examples include mathematics literacy, science literacy, and social science literacy. Applications related to each of these literacies can be found in subsequent chapters of this book.

Content area courses often require the use of textbooks that many adolescents have difficulty reading. Some of these reading difficulties can be traced back to problems with decoding, which students should have learned when they were much younger. Other students' reading difficulties might be related to poorly developed vocabularies and a lack of background knowledge (Schoenbach, Greenleaf, Cziko, & Hurwitz, 1999). Schools continue to use content area textbooks, even though the average high school student is reading below the level of many of the texts (Allington, 2002). Biancarosa and Snow, the authors of *Reading Next—A Vision for Action and Research in Middle and High School Literacy* (2006), conclude that students "lack the strategies to help them comprehend what they read" (p. 8).

To address this issue, Biancarosa and Snow (2006) recommend the explicit teaching of reading comprehension and intensive writing across the curriculum, as well as instruction in how to learn from texts. They also advocate for greater student motivation and more opportunities for small-group instruction—factors that should work well for our Millennial students. Santa (2006) agrees with these suggestions and adds that the most influential factor in student achievement is the teacher. The International Reading Association's Commission on Adolescent Literacy (2001) has suggested that home-school literacy connections should also be developed.

So, although many people may believe that reading and writing are becoming less prevalent in an age of multiple literacies, just the opposite seems to be true. As Leu (2000) has reported:

> It is likely that reading and writing ability will become even more important in the future than they are today. This is due to the increasing need for acquiring and communicating information rapidly in a world of global competition and information economies. In this context, success will often be defined by one's ability to quickly locate useful information to solve important problems and then communicate the solution to others. Proficient readers can acquire many types of information more rapidly by reading than they can by listening to speech or viewing a video. In an age when speed of information access is central to success, reading will be even more critical to our children's futures. (p. 760)

Using What We Know about Adolescent Literacy and Content Literacies in Teaching

In *Reading Next—A Vision for Action and Research in Middle and High School Literacy*, Biancarosa and Snow (2006) encourage us to use what we know to teach adolescent literacy and content literacies. They remind us there are more than 8 million students in grades 4–12 who are struggling readers—students who cannot comprehend. These authors suggest that meeting the diverse literacy needs of such students will require a comprehensive approach. Although they note that the "optimal mix" of the elements will vary, they suggest that middle and high school literacy programs should focus on the following instructional improvements:

1. *Explicit teaching of comprehension strategies and processes.* We know that comprehension strategies can be taught. Within our districts, we need to work to ensure that such instruction begins in the primary grades, so students can develop a repertoire of strategies they can use as needed while they are reading. It is also critical that we and teachers throughout the grades and across content areas focus on students' strategy use. (See Chapters 4–7 for additional information about comprehension processes such as activating background knowledge and teaching reading comprehension strategies).

2. *Embedding effective instructional principles in content.* This improvement proposes that we, as content area teachers, infuse discipline-related reading and writing into our teaching and provide opportunities for application. Examples of this can be found in subsequent chapters in this text. (For further information about reading and writing, see Chapters 4–8 and 10–13)

3. *Motivating students.* As teachers, we know that student motivation is essential for learning in all subjects. We know many ways to motivate our students, including helping them make connections between their personal experiences and content, providing opportunities for self-selection of research/project topics, and encouraging students to represent their thinking in a variety of ways. (For more information about alternative ways to represent thinking, see Chapter 13.)

4. *Using text-based, collaborative learning.* This supports the Millennials' tendency to gravitate toward working in groups. This type of learning can promote student interaction related to the topic being studied. It can also advance other benefits of collaborative learning, such as shared ideas, respect for the thoughts of others, negotiated meaning, positive interdependence, individual accountability, interpersonal communication skills, and risk taking, as well as working with diverse types and levels of text (see instructional improvement 6).

5. *Strategic, intensive tutoring.* As noted earlier, there are millions of struggling readers, but few programs to help them read better during adolescence. This improvement would provide such tutoring for adolescents in reading, writing, and content knowledge.

6. *Using diverse types and levels of text.* Using multiple types and levels of text motivates students and provides access that they may not experience when reading the course textbook. Using theme-related trade books provides opportunities for students to learn from different perspectives. (See Chapter 8 for more information about types of texts.)

7. *Intensive writing.* Reading and writing are inextricably linked, and we know the more students engage in them, the better they perform. Courses infused with intensive writing will benefit students. (For more information about integrating writing in the content areas, see Chapter 10. For additional examples of integrating writing, see Chapters 12, 13, and 14.)

8. *Using technology as a tool for, and a topic of, literacy instruction.* Technology use is a great motivator for students. Most learners have an intrinsic interest in it. This improvement suggests that we use technology to motivate and to inform. (For more information about integrating technology in the content areas, see Chapter 11.)

9. *Assessing students through informal measures.* Informal measures are those that we use to assess our students every day. They include observation, students' strategy applications, discussion, and informal written responses. (For more information about informal assessments, see Chapter 14.)

In addition to the instructional improvements, *Reading Next* suggests that the educational infrastructure should be improved by providing extended time for literacy, long-term professional development, summative (more formal) assessment of students and programs, interdisciplinary teacher teams, and leadership in teaching reading and writing to all students. (For more information about professional development, see Chapter 15.)

According to *Reading Next*, the suggested improvements should not be viewed in isolation, but rather as elements of a group that have dynamic and powerful interrelations. Although professional development and formative and summative assessment are described as essential to effect change, Biancarosa and Snow (2006) suggest that the elements should be used in optimal mixes, dependent on contexts.

Regardless of technological developments that occur in the future, adolescent literacy and content literacies will continue to be important issues for our students. As their teachers, we need to ensure that they have the processes, strategies, knowledge, and opportunities they need to be successful. (For more detailed information about such strategies and the reading process, see Chapters 4–7.)

What Do We Know about Critical Literacy?

Current thinking about literacy suggests that we should help our students to comprehend at deeper levels—levels that require them to understand beyond the information on the printed page and critically analyze the author's message (Pearson, 2001). Reading from a critical literacy perspective encourages our students and us to examine the connections between language, power, and knowledge; to transform relationships; and to reason and act responsibly. It involves thinking beyond the text to understand issues such as why the author wrote about a particular topic, wrote from a particular perspective, and chose to include some ideas about the topic and exclude others.

For example, when we were in elementary school, content area text authors may have shared some information about a topic, but not all. Many of us may remember learning that Christopher Columbus sailed the ocean blue in 1492 and that he had three ships: the *Nina*, the *Pinta*, and the *Santa Maria*. We probably also learned that Italy—Columbus's homeland—would not provide funding for his explorations. The money came instead from Queen Isabella of Spain.

What we have just read about Columbus is what many believe to be the essential history of his explorations, but it is not the whole story. A textbook company decided that what we should learn about Columbus was what I have just recounted. The same company also decided what we should not learn about Columbus—that he is viewed as the person responsible for destroying the Tainos people. From a critical perspective, we would question why the textbook from which we learned did not include the whole truth, as current history textbooks do. We would also question what right the author and the textbook company had to withhold the whole story, to discount the perspective of the Tainos people. We would then reflect and try to take action that would provide justice for the Tainos, perhaps by ensuring that their story is told or by working to help other indigenous peoples.

Critical literacy is grounded in Freire's (1983) belief that reading is much more than decoding language or accepting text as true—it is preceded by and intertwined with knowledge of the world. Because language and reality are dynamically interwoven, the understanding attained by the critical reading of a text implies perceiving the relation between text and context.

Freire (1970) suggests that instead of passively accepting the information presented, readers should not only read and understand the word, but "read the world" and understand the text's purpose to avoid being manipulated by it. "Reading the world" enables critically aware readers to comprehend beyond the literal level and think about the function and the production of texts. Reading the world means trying to understand *what* authors are trying to convey in their messages and *how* they are communicating those messages. It requires that readers not accept only superficial responses to the text, but rather reflect on the text's purposes and the author's style. This reasoning is often expressed through dialogue with others who are seeking to understand the hidden forces at work. This kind of reflection takes time and requires constant monitoring of the text.

Reading from this perspective requires both the ability and the deliberate inclination to think critically about—to analyze and evaluate—texts, meaningfully question their origin and purpose, and take action by representing alternative perspectives. Questioning plays an important role in this process. Examples of the types of questions that facilitate thinking from a critical perspective are featured in Figure 2.1. These questions require readers to think at evaluative levels, to question what message the author is trying to convey and how that message relates to the truth. (For more information about generating questions at multiple levels of thinking, see Chapter 8.)

FIGURE 2.1

Questions That Promote Reading from a Critical Stance

Print (e.g., books, newspapers, magazines, song lyrics, hypertext)
- Whose viewpoint is expressed?
- What does the author want us to think?
- Whose voices are missing, silenced, or discounted?
- How might alternative perspectives be represented?
- How would that contribute to your understanding the text from a critical stance?
- What action might you take based on what you have learned?

Television/Photographs
- Who is in the video/photograph?
- Why are they there?
- What does the videographer/photographer want you to think?
- Who/what is missing from the video/photograph? (Silenced? Discounted?)
- What might an alternative video show?
- What might an alternative photograph look like?
- How would that contribute to your understanding the video or photograph from a critical stance?
- What action might you take based on what you have viewed?

Source: McLaughlin & DeVoogd, 2004a.

It is important to note that critical theorists' expanded notion of texts isn't limited to words from a novel or a song or a newscast. Texts can also be conditions (sociocultural influences, state assessment-driven curriculums, funding or lack of it) or relationships and situations in everyday life (analyzing an occurrence from another person's perspective).

Critical literacy views readers as active participants in the reading process and invites them to move beyond passively accepting the text's message to question, examine, or dispute the power relations that exist between readers and authors—to ponder what the author wants readers to believe, take action, and promote fairness between people. It focuses on issues of power and promotes reflection, action, and transformation (Freire, 1970).

The Principles of Critical Literacy developed by McLaughlin and DeVoogd (2004a) include a number of essential understandings and beliefs about the power relationship that exists between the reader and the author. The four principles and related examples are summarized next.

- Critical literacy focuses on issues of power and promotes reflection, transformation, and action.

Whenever readers commit to understanding a text—whether narrative or informational—they submit to the right of the author to select the topic and determine the treatment of the ideas.

- Critical literacy focuses on the problem and its complexity.

Situations that are fairly intricate are often viewed from an essentialist (very simplistic) perspective. In critical literacy, rather than accepting an essentialist view, we engage in *problematizing*—seeking to understand the problem and its complexity. In other words, we raise questions and seek alternative explanations as a way of more fully acknowledging and understanding the complexity of the situation.

- Critical literacy strategies are dynamic and adapt to the contexts in which they are used.

There is no list of methods in critical literacy that work the same way in all contexts at all times. No technique that promotes critical literacy can be exported to another setting without adapting it to that context. As Freire (1998, p. xi) has observed, "It is impossible to export pedagogical practices without reinventing them."

Comber (2001) has observed that when teachers and students are engaged in critical literacy, "They ask complicated questions about language and power, about people and lifestyle, about morality and ethics, about who is advantaged by the way things are and who is disadvantaged" (p. 271). To participate in such a classroom environment, readers must play not only the roles of code breakers, meaning makers, and text users, but also the role of text critics (Luke & Freebody, 1999). In other words, readers need to understand that they have the power to envision alternative ways of viewing the author's topic, and they exert that power when they read from a critical stance.

- Critical literacy disrupts the commonplace by examining it from multiple perspectives.

Examining the point of view from which a text is written and brainstorming other perspectives that may or may not be represented challenge students to expand their thinking and discover diverse beliefs, positions, and understandings (McLaughlin, 2001). These techniques help students to transition from accepting the text as it is presented to questioning the author's intent and the information presented in the text.

The principles of critical literacy provide insight into what critical literacy is and how it functions. This dynamic process examines power relationships, acknowledges that all texts are biased, and encourages readers to explore alternative perspectives and take action. It expands our thinking, and it enlightens our perceptions as we read both the word and the world from a critical stance.

Reading from a critical stance requires both the ability and the deliberate inclination to think critically about—to analyze and evaluate—texts (books, media, lyrics, electronic text, life relationships), meaningfully question their origin and purpose, and take action by representing alternative perspectives. The goal is for readers to become text critics in everyday life—to become active thinkers rather than passive recipients of knowledge.

Making Connections | **Thinking about Critical Literacy**

■ Reflect on reading from a critical perspective. How could reading from a critical stance deepen your students' understanding of your content area?

■ Share your thoughts with others in small-group discussion.

It is important to realize that critical literacy is more complex than other literacies. We cannot just "become" critically literate. Instead, this process requires learning, understanding, and changing over time. It includes developing theoretical, research, and pedagogical repertoires, changing with time and circumstance, engaging in self-critical practices, and remaining open to possibilities (Comber, 2001).

Integrating What We Know about Critical Literacy into Teaching

Teachers, students, and texts play important roles in creating a context that fosters critical literacy— one in which reading from a critical stance is a natural occurrence that extends beyond the classroom to everyday life experiences (McLaughlin & DeVoogd, 2004b). Our role in initiating and developing critical literacy is multifaceted. It begins with personal understanding and use of critical literacy and extends to teaching students about critical literacy, modeling reading from a critical stance in everyday teaching and learning experiences, and providing access to a variety of texts that represent critical literacy.

Once we become critically aware, teaching students to read from a critical stance should be a natural process. First, as in any other act of reading, the teacher should ensure that students have the background knowledge necessary to read from a critical stance. The teacher might then choose to scaffold learning by using a five-step instructional framework: explain, demonstrate, guide, practice, and reflect (McLaughlin & Allen, 2002). This scaffolding, or gradual release of responsibility to students, provides time and opportunity for them to become comfortable with reading from a critical stance. To begin, we can explain what it means to be critically aware and then demonstrate by using a read-aloud and a think-aloud. During this process, we provide a critical perspective that questions and challenges the text. We may use questions such as, Whose viewpoint is expressed? Whose voices are missing, silenced, or discounted? What action might you take based on what you have learned? We might also introduce strategies such as juxtapositioning or alternative texts. After we explain and demonstrate, students—working in pairs or small groups—can offer responses as we guide their reading and as they practice reading from a critical stance. As a final step, we and the students reflect on what they know about being critically aware and how it helped them to understand the text. This often results in their making connections (text–self, text–text, text–world) and leads to discussions of how students can apply what they have learned to the reading of other texts.

Students who engage in critical literacy become open-minded, active, strategic readers who are capable of viewing text from a critical perspective. They understand that the information presented in texts, magazines, newspapers, song lyrics, and websites has been authored from a particular perspective for a particular purpose. They know that meaning is "grounded in the social, political, cultural and historic contexts of the reading event" (Serafini, 2003).

Although methods are something most critical scholars shy away from, there are a variety of starting points that we can use to help students develop a critical stance. The following ideas and resources provide some direction for initial engagement. As noted earlier, we need to take these ideas, adapt them to our particular contexts, and scaffold students' learning.

JUXTAPOSITIONING TEXTS. Juxtapositioning is a technique that helps demonstrate multiple perspectives. It can occur in a variety of formats, using a number of informational sources. For example, in a high school history course in which World War II was being studied, juxtapositioning was used in theme-based focus groups. The students were reading excerpts from *The Greatest Generation,* a theme-related text that represented the Allies' perspective, in a whole-class setting. They were also reading theme-based books that represented different perspectives of World War II—those of Holocaust victims, German soldiers, American and Japanese survivors of the bombing of Pearl Harbor, various political leaders of the time, and victims of the Japanese American Internment—in small groups. After the books were read and discussed, the students regrouped, so that one student representing each book would be in each of the newly formed groups.

In this scenario, discussions focused on multiple perspectives. Students reported that they had not considered perspectives such as those of the Japanese American victims of internment, nor had they thought about the perspectives of women working on the homefront or of people who had worked to help save the victims of the Holocaust. An interesting discussion of the media during the 1940s also emerged. It focused on the immediacy of information we experience now as compared to the radio news and handwritten letters used to communicate military developments during World War II. The discussion then moved on to a critical analysis of the media, focusing on issues such as who decides what information is included in and excluded from the news we see and read. After in-depth small-group discussion, pairs of students created posters on which they juxtaposed visual representations of the World War II perspectives they had read about. The posters were then shared and discussed in a whole-class setting. Students took action by inviting Holocaust survivors and U.S. soldiers who had participated in World War II to school to share their perspectives on World War II. Figure 2.2 contains a list of sample texts used for the theme-based focus groups on World War II.

ALTERNATIVE TEXTS. We create alternative texts to represent perspectives that are different from those that are present in the texts we read. The text can be narrative or informational and can consist of oral, written, visual, or imagined representations—including, but not limited to, drawings, oral descriptions, dramatizations, and songs. By creating an alternative text, the reader perceives the information in a different way and begins to understand the complexity of the issue examined. When using this technique, students can examine the message conveyed by a text, photo, or song and then write an alternative text, take or find an alternative photo, or create alternative lyrics. For example, after seeing a billboard of happy people having dinner in their expensive house, a student might choose to create an alternative text—which might also have a billboard design—about a sad person who is alone, homeless, and dependent on shelters for food and a bed. The student might then take action by encouraging peers to actively participate in the school's food and clothing drive for the homeless or by organizing a group of friends to work for that effort.

Students have also created alternative texts in other curricular areas. For example, they have created alternative texts in science class after reading newspaper articles about the effects of medical waste pollution on the ocean and developments in the use of cloning. In music class, students have examined family relationships by creating alternative lyrics to a variety of songs including "Cat's in the Cradle." In social studies, students created alternative texts for texts expressing views on a variety of political issues.

Teaching ideas such as juxtapositioning, theme-based focus groups, and creating alternative texts are adaptable across curriculum areas. They provide opportunities to situate critical literacy in a variety of contexts and encourage both our students and us to view critical literacy as a natural part of learning.

Critical literacy permeates every other kind of literacy. Information literacy, media literacy, multicultural literacy, and discipline-specific literacies provide examples of its broad influence.

Allen, T. B. (2001). *Remember Pearl Harbor: American and Japanese survivors tell their stories.* Washington, DC: National Geographic Society.

Personal recollections of Pearl Harbor survivors, both American and Japanese, military and civilian, are presented in this book. Maps, pictures, and timelines to help readers follow the events of Pearl Harbor and World War II in general are included.

Appleman-Jurman, A. (1989). *Alicia: My story.* New York: Bantam Books.

This autobiography recounts Alicia Appleman-Jurman's triumph over the terrifying, unrelenting brutality of the Nazi regime. After managing to escape and witnessing her own mother's murder, she helps others escape with her to Palestine.

Elliott, L. M. (2001). *Under a war-torn sky.* New York: Hyperion.

Set in France during World War II, this book is based on recollections of the author's father. A young American pilot's plane is shot down in Nazi-occupied France, and the French Resistance works to get him safely out of enemy territory.

Friedman, I. R. (1990). *The other victims: Non-Jews persecuted by the Nazis.* Boston: Houghton Mifflin.

Personal narratives tell the stories of the many non-Jews persecuted by Hitler and the Nazis, both before and during World War II. Some of the groups discussed include gypsies, homosexuals, blacks, physically challenged individuals, and political and religious activists.

Gold, A. L. (2000). *A special fate: Chiune Sugihara: Hero of the Holocaust.* New York: Scholastic.

This biography tells the story of a Japanese diplomat working in Lithuania, who chooses to ignore his orders and listen to his conscience. Despite the risks to himself and his family, Sugihara writes thousands of transit visas and saves the lives of countless Jews.

FIGURE 2.2
Young-Adult Novels about World War II That Represent Critical Literacy

Greene, B. (1973). *Summer of my German soldier.* New York: Puffin.

Patty, a young Jewish girl who is struggling to find herself, discovers Anton, a young German prisoner of war who has escaped. Patty takes incredible risks to conceal and protect Anton and learns a great deal about herself in the process.

Kuchler-Silberman, L. (1990). *My hundred children.* New York: Dell Laurel-Leaf.

A Holocaust survivor copes with the loss of her family by running an orphanage for 100 Jewish children who survived the Nazi occupation of Poland. The story recounts everyday victories like learning to laugh again as well as bigger issues such as leaving Poland for a safer home.

Lowry, L. (1989). *Number the stars.* Boston: Houghton Mifflin.

A ten-year-old Danish girl named Annemarie and her family risk their own safety to help Annemarie's best friend and her Jewish family escape to Sweden, where they will be safe from the Nazis.

Richter, H. P. (1987). *I was there.* New York: Viking Penguin/Puffin Books.

A young boy who is a member of the Hitler Youth Movement early in the Nazi era tells his story. The first-person account provides some insight into the people who were part of the Axis forces.

Talbott, H. (2000). *Forging freedom: A true story of heroism during the Holocaust.* New York: Putnam.

Jaap Penraat, a young Dutchman, helps save more than 400 Jews during World War II by using his father's printing press to forge identification papers for Jewish friends and neighbors. He then creates a bogus German construction company and smuggles his "construction workers" to phony job sites and safety.

Volavkova, H. (Ed.). (1971). *I never saw another butterfly.* New York: McGraw Hill.

Children of the Nazi concentration camp in Terezin, Czechoslovakia, created these haunting poems and drawings. Of the 15,000 children who went to Terezin, fewer than 100 survived.

Wiesel, E. (1982). *Night.* New York: Bantam Books.

This autobiography recounts the life of a young boy in a Nazi death camp. The book includes accounts of many tragic events, including the author witnessing the death of his own family.

What Do We Know about Information Literacy?

Abilock (2007) defines *information literacy* as a "transformational process in which the learner needs to find, understand, evaluate, and use information in various forms to create for personal, social, or global purposes." The easiest way to think about information literacy may be to imagine a long-term, student performance–based research project. The students would utilize information literacy to use the Internet to develop important questions, locate information, synthesize the information to answer their questions, and communicate the information to others (Leu et al., 2004, p. 1572).

In Figure 2.3, Abilock (2007) presents information literacy as a problem-solving process in which students use certain skills and strategies to achieve particular outcomes in given contexts. Notice how inquiry pervades the performance-based nature of the process.

Using What We Know about Information Literacy in Teaching

In Figure 2.3, Abilock suggests that we can make connections among information literacy, students' skills and strategies, student outcomes, and curriculum and teaching design. This integration supports our use of information literacy across the curriculum. For example, students using information literacy in science might engage in research projects about scientific developments such as global warming or the viability of life on Mars, while students in foreign language class might research the various dimensions of the culture they are studying.

FIGURE 2.3
Overview of Informational Literacy

Information Literacy	Student Skills and Strategies	Student Outcomes	Curriculum and Teaching Design
A problem-solving process for	The student uses habits of mind to	The student is a learner who is	The learning design provides
■ Exploring and questioning	■ Recognize problems	■ Independent	■ Authentic contexts
■ Defining an information need	■ Formulate hypotheses	■ Disciplined	■ Simulations, real applications, and problems
■ Creating a plan to locate relevant information	■ Make good predictions	■ Planful	■ Reiterative opportunities for unique performances
■ Reading the medium	■ Ask important questions	■ Self-motivated	
■ Synthesizing information to create knowledge	■ Locate, analyze, interpret, evaluate, and record information and ideas	■ Metacognitive	■ Ongoing assessments
■ Applying insight to personal, social, or global contexts to create wisdom	■ Assume multiple stances	■ Flexible	■ Longitudinal rubrics
■ Self-evaluating the process and the product	■ Apply heuristic strategies	■ Adventurous	■ Integration of information literacy
	■ Develop complex understanding		■ Creative roles for teachers
	■ Extend understanding through creative models		■ Collegiality
	■ Apply understanding to new problems		■ Culture of innovation

Source: Abilock, 2007.

Making Connections | Thinking about Information Literacy

■ Reflect on your content area and contemplate how your students might use information literacy.

■ Share your thoughts with others in a small-group discussion.

What Do We Know about Media Literacy?

According to Considine (1995), *media literacy* is "the ability to access, analyze, evaluate, and create information in a variety of media formats." Much like critical literacy, it moves beyond what we would generally consider as comprehension to analyzing and evaluating information. Media literacy applies critical perspectives to print and electronic media (Summers, 2000).

Media literacy fosters what Brown (1998) describes as "discriminating responsiveness" and what Singer and Singer (1998) term "critical viewers." In media literacy, viewers deconstruct media messages by analyzing the message, the product, and the influence (Scharrer, 2002–2003). We do this by raising questions similar to those we ask in critical literacy: Who chose the message that is being communicated? What does that person want us to believe? What perspectives may have been marginalized? What action might we take based on what we have viewed? Because media are pervasive in our lives and the lives of our students, questioning from a critical perspective is essential if we are to be able to interpret the messages we receive (Ivey, 2000).

Silverblatt (2000) suggests that we should use seven principles to guide the use of media literacy in our teaching:

1. Principle 1: Media literacy empowers individuals to make independent judgments about media consumption.
2. Principle 2: Media literacy focuses attention on the elements involved in the media communication process. Our online communication is both expressive and receptive, because we both impart and retrieve information.
3. Principle 3: Media literacy fosters an awareness of the impact of the media on the individual and on society as a whole.
4. Principle 4: Media literacy develops strategies with which to analyze and discuss media messages.
5. Principle 5: Media literacy promotes awareness of interactive media content as a "text" that provides insight into contemporary culture and ourselves.
6. Principle 6: Media literacy cultivates enhanced enjoyment, understanding, and appreciation of media content.
7. Principle 7: Media literacy challenges interactive media communicators to produce effective and responsible media messages.

Our goal is to teach our students to be active learners and to not passively accept media messages. Teaching media literacy will encourage our students to actively question the format, content, and intent of media communication.

Integrating Media Literacy into Teaching

Media literacy not only suggests that students learn from the media, resist media manipulation, and empower themselves in terms of media, but also promotes the development of skills that will motivate and empower students in everyday life. Critical discussions, analyses, and respect for inquiry play important roles in this process. When teaching our students about media literacy, Summers (2000) suggests that we use the three R's—*review, reflect,* and *react.* She describes these terms as follows:

- *Review:* examine, investigate, summarize, restate, describe, explain, analyze, deconstruct, and study
- *Reflect:* compare, contrast, personalize, apply, judge, debate, critique, defend, and evaluate
- *React:* support, subscribe to, reject, internalize, participate in, adopt, editorialize, and oppose

Our students can apply the three R's process to a variety of media, including news, controversial advertisements, and political message films. For example, science students might analyze messages about rainforests or cloning, while mathematics students might question the source and relevance of statistics about a particular issue. Because the media permeate our students' lives, it is increasingly important that the students know how to analyze messages from these sources.

What Do We Know about Multicultural Literacy?

Multicultural literacy is the ability to understand and appreciate the similarities and differences in the customs, values, and beliefs of one's own culture and the cultures of others (NCREL, 2003). Proponents of multicultural literacy

- *Value diversity.* They appreciate and accept similarities and differences in cultural beliefs, appearances, and lifestyles.
- *Exhibit an informed sensitivity.* They can take the perspectives of other cultural groups and can be sensitive to issues of bias, racism, prejudice, and stereotyping.
- *Actively engage in and with other cultures.* They communicate, interact, and work with individuals from other cultural groups, using technology where appropriate.

We live in a world in which communication with other cultures is instantaneous. To communicate cross-culturally in meaningful ways, we and our students not only need to understand and appreciate a variety of cultures, but also to develop the knowledge and skills necessary for positive interaction (Banks et al., 2001).

Integrating What We Know about Multicultural Literacy into Teaching

Communication seems to be the ultimate mode of engagement for multicultural literacy. We can communicate personally within our own communities or with cultures around the world through cyberspace. This includes classes using email, shared websites, or videoconferencing as formats for cultural exchange. For example, students in foreign language class can learn about particular cultures by communicating with students who actually live in those cultures. Students can also participate in shared class projects, such as animal extinction research with students in Greenland and Africa, or engage in moderated e-discussions of world issues, such as the economy or scientific discoveries.

FINAL THOUGHTS

Teaching in an age of multiple literacies is a complex, dynamic experience filled with challenges and rewards. Characterized by global innovation, evolving understandings of our content area subjects, and ever-emerging technologies, the time in which we live demands that we become critically aware and transition from passively accepting information to critiquing it, from relying on the author's intent to exploring multiple perspectives. Our goal: To make sense of the world in a time that is characterized by change.

In the next chapter we build upon what we have learned by examining standards-based teaching and learning. We explore national and state standards, situate them within a constructivist framework, and examine discipline-specific examples.

Teaching Connections

APPLYING WHAT WE HAVE LEARNED

E-Link

To gain a deeper understanding of the state of adolescent literacy, read *Reading Next—A Vision for Action and Research in Middle and High School Literacy*. In that report from the Alliance for Excellent Education, Biancarosa and Snow (2006) assess the state of adolescent literacy and make recommendations concerning how to address current challenges in the field. To find the document, visit www.all4ed.org/files/archive/publications/ReadingNext/ReadingNext.pdf.

Focus on the background information about struggling adolescent readers and the 15 suggestions to improve instruction and infrastructure. Remember that Snow and Biancarosa suggest that the 15 elements should be used in what they describe as an "optimal mix." Choose a school in which you have had a field experience or currently teach and develop what you perceive to be the optimal mix of elements that would benefit the adolescents in that school. Justify your thinking in a portfolio reflection.

Accountable Talk

Many of us grew up believing everything we read in a textbook. We never questioned who was writing the text, who was determining which topics would be included in it, or who was deciding what would be excluded from it. We never questioned if there was any perspective other than the one presented. As a result, we believed the information presented to us, which included that all inventors of importance were white men and excluded information about events such as the Japanese American Internment during World War II. Today's school students interact with many more information sources than we did at their age. They need to understand that critical literacy requires that we move beyond passively accepting information and question both the information and those who have created or compiled it. Consider critical literacy and explain how you would teach your students to think from a critical perspective. Choose a specific topic in your content area and offer an example of how you could use it to teach critical literacy. Discuss your ideas in small-group conversations and then share your group's thoughts in whole-class discussion.

 ### Portfolio/Performance Opportunity

Integrating multiple literacies is essential for quality teaching and learning. Consider information literacy, media literacy, and multicultural literacy. Explain how you would integrate each when teaching in your content area. Choose a specific topic and create a lesson plan that incorporates two of these literacies. Include the lesson plan in your portfolio.

3

Chapter Overview

Standards-Based Teaching and High-Stakes Assessments

S tandards and high-stakes assessments greatly influence our teaching. From the national level to states and local districts, there are directives for us to follow to ensure that our teaching is standards based and that our students are prepared to take the necessary assessments.

As educators, we often struggle to balance the demands of educational standards with the student-centered, constructivist nature of our teaching. On one hand, we must ensure that we have enough time to teach all the content necessary to meet state standards. On the other hand, we want our students to experience in-depth, inquiry-based learning. This has resulted in a "coverage versus depth" debate—whether it is better to cover as many topics as possible to accommodate standards and prepare for related assessments or whether it is better to teach selected topics in depth. Regardless of the outcome of this debate, most school districts require teachers to create lessons based on state standards and prepare students for the related state assessments.

High-stakes testing has existed for decades. In the 1970s and 1980s, it was associated with minimum competency testing; its relation to the standards movement emerged in the 1990s. Minimum competency testing assessed students' abilities to demonstrate specified basic skills. The question was, "Can each student do the minimum?" Reading and mathematics were the subjects most frequently measured. Now high-stakes tests are usually associated with state standards that focus on students achieving their greatest potential. The question now is, "How much can students achieve?" In high-stakes testing, the results of one test are used for a variety of high-stakes purposes. These include school success, placement in courses, graduation, and funding. Although students are usually required to engage in it, high-stakes testing is a controversial issue that seems to have very little support from teachers and educational organizations.

In this chapter, we focus on educational standards and high-stakes testing. We begin by exploring state standards and examining their impact on teaching and learning. Next, we demonstrate how state standards can be integrated into meaningful lessons for a variety of subject areas. Then we extend our focus by examining high-stakes testing, an enduring component of the standards movement.

What Do We Know about Educational Standards?

The standards movement began after the publication of *A Nation at Risk* in 1983. The content of that report prompted questions about what students should know and be able to do (Lefkowits & Miller, 2006). That line of inquiry eventually led to the development of standards by content-specific national educational organizations, such as the National Council of the Teachers of Mathematics, which in turn encouraged the development of standards at the state and school district levels.

Academic standards are statements of what students should know and be able to do as a result of their learning. They are often described as goals or proficiency levels students should strive to reach (Noddings, 1997). The National Council of Teachers of Mathematics (NCTM) was the first professional organization to develop standards. In 1989, NCTM published *Curriculum and Evaluation Standards for School Mathematics.* Figure 3.1 features an excerpt from the NCTM geometry standards. Notice that although this figure shows expectations for students in grades 9 through 12, NCTM expects students to build on their knowledge from prekindergarten through grade 12 to meet these standards.

Today, most content areas, including mathematics, science, social science, physical education and health, fine arts, and foreign languages have standards in place. In addition, other standards permeate all content areas. Examples include the National Educational Technology Standards (2007), the English Language Arts Standards (1996), and the Teachers of English to Speakers of Other Languages PreK–12 English Language Proficiency Standards in the Core Content Areas (TESOL, 2006). The National Educational Technology Standards (2007), which were developed by the International Society for Technology in Education, address grade levels preK–12 and are organized in six categories: Creativity and Innovation; Communication and Collaboration; Research and Information Fluency; Critical Thinking, Problem Solving, and Decision Making; Digital Citizenship; and Technology Operations and Concepts. The Language Arts Standards, which were developed jointly by the International Reading Association and the National Council of Teachers of English, pervade all of the content areas. Those standards, which are presented in Figure 3.2, focus on what students should know and be able to do in literacy. The Language Arts Standards are based on the beliefs that standards are needed to prepare students for literacy requirements, communicate a shared vision, and promote high educational expectations for all students.

As content area teachers, we also need to have knowledge of the TESOL PreK–12 English Language Proficiency Standards in the Core Content Areas (2005). A brief overview of these standards is featured in Figure 3.3. To learn more about teaching English learners in the content areas, see Chapter 9.

States and many school districts have *designed down* or *backward mapped* from the national standards and created standards at their respective levels. In other words, they have used the broad national standards as a starting point and adapted the standards to be more specific to their purposes. Figure 3.4 features the California State Standards for history–social science. In its prelude to these standards, the California State Board of Education provides an overview of what students should learn and be able to do in grade 10. Members of the California State Board state:

> Students in grade ten study major turning points that shaped the modern world, from the late eighteenth century through the present, including the cause and course of the two world

Examine the national and state standards for your content area and for reading by visiting the Resources tab in the MyEducationLab for your course and clicking on Licensure and Standards.

FIGURE 3.1 NCTM Geometry Standard and Expectations for Grade 9–12 Students

Instructional programs from prekindergarten through grade 12 should enable all students to	Expectations In grades 9–12 all students should
Analyze characteristics and properties of two- and three-dimensional geometric shapes and develop mathematical arguments about geometric relationships	■ Analyze properties and determine attributes of two- and three-dimensional objects ■ Explore relationships (including congruence and similarity) among classes of two- and three-dimensional geometric objects, make and test conjectures about them, and solve problems involving them ■ Establish the validity of geometric conjectures using deduction, prove theorems, and critique arguments made by others ■ Use trigonometric relationships to determine lengths and angle measures
Specify locations and describe spatial relationships using coordinate geometry and other representational systems	■ Use Cartesian coordinates and other coordinate systems, such as navigational, polar, or spherical systems, to analyze geometric situations ■ Investigate conjectures and solve problems involving two- and three-dimensional objects represented with Cartesian coordinates
Apply transformations and use symmetry to analyze mathematical situations	■ Understand and represent translations, reflections, rotations, and dilations of objects in the plane by using sketches, coordinates, vectors, function notation, and matrices ■ Use various representations to help understand the effects of simple transformations and their compositions
Use visualization, spatial reasoning, and geometric modeling to solve problems	■ Draw and construct representations of two- and three-dimensional geometric objects using a variety of tools ■ Visualize three-dimensional objects and spaces from different perspectives and analyze their cross sections ■ Use vertex-edge graphs to model and solve problems ■ Use geometric models to gain insights into, and answer questions in, other areas of mathematics ■ Use geometric ideas to solve problems in, and gain insights into, other disciplines and other areas of interest such as art and architecture

wars. They trace the rise of democratic ideas and develop an understanding of the historical roots of current world issues, especially as they pertain to international relations. They extrapolate from the American experience that democratic ideals are often achieved at a high price, remain vulnerable, and are not practiced everywhere in the world. Students develop an understanding of current world issues and relate them to their historical, geographic, political, economic, and cultural contexts. Students consider multiple accounts of events in order to understand international relations from a variety of perspectives.

After creating standards, many states use the "designed down" information to create benchmarks—expectations of what students would achieve by particular points in their learning. Reviewing K–12 benchmarks demonstrates how students begin to achieve the standards in prekindergarten and progress throughout their academic careers to high school graduation. This gives direction to teaching and learning at all levels. Figure 3.5 features benchmarks for the Pennsylvania State Mathematics Standard for Geometry. You will notice that these benchmarks address expectations at periodic points in students' learning—grades 3, 5, 8, and 11—not at each grade level. Grade-level benchmarks are often developed at the local level.

Ravitch (1995) suggests that three interrelated categories of standards exist: (1) content or curriculum standards—what we teach and students learn; (2) performance standards—what

FIGURE 3.2

IRA/NCTE Language Arts
Standards

Although we present these standards as a list, we want to emphasize that they are not distinct and separable. They are, in fact, interrelated and should be considered as a whole.

1. Students read a wide range of print and nonprint texts to build an understanding of texts, of themselves, and of the cultures of the United States and the world; to acquire new information; to respond to the needs and demands of society and the workplace; and for personal fulfillment. Among these texts are fiction and nonfiction, classic and contemporary works.

2. Students read a wide range of literature from many periods in many genres to build an understanding of the many dimensions (e.g., philosophical, ethical, aesthetic) of human experience.

3. Students apply a wide range of strategies to comprehend, interpret, evaluate, and appreciate texts. They draw on their prior experience, their interactions with other readers and writers, their knowledge of word meaning and of other texts, their word identification strategies, and their understanding of textual features (e.g., sound–letter correspondence, sentence structure, context, graphics).

4. Students adjust their use of spoken, written, and visual language (e.g., conventions, style, vocabulary) to communicate effectively with a variety of audiences and for different purposes.

5. Students employ a wide range of strategies as they write and use different writing process elements appropriately to communicate with different audiences for a variety of purposes.

6. Students apply knowledge of language structure, language conventions (e.g., spelling and punctuation), media techniques, figurative language, and genre to create, critique, and discuss print and nonprint texts.

7. Students conduct research on issues and interests by generating ideas and questions, and by posing problems. They gather, evaluate, and synthesize data from a variety of sources (e.g., print and nonprint texts, artifacts, people) to communicate their discoveries in ways that suit their purpose and audience.

8. Students use a variety of technological and informational resources (e.g., libraries, databases, computer networks, video) to gather and synthesize information and to create and communicate knowledge.

9. Students develop an understanding of and respect for diversity in language use, patterns, and dialects across cultures, ethnic groups, geographic regions, and social roles.

10. Students whose first language is not English make use of their first language to develop competency in the English language arts and to develop understanding of content across the curriculum.

11. Students participate as knowledgeable, reflective, creative, and critical members of a variety of literacy communities.

12. Students use spoken, written, and visual language to accomplish their own purposes (e.g., for learning, enjoyment, persuasion, and the exchange of information).

FIGURE 3.3

PreK–12 English
Language Proficiency
Standards in the Core
Content Areas

Standard 1: English language learners communicate for social, intercultural, and instructional purposes within the school setting.

Standard 2: English language learners communicate information, ideas, and concepts necessary for academic success in the area of language arts.

Standard 3: English language learners communicate information, ideas, and concepts necessary for academic success in the area of mathematics.

Standard 4: English language learners communicate information, ideas, and concepts necessary for academic success in the area of science.

Standard 5: English language learners communicate information, ideas, and concepts necessary for academic success in the area of social studies.

Source: TESOL, 2006.

FIGURE 3.4
California State
Standards—Grade 10:
World History, Culture,
and Geography: The
Modern World

10.1   Students relate the moral and ethical principles in ancient Greek and Roman philosophy, in Judaism, and in Christianity to the development of Western political thought.

10.2   Students compare and contrast the Glorious Revolution of England, the American Revolution, and the French Revolution and their enduring effects worldwide on the political expectations for self-government and individual liberty.

10.3   Students analyze the effects of the Industrial Revolution in England, France, Germany, Japan, and the United States.

10.4   Students analyze patterns of global change in the era of New Imperialism in at least two of the following regions or countries: Africa, Southeast Asia, China, India, Latin America, and the Philippines.

10.5   Students analyze the causes and course of the first World War.

10.6   Students analyze the effects of the first World War.

10.7   Students analyze the rise of totalitarian governments after World War I.

10.8   Students analyze the causes and consequences of World War II.

10.9   Students analyze the international developments in the post–World War II world.

10.10   Students analyze instances of nation-building in the contemporary world in at least two of the following regions or countries: the Middle East, Africa, Mexico and other parts of Latin America, and China.

10.11   Students analyze the integration of countries into the world economy and the information, technological, and communications revolutions (e.g., television, satellites, computers).

students should demonstrate to show proficiency; and (3) opportunity to learn standards—also referred to as delivery standards—that define the quality of the programs, staff, and other resources that schools, districts, and states provide to enable students to meet the content and performance standards. Although the content and performance standards appear prevalent in our teaching, the opportunity to learn or delivery standards do not seem to be equally valued.

Positive and Negative Views of Standards

As with all educational practices, the standards have received both praise and criticism. Some believe the standards provide a focus for education; others suggest that they may cause greater failure among students who are already at risk.

Supporters note that the standards give direction to teaching and help students to focus their achievement. Falk (2002) reports that working with standards can stimulate teachers and students to use a variety of instructional strategies that support multiple approaches to learning and to develop clear purposes and sound learning goals. She further notes that assessing students' work in relation to standards has helped teachers understand what students know and can do. Lefkowits and Miller (2006) suggest that we can help students achieve high standards by providing the necessary resources, ensuring accountability, and maintaining flexibility and control at the local level.

Those who question the value of standards raise issues such as accommodating varying ways for students to learn, diverse populations, and accountability. For example, Reigeluth (1997) suggests that if the purpose of the standards is to accelerate learning for all students, then we must recognize that students learn at different rates and accommodate individual needs when working with the standards. Falk (2002) focuses on the needs of diverse populations, noting that teachers working with standards struggle to help such students to reach their full potential. Many believe the standards require teachers to cover a wide spectrum of topics, rather than

FIGURE 3.5 Benchmarks for Pennsylvania's Mathematics Standard for Geometry

2.9. Geometry

2.9.3. Grade 3	2.9.5. Grade 5	2.9.8. Grade 8	2.9.11. Grade 11

Pennsylvania's public schools shall teach, challenge, and support every student to realize his or her maximum potential and to acquire the knowledge and skills to

2.9.3. Grade 3	2.9.5. Grade 5	2.9.8. Grade 8	2.9.11. Grade 11
A. Name and label geometric shapes in two and three dimensions (e.g., circle/sphere, square/cube, triangle/pyramid, rectangle/prism).	A. Give formal definitions of geometric figures.	A. Construct figures incorporating perpendicular and parallel lines, the perpendicular bisector of a line segment, and an angle bisector using computer software.	A. Construct geometric figures using dynamic geometry tools (e.g., Geometer's Sketchpad, Cabri Geometry).
B. Build geometric shapes using concrete objects (e.g., manipulatives).	B. Classify and compare triangles and quadrilaterals according to sides or angles.	B. Draw, label, measure, and list the properties of complementary, supplementary, and vertical angles.	B. Prove that two triangles or two polygons are congruent or similar using algebraic, coordinate, and deductive proofs.
C. Draw two- and three-dimensional geometric shapes and construct rectangles, squares and triangles on the geoboard and on graph paper satisfying specific criteria.	C. Identify and measure circles, their diameters, and their radii.	C. Classify familiar polygons as regular or irregular up to a decagon.	C. Identify and prove the properties of quadrilaterals involving opposite sides and angles, consecutive sides and angles, and diagonals using deductive proofs.
D. Find and describe geometric figures in real life.	D. Describe in words how geometric shapes are constructed.	D. Identify, name, draw, and list all properties of squares, cubes, pyramids, parallelograms, quadrilaterals, trapezoids, polygons, rectangles, rhombi, circles, spheres, triangles, prisms, and cylinders.	D. Identify corresponding parts in congruent triangles to solve problems.
E. Identify and draw lines of symmetry in geometric figures.	E. Construct two- and three-dimensional shapes and figures using manipulatives, geoboards, and computer software.	E. Construct parallel lines, draw a transversal, and measure and compare angles formed (e.g., alternate interior and exterior angles).	E. Solve problems involving inscribed and circumscribed polygons.
F. Identify symmetry in nature.	F. Find familiar solids in the environment and describe them.	F. Distinguish between similar and congruent polygons.	F. Use the properties of angles, arcs, chords, tangents, and secants to solve problems involving circles.
G. Fold paper to demonstrate the reflections about a line.	G. Create an original tessellation.	G. Approximate the value of π (pi) through experimentation.	G. Solve problems using analytic geometry.
H. Show relationships between and among figures using reflections.	H. Describe the relationship between the perimeter and area of triangles, quadrilaterals and circles.	H. Use simple geometric figures (e.g., triangles, squares) to create, through rotation, transformational figures in three dimensions.	H. Construct a geometric figure and its image using various transformations.
I. Predict how shapes can be changed by combining or dividing them.	I. Represent and use the concepts of line, point, and plane.	I. Generate transformations using computer software.	I. Model situations geometrically to formulate and solve problems.
	J. Define the basic properties of squares, pyramids, parallelograms, quadrilaterals, trapezoids, polygons, rectangles, rhombi, circles, triangles, cubes, prisms, spheres, and cylinders.	J. Analyze geometric patterns (e.g., tessellations, sequences of shapes) and develop descriptions of the patterns.	J. Analyze figures in terms of the kinds of symmetries they have.
	K. Analyze simple transformations of geometric figures and rotations of line segments.	K. Analyze objects to determine whether they illustrate tessellations, symmetry, congruence, similarity, and scale.	
	L. Identify properties of geometric figures (e.g., parallel, perpendicular, similar, congruent, symmetrical).		

teach selected topics on an in-depth basis. Still others suggest that the standards have reduced curriculums to mere "test preparations" and changed students into test takers.

Darling-Hammond and Falk (1997) suggest that we should focus on the essence of the standards and the assessments. They also propose that we should examine the purposes for which the standards and assessments may be used. These authors note that students' ability to meet standards is directly connected to issues of teaching, assessment, school organization, professional development, and funding.

In addition, Falk (2002) draws our attention to the issue of accountability. She suggests that, "Fair and equitable accountability policies and practices are needed if standards-based reforms are to serve the learning of students and teachers" (p. 614). She proposes that fair accountability

- Acknowledges the social inequities in the United States.
- Uncouples high stakes from high standards.
- Uses standards and assessments to give educators information that can be used to improve student learning.
- Relies on standards and assessments as just one source of information that can be used, in conjunction with other kinds of information, to make decisions about students' futures and to allocate support for students and schools (Falk, 2002, p. 617).

Making Connections | Thinking about the Standards

- Reflect on the role that standards play in your teaching. Consider what you perceive to be the good points about standards-based teaching. Then think about whether standards drive your curriculum. Focus on specific examples.
- Share your thoughts with others in small-group discussion.

How Can We Use What We Know about the Standards in Teaching?

Generally, we can use educational standards to help us make decisions about what to teach, what to assess, and what to eliminate from the curriculum. Deciding which content to teach and which to eliminate can be a challenge (Schmoker & Marzano, 1999; Wiggins & McTighe, 1998; Zemelman, Daniels, & Hyde, 2005). Teachers often use "backward mapping" to facilitate this process. That is, they turn the standards into questions and allow those queries to serve as the focus of teaching and learning. After the questions have been developed, teachers design performance assessments. Next, they develop their lessons. This process aligns standards, performance assessments, and teaching.

Of course, teachers who use "backmapping" need to base the process on what they know about best practice for teaching and learning. As Tomlinson (2000) notes, "The conflict between focusing on standards and focusing on individual learners' needs exists only if we use standards in ways that cause us to abandon what we know about effective curriculum and instruction" (p. 6).

Noddings (1997) reminds us that if we want to raise standards, we need to explain the standards to our students and detail how they relate to students' learning. Falk (2002) agrees, noting:

Standards can support better learning if they are used to direct teaching toward worthy goals, to promote teaching that is responsive to the way students learn, to examine students in ways that can be used to inform instruction, to keep students and parents apprised of progress, to trigger special supports for students who need them, and to evaluate school practices. (p. 620)

Of course, the responsibility for motivating our students to engage in standards-based learning also rests with us. As George Murphy, a biology teacher who emphasizes inquiry, explains:

> It's not the standards that will make school relevant and vital for students. I want to get them interested in what they're doing. I'm not up front to dance for them. I want to present the students with a challenge, see them rise to the challenge, see them want to learn. I want to dare them to have a good time with science. (Tomlinson & Doubet 2005, p. 12)

Making Connections | Thinking about Teaching with Standards

- Reflect on what you would do to help your students understand the state standards and the role they play in teaching and learning.
- Share your thoughts with others in a small-group discussion.

Standards-Based Lessons

In this section, we examine standards-based lessons in everyday teaching. Excerpts from standards-based lessons in science, mathematics, world language, and literature are featured. Each plan lists the lesson's goals and the state standards to which they relate. The goals or expectations indicate what students should be able to demonstrate by the end of the lesson. In addition to the standards and goals (or objectives), each excerpt includes the topic of the lesson, the author(s), suggested grade levels, materials/technology, time required, and assessment. The first two lessons reference the Montana State Standards, the latter two reference the Pennsylvania State Standards.

LESSON I. SCIENCE: THE GREAT FLATHEAD LAKE ECOSYSTEM MYSTERY. Dan O'Brien and Dave Fitzpatrick, high school teachers in the Polson and Charlo School Districts in Western Montana, authored this science lesson for grades 10–12. They based the lesson on an actual, large-scale, ecosystem crash that occurred in their area during the late 1980s. They estimate the lesson will take two to four 50-minute class periods, depending on depth of discussion and research.

Prior to beginning this science lesson, Dan and Dave tell students about the "good old days" when more than 600 bald eagles could be counted on a single day feeding on the local, spawning Kokanee salmon. Local historians described the salmon as being so plentiful that one could cross a stream simply by walking across on their backs. The daily catch limit was 70 fish per person every two days, and plans had been made to build two salmon canneries in the area. Then sadly the eagles and salmon suddenly disappeared, almost overnight. Now Dan and Dave ask students to study all of the data known about the animals involved to try to solve this amazing mystery.

In this lesson, the students use their prior knowledge to construct detailed food webs of the problem ecosystem while looking for factors that may have contributed to its instability. They use these data to construct a formal problem statement and then offer a hypothesis as to the probable cause of that problem. Finally, students offer their own suggestions for a management plan that would best promote the survival of the culturally significant bull trout.

Materials needed by students include graph paper or spreadsheets and lab response sheets. Note the relation between the lesson goals and the state standards addressed, as well as the performance nature of the lesson.

LESSON GOALS

Students will:

1. Develop skills in data manipulation (graphing and web diagramming) and interpretation.
2. Use available information to propose a mitigation plan for a local ecological problem.

MONTANA SCIENCE STANDARDS ADDRESSED

1. Students design, conduct, evaluate, and communicate scientific investigations.
2. Students demonstrate knowledge of characteristics, structures, and function of living things, the process and diversity of life, and how living organisms interact with each other and their environment.

ASSESSMENT

To assess, Dan and Dave observe students as they work and comment on their completed graphs and food webs as well as the step-by-step, cause-and-effect analysis of the food web collapse and its best future management plan. They provide a checklist to students at the start of the lesson.

To read Dan and Dave's lesson, please go to http://www.polson.k12.mt.us/phs/staff/dobrien/biology/eco_mystery.pdf.

LESSON 2. GEOMETRY: TRADITIONAL NATIVE AMERICAN (INDIAN) LODGES. Teachers Sue Moore, Glenn Blake, and Polly Dupuis created this lesson for grades 8–10. This is one of a set of five lessons in which students use the designs of traditional Native American (Indian) lodges to explore geometric shapes and their properties such as volume and surface area. The lessons can be done separately or can be grouped and completed as a unit. Each lesson takes approximately one 50-minute class period. Materials needed include calculators, meter sticks, crepe paper or flagging tape, and research tools such as books and websites. Notice the following points: (1) how the lesson goals reflect the state standards; (2) the student-centered nature of the lesson; and (3) the use of a rubric for the final project. (For more information about rubrics, see Chapter 14.)

LESSON GOALS

Students will:

1. Explain circles as the limiting shape for an inscribed regular polygon.
2. Determine the surface area and volume of prisms, cones, and cylinders.
3. Find ratios between volume and surface areas.
4. Research traditional Native American (Indian) lodges.
5. Describe and discuss the mathematical properties of traditional Native American (Indian) lodges.

MONTANA MATH STANDARDS ADDRESSED

1. Students engage in the mathematical processes of problem solving and reasoning, estimation, communication, connections and applications, and using appropriate technology.
2. Students demonstrate understanding of shape and an ability to use geometry.

ASSESSMENT

To assess learning at the end of the unit, students complete a project in which they are asked to choose one type of Native American (Indian) lodge to research. They describe the dwelling's design and then define it from a mathematical perspective, applying the concepts learned in this unit, including geometric shape, surface area, and volume. Figure 3.6 features a rubric for the end-of-unit project. Note that the Montana State Math Standards referenced in this unit are reflected in the evaluative criteria used in the traditional Native American (Indian) lodges project rubric. This provides evidence that state standards are not isolated documents. In most school districts, they are required parts of daily lesson plans, and teachers are asked to share the standards with the students they teach. Including the standards in the rubric helps extend that understanding. Students receive the rubric prior to beginning the project. For more information about rubrics, see Chapter 14.

LESSON 3. FRENCH: LE VERBE ÊTRE AND ADJECTIVES. Edit Vergara, a French teacher, wrote this lesson for French I class in grade 9. During this class, students learn the different forms

FIGURE 3.6   The Traditional Native American (Indian) Lodges Geometry Project Rubric

Category	4	3	2	1
Describe and illustrate a traditional Native American (Indian) lodge using appropriate geometry concepts	Outstanding description and illustration	Thorough description and illustration	Adequate description and illustration	Inadequate description and illustration
Describe the mathematical properties of a traditional Native American (Indian) lodge, including geometric shape, surface area, and volume	Excellent use of mathematical properties to describe a traditional Native American (Indian) lodge	Very good use of mathematical properties to describe a traditional Native American (Indian) lodge	Acceptable use of mathematical properties to describe a traditional Native American (Indian) lodge	Poor use of mathematical properties to describe a traditional Native American (Indian) lodge
Problem solve and reason	Outstanding evidence of problem solving and reasoning	Thorough evidence of problem solving and reasoning	Adequate evidence of problem solving and reasoning	Inadequate evidence of problem solving and reasoning
Use technology	Excellent use of technology	Very good use of technology	Acceptable use of technology	Poor use of technology
Organize and present information logically	Outstanding organization and presentation	Thorough organization and presentation	Adequate organization and presentation	Inadequate organization and presentation

of the French verb *être*—"to be." They also use vocabulary they have recently learned to describe photos and advertised items from newspapers and magazines. Finally, they engage in translating short passages that include "être" and adjectives. Discussion permeates the lesson. According to Edit, the class time required for this lesson is one 50-minute class period. Students need additional time outside of class to complete the assessment. Materials needed include markers, a chalkboard or whiteboard, pictures, textbooks, and response sheets. As noted in the assessment section, the project to extend students' learning requires students to write a poem in French, demonstrating their knowledge of "être" and adjectives. Notice the relation between the lesson goals and the state standards, as well as the performance assessment used to extend students' thinking. (To learn more about performance assessments, see Chapter 14.)

LESSON GOALS

Students will:

1. Conjugate the verb être in the present tense.
2. Describe pictures using new vocabulary.
3. Translate text.
4. Engage in discussion.
5. Complete a project about French culture.

PENNSYLVANIA STANDARDS ADDRESSED

Communications

1.1. Provide and obtain information, express feelings, exchange opinions.
1.2. Interpretation of written and spoken language.
1.3. Present information and ideas to an audience.

Cultures

2.1. Relation between practices (the way people interact) and perspectives.
2.2. Relation between products (physical reality) and perspectives.

Comparisons

4.1. Demonstrate understanding of the nature of language through comparing French and English.

ASSESSMENT

As a follow-up to lessons on "être" and adjectives, students learn how to create repeated phrase poems in French. They then work with partners to create repeated phrase poems (see Chapter 13) about different aspects of French culture. The poems focus on topics of students' choosing and include a repeated phrase. For example, if students choose to write about Paris, the poem might include city sites ranging from the Opera to the Louvre and the repeated phrase might be, "Paris is a creative city." As demonstrated in the repeated phrase, students use "être" and adjectives throughout their poems. As an alternative assessment, students create tourist guides to various regions of France.

LESSON 4. LITERATURE: *THE GLASS MENAGERIE.* Kristi Streightiff, a high school English teacher, created this lesson for her eleventh-grade Honors English class. She begins the class by encouraging students to share their opinions about the work of Tennessee Williams, a playwright they have been studying. She uses the discussion of Williams' work to introduce the focus of today's lesson: challenging the students to create a dramatic scene with peers. The class is divided into three groups of five students, with each person in the group choosing a specific part of the play production to focus on and design (character voice, actions, and expressions; make-up and costumes; set design; producer/casting director; director of lighting and music). Finally, as a group, students come together and collaborate to produce the whole scene. Kristi suggests that this lesson will require one 50-minute class period and that students will need materials such as markers, crayons, colored pencils, magazines, books, and construction paper. Notice (1) how the lesson goals relate to the state standards addressed and (2) the student-centered, performance-based nature of the lesson.

LESSON GOALS

Students will:

1. Demonstrate knowledge of the elements of drama and how they contribute to production.
2. Create and design a scene.
3. Engage in discussion.
4. Present a scene to the class.
5. Engage in peer assessment.

PENNSYLVANIA STANDARDS ADDRESSED

1.1.11.B. Analyze the structure of informational materials, explaining how authors used these to achieve their purposes.
1.2.11.C. Produce work in at least one literary genre that follows the conventions of the genre.
1.6.11.E. Participate in small-and large-group discussions and presentations.

ASSESSMENT

The students and teacher assess the scenes they create and perform. A performance checklist designed to facilitate peer assessment is shared with students at the beginning of class.

As demonstrated in the lessons in this section, standards can provide a focus for teaching and learning. As Darling-Hammond and Falk (1997) note:

The standards are intended to provide educators with guidelines for curriculum and teaching that will ensure that students have access to the knowledge believed necessary for their later success. When thoughtfully developed to integrate what we know about learning with key concepts and modes of inquiry within the disciplines, standards can help educators rethink curriculum, teaching, and assessment practices. (pp. 190–191)

Making Connections | Thinking about State Standards and Lesson Plans

■ Reflect on developing standards-based lesson plans in your content area. Choose a topic and develop instructional goals (objectives) for a lesson, and then list the state standards to which the objectives relate. Examine how the objectives and the standards are related.

■ Share your ideas with others in a small-group discussion.

What Do We Know about High-Stakes Assessments?

High-stakes assessments use the results of a single measure to make important decisions about student progress or the effectiveness of instruction. They are called "high stakes" because they are used to make important decisions about individual students, teachers, or schools. Proponents of this type of assessment believe that it is a catalyst for reform that promotes higher expectations for student performance. Developed by policy makers with the intention of improving education, high-stakes tests are designed for numerous purposes, including making comparisons of students across the United States. These types of assessments are most frequently developed at the state level and administered annually to a number of different grades. Florida's Comprehensive State Assessment, Pennsylvania's System of School Assessment, and Virginia's Standards of Learning Tests are examples of such measures.

High-stakes assessments at the state level have been designed to report school performance, change curriculum and assessment practices, evaluate curricular changes, and monitor program effectiveness. Nearly all states have such measures in place. The most frequently used types of questions are performance-based, open-ended, and selected-response. Writing essays in response to prompts or creating math problems and solutions based on test-provided information are examples of performance tasks. Open-ended questions require students to provide their own answers, whereas selected-response items allow students to choose their answers from several test-provided possibilities. Most states began high-stakes testing by measuring students' abilities in reading, writing, and mathematics. Over time, the assessments have expanded to include science and social studies, with many states currently developing tests for an even more extensive list of subject areas.

High-stakes tests may consist of traditional standardized tests or more performance-based measures. Administrators usually value high-stakes testing and use its results to plan curriculums and guide instruction. They often prefer multiple-choice tests because they are easier to score than performance-based measures (Guthrie, 2005, p. 286).

Criticisms of High-Stakes Testing

Opponents of high-stakes assessment focus on its structure and misuse. They believe that it is not sound practice to make any educational decision on the basis of one test score. Thompson (2001) reports that whenever a high-stakes, standardized measure is imposed as the sole criterion for judging student success, it replaces existing content or performance standards. Opponents also note that high-stakes tests do not have sufficient reliability and validity for the purposes for which they are being used. To correct this deficiency, Gratz (2000) proposes standards for testing. These would ensure that the constructs (e.g., academic standards) the test measures are relevant and fair and that the test assesses what it purports to assess.

Many researchers report that high-stakes assessments often fail to accurately evaluate students' knowledge. Because reading is such a complex process, literacy professionals, in particular, believe that high-stakes tests do not provide a full and accurate view of students' abilities. They suggest that policy makers should design assessment plans that take into consideration issues related to reading, learning to read, and the teaching of reading. They further note that policy makers should rely on multiple measures and use sampling when possible, but not use incentives or attempt to manipulate instruction (Guthrie, 2005; Hoffman, Assaf, & Paris, 2001).

Other controversies regarding high-stakes assessment have arisen because the results have been used for a wide variety of purposes. These include meeting a consumer demand for credentialing, transferring control of curriculum and graduation standards from the local level to state departments of education, describing publicly the performance of individual students, and defining the nature of educational priorities (Madaus & Kellaghan 1993). The outcomes of such assessments affect students, teachers, administrators, and school districts by affecting promotion, retention, instructional effectiveness, teacher salary, and the school district's funding. For example, as teachers, we often need to contend with the pressures associated with student success on such assessments. This includes the need to spend many hours teaching the test's content and the skills the students need to complete it. For this reason, high-stakes tests are often viewed as being misused in evaluating teachers and schools because they have no connection to the school's content standards or curriculum (Thompson, 2001).

In addition to the doubts voiced by numerous individual researchers, professional educational organizations—including the International Reading Association (IRA), the National Reading Conference, the National Council of Teachers of English (NCTE), and the National Council of Teachers of Mathematics (NCTM)—have questioned the value of high-stakes testing. These organizations have issued position statements either expressing their opposition to such testing or calling for it to be only one of multiple ways in which students are assessed. Assessing students through the administration of one standardized test is not an idea these professional organizations support. See the E-Links section at the end of the chapter for further information about their position statements.

Connection to State Standards

High-stakes assessments at the state level are usually correlated with state standards and designed to measure student progress in attaining them. School districts often design down from the state standards to create benchmarks or grade-level indicators of expected student performance. As a consequence, high-stakes testing influences everyday teaching and learning.

The relation between state assessments and state standards can also be viewed as problematic. The control of curriculum and limitation of instruction are two examples. Because high-stakes testing is inextricably linked to important rewards and sanctions, school districts often tailor the curriculum to accommodate subject areas and topics addressed in the tests. This can result in a narrowing of the school district's curriculum, which can affect what the students learn. In the classroom, teachers may find themselves not only teaching to the test, but also spending inordinate amounts of time on test preparations, including the use of instructional materials that mirror high-stakes testing formats, content, and question types (Guthrie, 2005). Such practices can diminish students' access to meaningful instruction and achievement of state standards.

Issues related to administering high-stakes tests are also problematic. For example, high school students often do not put forth their best efforts when taking the tests (Guthrie, 2005); students often need to be taught how to complete the tests; teachers do not receive the test results quickly enough; and the results that teachers receive usually lack the level of detail needed to target specific improvements (Barton, 2002; Kifer, 2001).

Despite its controversial nature, high-stakes assessment is widely practiced. Virtually every state in the nation engages in this type of assessment.

FINAL THOUGHTS

All that we have learned about standards seems to indicate that they will be a part of our educational practice for some time to come. Falk (2002) sees three challenges related to this standards-based reform: (1) developing worthy standards; (2) teaching the way students learn; and (3) assessing to inform and support student learning, using multiple measures.

High-stakes testing seems to be another issue with which we will need to continue to contend. In this case, our goals are to work to ensure that the assessments are correlated with the standards and that they are designed to enable our students to perform to their maximum potential.

In Chapter 4, we examine what we know about reading comprehension and how we can teach our students to use essential strategies. We focus particularly on those strategies designed to engage thinking.

Teaching Connections
APPLYING WHAT WE HAVE LEARNED

E-Links

This E-Links activity has two parts. The first deals with state standards. The second addresses professional organizations' position statements on high stakes testing.

PART ONE: STATE STANDARDS

Figure 3.7 features websites that provide access to state standards. These websites either provide links to the individual state standards or a list of the websites through which to access state standards. Use one of the websites to access your state's standards for the subject you either plan to teach or currently teach. Focus on the standards for middle school or high school. Work with a partner to critique those standards. Do you think the standards are appropriate as they are written? Do you think other standards should be added to the list? Do you think some standards should be deleted from the list? In response to each question, provide examples and justify your thinking in a portfolio reflection.

PART TWO: PROFESSIONAL EDUCATIONAL ORGANIZATIONS AND HIGH-STAKES TESTING

1. Read the position statements that the following professional organizations have issued regarding high-stakes testing: IRA, NRC, NCTE, and NCTM. (See Figure 3.8 for some links.) Then consider what you have learned about high-stakes testing and your own experiences with such measures. What is your position on high-stakes testing? Justify your thinking in a portfolio reflection.
2. In some school districts, high-stakes testing seems to be determining schools' curriculums. Teachers are not only teaching the content of the test, but are also required to teach the students how to take the test. This limits the focus on standards-based learning. As an inservice or preservice teacher, reflect on how you believe curriculum should be determined. Justify your response in a portfolio reflection.

Accountable Talk

Standards and high-stakes testing permeate our teaching.

1. Consider the state standards in your content area. Think about how you can use them to teach more effectively. Focus on specific examples.
2. Consider the high-stakes tests your students are required to take. Discuss whether you believe those tests relate to your state standards and how they may or may not be beneficial for your students. Focus on specific examples.
3. Meet in small groups and discuss your ideas.

Portfolio/Performance Opportunity

Review and revise two lesson plans you have created while studying your content area. Make certain that the lessons are correlated to state standards. Consider (1) how each lesson helps students progress toward meeting the standards and (2) how the assessments you used measure that progress. Revise the lessons as needed. Meet in small groups to discuss the lessons, focusing on state standards, as well as points 1 and 2. Provide feedback for peers and receive feedback for your work. Revise as necessary. Discuss how peer input influenced the final lessons. Share your thoughts in whole-class discussion and include your revised lesson plans in your portfolio.

FIGURE 3.7

Links to Comprehensive Listings of State Standards

Education World
http://www.education-world.com/standards

State Content Standards: A 50-State Resource
www.ccsso.org/content/pdfs/StateContentStandards.pdf

This PDF document lists the individual state websites but does not provide a direct link to them.

FIGURE 3.8

Links to Professional Educational Organizations' Position Statements on High-Stakes Testing

International Reading Association, *High Stakes Testing in Reading: A Position Statement of the International Reading Association* (1999)
http://www.reading.org/downloads/positions/ps1035_high_stakes.pdf

National Reading Conference, *National Reading Conference Policy Brief High Stakes Testing and Reading Assessment* (2004)
http://www.nrconline.org

National Council of Teachers of English, *Framing Statements on Assessment* (2004)
http://www.ncte.org/positions/statements/assessmentframingst

National Council of Teachers of Mathematics, *High-Stakes Tests* (2006)
http://nctm.org/about/content.aspx?id=6356

4

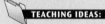
Comprehending Content Area Text

I magine trying to read a textbook, a novel, a newspaper, or a computer screen and not being able to understand it. Think about how frustrating it would be if you could not comprehend text and how that would affect your life—from everyday occurrences such as reading the newspaper or email to reading novels or textbooks. Then think about students who may find themselves in that same situation. As teachers, we want our students to be active, independent, strategic learners, but that is not possible if they cannot comprehend text. In this chapter, we examine ways to help students understand what they read in their content area classes. Our discussion focuses on three topics: what reading comprehension is, what contributes to successful reading experiences, and how we can help students use strategies to think through the reading process.

In this chapter, we explore these issues through theory and practice. We begin by focusing on what we know about reading comprehension. We examine reading from a social constructivist perspective and as a thinking process. Then we describe factors that contribute to successful reading experiences. Next, we investigate what we, as teachers, can do to contribute to students' understanding of content area text. After that, we take a closer look at reading comprehension strategies, paying particular attention to strategies for engaging student thinking.

What Do We Know about Reading Comprehension?

Every worthwhile educational practice has a strong theoretical foundation. So we begin our quest to understand reading's role in content area teaching by examining its roots—the theories and beliefs that support it. As Brian Cambourne (2002, p. 25) notes, "There is nothing so practical as a good theory."

Our theoretical investigation of the reading process focuses on two current beliefs: (1) that reading is a social constructivist process and (2) that readers think their way through the construction of meaning. We begin our discussion by noting that comprehension is an essential component of teaching and learning. One of our primary goals as content area teachers is to ensure that our students know how to comprehend text. This is a complex task, but as Duke and Pearson (2002) note, "Comprehension is a consuming, continuous, and complex activity, but one that, for good readers, is both satisfying and productive" (p. 206).

Comprehension of Text as a Social Constructivist Process

Savery and Duffy (1995, p. 31) suggest that constructivism is a "philosophical view on how we come to understand or know." Constructivists believe that students construct knowledge by linking what they already know to new information. In reading, this concept is reflected in schema-based learning development, which suggests that learning takes place when prior knowledge—what is already known—is integrated with new information—what is currently being read. The more knowledge and experience learners have with a particular topic, the easier it is for them to make connections between what they know and what they are learning (Anderson, 1994). As noted in Chapter 1, Brian Cambourne suggests that knowledge and meaning are socially constructed through the processes of negotiation, evaluation, and transformation.

We refer to reading comprehension as a *social* constructivist process because readers often share ideas about what they are reading to negotiate meaning. Such discussions are "forums for collaboratively constructing meaning and for sharing responses" (Almasi, 1996, p. 2). Gambrell (1996) notes that these collaborations integrate listening, speaking, and thinking skills. Because of the dynamic nature of these discussions, the meanings that readers construct are continually transformed by their experiences, interactions with others, and information from the text (Almasi, 1996). This social interaction is another aspect of literacy that is underpinned by Vygotsky's (1978) theoretical framework. His work suggests that social interaction plays a fundamental role in the development of cognition. His beliefs support that students' thinking abilities develop more fully when students work with teachers or peers.

Multiple Literacies as Comprehension

In Chapter 2, Teaching and Learning in an Age of Multiple Literacies, we discussed the current focus on adolescent, content, critical, information, media, and multicultural literacies. These literacies are distinctive in nature, yet similar in that one of the outcomes of each is comprehension. For example, adolescent literacy involves understanding and applying knowledge in a variety of contexts, content literacy involves understanding through the uniqueness of each discipline, and critical literacy involves questioning the author and the message to move beyond everyday understanding to comprehend at deeper levels. (For more information about multiple literacies, see Chapter 2.)

Reading online, which is an integral part of today's literacies, is a constructivist process, just as reading offline is. Online reading comprehension is a problem-based, inquiry process (Coiro, Knoebel, Lankshear, & Leu, 2008; Leu, Kinzer, Coiro, & Cammack, 2004). Readers construct meaning based on their personal paths of inquiry and discovery (Schmar-Dobbler, 2003). (For more information about reading online and offline, see Chapter 11.)

Reading as a Thinking Process

Decades ago, Dolores Durkin (1978–1979) defined reading as comprehension, indicating that the focus of instruction should be the strategies readers use to make sense of text. Frank Smith (1997) extended this idea by defining reading as "thinking, cued by print." Suggesting that reading is a thinking process indicates that the focus of instruction should not be on the print, but rather on how readers connect with the print. Hiebert, Pearson, Taylor, Richardson, and Paris (1998) endorse this idea: "Teachers support their students' strategic reading through lessons that attend explicitly to how to think while reading" (p. 4). Harris and Hodge (1995) also support the idea of reading as a thinking process, noting that the meaning readers construct "resides in the intentional problem-solving, thinking processes of the interpreter during such an interchange" (p. 39).

Describing reading as a thinking process seems quite logical and natural if we examine a reader's interaction with text. To begin, the student contemplates text selection and uses a variety of thought processes to activate prior knowledge and make connections to the text. The reader previews the text by making predictions about the content and setting purposes for reading. During reading, the student may self-question, visualize, monitor, make connections, summarize the text read so far, and evaluate the author's purpose and the consistency of text. After reading, the learner may summarize, evaluate, and make connections, again engaging in cognitive processes. To successfully interact with text, students need to be thinkers. To effectively think through the reading process and interact with a variety of types and levels of text, students need to know how to use reading comprehension skills and strategies.

Although many factors appear to contribute to reader comprehension, three influences seem most prominent: influential teachers, good readers, and quality contexts. In the remainder of this section, we learn that influential teachers are described as knowledgeable—not only about content, but also about their students; good readers are represented as motivated and strategic; and contexts are viewed as meaningful teaching and learning environments.

Influential Reading Teachers Affect Students' Learning

As detailed in Chapter 1, researchers and professional organizations report that teachers are the single most influential factor in students' learning (International Reading Association, 2000; Ruddell, 2004). Characteristics of such teachers, who are commonly described as "influential" or "excellent," are featured in Figure 4.1.

As noted in the figure, these teachers know their content and how to teach it. They are aware of students' individual needs and the importance of motivation. They also use multiple grouping patterns and a variety of teaching and assessment methods.

What Good Readers Do

Reading researchers report that much of what we know about comprehension is based on studies of "good readers" (Duke & Pearson, 2002; Pearson, 2001; Pressley, 2000). They describe good readers as active participants in the reading process, who have clear goals and constantly monitor the relation between the goals they have set and the text they are reading. Good readers use a repertoire of comprehension strategies to facilitate the construction of meaning. These strategies include previewing, monitoring, making connections, self-questioning, visualizing, summarizing, and evaluating. Students should know how to use these strategies, so they can call upon them as needed when they are reading.

FIGURE 4.1
Characteristics of Influential Reading Teachers

- Believe all students can learn
- Motivate their students
- Teach in concept-rich environments
- Have in-depth knowledge of literacy
- Use diverse teaching methods
- Use multiple grouping patterns
- Are participants in the reading process

- Teach to the needs of individual learners
- Use multiple kinds and levels of text
- Have in-depth knowledge of content
- Teach for a variety of purposes
- Use a variety of materials
- Teach reading strategies
- Assess in multiple ways

Good readers read from aesthetic or efferent stances and have an awareness of the author's style and purpose (Rosenblatt, 1978). The aesthetic stance depicts a predominantly emotional perspective; the efferent stance, a predominantly factual one. Rosenblatt (2002) notes that no reading experience is purely aesthetic or purely efferent, but rather that readers continually make choices about their thinking, focusing on both stances, and sometimes more on one than the other. For example, if we were reading about the Holocaust and learned that 1.5 million Jewish children died in concentration camps during that time, we might choose an aesthetic stance in our emotional response to the deaths of the children and an efferent stance when noting the number of children who perished.

Making Connections
TO MULTIPLE LITERACIES

Reader stance is an issue of particular interest within multiple literacies, because in addition to reading from Rosenblatt's aesthetic and efferent stances, researchers suggest that we can read from a critical stance (McLaughlin & DeVoogd, 2004). When reading from a critical literacy perspective or critical stance, readers use their background knowledge to understand the power relationships between their ideas and the ideas presented by the author of the text. In this process, readers play the role of text critics (Luke & Freebody, 1999). In other words, readers have the power to question, to problematize, and to envision alternative ways of viewing the author's topic. Readers exert that power when they read from a critical stance. ■

The critical stance functions just as the aesthetic and efferent stances do during reading: Our reading experiences may involve one stance more than the others, but all three are represented during reading. For example, when reading about the Holocaust, we may respond aesthetically to the poetry and drawings the children created in the concentration camps, efferently to the number of children who died during the Holocaust, and critically to the issues of justice associated with this event.

Good readers read both narrative or story-based text and informational or fact-based text. They have ideas about how to figure out unfamiliar words. They often preview what they are about to read and use their knowledge of text structure to efficiently and strategically think through text. This knowledge develops from experiences with different genres and is correlated with age and time spent in school (Goldman & Rakestraw, 2000).

Making Connections
TO STRUGGLING READERS

When teaching struggling readers, we should check to ensure that the students know and can use the skills that underpin the reading comprehension strategies and the strategies themselves. For example, these students need to know the elements of narrative text and to recognize the various patterns associated with informational text. It is helpful for us to preteach struggling readers, so they will have some knowledge prior to the whole-class instruction. This often enables these students to gain a better understanding and participate in class discussions in more meaningful ways. For detailed information about how to teach skills such as text patterns and generating questions, see Chapter 8. ■

Good readers also read widely. This helps them to understand a variety of genres and text formats, while accommodating their interests. It also provides opportunities for students to use reading strategies, increase their understanding of vocabulary, and engage in discussion and meaning negotiation.

FIGURE 4.2
Characteristics of Good Readers

- Use their prior knowledge
- Negotiate meaning
- Spontaneously generate questions
- Integrate reading, writing, speaking, and listening
- Read different kinds of text differently
- Set goals
- Are motivated and engaged
- Are problem solvers
- Use comprehension strategies
- Know text structures
- Make strategic decisions
- Adapt their thinking

Like influential teachers, good readers have numerous other characteristics (Block, Schaller, Joy, & Gaine, 2002; Duke & Pearson, 2002; Pressley & Afflerbach, 1995). Examples of those frequently cited are featured in Figure 4.2.

Making Connections | Thinking about Good Readers

- Think about when you were in high school. How would you have described a "good reader" then? At that time, did you consider yourself to be a good reader? Explain your response. Did you choose to read, or was your reading limited to your teachers' assignments? Did you think about reading as part of your learning in the content areas? Do you think today's middle and high school students are good readers? Justify your response.
- Share your thoughts in small-group discussions.

A Quality Context: An Integral Part of Meaningful Literacy Instruction

Context has been viewed as a broad concept that encompasses instructional settings, resources, approaches, and tasks (Lipson & Wixson, 2009). The instructional settings include facets such as teacher beliefs, literacy environment, classroom organization, classroom interaction, and grouping patterns. Instructional resources comprise elements such as text types and text structures. Instructional approaches include the curriculum, teaching methods, and assessment practices. Task type, content, form, and implementation are the elements of the instructional tasks. Duke (2001) has suggested that we expand our understanding of context and view curriculum, activity, classroom environment, teaching, discussion, text and society as context. Researchers and practitioners agree that both teaching and learning are greatly influenced by the contextual choices we make.

Making Connections | Thinking about the Contexts in Which We Teach

- Close your eyes and imagine the context in which you would like to teach. Open your eyes and sketch some of the ideas you visualized. Think about how you might create such a context while coping with influences such as pressure for your students to do well on state assessments.
- Share your sketches and ideas in small-group discussions.

What Can We Do to Foster Students' Comprehension of Content Area Text?

To help our students understand content area texts, we need to help them make connections between what they know and what they are reading. We must move beyond the traditional, "Read the next chapter" assignment and help students to become actively engaged in the text. To do so, we might provide a chapter overview and engage students in discussion about what they already know about the topic. We might motivate students by reading aloud, providing opportunities to view short videos, or sharing an array of related photos. We might also offer opportunities for self-selection of related readings or project topics.

Once our students are motivated, we need to continue to encourage them:

- *To activate and continue to expand their prior knowledge.* The constructivist view of reading focuses on the reader's prior knowledge interacting with the text that is being read. The more widely students read and the more they experience, the greater their prior knowledge will be and the better they will comprehend. To help students continue to increase their prior knowledge, we can provide them with a variety of content area experiences, types and levels of text, technology access, and opportunities for discussion.

- *To deepen their understanding of how language works.* Students often complain that they don't need to study grammar, because their computers will offer suggestions to correct it when they write. What they don't understand is that knowing how language works—parts of speech, word order, sentence structures—helps us to read more fluently, determine word meanings, and comprehend text.

- *To enhance their understanding of everyday and academic vocabularies.* Well-developed vocabularies help us to comprehend what we read. To help students increase their vocabularies, we can encourage them to read widely, teach them effective ways to learn new words, provide opportunities to use context clues, and support them while they use the terms while they read, write, and speak.

- *To read and respond to text.* The more our students read and respond to what they have read, the better they will comprehend. As teachers, we can provide students with frequent opportunities to read and communicate about what they have read. In the process, we should remain open to student thinking and offer access to multiple modes of presentation.

- *To develop and use a repertoire of comprehension strategies that they can call upon as needed to think through text.* We can explicitly teach these strategies; in the next section, we begin to focus on how to do that effectively.

Making Connections
TO ENGLISH LEARNERS

We expect all students to continually expand their knowledge, respond to what they read, and use strategies as needed, but these tasks can prove challenging for English learners. These students often need more support as they learn. We can provide this assistance in many ways, including (1) supplying text on tape or CD; (2) preteaching skills, strategies, and content as needed; and (3) simplifying or numbering graphic organizers. For more information on teaching English learners, see Chapter 9. ■

How Can We Teach Students to Think through the Comprehension of Text?

To help students think through the comprehension process, we can teach them reading comprehension strategies. We use a repertoire of these strategies as needed when we read text. The comprehension strategies that we use include these:

- *Previewing.* This strategy includes activating prior knowledge (What do I already know about this topic?), setting purposes for reading (Why am I reading this text?), and predicting/inferring (Based on what I know and what I have read, what do I think will happen in this text?).

- *Making connections.* When reading, we make three kinds of connections: text–self, text–text, and text–world (connections to others).
- *Monitoring/clarifying.* This strategy involves asking ourselves, "Does this make sense?" as we read, and, if it doesn't, adapting strategic processes to make it clear.
- *Self-questioning.* This strategy comprises generating questions to guide reading.
- *Visualizing.* We visualize by creating mental pictures of the text while reading.
- *Summarizing.* This strategy involves synthesizing important ideas. When we read narrative text, such as novels or short stories, we focus on elements such as characters, setting, problem, attempts to resolve the problem, and resolution. This process changes when we read informational or factual text, which is based on different text patterns, such as cause and effect and comparison/contrast. (To learn more about text patterns, see Chapter 8.)
- *Evaluating.* We evaluate or make judgments about text as we read. Examples include questioning the author's purpose and the consistency of the author's message.

Later in this chapter and in Chapters 5 and 6, we discuss each of these strategies in detail and provide multiple examples of how we can teach our students to use them. We discuss the strategies in three categories: engaging, guiding, and extending thinking. When we use strategies to engage thinking, we motivate the students to read by activating background knowledge, setting purposes for reading, and making predictions about the text. We teach students to use these strategies *before* reading. When we use strategies to guide thinking, we help students to transact with the text to comprehend it. We teach students to use these strategies *during* reading. When we use strategies to extend thinking, we encourage students to synthesize their thoughts and transfer what they have learned to other subject areas. We teach students to use these strategies *after* reading. Of course, although we learn the strategies as before, during, or after reading or as engaging, guiding, and extending thinking, they can be used *throughout* the reading process. Our overall goal is to help students develop a repertoire of reading comprehension strategies that they can call upon as needed to think through text.

Teaching ideas that support these strategies are featured in the next section, as well as in Chapters 5 and 6. In each example, we explain and demonstrate each idea using content area text. Then we guide students as they (and a partner) try using the strategy. We offer support as requested when students practice using the strategies on their own. Finally, we join the students in reflecting about the strategy and how we will use it over time. Some ideas involve alternative modes of response such as sketching, dramatizing, and singing. Offering alternative modes of response provides variety and accommodates students' varying learning styles. (For additional information about learning styles, see Chapter 1. For more comprehension-based teaching ideas and their related graphic organizers, see Chapters 5 and 6. For reproducible graphic organizers designed to support the strategies, see the Appendix.)

When we teach the reading comprehension strategies, we use the five-step explicit instruction process from the Guided Comprehension Model (McLaughlin & Allen, 2002a). The five steps in which we engage are explain, demonstrate, guide, practice, and reflect. When we use this Model, we can scaffold students' learning, gradually releasing responsibility from teacher to student (McLaughlin & Allen, 2002a). The Guided Comprehension Model is supported by Vygotsky's (1978) beliefs about scaffolding, the gradual relinquishing of support as the students become more competent in using the strategy. For example, when using the Guided Comprehension Model, we offer students full support when we explain and demonstrate the strategies. Then we gradually release responsibility for learning to the students. We guide their learning, offering support as needed when they practice the strategies with partners. Finally, we offer little or no support as students use the strategies on their own.

Strategies are more complex than skills, but they often integrate several skills. For example, we use skills such as questioning and sequencing when we engage in the comprehension strategy of summarizing. Linking skills and strategies facilitates comprehension. For a more detailed discussion of reading skills, including questioning, see Chapter 8.

How Can We Use Comprehension Strategies to Engage Thinking?

We use comprehension strategies throughout the reading process. We often describe this practice as using comprehension strategies before, during, and after reading. In this part of the chapter, we focus on strategies we can use *before* reading to engage student thinking. We use these strategies to activate background knowledge, make connections to text, and predict what may happen in the text based on what we already know or have read in the text.

In the examples that follow, we describe a variety of ways to support students' use of comprehension strategies before reading. Although we use previewing and making connections as examples of strategies that can be used to engage thinking, both strategies can also be used at other times during the reading process. In each step-by-step sequence, we begin by explaining the strategy and the teaching idea. Then we demonstrate it, using a think-aloud and a visual. Next, we guide students as they work with partners. Then the students attempt to use the strategy on their own. Finally, we reflect on what we have learned and how we can use the strategy in the content areas. Each sequence is followed by an example to support teaching in the content areas.

Making Connections
TO MULTIPLE LITERACIES

Although content literacy examples are featured in the sections that follow as well as in Chapters 5 and 6, the reading comprehension strategies we are learning how to teach are applicable in all literacies. In media literacy, examples of how we use the strategies include analyzing and evaluating information. Examples of how we use the strategies in information literacy include questioning to guide our inquiry and summarizing the information we locate. ■

Previewing

Previewing is a comprehension strategy that includes activating prior knowledge (What do I already know about this topic?), setting purposes for reading (I will read this text to learn . . .), and predicting and inferring (What can I hypothesize based on what I already know and what I am able to assume from the text?). Many teaching ideas support this strategy, including the seven featured in this section. For related graphic organizers, see Appendix A.

TEACHING IDEA ANTICIPATION/REACTION GUIDE. Students can use an Anticipation/Reaction Guide (Readence, Bean, & Baldwin, 2000) to preview what they are about to read and to monitor their thinking while reading. Specifically, this idea helps students activate their prior knowledge, make connections to text, set purposes for reading, and develop more accurate understandings of informational text. An Anticipation/Reaction Guide consists of several statements related to the text; the statements may or may not be true. Before reading, students indicate whether they agree or disagree with each statement and share their responses through partner, small-group, or whole-group discussion. After reading, students revisit the statements, decide whether their thinking has changed, and mark the statements accordingly. Then we discuss again and students explain any changes in their thinking that may have occurred. We use Anticipation/Reaction Guides before and after reading informational texts.

To teach students how to use an Anticipation/Reaction Guide, follow these steps:

1 **Explain:** Explain the strategy of previewing and how the Anticipation/Reaction Guide works. For example, you might say, "Previewing is a comprehension strategy that includes activating background knowledge, setting purposes for reading, and predicting what will come next, based on what has been read. Anticipation/Reaction Guides involve reading a

FIGURE 4.3 Biology Anticipation/Reaction Guide

Agree	Disagree	Statement
✓		1. An organ is a group of tissues that work together.
✓		2. There are ten organ systems in the human body.
✓	✗	3. Motor neurons are the only class of neurons in the body.
✓		4. An impulse is similar to the flow of an electrical current through a wire.

set of statements and determining whether we agree or disagree with them. After completing the guide, we discuss it. Then we read a text. Next, we revisit the Guide and record how our thinking may have changed based on what we have read (our reactions)."

2 **Demonstrate:** Demonstrate by using an Anticipation/Reaction Guide that you created prior to the lesson. The Guide should contain 3 to 5 statements that relate to the text. The statements may be facts or statements that are not accurate. Read the first statement in the Anticipation/Reaction Guide and think aloud about why you might agree or disagree with it. Put a check mark under the Agree or Disagree column at the start of the statement. For example, in the Anticipation/Reaction Guide shown in Figure 4.3, you might read the first statement, "An organ is a group of tissues that work together." Then you might say, "I will place a check mark in the Agree column, because we have already learned that organs are groups of tissues that work together."

3 **Guide:** Guide students to work with partners to read and respond to the next two statements, marking either Agree or Disagree, and discussing their reasoning.

4 **Practice:** Invite students to practice by working on their own to respond to the remaining statements. Discuss their responses. Introduce the text and read aloud the section of the text to which the statements relate. Discuss the text. Invite the students to revisit (react to) their original responses and place an "X" in the Agree or Disagree column to indicate their thinking has changed. Discuss students' responses.

5 **Reflect:** Encourage students to reflect on what they have learned about previewing and how they can use the Anticipation/Reaction Guides in other content areas.

In Figure 4.3, Michael Gress, a biology student, responded to an Anticipation/Reaction Guide based on a chapter in his biology textbook. As you can see, Michael originally agreed with all four statements, but, after listening to the text being read (or reading it on his own), he changed his thinking about the third statement and marked it with an "X." While reading, Michael discovered that statements 1, 3, and 4 were true, but statement 2 was not. He learned that there are three different classes of neurons in the body: sensory neurons, interneurons, and motor neurons.

 **TEACHING IDEA**

SEMANTIC MAP. We use Semantic Maps (Johnson & Pearson, 1984) to activate prior knowledge, introduce content specific vocabulary, and organize information about a topic. When teaching students how to use this map, we choose a focus word, engage students in brainstorming, and create and complete a graphic organizer that features categories and details. We can use completed Semantic Maps to create summaries. Because the design of the Semantic Map depends on students' responses, the structure of each map is different. We usually use Semantic Maps before and after reading either narrative or informational text.

To teach your students how to use Semantic Maps, follow these steps:

1 Explain: Begin by explaining the strategy of previewing and the use of a Semantic Map. For example, you might say, "Previewing is a comprehension strategy that includes activating background knowledge, setting purposes for reading, and predicting what will come next, based on what we have already read. Semantic Maps involve our brainstorming about a focus word and determining categories that emerge from our responses." We usually complete Semantic Maps before reading a text, and revisit them after reading.

2 Demonstrate: Begin the demonstration by choosing a focus word and writing it on a chart, chalkboard, or computer screen. Draw an oval around it. For example, if the focus word were *baseball*, we would write that word and draw an oval around it. Then think aloud about what word comes to mind when you read the focus word. For example, your response might be *pitcher*. Write that word on a different section of the chart paper, board, or computer screen where you will also list students' responses.

3 Guide: Guide students to work with a partner and think about what word comes to mind when they read the focus word. Write the students' responses beneath your response— *pitcher*—on the separate section of the board. Next, read the focus word and the list of responses. Think aloud about one category that you think emerges from the responses. For example, if the focus word were *baseball,* an emerging category might be *leagues.* Draw a line from the focus word oval to a satellite oval and write the category (*leagues*) within that oval. Underneath the oval, write the words from the list of responses that support that category. For example, in the *baseball* example, you might list *American League* and *National League.* Revisit the list of words on the separate board. Put a line through *American League* and *National League* to indicate that those responses have been used. Then invite the student partners to determine another category they think emerges from the list of responses. They might suggest *teams* as a category. Follow the same procedure of drawing a line through the student responses that have been used, adding a satellite oval, and listing the words beneath it.

4 Practice: Invite students to work on their own to determine other categories (e.g., *positions, players, stadiums*) and suggest which words should be listed beneath it. Add the students' suggestions to the Semantic Map about baseball. Continue this process until all of the words on the list of responses on the separate board have been used. Discuss the completed map and show students how the information on the map can be used to create a summary about the focus word. Then introduce the text, read it aloud, and discuss how the focus word relates to it. After the discussion, revisit the map to ensure it provides full and accurate information about the focus word. Revise as necessary. Use the completed map to summarize the topic.

5 Reflect: Encourage students to reflect on what they have learned about previewing and activating their background knowledge before reading. Engage them in discussion about how they can use Semantic Maps to preview text and learn vocabulary in other content areas.

Figure 4.4 shows a Semantic Map that Venetta Hurley and her students completed in geometry class. The figure focuses on the various types of triangles, which are classified by sides and angles. The map is simple in structure and was used to promote a class discussion of triangles. After the information contained on the map was verified through discussion, students worked with partners to illustrate each type of triangle.

For other examples of Semantic Maps as well as information about Semantic Question Maps and Concept of Definition Maps, see Chapter 7. For related reproducible graphic organizers, see the Appendix.

 **TEACHING IDEA** PREREADING PLAN. We use the Prereading Plan (PreP) (Langer, 1981) to activate prior knowledge about a topic, introduce new vocabulary, and make connections. When teaching students how to use PreP, we provide a cue word or idea and invite students to brainstorm related words or concepts. We record all ideas and then ask students why they suggested a particular word.

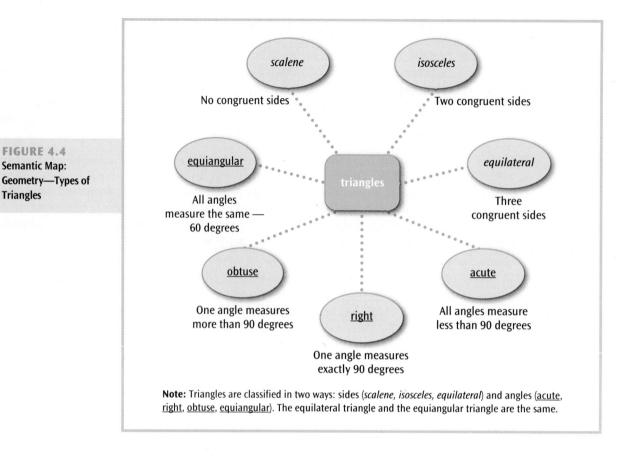

FIGURE 4.4
Semantic Map: Geometry—Types of Triangles

Note: Triangles are classified in two ways: sides (*scalene, isosceles, equilateral*) and angles (<u>acute</u>, <u>right</u>, <u>obtuse</u>, <u>equiangular</u>). The equilateral triangle and the equiangular triangle are the same.

Next, we read a text and revise the original list as necessary. We usually use PreP before and after reading informational text.

To teach your students how to use the Prereading Plan, follow these steps:

1 **Explain:** Begin by explaining that previewing is a comprehension strategy that includes activating background knowledge, setting purposes for reading, and predicting what will come next, based on what we have already read. Then explain how PreP works. For example, you might say, "PreP provides us with an opportunity to brainstorm words or ideas related to a topic and explain why we suggested particular words. After clarifying the words or ideas, we read a related text, revisit the terms, and revise as necessary."

2 **Demonstrate:** Begin the demonstration by providing a cue word or idea to stimulate thinking. Then think aloud about which related word comes to mind. Write the word or idea on the board or overhead screen. Then explain why you suggested it. For example, if the cue word or phrase is "U.S.S. *Maine*," the word that comes to mind might be *battleship*, and the reason might be "It was considered a floating tank."

3 **Guide:** Invite students to work with partners and brainstorm words or ideas related to the cue word and why they suggested them. Write down their responses.

4 **Practice:** Encourage students to practice by contributing other terms related to the cue word. Next, ask students to explain why they suggested them. Elaborate on the listed words. Then introduce the text and read it aloud. Join the students in reviewing the list of related words and the reasons they were offered. Revise as necessary.

5 **Reflect:** Encourage students to reflect on how PreP helps us to activate our background knowledge and predict what might appear in the text. Invite students to reflect on how they can use PreP in other content areas.

FIGURE 4.5

Excerpt from PreP about U.S.S. *Maine*

Cue Idea: U.S.S. *Maine*

Brainstormed Responses	Reasons
battleship	It was considered a floating tank.
Spanish–American War	The sinking of the U.S.S. *Maine* was a cause of this war.
unknown cause of explosion	No one knows how the explosion was caused.
Alfonso XII	This is the ship that sent rescue crews to the U.S.S. *Maine*.

Figure 4.5 features an excerpt from a PreP about the U.S.S. *Maine*, that Jim Burke completed in history class. The sinking of the battleship was a cause of the Spanish-American War.

TEACHING IDEA

BIO-IMPRESSIONS. Bio-Impressions are adapted from the Story Impressions created by McGinley and Denner (1987). We use Bio-Impressions before reading to predict which information the text will contain. They provide a framework for biographical writing, encourage predictions about people's lives, and help us to make connections between vocabulary and biographical structure. To create Bio-Impressions, we choose a person and structure a list of clues about his life connected by downward arrows. Then we encourage pairs of students to use the clues in sequential order, as they write their Bio-Impressions—what they predict the content of the biography will be. The maximum number of clues is ten; the maximum number of words per clue is five. When students finish writing their Bio-Impressions, they share them with another pair of students. Next, each pair reads a biography about the person featured in their Bio-Impression. After reading, they revisit the Bio-Impression and revise it as necessary. Then the students add facts from their reading to their Bio-Impressions and share them with another pair of students.

We create Bio-Impressions before reading biographical (informational) text and insert additional facts after reading. We can also use this format to create Poem Impressions based on story poems or Story Impressions based on the narrative elements: characters, setting, problem, attempts to resolve and resolution.

To teach your students how to create Bio-Impressions, follow these steps:

1   **Explain:** Begin by explaining that previewing is a comprehension strategy that includes activating background knowledge, setting purposes for reading, and predicting what will come next, based on what we have already read.

   Next, explain how Bio-Impressions work. For example, you might say, "We work with a partner and use a list of sequential clues to write Bio-Impressions. After writing the impressions, we share them with another pair of students. Next, we read a biography of the person whose life is the focus of the impression. Then we revisit the Bio-Impression and revise it as necessary. Finally, we either insert additional facts or sketch at least two ideas from the biography to enhance our Bio-Impressions."

2   **Demonstrate:** Model how to create a Bio-Impression by using a list of sequential clues connected by downward arrows (see Figure 4.6.). Include the sequential information as you write your Bio-Impression, beginning with the first clue. When the impression is complete, read it to the students. Then read a brief biography about the person who is the focus of the Bio-Impression. Revisit your impression and revise it as necessary. Include additional facts or a minimum of two sketches to represent ideas gleaned from reading. Discuss the process with your students.

3   **Guide:** Invite students to work with a partner to create Bio-Impressions using a new list of sequential clues. Encourage each pair to share and discuss their impressions with another pair of students.

4   **Practice:** Encourage students to practice by reading along silently as you read aloud a brief biography of the person who is the focus of the example Bio-Impression. Invite them to

Bio-Impression Clues

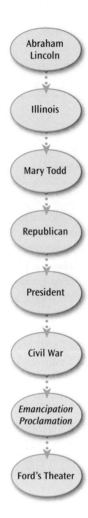

FIGURE 4.6
Bio-Impression
about Lincoln

**Bio-Impression
(Before Reading)**

Abraham Lincoln grew up in Illinois. He married Mary Todd and they had several sons. Lincoln was a member of the Republican Party. He was elected President and supported the abolition of slavery. The Union states fought the Confederacy during the Civil War and won. Lincoln freed the slaves by issuing the *Emancipation Proclamation*. He was later assassinated by John Wilkes Booth in Ford's Theater.

**Bio-Impression with Additional Facts
(After Reading)**

Abraham Lincoln grew up in Illinois. He married Mary Todd and had four sons. In 1836, he began to practice law. Twenty years later, he was known as a distinguished and successful lawyer in Illinois. Andrew Jackson was president when Lincoln first entered politics. Lincoln was elected to the Illinois State Legislature four times and to Congress once. Lincoln became a member of the Republican Party in 1856, the Republican presidential nominee in 1860, and President in 1861. During his time in office, the Union states fought the Confederacy during the Civil War. In 1864, Lincoln put Ulysses S. Grant in command of all federal armies, and that led to victory for the Union. Lincoln freed the slaves by issuing the *Emancipation Proclamation*. He was later assassinated by John Wilkes Booth in Ford's Theater.

revise their Bio-Impression as necessary. Discuss the biography with the students and invite them to add facts to enhance their Impressions.

5 **Reflect:** Encourage students to reflect on how Bio-Impressions help us predict the information included in a biography. Ask them to think about how they could use Bio-Impressions in other content areas.

The Bio-Impression about Abraham Lincoln shown in Figure 4.6 was created by students studying American history. The teacher, James Phillips, prepared Bio-Impression clues about ten influential people during the time of the Civil War, and pairs of students chose one who interested them. The Bio-Impression featured in Figure 4.6 was created by Sonia Hernandez and Elizabeth Burke.

Making Connections | Thinking about Previewing

- Previewing focuses on these essential processes: activating prior knowledge, setting purposes for reading, and predicting and inferring. Compare and contrast the value of teaching students how to preview with the past practice of simply assigning text for students to read. Consider specific examples.
- Share your thoughts with others in small-group discussions.

Making Connections
TO STRUGGLING READERS

When teaching English learners or struggling readers in content areas, it is important to remember that prior knowledge plays a critical role in understanding text. There are many things we can do to help develop students' background knowledge, including (1) encouraging them to read widely and making available a variety of types and levels of content-related text; (2) creating cross-age partnerships between current students and those who have already completed the course; and (3) providing access to a variety of interactive websites that feature photographs and short video clips to support student learning. ■

Making Connections

Making connections is a reading comprehension strategy in which students activate their prior knowledge and make a variety of connections or associations to the text they are reading. There are three kinds of connections: text–self, text–text, and text–world (others). Connection Stems, Save the Last Word for Me, Coding the Text, and Sketch and Label Connections are the teaching ideas featured in this section. Details about how to teach them follow. Related graphic organizers can be found in the Appendix, along with other teaching ideas that will help students to make connections.

CONNECTION STEMS. Connection Stems (Harvey & Goudvis, 2000) provide a way for students to make connections or associations between the texts they are reading and themselves, other texts, and the world (others). The purpose of Connection Stems is to provide a structure to encourage students to make connections while reading and to encourage students to reflect on their reading. They can be used before, during, or after reading narrative or informational text.

To teach students how to use Connection Stems, follow these steps:

1 **Explain:** Begin by explaining making connections as a reading comprehension strategy in which students activate their prior knowledge and make a variety of connections or associations to the text they are reading. Note that there are three kinds of connections: text–self,

text–text and text–world (others). Then explain Connection Stems, including a variety of stems. For example, you might say, "Connection Stems, such as 'That reminds me of . . .' or 'I remember when . . .', help us to make connections or associations between the texts we are reading and ourselves, other texts, and the world (others)."

Here are examples of Connection Stems:

- That reminds me of . . .
- I remember when . . .
- I have a connection . . .
- An experience I have that was similar to that . . .
- I felt like that person when . . .
- If I were that person, I would . . .

2 **Demonstrate:** After introducing a text, show students a sentence stem and think aloud about how to complete it. Use the text and personal experiences to explain the connection. For example, you might say, "I am going to use the Connection Stem 'That reminds me of . . .' So I will say, 'This text reminds me of my grandfather, because he was a soldier in World War II.' I have made a text-to-self connection, because I have related our text about World War II to my life."

3 **Guide:** Read a section of the text aloud or invite students to read a section silently. Then guide the students to work with a partner to complete one of the other connection stems. Invite partners to share their connections with the class, noting which type of connection they have made.

4 **Practice:** Encourage students to practice by reading a short text and completing Connection Stems. Discuss how they chose to complete the Connection Stems and which kinds of connections they made.

5 **Reflect:** Invite the students to think about how well they can use Connection Stems and how they might extend their use to other content areas.

Figure 4.7 shows two sets of connection stems, which were completed by students studying history and trigonometry.

 **TEACHING IDEA**   **SAVE THE LAST WORD FOR ME.** Save the Last Word for Me (Short, Harste, & Burke, 1996) is designed to help students make connections to the text, evaluate information in the text, and provide a structure for discussion of the text. When students use this technique, they select a quote, fact, or idea from the text and record it and the page number on which it is located on the front side of an index card. On the back of the card, they explain why they chose the information and which connections they can make to it. After reading, they gather in small groups and one at a time, students share the information on the front of their cards with the rest of the

---

FIGURE 4.7

Connection Stems Completed in History and Trigonometry Classes

These connection Stems were completed by students in history class while reading about World War II:

- That reminds me of . . . my grandmother, who was a nurse in World War II.
- I remember when . . . I saw *Schindler's List* and realized how horribly people were treated in the concentration camps during World War II.
- An experience I have had that was similar to soldiers being drafted into the Army was . . . when my brother enlisted in the Army.

These connection stems were completed by students beginning to study trigonometric functions in trigonometry class:

- The hypotenuse reminds me of . . . when we learned it was the side opposite a triangle's right angle in geometry.
- I remember when . . . we first learned about Pythagoras and now we are using his theorem.
- I have a connection . . . to SOH. I know it stands for "sine equals opposite over hypotenuse."

group. Each member of the group comments on the quote or idea. The student who wrote that card speaks last and shares the thoughts he/she has recorded on the back of the card (hence the title, Save the Last Word for Me). This technique is usually used after reading with either narrative or informational text.

To teach students how to use the Save the Last Word for Me strategy, follow these steps:

1 Explain: Begin by explaining making connections as a reading comprehension strategy in which students activate their prior knowledge and make a variety of connections or associations to the text they are reading. Then explain how Save the Last Word for Me works. For example, you might say, "Save the Last Word for Me is designed to help us make connections to the text, evaluate information in the text, and provide a structure for discussion of the text. We read a segment of text. Then we write a quote or idea from the text on one side on an index card (or at the top of the blackline) and the reason that we chose that quote or idea on the other side of the index card (or the bottom of the blackline). We share the quotes or ideas in small group, where each member comments on them. The last person to comment is the person who selected the quote or idea—hence the title, 'Save the Last Word for Me.'

2 Demonstrate: Use a short text, an index card or blackline, a pen, and a think-aloud to demonstrate how to use the Save the Last Word for Me strategy. Before beginning to read, think aloud about needing to find a quote, a fact, or an idea to write on the front of the index card. Read the text and then think aloud as you write the necessary information—including the page number on which the information is located— on the front of the card. Think aloud about why you chose the quote, fact, or idea, and which connection(s) you can make to it. Write that information on the back of the index card.

Next, model how to use Save the Last Word for Me by inviting three or four students to sit with you in a small group. Read the front of your card (or top of the blackline) and invite each of the students to respond to what you wrote. After each has had a chance to comment, read what you wrote on the back on the index card (or the bottom of the blackline) to make connections to the quote, fact, or idea that you selected. After the demonstration, discuss Save the Last Word for Me with the class.

3 Guide: Guide students to work with partners as they try Save the Last Word for Me. Provide students with index cards (or blacklines) and a copy of the short text. Read the short text aloud and provide time for the students to complete their index cards or blacklines. Remind students that what they write on the front of the index card may be something new, something that confirms previous ideas, something they disagree with, and so on. Also remind them to include the page number on which the information appears on the front of the card. Ask each pair of students to share with another pair, so each will have a group of four as they complete Save the Last Word for Me. Discuss the process.

4 Practice: Provide copies of a short text and invite students to practice by listening for a quote, fact, or idea to which they can make connections. When you have finished reading and they have completed their index cards or blacklines, ask students to meet in groups of four and participate in "Save the Last Word for Me." Discuss their efforts.

5 Reflect: Reflect on what the students know about making connections and how they can use Save the Last Word for Me when learning about other content area topics.

Figure 4.8 features Save the Last Word for Me information that John McGraw wrote while reading about global warming in science class.

CODING THE TEXT. Coding the Text (Harvey & Goudvis, 2000) was developed to help us actively engage in reading by make connections. During reading, we use small sticky notes to indicate the points in the text where we are able to make text–self, text–text, and text–world (others) connections. We use a code for each type of connection (T-S, T-T, and T-W, respectively) and include a few words to describe each connection. We can use Coding the Text while reading narrative and informational text.

FIGURE 4.8
Save the Last Word for
Me: Global Warming

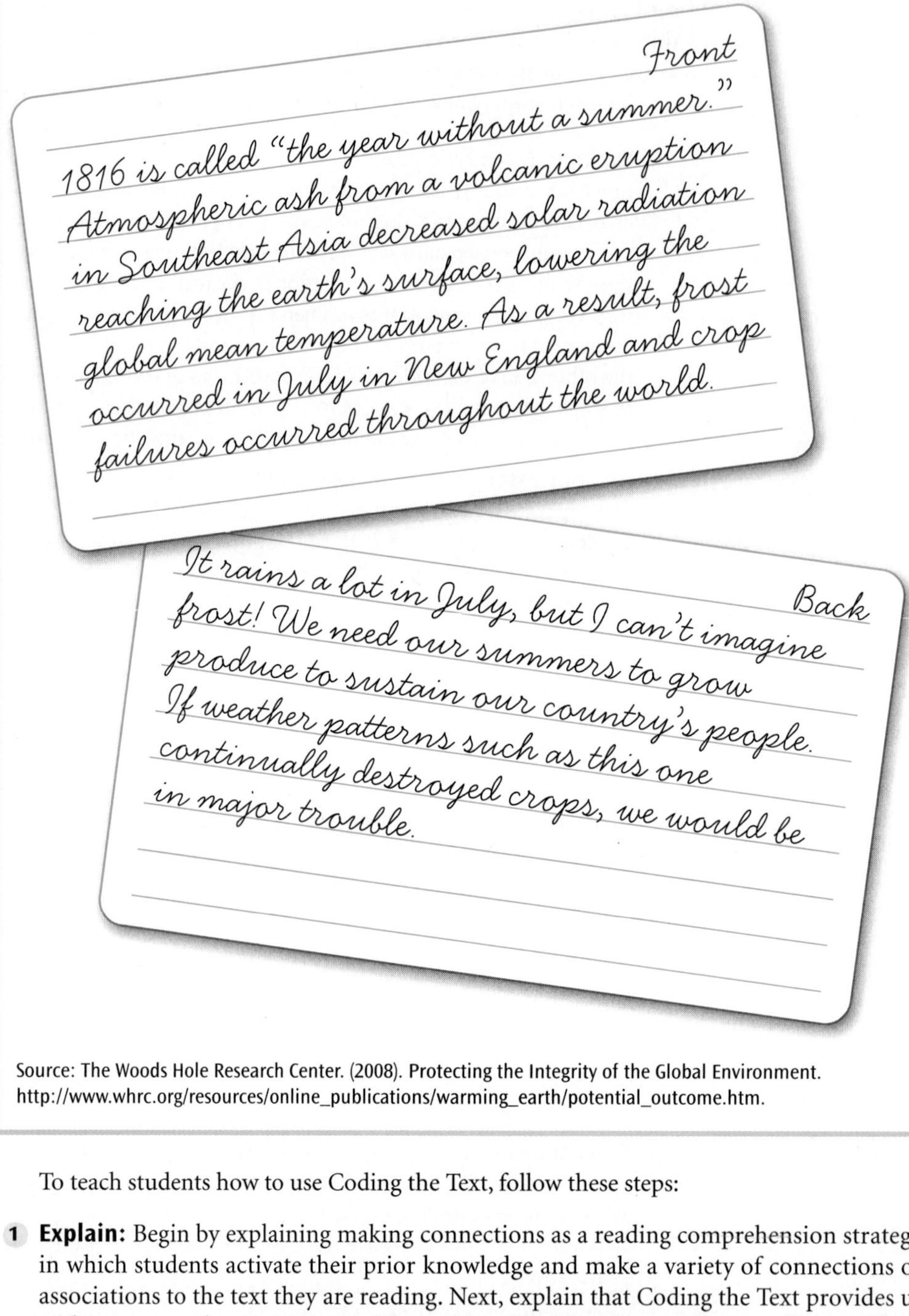

Front

1816 is called "the year without a summer." Atmospheric ash from a volcanic eruption in Southeast Asia decreased solar radiation reaching the earth's surface, lowering the global mean temperature. As a result, frost occurred in July in New England and crop failures occurred throughout the world.

Back

It rains a lot in July, but I can't imagine frost! We need our summers to grow produce to sustain our country's people. If weather patterns such as this one continually destroyed crops, we would be in major trouble.

Source: The Woods Hole Research Center. (2008). Protecting the Integrity of the Global Environment. http://www.whrc.org/resources/online_publications/warming_earth/potential_outcome.htm.

To teach students how to use Coding the Text, follow these steps:

1. **Explain:** Begin by explaining making connections as a reading comprehension strategy in which students activate their prior knowledge and make a variety of connections or associations to the text they are reading. Next, explain that Coding the Text provides us with a way to make connections while reading. For example, you might say, "We use Coding the Text to mark different points in our reading where we are able to make text–self, text–text, or text–world (others) connections. We write the code for a type of connection—T-S, T-T, or T-W—and a brief description of the connection on a small sticky note. Then we stick the sticky note in the section of the text where we are able to make the connection."

2. **Demonstrate:** Begin the demonstration by showing students how to label the different kinds of connections on sticky notes. Then read aloud a section of text and pause when you are able to make a connection. Think aloud about which kind of connection you are able to make. Code the sticky note, write a brief description, and stick it next to the section of text

where you were able to make the connection. Continue to read the section of text aloud and code your connections. Discuss the text and your connections with your students.

3 **Guide:** As students read a new section of text, encourage them to work in pairs, and guide them to make text–self, text–text, or text–world connections. Ask them to code the type of connections and brief descriptions on the sticky notes. Then guide them to insert the sticky notes at the correct points in the text. Discuss the text and the students' connections.

4 **Practice:** Invite students to practice on their own by continuing to read another segment and Coding the Text. Discuss the text and connections students made.

5 **Reflect:** Encourage students to reflect on how Coding the Text helps us to make connections while we are reading. Invite students to think about how they can use it when reading in other content areas.

Figure 4.9 shows sticky notes of text–text and text–self "Coding the Text" examples from Chapter 17, The History of Life, in *Biology* (Miller & Levine, 2008).

 **TEACHING IDEA**   SKETCH AND LABEL CONNECTIONS.   Sketch and Label Connections (McLaughlin & Allen, 2002) is designed to help us use labeled visual representations to express connections. When using this approach, we read a section of text and think about a connection we can make. Then we sketch the connection, label it "text–self," "text–text," or "text–world," and write an explanation of why it is that type. We usually use "Sketch and Label Connections" before, during, and after reading narrative or informational text.

To teach students how to use Sketch and Label Connections, follow these steps:

1 **Explain:** Begin by explaining making connections as a reading comprehension strategy in which students activate their prior knowledge and make a variety of connections or associations to the text they are reading. Then explain Sketch and Label Connections as a way to use visual representations to express connections. For example, you might say, "When we use 'Sketch and Label Connections,' we use simple lines and shapes to represent our connections and then we label them. We indicate the type of connection and explain why it is that type."

2 **Demonstrate:** Begin demonstrating by introducing the text and thinking about connections you can make. Demonstrate how to sketch using simple lines and shapes. (This is a good time to remind students that we do not need to be talented artists to be able to sketch.) Think about the kind of connection you will make. Then think aloud as you sketch your connection. After you have sketched your connection, label the type of connection and explain why it is that type. Discuss your sketched and labeled connection with your students.

FIGURE 4.9
Coding the Text in Biology Class

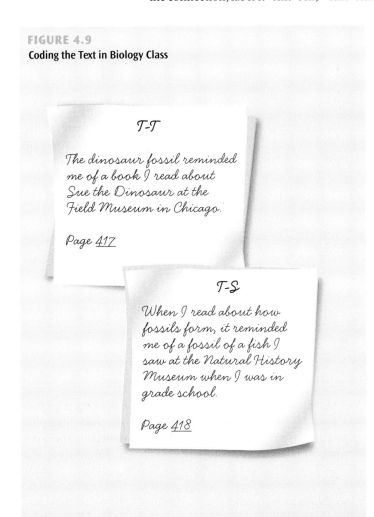

T–T

The dinosaur fossil reminded me of a book I read about Sue the Dinosaur at the Field Museum in Chicago.

Page 417

T–S

When I read about how fossils form, it reminded me of a fossil of a fish I saw at the Natural History Museum when I was in grade school.

Page 418

FIGURE 4.10
FIGURE 4.10
Sketching Connections: "Because I Could Not Stop for Death"

I drew a picture of a clock after reading the first stanza, because to me the first stanza describes how we get so caught up in our lives that time passes without our knowing it. The narrator was so caught up in living her life that she didn't realize the end had come.

3 **Guide:** Provide the students with copies of the text and guide them to work in pairs to Sketch and Label Connections as you read a segment aloud. Encourage the students to discuss their connections with another pair. Then discuss the text and student responses with the class. Repeat this process with additional segments of text.

4 **Practice:** Encourage students to practice by working on their own to sketch their connections. Invite them to share their connections with a partner. Repeat this process using multiple segments of text.

5 **Reflect:** Encourage students to reflect on how Sketching and Labeling Connections helps us to understand what we read. Ask students how they can use it in other content areas.

In Figure 4.10, Rosario Pinto sketches and explains her connection to the opening stanza of Emily Dickinson's poem, "Because I Could Not Stop for Death."

FINAL THOUGHTS

When we engage students' thinking, we motivate them to make connections between what they already know and what they are learning. Activating background knowledge and setting purposes for reading are essential components of comprehension. Making connections between background knowledge and what we are learning supports our belief that reading is a constructivist process.

In the next chapter, we expand our discussion of strategies to those we use to guide our thinking during reading. Our focus shifts to approaches that are designed to help students transact with text and monitor their understanding.

Teaching Connections

APPLYING WHAT WE HAVE LEARNED

E-Links

Because we are mature, sophisticated readers, we use reading comprehension strategies unconsciously. Work with a partner and choose a website such as those listed to locate text related to your content area. As you read, consciously use comprehension strategies such as previewing and making connections. Discuss with your partner how using these strategies helped you understand the text. Record your thoughts as a reflective entry in your portfolio.

EXAMPLE WEBSITES

Absolute Shakespeare (English)
http://absoluteshakespeare.com

Biography
http://www.biography.com

Discovery Channel
http://dsc.discovery.com/news

Science Daily: Your Source for the Latest Research News
http://www.sciencedaily.com/articles

Accountable Talk

As content area teachers of the 21st century, we need to ensure that our students can read text effectively. Meet in small groups and discuss (1) how you will use reading comprehension strategies in your teaching and (2) how you will motivate your students to use reading strategies. Record your ideas and share what you believe to be the best suggestions in a class discussion.

 ### Portfolio/Performance Opportunity

Work with a partner in your content area to develop a standards-based lesson plan that focuses on dual purposes: (1) to teach course content and (2) to help students use comprehension strategies as they read. Meet in small groups and teach your lesson to the group. Engage in peer feedback and revise the lesson plan as necessary. Discuss how including reading strategies and receiving peer feedback affected your lesson. Reflect on your work and include your lesson plan in your portfolio.

Chapter Overview

Using Comprehension Strategies to Guide Thinking

In this chapter, we continue to learn comprehension strategies we can use to think through text. Our specific focus is strategies to use *during* reading. Our goal is to help students develop a repertoire of strategies that they can use as needed while reading.

We begin by exploring how to use strategies such as self-questioning, monitoring, and visualizing to guide thinking. We learn how to teach the strategies by using a step-by-step model of explicit instruction. Student examples are featured throughout the chapter.

How Can We Use Comprehension Strategies to Guide Thinking?

We know that we use comprehension strategies to engage, guide, and extend thinking throughout the reading process. The strategies we use during reading help to guide our thinking—to monitor our understanding of text, make connections to text, clarify meaning, and respond actively. Although the strategies in this chapter are cited as examples to use during reading, we can also use them at other points during the reading process.

In the examples that follow, we describe a variety of ways to support students' use of comprehension strategies during reading. In each step-by-step sequence, we begin by explaining the strategy and the teaching idea. Next, we demonstrate it. Then, we guide students as they work with partners. After that, we provide support as requested as students attempt to use the strategies on their own. Finally, we reflect on what we have learned and how we can use the strategy in the content areas. Each teaching sequence is followed by a student example. Reproducible graphic organizers for these techniques can be found in the Appendix.

Self-Questioning

Self-questioning is a reading comprehension strategy that involves generating questions to guide thinking while reading. For example, if we are reading a science experiment, we may wonder what the next step will be, what the outcome of the previous step might be, what effect a particular action might cause, or what the result of the experiment might be. Many teaching ideas support this strategy, including those featured in this section. Descriptions of these ideas and step-by-step directions for teaching them follow. (For information about how to teach students the skill of generating questions at a variety of levels, see Chapter 8.)

QUESTION–ANSWER RELATIONSHIPS. Question–Answer Relationships (Raphael, 1986) is a teaching idea that helps students understand how to self-question. Students learn that there are two information sources: text and prior knowledge. Within each information source, there are two question–answer relationships (QAR). This teaching idea helps students to develop self-questioning abilities by focusing on the information source needed to answer the question. QAR can be used when reading narrative and expository text.

To teach students how to use QAR, follow these steps:

1 **Explain:** Begin by explaining self-questioning as a reading comprehension strategy in which we generate questions to guide thinking. Then explain the QAR concept and terminology:
   - There are two kinds of information:

     In the book: Answers are found in the text (e.g., book, video, website).

     In my head: Answers require input from students' understandings and prior knowledge.
   - There are two kinds of QARs for each kind of information:

     In the Book:
     - Right There: The answer is stated in the passage.
     - Think and Search: The answer is derived from more than one sentence or paragraph but is stated in the text.

     In My Head:
     - On My Own: The answer is contingent on information the reader already possesses in his prior knowledge.
     - Author and Me: The answer is inferred in the text, but the reader must make the connections with his own prior knowledge.

2 **Demonstrate**: Think aloud as you demonstrate how to use QAR with a text. Model choosing the appropriate QAR strategy, answering from the designated source, and writing or saying the answer. Introduce a short passage and related questions.

3 **Guide:** Guide students to work with partners to use QAR with the passages and the questions. Encourage students to answer the questions and explain which QAR strategy they used. Any justifiable answer should be accepted.

4 **Practice:** Ask students to work on their own to use QAR. Discuss their responses.

5 **Reflect:** Invite students to reflect on what they have learned about self-questioning and how to use QAR in the content areas.

The question–answer relationships featured in Figure 5.1 were created by high school student Grace Fisher based on a chapter in her Spanish language and culture course text.

FIGURE 5.1 Question–Answer Relationships Created in a Spanish Language and Culture Course

In the Book:

Right There: What are some elements of Spanish culture?
Art, dance, music, writing, customs, and food are some elements of Spanish culture. (This information is directly stated in one sentence in the text.)

Think and Search: Which artists are considered to have made the greatest contributions to Spanish culture?
Artists who have contributed greatly to the Spanish culture have spanned several centuries and include El Greco, Velazquez, Goya, Picasso, Gris, Miró, and Dalí. (This information appears in the text, but is located in more than one sentence.)

In My Head:

On My Own: Which of the Spanish authors we have studied interests you the most? Justify your thinking.
Arturo Perez-Reverte is an author I would like to learn more about. He started out as a journalist but then became a novelist. He is also credited with motivating a lot of Spanish citizens to read. (This information was provided through the student's prior knowledge.)

Author and Me: Do you think Spanish culture has influenced American culture? Justify your response.
Spanish culture has influenced American culture. Evidence of this can be seen in the impact of Spanish architecture on American structures, the way we value the work of Spanish artists such as Picasso, and the increasing use of the Spanish language in our country. (This response was based on information in the text as well as the student's prior knowledge.)

TEACHING IDEA

"I WONDER . . ." STATEMENTS. "I Wonder . . ." Statements (Harvey & Goudvis, 2000) are designed to encourage students to generate questions and to provide a model for active thinking during the reading process. These statements can be used with either narrative or informational text, before, during, and after reading. "I Wonder . . ." Statements can be shared orally, through sketching, or in writing. In this section, the student example features "I Wonder . . ." Bookmarks that were created *during* reading.

To teach students how to use "I Wonder . . ." Statements, follow these steps:

1. **Explain:** Begin by explaining self-questioning as a reading comprehension strategy in which we generate questions to guide thinking. Then explain that we can use "I Wonder . . ." Statements to help us engage in active thinking and generate questions while reading.

2. **Demonstrate:** Think aloud about the text and the prior knowledge you have about the topic. Introduce the text and create "I Wonder . . ." Statements about the title, both orally and in writing. Read a segment of the text aloud and think aloud about whether your "I Wonder . . ." Statements were confirmed or disconfirmed.

3. **Guide:** Invite students to work with partners to create "I Wonder . . ." Statements. Ask selected students to share their "wonders." Ask students to listen to determine whether their statements are confirmed or disconfirmed as you read another segment of text. Discuss whether the students' statements were confirmed or disconfirmed.

4. **Practice:** Invite students to work on their own to create "I Wonder . . ." Statements in writing. Briefly discuss the students' wonders and then read another segment of text. Encourage the students to listen to determine whether their statements are confirmed or disconfirmed. Discuss this when you have finished reading the segment. Continue this process until you have finished reading the text.

5. **Reflect:** Encourage students to reflect on what they have learned about "I Wonder . . ." Statements and how they help us to engage in self-questioning while reading. Discuss how students can use "I Wonder . . ." Statements while reading texts in the content areas.

Maria Fernandez completed the "I Wonder . . ." Bookmarks featured in Figure 5.2 while reading "The Pedestrian" by Ray Bradbury in her literature anthology class.

 **TEACHING IDEA**

REQUEST. When engaging in ReQuest (Manzo, 1969), students actively participate in the discussion of the text. After observing teacher modeling, they practice generating questions at multiple levels. Teachers and students also answer questions. This provides opportunities to engage in the social construction of knowledge and learn the content.

When teaching ReQuest, follow these steps:

1 **Explain:** Begin by explaining self-questioning as a reading comprehension strategy in which we generate questions to guide thinking. Focus on ReQuest as a type of reciprocal questioning that involves reading silently, generating questions at multiple levels, predicting, and discussing. Explain that the students and the teacher engage in ReQuest by reading silently and asking one another questions.

2 **Demonstrate:** Introduce the text, and then invite students to participate in the demonstration. Join them in reading a designated section of text (usually a few paragraphs) silently. Then ask the students to close their books while you ask them questions about the text they read. Comment on the quality of responses. Then close your book and encourage the students to ask you questions. Comment on the quality of the questions.

3 **Guide:** Guide students to engage in ReQuest by silently reading another section of text. Then question the students and encourage them to question you.

4 **Practice:** After students have read an appropriate amount of text, invite them to stop questioning and begin predicting. Provide prompts, such as "I think . . ." or "I wonder . . . ," to encourage predictions. Invite the students to read the remaining text silently. After they have finished reading the text, facilitate a discussion based on the text and students' predictions.

5 **Reflect:** Encourage students to think about how ReQuest helps us to use reciprocal questioning and prediction to understand text. Discuss other content areas in which students could use ReQuest.

When engaging in ReQuest, we may find that students ask too many memory-level questions. If we teach Ciardiello's (1998) four levels of questioning before we teach ReQuest, students will be able to use the signal words to generate questions at all levels of thinking. Although memory-level questions are certainly important, we should also encourage our students to think at higher levels. For example, if students are researching the biography of someone who is well respected in a content area—such as Churchill in history, Banneker in mathematics, Hemingway in literature, or

FIGURE 5.2
"I Wonder . . ." Bookmarks Based on "The Pedestrian" by Ray Bradbury (1964)

"I Wonder..." Bookmark

Page 173
I wonder... why Leonard Mead most dearly loves to look out at the intersection.
because... this seems to be an unusual thing to do in your spare time.

Page 173
I wonder... what the world is like in this story.
because... it is set in 2053.

Page 174
I wonder... where all the people went.
because... Leonard says that in 10 years of walking night and day and covering thousands of miles he has never met another person.

"I Wonder..." Bookmark

Page 174
I wonder... how the intersection can be such "a thunderous surge of cars" during the day.
because... I thought that there were no people. Who is driving the cars?

Page 176
I wonder... how the obsession with television got so intense that people don't do anything.
because... the police think Leonard has done something wrong because he isn't at home stuck in front of the television. They think he is a criminal because he walks, writes, and isn't married.

Page 176
I wonder... if Leonard will ever get out of the Psychiatric Center
because... it doesn't seem that he truly has done anything "crazy" to be there in the first place.

Einstein in science—memory levels questions about where and when the person was born provide some background information. We also want students to ask how that person's contribution to the field compared and contrasted to other contributions (convergent level), how students might imagine themselves making such a contribution (divergent thinking), and how students would defend or justify the person's contribution (evaluative level).

PAIRED QUESTIONING. In Paired Questioning (Vaughn & Estes, 1986), students engage in actively generating questions during reading. To teach students how to use Paired Questioning, follow these steps:

1. **Explain:** Begin by explaining self-questioning as a reading comprehension strategy in which we generate questions to guide thinking. Then explain that Paired Questioning involves students taking turns in generating text-related questions and responding to them. When the students have finished generating and responding to questions while reading segments of the text, one partner summarizes the important ideas in the text and the other agrees or disagrees and justifies his or her thinking.

2. **Demonstrate:** Arrange in advance to have a student volunteer to be your partner during the demonstration. Introduce the text and demonstrate how you and your partner read the title or subtitle of a section of text, set the text aside, and then respond to the questions each of you generate. Remind students that asking questions about the title or subtitle helps readers set purposes for reading. For example, if the title was *The Civil War* and the subtitle was *Causes of the Civil War,* the questions raised might be "What was the Civil War?" and "What were the causes of the Civil War?" Next, repeat this process, reading a section of text instead of the title or subtitle. After you and your partner have responded to the questions, discuss how generating questions as we read helps us to understand the text.

3. **Guide:** Invite students to work with a partner and new section of text to engage in Paired Questioning, first with a subtitle and then with a section of text. Encourage discussion.

4. **Practice:** Invite students to finish reading the text by engaging in Paired Questioning. Stop periodically to discuss the text and the questions that have been raised. When the students have finished reading the text, invite one partner to share the important ideas in the text with the other. Then encourage the other partner to agree or disagree and justify his response.

5. **Reflect:** Invite students to share their thoughts about Paired Questioning and how it can help us understand text.

Figure 5.3 features examples of Paired Questioning that students created in their earth science class.

Monitoring/Clarifying

Monitoring/clarifying is a reading comprehension strategy that involves constantly asking ourselves, "Does this make sense?", and adapting strategic processes to make the message clear. For example, if our reading makes sense, we continue reading. If our reading does not make sense, we might go back and reread the material, read that passage more slowly, examine a difficult vocabulary word more closely, or use other ideas that will help us clarify the meaning. A number of teaching ideas support this strategy. Information about how to teach several of them follows. We use this strategy during the reading of narrative or expository text. Reproducible graphic organizers related to monitoring/clarifying are found in the Appendix.

BOOKMARK TECHNIQUE. Readers can use Bookmark Technique (McLaughlin & Allen, 2002b) to help monitor their comprehension while reading and make evaluative judgments about aspects of the text. This technique can be used with narrative and expository text, and it works well with both in-class reading and homework assignments.

To teach your students how to use Bookmark Technique, follow these steps:

1. **Explain:** Begin by explaining that monitoring/clarifying is a reading comprehension strategy that involves constantly asking ourselves, "Does this make sense?", and adapting strategic processes to make the message clear. Begin by distributing the four Bookmarks (see the

FIGURE 5.3
Students' Paired
Questioning Example
about "Structure of the
Earth" in Earth Science

Student 1: How many layers of the earth are there?
Student 2: There are four layers of the earth.
Student 2: What is the outermost layer called?
Student 1: The outermost layer is called the crust.

After reading a selection:
Student 1: What is an example of the earth's crust?
Student 2: The continents are examples of the earth's crust.
Student 2: How thick is the earth's crust?
Student 1: The thickness of the earth's crust varies. It can be anywhere between 5 and 70 kilometers.
Student 1: The outermost layer of the earth is called the crust. This layer consists of the continents and ocean basins. It varies in thickness.
Student 2: I agree, but I would add that the earth's crust is made up of mostly alumino-silicates.

Appendix for graphic organizers). Introduce the text and explain what monitoring is and how the Bookmark Technique can help us monitor our reading. Explain the four bookmarks, noting the information required for each:

- **Bookmark 1:** What was the most important part? Why?
- **Bookmark 2:** Which vocabulary word do you think the whole class should discuss? Why? Include predicted meaning of the word.
- **Bookmark 3:** What was confusing in this text? Why?
- **Bookmark 4:** Which chart, map, graph, or illustration helped you to understand what you read? Why?

There is a place for students to include page numbers on all Bookmarks. There is also a place for paragraph numbers on all Bookmarks except the fourth one. Providing page and paragraph numbers helps the class to locate the information during discussion.

2 **Demonstrate:** Read a short text to the students. Think aloud as you complete the first Bookmark. For example, if you are using the Bookmarks in biology class and the text was about DNA, you might say, "I think the double helix model was the most important part of the text, because it showed the structure of DNA."

3 **Guide:** Guide students to work with a partner to complete Bookmark 2 and 3. Discuss their vocabulary choices. Revisit the text to locate the words and assess whether the students' thoughts about the words' meanings are appropriate in the contexts. If needed, use a dictionary to clarify the meanings.

4 **Practice:** Ask students to work on their own to complete the fourth Bookmark. Discuss their choices.

5 **Reflect:** Invite students to reflect on what they know about monitoring and how they can use the Bookmark Technique in other aspects of their content area learning.

Bookmark Technique helps students focus on what they are reading and develop at least four points of information to contribute to class discussion. Figure 5.4 features Connor Watkins' responses using Bookmark Technique; Connor is a high school student who is studying biology.

SAY SOMETHING. Readers can use Say Something (Short, Harste, & Burke, 1996) to help monitor their understanding. When using this technique, students work in pairs to read a text, stopping at designated points to turn and Say Something to their partners. Say Something can be used with narrative or informational text during and after reading. When participating in Say Something while reading informational text, students might make a comment, ask a question, make a prediction, clarify a point, or make a connection. When using the technique while reading narrative text, students might extend their comments to include narrative elements such as setting, characters, and theme.

FIGURE 5.4
Bookmark Technique: Biology—Student Responses When Reading about DNA

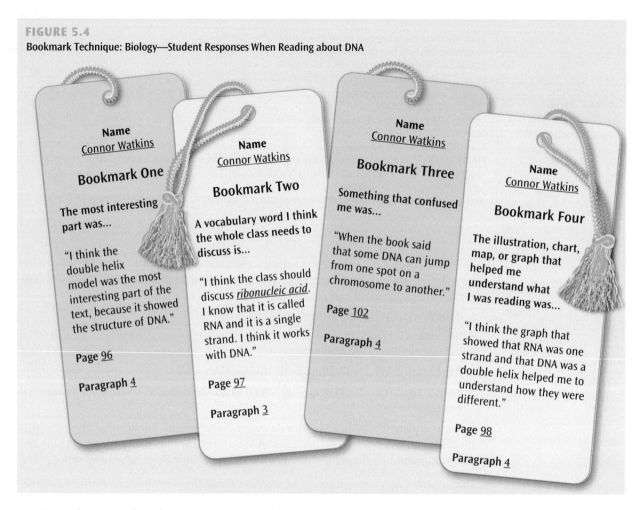

FIGURE 5.4
Bookmark Technique: Biology—Student Responses When Reading about DNA

To teach your students how to use Say Something follow these steps:

1. **Explain:** Begin by explaining monitoring/clarifying as a comprehension strategy that involves constantly asking ourselves, "Does this make sense?" and adapting strategic processes to make the message clear. Then explain how Say Something helps students monitor their understanding. Next, introduce the text and invite a student to work with you to demonstrate this approach. (The designated stopping points in the text should have been labeled prior to the start of the lesson.)

2. **Demonstrate:** Read a designated segment of text, turn to your student partner, and Say Something. Next, your student partner should read a designated segment of text and Say Something to you. Model this with four segments of text. Remember to discuss the text periodically.

3. **Guide:** Ask students to work with a partner while using Say Something. Guide their practice by continuing to read aloud designated segments and inviting them to Say Something to their partners. Do this for four segments of text.

4. **Practice:** Encourage students to practice on their own by reading the remaining designated segments and continuing to Say Something to their partners. Remind students to discuss the text periodically. The students should continue this process until they come to the end of the text.

5. **Reflect:** Encourage students to reflect on what they know about monitoring their understanding and how they can use Say Something to help them do that. Discuss how the students can use Say Something as they study the content areas.

> **Stopping Point 1**
> Student 1: I didn't know *cryogenics* came from the Greek words for "frost" and "to produce."
> Student 2: I knew cryogenics involved low temperatures, but I didn't know it referred to temperatures below −150 °C.
>
> **Stopping Point 2**
> Student 1: The lowest temperature that can be approached but not achieved is absolute zero.
> Student 2: Absolute zero is equal to −273.15 °C.
>
> **Stopping Point 3**
> Student 1: I didn't know that normally mercury freezes and becomes useless at low temperatures.
> Student 2: I didn't know some types of ceramics are high-temperature superconductors.
>
> **Stopping Point 4**
> Student 1: Cryogenics can be used for flash freezing some foods.
> Student 2: It can also be used to treat cancers.

FIGURE 5.5

Examples of Say Something from Science Class

In Figure 5.5, Javier Martinez and Paul Romano engaged in "Say Something" while reading about cryogenics in science. The teacher had designated four stopping points and the students exchanged ideas at each point.

TEACHING IDEA

Go to the Activities and Applications section under the topic *Activating Prior Knowledge and Interest* in the MyEducationLab for your course and complete the activity entitled *Using K-W-L in 8th Grade Math* to learn how to use this important graphic organizer to help build student interest.

KWL AND KWLS. KWL supports multiple reading comprehension strategies. Its purposes include activating students' prior knowledge about a topic, setting purposes for reading, and confirming, revising, or expanding original understandings of a topic. In the traditional form of KWL, developed by Donna Ogle in 1986, readers ask themselves, "What do I <u>k</u>now?" "What do I <u>w</u>ant to know?" and "What have I <u>l</u>earned?". Sippola (1995) suggested that we add a fourth column to the KWL to create the KWLS. The first three questions are the same; the new question is "What do I still want to know?". The fourth column of the KWLS graphic organizer (see the Appendix) encourages students to examine whether they have found answers to all of the questions they raised in response to "What do I need to know?". If students have not found responses to all of these questions, they move the unanswered questions to the fourth column and research responses to them. Other adaptations to the KWL—such as KWDL ("What I know," "What I want to know," "What I did," and "What I learned"), which is often used in science and mathematics—can be found in Appendix A.

To teach your students how to use KWL, follow these guidelines and encourage discussion throughout the process:

1. **Explain:** Explain that the KWL supports the reading strategies of self-questioning, monitoring, and summarizing. Then focus on the three steps involved in KWL: What I Know, What I Want to Know, and What I Learned.

2. **Demonstrate:** Introduce the topic and a short text. Share the KWL graphic organizer with students (see the Appendix). Think aloud as you brainstorm what you know in the K column. Then move to the W column and list what you want to know. Discuss what you wrote in the K and W columns. Then read the text. After reading, record what you learned in the L column. Discuss what you learned with the class. Then revisit the K column to determine if what you knew was verified in the text and the W column to ensure that all of your questions were answered. Summarize what you learned.

3. **Guide:** Introduce a new text and guide students to work with a partner as each completes the K and W columns. Discuss the students' responses. Provide time for them to read the text and complete the L column. Discuss their responses. Then ask students to check the K and W columns to ensure that what they knew was verified by the text and that all of their questions were answered. Finally, encourage the pairs of students to summarize what they have learned.

4. **Practice:** Invite students to work on their own to complete a KWL for another short text. Monitor students as they complete each step, and discuss their work as noted earlier in the

K (What I know or think I know)	W (What I want to know)	L (What I learned)
Atoms have protons, neutrons, and electrons.	How do these work together?	Protons, neutrons, and electrons are subatomic particles. Each carries a charge. The proton is positive. The neutron is neutral. The electron is negative. The protons and neutrons together form the nucleus, which is in the middle of the atom.
A chemical compound is a combination of elements.	Can this be more than two elements combined?	A chemical compound is a substance formed by the combination of 2 *or more* elements.
There are two kinds of chemical bonds: covalent and ionic.	What is an ion?	An ion is either an atom that loses electrons (so it has a positive charge) or an atom that gains electrons (so it has a negative charge).
	How are they different?	If atoms are sharing electrons, then the bond between them is covalent. If an atom gives an electron to another atom, then they have an ionic bond.

FIGURE 5.6 KWL: Chemistry—The Nature of Matter

process. After the students have discussed the completed KWL chart, encourage them to revisit the K and L columns as noted in steps 2 and 3. Then invite students to share their oral summary of what they learned with a partner.

5 Reflect: Invite students to think about how the KWL helps us comprehend by providing opportunities to self-question, monitor, and summarize text.

Figure 5.6 features a KWL form that Melanie Younger completed when her chemistry class was studying matter.

Making Connections
TO MULTIPLE LITERACIES

Students can use ideas such as Say Something and KWLS to set purposes for reading, monitor understanding, and provide information for discussion. These approaches apply to multiple literacies. For example, when students engage in information literacy to research an issue, they can use these techniques to gain understanding of the facts presented on websites, which in turn may lead them to search for other sites and locate additional information. Students can also use the information gleaned from the strategy applications to interact with peers in small-group discussions or Internet Workshop (see Chapter 11). ■

TEACHING IDEA

INTERACTIVE NOTATION SYSTEM TO EFFECTIVE READING AND THINKING (INSERT). The Interactive Notation System to Effective Reading and Thinking (INSERT) method was developed to encourage students to become active readers. When using this technique, students insert a number of symbols into the text. INSERT provides students with opportunities to reflect about what they know and encourages them to make some decisions about the ideas expressed in the text. We have adapted the original INSERT for our students' use; the revised version requires the reader to insert fewer symbols than does the original version.

To teach students how to use INSERT, follow these steps:

1 Explain: Begin by explaining that monitoring/clarifying is a reading comprehension strategy that involves our constantly asking ourselves, "Does this make sense?" and adapting strategic processes to make the message clear. Then explain that INSERT helps us to self-question, monitor, and summarize as we read. Focus on how INSERT begins with readers brainstorming a list of what they know about the topic, reading the text, and inserting four symbols as they read. Introduce the four symbols to be inserted into the text and explain what each means:

- Place a check mark (✓) in the margin if the information in the text verifies what is on the brainstormed list.
- Place a plus sign (+) in the margin if the information is new—that is, not on the reader's list.
- Place a minus sign (−) in the margin if the information contradicts or disproves information on the brainstormed list.
- Place a question mark (?) in the margin if there is something in the text that is confusing.

Explain that if the students are completing the INSERT Bookmarks, they will write information on each Bookmark, rather than in the margin of the text. Share the INSERT Bookmarks with the students and use the Bookmarks throughout the remainder of the lesson.

2 **Demonstrate:** Introduce a short text and think aloud as you brainstorm what you know about the topic. Write your brainstormed list on the board, on an overhead transparency, or on a computer. Then read the text and complete an INSERT Bookmark each time you insert a notation.

For example, in Figure 5.7, when David Bishop wanted to indicate that he read something that confirmed what he had brainstormed, he wrote the page and paragraph numbers and what was confirmed on the ✓ (check symbol) Bookmark. When he encountered information that was new to him, he wrote on the + (plus symbol) Bookmark. When he read something that did not support what appeared on his brainstormed list, he wrote it on the - (minus symbol) Bookmark. When he read something that confused him, he wrote it on the ? (question mark symbol) Bookmark.

After you have finished reading, discuss the notations you inserted and how they related to your brainstormed list. Then summarize the text.

3 **Guide:** Introduce another short text and invite students to work with a partner to brainstorm what they know about the topic. Then encourage the students to complete the INSERT Bookmarks, indicating when the text supported what they had brainstormed, when the text contained new information, when the text disconfirmed something that appeared on the brainstormed list, and when they found text information confusing. After the students complete the Bookmarks, invite them to discuss their ideas and summarize the text.

4 **Practice:** Invite students to work on their own to complete INSERT Method. Introduce another short text and encourage students to brainstorm what they know. Then monitor students, assisting as needed, as they read the text and complete the INSERT Bookmarks. Encourage them to discuss their completed Bookmarks and summarize the text.

5 **Reflect:** Invite students to reflect on how using INSERT helps us to self-question, monitor, and summarize as we read. Encourage students to think about other situations in which they can use INSERT.

In the following example, David Bishop, a high school history student, used INSERT while reading about the Louisiana Purchase. He began by brainstorming what he knew about the historic event before he began to read. David's brainstormed list included the following five statements:

1. The United States wanted the right to use the Mississippi River for shipping.
2. The United States purchased Louisiana.
3. The land was bought from France.
4. The land was bought for $15 million.
5. Napoleon, Monroe, and Livingston negotiated the deal.

FIGURE 5.7

INSERT Bookmarks about the Louisiana Purchase

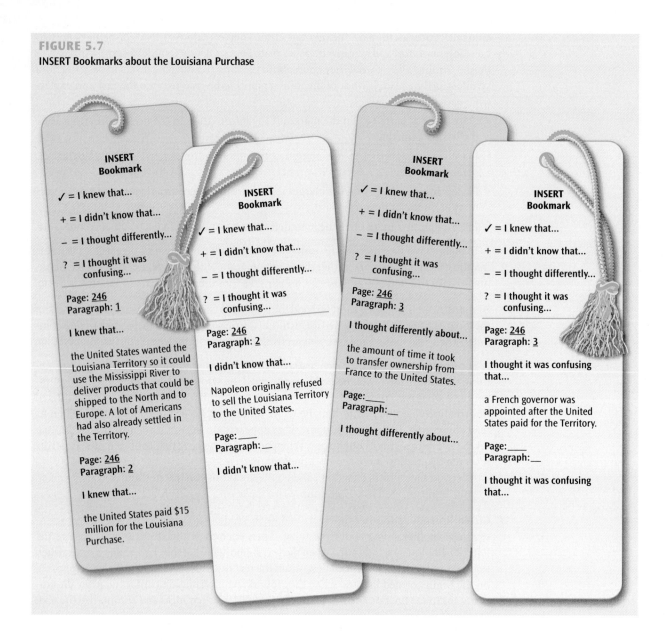

After brainstorming what he already knew, David read the section about the Louisiana Purchase in his history textbook. As he read, he completed the INSERT Bookmarks (McLaughlin & Allen, 2002b) as shown in Figure 5.7.

Visualizing

Visualizing is a reading comprehension strategy that involves creating mental images of the text as we read. When readers visualize, they often express their *mental pictures* through sketching. It is important that students understand that they do not need to be great artists to be able to sketch: They can use simple lines and shapes to communicate their thoughts. We can use this strategy while reading narrative or expository text. Detailed information about teaching ideas that help students to engage in visualization while reading follows.

 **TEACHING IDEA** **PHOTOGRAPHS OF THE MIND.** We can use Photographs of the Mind (Keene & Zimmerman, 1997) to help students to share the mental images they create while reading. While reading text, students stop at four designated points and sketch their visualizations. The graphic organizer we use with

this teaching idea is divided into four sections, one for each time the students sketch their visualizations. Students can also use the organizer to create Photographs of the Mind during specific content area tasks, such as different steps used to conduct experiments in science.

To teach your students how to use Photographs of the Mind, follow these steps:

1 **Explain:** Explain visualizing as a comprehension strategy that involves creating mental images of text as we read. Then explain that when we use Photographs of the Mind, we can stop periodically while reading to express our visualizations through sketching.

2 **Demonstrate:** Before reading, divide a short selection into four sections. Read the first section and think aloud about the mental picture you have created. Then sketch the picture you have in your mind. Briefly discuss it with the students.

3 **Guide:** Read the next section and ask students to work with a partner to create and discuss their mental images and sketches. Briefly discuss the results as a class.

4 **Practice:** Read the third section. Invite students to create mental images and sketch on their own, and then share those images with a partner. Read the fourth section, and follow the same procedure.

5 **Reflect:** Ask students to reflect on what they know about visualizing and how they can use Photographs of the Mind when reading content area text.

Figure 5.8 shows Photographs of the Mind that Caitlin McLaughlin created in response to Margarita Engle's poem "Juan" about the life of Juan Francisco Manzano, the poet slave of Cuba, who was born in 1797 and died in 1854.

Making Connections
TO ENGLISH LEARNERS

Teaching English learners to create mental pictures and share them through sketching supports their ability to communicate their thoughts through an alternative mode of representation. Providing opportunities for English learners to use sketching, dramatizing, and singing to represent their ideas encourages these students to express themselves and their understandings. ■

GUIDED IMAGERY. Guided Imagery (Long, Winograd, & Bridge, 1989) helps readers to activate prior knowledge, create visualizations, solve problems, and use their imaginations. We can use this teaching idea with narrative or informational text that evokes images.

To teach students how to use Guided Imagery, follow these steps:

1 **Explain:** Begin by explaining visualizing as a comprehension strategy that involves creating mental images of the text as we read. Next, describe the process of Guided Imagery, noting that it helps readers to activate prior knowledge, create visualizations, solve problems, and use their imaginations. Then introduce the text. Remember to use a text that will evoke images.

2 **Demonstrate:** Ask a student to read a segment of text aloud as you demonstrate Guided Imagery. Close your eyes and create sensory images while listening to a segment of text. Stop periodically and use a think-aloud to describe what you are visualizing and sensing. At the end of the text, talk about the images you created, including how they helped you to understand the text.

3 **Guide:** Invite the students to work with partners as they close their eyes and listen to another segment of text. As you read aloud, stop periodically and ask the students to share what they are visualizing and sensing with their partners. When you finish reading, ask students to talk about the images they created and describe how their images helped them to understand the text. Record their thoughts on a chalkboard, overhead transparency, or computer.

4 **Practice:** Encourage students to create images on their own, as you continue to read the text aloud. Stop at designated points so that students can share the images they have

FIGURE 5.8 Photographs of the Mind: "Juan" (The Life of Juan Francisco Manzano)

created. When the students finish reading, ask them to discuss the images they created and describe how their visualizations helped them to comprehend the text. Discuss the importance of visualizing while we read.

5 **Reflect:** Ask students to reflect on what they learned about visualizing and discuss how they can use Guided Imagery throughout the content areas.

FIGURE 5.9

Holocaust Survivor Guided Imagery Example

> I could see Eva's family gathered together as her parents decided who might survive if they jumped from the train. I felt afraid for them. When they jumped, I could see the bullets flying from the roof of the train as it continued to move. When Eva found her brother and sister dead, I saw a field of high brown grass dotted by dead bodies. I cringed. When she talked about pretending not to be Jewish and working on a farm during the rest of the war, I pictured a farm in the country where she waited to one day reclaim her identity. Creating images in my mind helped me to see what Eva experienced and to understand how horrible life was for all who were taken from their homes and sent to concentration camps during the Holocaust.

FIGURE 5.10

Poetry Guided Imagery Example

> While I listened to the poem being read, I could picture all of the people and things that Maya Angelou knows can be frightening. Then every time I heard the phrase, "Life doesn't frighten me at all," those images would disappear and I would start picturing the next items Maya Angelou included in the poem. For example, when I heard "Mean old Mother Goose, Lions on the loose," I pictured a book of fairy tales I had when I was in first grade and remembered how some of the stories like "Rumplestiltskin" did frighten me, but then the image disappeared when I was reminded it didn't frighten Maya Angelou. Creating images helped me to understand that none of the things mentioned frighten Maya Angelou and that we should all meet our fears and not let them frighten us anymore.

Figure 5.9 provides an example of Guided Imagery in which Tomas describes the images he created when he closed his eyes and listened as his European history teacher, Venetta Hurley, read Eva Galler's Holocaust survivor story to his class. Galler described how her parents encouraged her brother, her sister, and her to jump from a moving train as it transported her family and others to concentration camps. At predetermined stopping points, the students described their images to a partner. At the conclusion of the reading, they shared their images with the class.

In the example featured in Figure 5.10, Adelina describes the images she created while listening to her English teacher reading a poem. The poem was "Life Doesn't Frighten Me at All," by Maya Angelou.

Making Connections
TO STRUGGLING READERS

When teaching Guided Imagery to students who struggle with organizing, storing, and retrieving information, encourage them to activate all of their senses during reading—not just seeing. For example, encourage students to ask themselves what they are hearing, smelling, tasting, and touching. ■

TEACHING IDEA

GALLERY IMAGES. Gallery Images (Ogle, 2000) help us to create visualizations while reading and provide a format for sharing our mental images. This technique is usually used after reading informational text.

To teach your students how to create Gallery Images, follow these steps:

1 **Explain:** Begin by explaining that visualizing is a reading comprehension strategy that involves creating mental images of the text as we read. Then explain that we visualize when using Gallery Images, which provides us with a format for sharing our visualizations.

2 **Demonstrate:** Begin the demonstration by sharing a number of images that represent a variety of content area concepts. Next, visualize as you read a section of text. Think aloud about how to represent your mental pictures through sketching. Then use simple lines and shapes as you sketch on poster-size paper. Write a sentence or two below the sketches to explain the visualizations.

FIGURE 5.11 **Gallery Images about the Water Cycle in Science Class**

Evaporation   Condensation   Precipitation   Collection

3 **Guide:** Ask students to work in pairs and visualize at least two images as you read another segment of text. Encourage the students to sketch their mental pictures on poster-size paper, write a description, and share their images with their partner. Then engage the students in a discussion about their visualizations.

4 **Practice:** Encourage students to practice by creating at least two more mental pictures as you read another segment of text. Then invite them to sketch and label their visualizations on the poster-size paper. Use the classroom wall to create Gallery Images, as the students display their sketches and discuss them with other students.

5 **Reflect:** Encourage students to reflect on how creating visualizations, and specifically Gallery Images, helps us to understand what we read. Ask students to reflect on how they can use Gallery Images in other content areas.

Figure 5.11 features examples of Gallery Images about the water cycle that were created in a science class.

Making Connections | Thinking about Engaging Students *during* Reading

■ Think about when you were in middle school or high school. Do you remember teachers activating background knowledge and making connections to engage you in reading? Do you remember their providing creative writing options or hands-on projects to extend thinking after reading? Engaging and extending thinking strategies are more commonly used than strategies such as monitoring, self-questioning, and visualizing, which guide our thinking during reading. Consider how you will integrate these strategies in your teaching and help your students think through the comprehension process.

■ Share your thoughts in small-group discussions.

FINAL THOUGHTS

Using reading comprehension strategies to guide our thinking helps us to focus on content and construct meaning. We use strategies such as self-questioning, monitoring, and visualizing during reading to help us engage with text and monitor our understanding.

In the next chapter, we focus on reading comprehension strategies we can use to extend our thinking. Summarizing and evaluating are examples of these. Of course, as noted earlier, we can use all of the strategies we have learned as needed while reading.

Teaching Connections

APPLYING WHAT WE HAVE LEARNED

E-Links

Work with a partner and choose a website such as those listed to locate text related to your content area. As you read, consciously use comprehension strategies such as monitoring and visualizing. Complete strategy-based ideas such as Bookmark Technique and Photographs of the Mind (see the Appendix for graphic organizers). Discuss with your partner how using these strategies helped you understand the text. Record your thoughts as a reflective entry in your portfolio.

EXAMPLE WEBSITES

American History: USA.gov
http://www.usa.gov/Citizen/Topics/History_American.shtml

Calculus—from Wolfram Math World
http://mathworld.wolfram.com/Calculus.html

Ernest Hemingway: His Life and Works
www.ernest.hemingway.com

Physics Central
www.physicscentral.com

Poets.org
http:www.poets.org

Profiles of Spanish Speaking Countries
http://www.donquijote.org/tourist/profiles

Smithsonian's History Explorer (National Museum of American History)
http://historyexplorer.americanhistory.si.edu

Accountable Talk

Consider why it is important to motivate students to engage with text during reading. Think about how strategies, such as those we learned in this chapter, support students' transaction with text and promote reader response. Consider how these strategies help students to construct meaning and what students' responses can tell us about their understanding of text. Record your ideas and share what you believe to be the best suggestions in the class discussion.

 ### Portfolio/Performance Opportunity

Work with a partner in your content area to develop a standards-based lesson plan that focuses on (1) teaching course content and (2) using reading comprehension strategies to engage and guide student thinking (before and during reading). Meet in small groups and teach your lesson to the group. Engage in peer feedback, and revise the lesson plan as necessary. Discuss how you can work with other content area teachers to support students' use of comprehension strategies to guide their thinking. Reflect on your work and include your lesson plan in your portfolio.

6

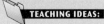

■ **How Can We Use Comprehension Strategies to Extend Thinking?**
Summarizing
Evaluating

■ **Who Will Work with Us to Help Our Students Become Strategic Readers?**

TEACHING IDEAS:
• BIO-PYRAMID • NARRATIVE PYRAMID • PAIRED SUMMARIZING • SKETCH TO STRETCH • QUESTIONS INTO PARAGRAPHS (QuIP) • DISCUSSION WEB • MIND AND ALTERNATIVE MIND PORTRAITS • EVALUATIVE QUESTIONING • VENN DIAGRAM

Using Comprehension Strategies to Extend Thinking

In this chapter, we continue our quest to help students learn a variety of comprehension strategies to use as needed while reading. Our focus is strategies to use *after* reading to extend student thinking. We use these strategies to elaborate on what we have learned, extend learning beyond the classroom, and clarify understandings.

We begin by discussing how we can use strategies to extend thinking. Then we focus on summarizing and evaluation—both strategies that help us to extend our understanding. Next, we consider which literacy professionals and school administrators will support us in our quest to teach students a repertoire of strategies they can use while reading.

How Can We Use Comprehension Strategies to Extend Thinking?

In the examples that follow, we describe a variety of ways to support students' use of comprehension strategies *after* reading. In each step-by-step sequence, we begin by explaining the strategy and the teaching idea. Next, we demonstrate it. Then, we guide students as they work with partners. After that, the students attempt to use the strategies on their own. Finally, we reflect on what we have learned, including how we can use the strategies in the content areas. Each teaching sequence is followed by a student example. Related reproducible graphic organizers can be found in the Appendix.

78

Summarizing

Summarizing is a reading comprehension strategy that involves extracting essential information from text. This strategy is often used formally after reading to provide students with the opportunity to gather important information about a topic, but as we read we often summarize informally—thinking about what the author has said to that point before we read on. Many teaching ideas support this strategy, including those featured in this section. Descriptions of these ideas and step-by step directions for teaching them follow. Detailed information about scaffolding students' writing of summaries can be found in Chapter 10. Strategy-based examples found in that chapter include the Concept of Definition Map Summary and Questions into Paragraphs (QuIP). In Chapter 13, Lyric Summaries and Rapping for Review—two ideas for summarizing that integrate singing—are featured. Reproducible copies of related graphic organizers can be found in the Appendix.

TEACHING IDEA

BIO-PYRAMID. The Bio-Pyramid (Macon, 1991) is a summary format for a person's life that requires particular information and a specific number of words per line. It involves a graphic organizer that appears as a pyramid. In addition to helping students learn how to summarize, the Bio-Pyramid helps them monitor and make connections to the text they are reading.

To teach your students how to complete a Bio-Pyramid, follow these guidelines:

1 **Explain:** Explain summarizing as a comprehension strategy that involves extracting essential information from text. Then describe how Bio-Pyramids work, noting that there are 8 lines and that each can accommodate only a certain number of words. Then explain that what we write on each line needs to accommodate the description that appears below the line. Finally, distribute copies of the graphic organizer (see the Appendix).

2 **Demonstrate:** Begin by distributing a short biography to the students. Introduce the text. Read the biography aloud to the students and briefly discuss the person's life. Then think aloud as you complete the first 2 lines of the Bio-Pyramid. For example, if you were creating a Bio-Pyramid about Dr. Martin Luther King, Jr., you might say, "I see that the first line requires the person's name. It provides only one space, so I will write 'King.' The second line asks for two words describing the person, so I will write 'educated' and 'dedicated,' because Dr. King was well educated and very dedicated to the Civil Rights Movement."

3 **Guide:** Ask the students to work with partners as they complete lines 3, 4, and 5 of the Bio-Pyramid. Encourage several partners to share their lines with the class. Then complete lines 3, 4, and 5 on the Bio-Pyramid you began about Dr. King. For example, you might write, "Brother, Son, Grandson" on line 3, "Prejudice in United States" on line 4, and "He was a Baptist minister" on line 5.

4 **Practice:** Invite the students to work on their own to complete lines 6, 7, and 8. Encourage several students to share their lines with the class. Then complete the remaining lines on the Bio-Pyramid about Dr. King. For example, you might write, "He worked for American civil rights" on line 6, "Gave the 'I Have a Dream' speech" on line 7, and "We learned to celebrate the equality of all" on line 8.

5 **Reflect:** Encourage students to reflect on how well they can summarize and how they can use Bio-Pyramids in other content areas.

Figure 6.1 shows a Bio-Pyramid about Pythagoras that was completed in mathematics class by Daisy Herrera.

TEACHING IDEA

NARRATIVE PYRAMID. The Narrative Pyramid (Waldo, 1991) is a retelling or summary format for texts such as short stories and novels. Much like the Bio-Pyramid, the graphic organizer requires particular information and a specific number of words per line. In this case, each line includes information linked to the narrative elements: characters, setting, problem, events, and solution. The Narrative Pyramid is used after reading.

Go to the Activities and Applications section under the topic *Writing* in the MyEducationLab for your course and complete the activity entitled Summarizing to better understand the importance of teaching students to summarize information.

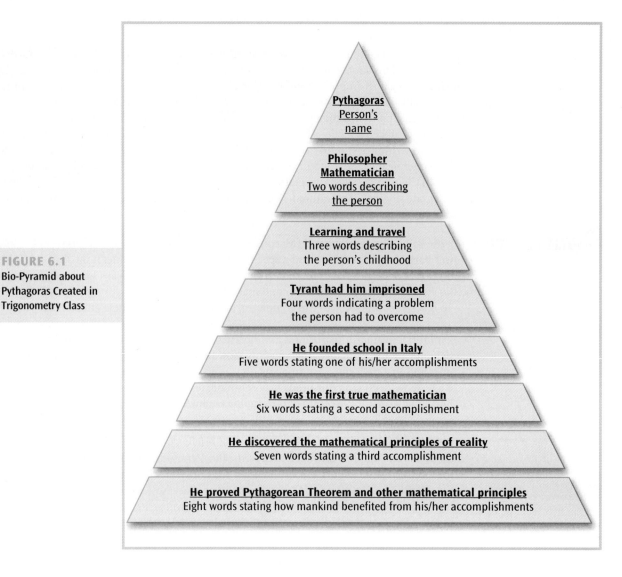

FIGURE 6.1

Bio-Pyramid about
Pythagoras Created in
Trigonometry Class

To teach your students how to complete a Narrative Pyramid, follow these guidelines:

1 **Explain:** Explain summarizing as a comprehension strategy that involves extracting essential information from text. Then explain how Narrative Pyramids help us to summarize stories. Note the number of lines, the number of words we can write per line, and the use of descriptions beneath each line to determine what we write. Distribute copies of the graphic organizer (see the Appendix).

2 **Demonstrate:** Engage students in completing a Narrative Pyramid after they have read a short story or novel. Briefly review the text. For example, you might say:

> The text we will use while learning about the Narrative Pyramid is the novel we have just finished reading: *To Kill a Mockingbird.* I see that I will need to provide specific information about the narrative elements on the graphic organizer. So, I will think about the characters, setting, problem, attempts to resolve the problem, and resolution. Atticus, Scout, Jem, Boo Radley, and Tom Robinson are the characters that come to mind. I remember the story took place in a poor rural community in Alabama and that the people in the community supported white people when it came to justice. Atticus Finch defended Tom Robinson, a black man, against rape charges, and, as a result, Atticus's

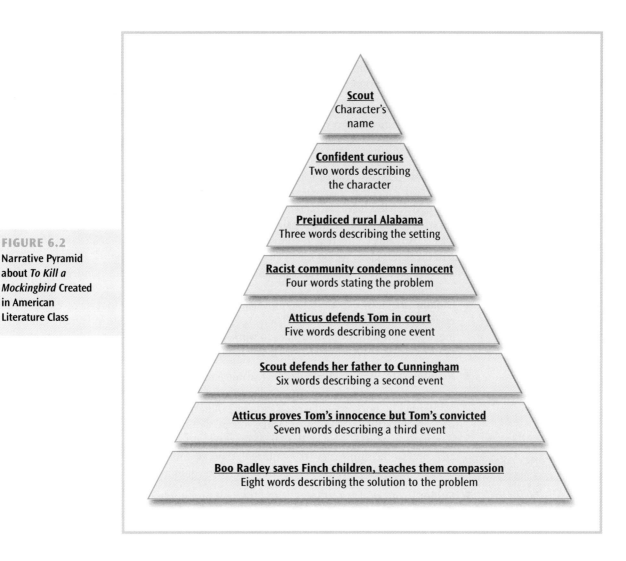

FIGURE 6.2
Narrative Pyramid
about *To Kill a*
Mockingbird Created
in American
Literature Class

children were harassed by Mr. Cunningham. Boo Radley came to the children's rescue, after Tom Robinson, who was innocent, was convicted.

Next, think aloud as you complete the first four lines of the Narrative Pyramid (Figure 6.2). For example, you might say, "I see that the first line requires the character's name. It provides only one space, so I will write <u>Scout</u>. The second line asks for two words that describe the character, and I know that Scout was <u>confident</u> and <u>curious</u>, so I will write those words in the two spaces in line 2." The setting needs to be described in line 3, so I might say, "The novel took place in rural Alabama during a time when prejudice was prevalent. I know I can use only three words, so I will write <u>prejudiced</u> <u>rural</u> <u>Alabama</u>." The problem needs to be stated in four words in line 4, so I might say, "<u>Racist</u> <u>community</u> <u>condemns</u> <u>innocent</u>."

3 Guide: Ask the students to work with partners to complete lines 5 and 6 of the Narrative Pyramid, each of which refers to an event in the novel. Encourage several partners to share their responses with the class. Then write responses on lines 5 and 6 on the Narrative Pyramid you have been completing. You may use student responses or create your own. For example, you might write "<u>Atticus</u> <u>defends</u> <u>Tom</u> in <u>court</u>" on line 5 and "<u>Scout</u> <u>defends</u> <u>her</u> father <u>to</u> <u>Cunningham</u>" on line 6.

4 Practice: Invite the students to work on their own to complete line 7, seven words describing another event, and line 8, eight words describing the solution to the problem. After a few students share their responses, complete the Narrative Pyramid you have been using for demonstration. For example, you might write, "<u>Atticus</u> <u>proves</u> <u>Tom's</u> <u>innocence</u> <u>but</u> <u>Tom's</u> <u>convicted</u>" on line 7 and "<u>Boo</u> <u>Radley</u> <u>saves</u> <u>Finch</u> <u>children,</u> <u>teaching</u> <u>them</u> <u>compassion</u>" on line 8. The completed demonstration Narrative Pyramid is featured in Figure 6.2.

5 **Reflect:** Encourage students to reflect on what they know about summarizing and how to use story elements to complete Narrative Pyramids. Discuss how the Narrative Pyramid can be used to summarize information when reading literature in the content areas.

PAIRED SUMMARIZING. Paired summarizing (Vaughn & Estes, 1986) provides a format for two students to work together to express their understandings and summarize narrative or informational text. After a text is selected and introduced, each student reads a segment and writes a summary of what she has read. Then the paired students read each other's summaries and summarize them. Next, students compare and contrast their summaries and share their ideas with a small group or the whole class. We engage in Paired Summarizing after reading.

To teach your students how to use Paired Summarizing, follow these guidelines:

1 **Explain:** Begin by explaining summarizing as a reading strategy that involves extracting essential information from text. Then explain that when we engage in Paired Summarizing, we have multiple opportunities to work with a partner to extract important information from text, determine what we understand, and generate questions we may have.

2 **Demonstrate:** Prior to demonstrating, arrange to have a student engage in Paired Summarizing with you. Think aloud as you follow each step in the process. To begin, you and your partner read a short text and write a summary of it. You may refer to the article, but you may not have the article in front of you while you are writing. When you finish writing, exchange summaries with your partner. Read that summary and write a summary of it. Then compare and contrast the summaries you wrote with those of your partner. Discuss what you do and do not understand. Create and respond to clarifying questions.

3 **Guide:** Invite students to work with a partner and guide them as they engage in Paired Questioning. Provide a short content area text they can read and summarize. Then observe as they exchange summaries and write summaries based on those they read. Encourage students to focus on what they understand and what questions they have. Guide them to discuss their summaries and questions in small groups. Contribute as requested. Repeat the process with another short text. Discuss Paired Summarizing with the students.

4 **Practice:** Encourage students to work with partners to independently engage in Paired Summarizing.

5 **Reflect:** Invite students to reflect on how Paired Summarizing helps us understand text. Encourage them to reflect on and discuss how they can use Paired Summarizing in other content area classes.

In the example featured in Figure 6.3, Brandon and Javier use Paired Summarizing as they are reading *Fields of Fury: The American Civil War* (McPherson, 2002), a content area trade book in American History class.

SKETCH TO STRETCH. Sketch to Stretch (Short, Harste, & Burke, 1996) involves using sketching to create, represent, and share personal understandings of text. Sketch to Stretch is usually used in small groups after reading narrative or informational text.

To teach your students how to use Sketch to Stretch, follow these steps:

1 **Explain:** Begin by explaining summarizing as a reading strategy that involves extracting essential information from text. Then explain Sketch to Stretch as a way to represent personal meaning through sketching after reading.

Brandon's Summary

March 4, 1865, began the Reconstruction period. After the Civil War, the South lay in ruins. President Lincoln asked that the high-ranking officials be pardoned because he wanted to create peace with the South. However, Lincoln never got to establish his Reconstruction ideas, because he was assassinated by John Wilkes Booth. His Vice-President, Andrew Johnson, took over. President Johnson was too lenient with the South, and Southerners reelected the same political parties and created black codes so they could almost use African Americans as slaves again. Congress got angry and took control of the Reconstruction. Southerners still resented African Americans and found new ways to keep them as second-class citizens. They enforced Jim Crow laws and segregation. Reconstruction ended in 1877.

Javier's Summary of Brandon's Summary

Reconstruction of the South began after the Civil War. The South was destroyed and President Lincoln was in charge of rebuilding it. Lincoln, however, was assassinated and so the job fell to his Vice-President, Andrew Johnson. Johnson attempted to bring order to the South, but he ran into problems. The South kept creating laws to keep African Americans in their control.

FIGURE 6.3
Brandon and Javier's Examples of Paired Summarizing

2 Demonstrate: Begin the demonstration by introducing and reading a short selection and thinking about what the text means to you. Next, express your thoughts through sketching. Share your sketch with a few students and ask them what they think it means. Then explain what you think it means.

3 Guide: Invite students to work in small groups of 3 to 5. Introduce another short text and either read the text aloud or encourage the students to read it. After reading, ask them to express what the text meant to them through a sketch. Then invite the students to engage in Sketch to Stretch, by sharing their sketches one at a time. After each group member comments on a sketch, the student who created it offers her interpretation.

4 Practice: Encourage students to practice by continuing to share and discuss their sketches, until everyone in the group has had a turn.

5 Reflect: Invite students to reflect on how expressing personal meaning of text through sketching helped them to comprehend. Encourage students to reflect on how they can use Sketch to Stretch in other content areas.

Figure 6.4 features the sketch Chrissy created in American story class when studying the *Brown v. Board of Education* decision. When it was her turn to share her interpretation, she said, "I drew a protest sign supporting the Fourteenth Amendment because *Brown v. Board of Education* was about ending segregation in places such as schools. Segregation violated the Fourteenth Amendment and needed to be abolished."

 **TEACHING IDEA**

QUESTIONS INTO PARAGRAPHS (QuIP). Questions into Paragraphs (QuIP) (McLaughlin, 1987) provides a framework for initiating research, structuring writing, and summarizing. Students choose a topic and develop three related research questions. Then they respond to each question from two sources. When the graphic organizer is complete, students use the information to write a paragraph. We use QuIP before reading (generating questions), during reading (reading the information provided by the two sources), and after reading (writing the summary).

To teach your students how to use QuIP, follow these guidelines:

1 Explain: Begin by explaining summarizing as a reading strategy that involves extracting essential information from text. Then explain QuIP as a framework for questioning, researching, and summarizing that focuses on developing three questions and responding to them from two different sources.

FIGURE 6.4 Sketch to Stretch – *Brown v. the Board of Education*

The 14th Amendment means equal protection for all.

2 Demonstrate: Begin demonstrating by sharing the graphic organizer (see the Appendix) and selecting a topic. Then remind students about the importance of generating higher-level questions (see Chapter 8) and develop three research questions. For example, if the topic you chose was Mars, you would raise three questions about it. Question 1 might be "How did Mars get its name?"

3 Guide: Invite students to work with a partner and guide them as they generate two additional questions. For example, Question 2 might be "Why do scientists believe there could be life on Mars?" Question 3 might be "What do scientists predict we will learn about Mars in the future?" Continue to guide the students as they use bookmarked websites to respond to the three research questions from two sources. Encourage the students to continue to complete the graphic organizer and discuss their responses.

4 Practice: Encourage students to work on their own to write a paragraph based on the completed graphic organizers. Invite them to share their completed paragraphs with their partners. Discuss completed QuIPs with the class.

5 Reflect: Invite students to reflect on how QuIP helps us to summarize and comprehend. Encourage students to think of other ways they can use QuIP in the content areas.

Figure 6.5 shows the QuIP and paragraph about Mars that Earth Science teacher Edward Puchalski completed during the Guided Comprehension demonstration.

FIGURE 6.5 Questions into Paragraphs about Mars QuIP Research Grid

Topic: Mars _____

Questions	Answers	
	Source 1: http://www.nineplanets.org/mars.html	Source 2: http://www.nasa.gov/worldbook/mars_worldbook.html
A. How did Mars get its name?	Mars was named after the god of war. It is also referred to as the red planet because of its coloring.	Mars was named after the Roman god of war. The Greeks and Romans named the planet after the god of war because the planet was blood colored.
B. Why do scientists believe there could be life on Mars?	In 1996, scientists discovered evidence of ancient Martian microorganisms in a meteorite.	Researchers found evidence of life in certain materials in meteorites found on Earth.
C. What do scientists predict we will learn about Mars in the future?	Scientists are still not convinced that there is/was life on Mars. Scientists will continue to search for answers.	Scientists are still attempting to prove that there is life on Mars through research.

QuIP Paragraph

Mars was named after the Roman god of war. The Romans named the planet after the god of war because the planet was red or blood colored. Scientists have discovered microorganisms in a meteorite that landed on Earth. Some researchers believe this indicates that there was life on Mars at one point, while others are skeptical. Scientists are still studying Mars today in hopes of proving that life does or did exist on Mars.

Making Connections
TO STRUGGLING READERS

Summarizing plays an essential role in student learning. Whether students are summarizing text as they read, creating summaries after reading, or representing summaries through alternative modes, students—and especially struggling learners—need to know how to summarize. For ideas about how to scaffold students' learning of how to summarize and, in particular, how to write summaries, see Chapter 10. For ideas about how to use music when summarizing, see the descriptions of Summary and Rapping for Review found in Chapter 13. ■

Evaluating

Evaluating is a reading comprehension strategy that involves making judgments during and after reading. Issues we focus on include these questions: (1) Is the author's message consistent? and (2) Whose perspective is presented in the text? This strategy is used with narrative and expository text. A variety of teaching ideas support this strategy, including the four that are featured in this section. Related reproducible graphic organizers are located in the Appendix.

DISCUSSION WEB. The Discussion Web (Alvermann, 1991) provides students with a structure to discuss and evaluate given texts. To complete the Web, students investigate both sides of an issue and think critically about a topic with varying points of view. The Discussion Web begins with a question and ends when students come to consensus about the issue. Used with informational text, this technique is designed to spark discussion and debate in all content areas.

To teach your students how to complete a Discussion Web, follow these steps:

1 Explain: Begin by selecting a text—or two, if necessary—that provides information about two perspectives on a topic. Share the text(s) with the students. Explain evaluating as a reading comprehension strategy that involves making judgments while reading. Then explain how Discussion Webs focus on questions or statements that have pro and con perspectives and how pairs and ultimately the whole class come to consensus on such issues.

2 Demonstrate: Think aloud about the topic of the text(s) and a question that might be raised that would require readers to investigate pro and con perspectives. For example, if the topic was school violence, the question might be, "Do the media contribute to school violence?" Introduce each of the related texts and invite the students to take a few minutes to read the information. Continue demonstrating by writing the brainstormed question on the graphic organizer. Then take one fact from each perspective and write it in either the Pro (yes) or Con (no) column. For example, in the Pro column you might write, "The media report on many violent acts during the daily news," and in the Con column you might write, "People don't need to listen to the media. They can turn off or ignore the media outlets."

3 Guide: Ask students to work with a partner and add two more facts to each column. Discuss the information they add to the graphic.

4 Practice: Ask students to continue working with partners until they have exhausted the facts they would like to include. Then invite them to discuss the information they have compiled and come to an agreement on their position about the topic. Invite the partners to share their positions with the class and then engage in class discussion until consensus is reached. Record the class's perspective on the graphic organizer. Finally, ask students to provide a rationale and record that on the graphic organizer. For example, when discussing whether the media are responsible for school violence, the class might reach this conclusion: "Yes, the media are responsible for school violence." Then they might offer the

FIGURE 6.6 Discussion Web about Changing the Constitution

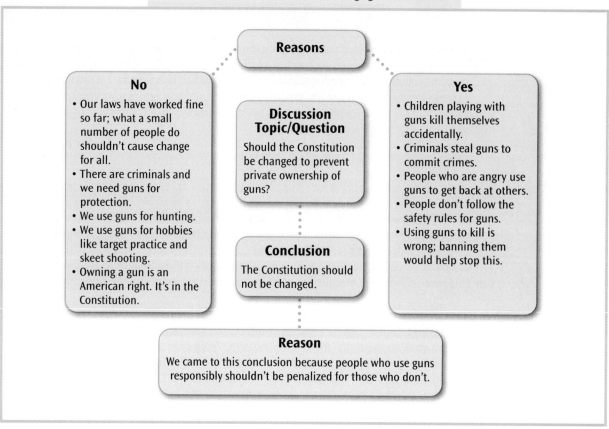

FIGURE 6.6 Discussion Web about Changing the Constitution

following rationale: "We came to this conclusion because students are exposed to so much violence in music, video games, and television, and on the Internet that when they react to real-life situations, they become violent just like the people they see in the media."

5 **Reflect:** Invite students to reflect on evaluating and how to use the Discussion Web in other content areas.

Figure 6.6 shows a Discussion Web focused on the following question: Should the Constitution be changed to prevent private ownership of guns? This Discussion Web was completed in Madeline Apfel's American History class.

TEACHING IDEA   MIND AND ALTERNATIVE MIND PORTRAITS.   Mind and Alternative Mind Portraits (McLaughlin, 2001) is designed to help readers examine a topic from two viewpoints. This technique helps us to evaluate the perspectives that exist within a text. Mind and Alternative Mind Portraits, which are used with informational text, are usually completed after reading. Alternatives to Mind and Alternative Mind Portraits include Narratives and Alternative Narratives, Photographs and Alternative Photographs, and Videos and Alternative Videos.

To teach your students how to use Mind and Alternative Mind Portraits, follow these steps:

1 **Explain:** Begin by explaining evaluating as a reading comprehension strategy that involves making judgments while reading. Then explain how Mind and Alternative Mind Portraits represent two different perspectives. Introduce the text, noting that it contains multiple perspectives, and share the graphic organizer.

2 **Demonstrate:** Use a think-aloud and a read-aloud to demonstrate Mind and Alternative Mind Portraits. Read the text and think aloud about the ideas it presents. Choose the two

FIGURE 6.7 Mind and Alternative Mind Portraits

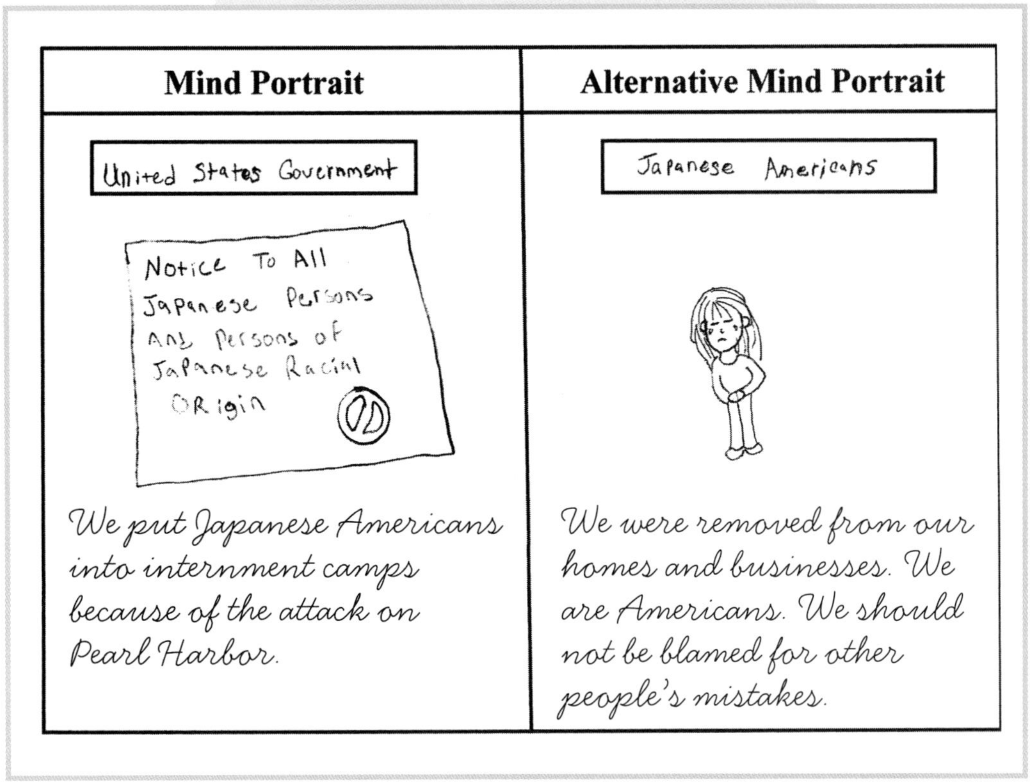

perspectives you will represent in Mind and Alternative Mind Portraits. For example, if the text is about the Japanese American internment during World War II, you might choose the predominant perspective of the U.S. government and the perspective of Japanese Americans living on the West Coast between 1942 and 1945, which may not be equally represented or may be missing in the text. Think aloud as you label the Mind Portrait on the graphic organizer. Inside the Mind Portrait, write or sketch ideas and experiences that describe the U.S. government's perspective. Next, label the Alternative Mind Portrait and think aloud as you write or sketch ideas inside that portrait that are characteristic of the Japanese Americans interned during World War II. (See the completed Portraits in Figure 6.7.) Think aloud as you contrast the Mind and Alternative Mind Portraits, noting which perspective is more predominant and pointing out that the Alternative Mind Portrait features a perspective that was not equally presented in the text.

3 **Guide:** Invite students to work with partners to begin Mind and Alternative Mind Portraits about another topic. Distribute copies of a short text in which multiple perspectives are represented. Introduce the text and read it aloud. After you have finished reading, encourage students to select two different perspectives on the topic and label the Portraits. Then invite the partners to discuss both perspectives and add two ideas each to the Mind Portrait and Alternative Mind Portraits. Invite the students to discuss their Portraits and share their reasoning.

4 **Practice:** Encourage students to work on their own to complete the Mind and Alternative Mind Portraits they began with their partners. After the graphic organizers are complete, encourage students to share their reasoning.

5 **Reflect:** Ask students to reflect on what they know about evaluating and how they can use Mind and Alternative Mind Portraits to help them evaluate as they read text in the content areas.

Figure 6.7 features the Mind and Alternative Mind Portraits that Jesse created in history class when they were studying the Japanese American internment.

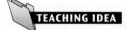

EVALUATIVE QUESTIONING. Evaluative questioning (Ciardiello, 1998) provides a format for us to express ideas and to defend, judge, or justify our thinking. When using this approach, students work in small groups, read text, and generate and respond to evaluative questions. We can use Evaluative Questioning after reading, but we can also use it before and during the reading of narrative and informational text.

To teach your students how to use Evaluative Questioning, follow these guidelines:

1. **Explain:** Begin by explaining evaluating as a reading comprehension strategy that involves making judgments while reading. Then explain that Evaluative Questioning involves developing ideas and defending or justifying our thinking.

2. **Demonstrate:** Begin demonstrating by reminding students about Ciardiello's levels of questioning (see Chapter 8), noting that we will focus on the highest level—evaluating. Read a short text, and create an evaluative question. For example, if you were reading about the contributions Leonardo DaVinci and the Wright Brothers made to flight, a question you would generate might be, "In your opinion, who contributed more to flight, DaVinci or the Wright Brothers? Defend your response." Then you should continue the demonstration by responding to the question you raised. Discuss Evaluative Questioning with the students.

3. **Guide:** Introduce a short text to your students and read it aloud. Before reading, remind the students that they will be generating evaluative questions. After reading, guide students to work in pairs to generate and respond to evaluative questions. For example, if the text you read focused on the Japanese American internment, a question students would raise might be, "Was the U.S. government justified in mandating the Japanese American internment after the bombing of Pearl Harbor?" Defend your response. Encourage students to generate and respond to at least two evaluative questions.

4. **Practice:** Invite students to practice by reading a short text on their own and generating two evaluative questions. Then ask them to share their questions with their partners, who will respond to them. Reverse the process, so that both students have opportunities to generate and respond to evaluative questions. Discuss Evaluative Questioning with the students.

5. **Reflect:** Encourage students to reflect on how Evaluative Questioning helps us to understand text. Then ask students how they might use Evaluative Questioning in other content areas.

VENN DIAGRAM. The Venn Diagram is named for its creator, John Venn, who used it to express thoughts about logic. The diagram, which is represented by two interlocking circles, provides a format for us to note similarities and differences or two perspectives about a topic. The similarities appear in the overlapping sections of the circles; the differences appear in the outer sides of each circle.

To teach your students how to complete a Venn Diagram, follow these guidelines:

1. **Explain:** Begin by explaining evaluating as a comprehension strategy that involves making judgments while reading. Then explain that the Venn Diagram provides us with a format to express the similarities and differences associated with two topics.

2. **Demonstrate:** Read a short text that clearly represents two different perspectives or similarities and differences about a topic. For example, in Figure 6.8, the Venn Diagram focuses on two types of volcanoes. Demonstrate this technique by listing the topics to be compared and contrasted in the spaces provided on the graphic organizer. For example, in the Venn Diagram in Figure 6.8, the topics are cinder cones and composite volcanoes.

FIGURE 6.8 Venn Diagram about Two Types of Volcanoes

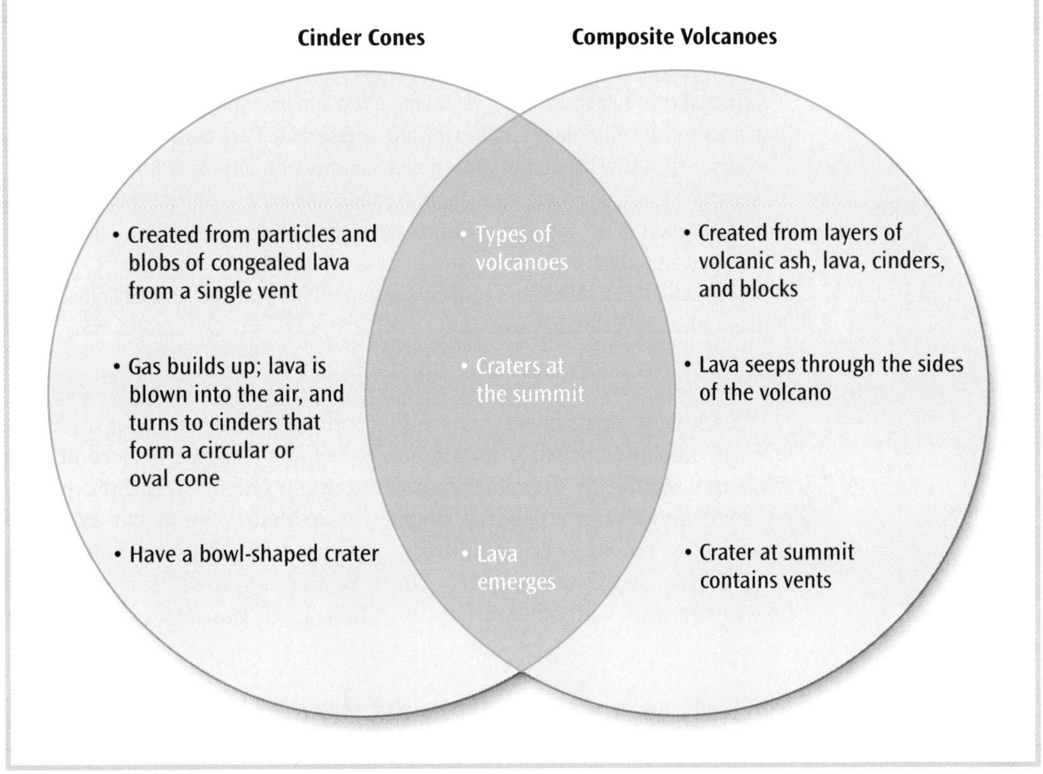

Cinder Cones   **Composite Volcanoes**

- Created from particles and blobs of congealed lava from a single vent

- Gas builds up; lava is blown into the air, and turns to cinders that form a circular or oval cone

- Have a bowl-shaped crater

- Types of volcanoes

- Craters at the summit

- Lava emerges

- Created from layers of volcanic ash, lava, cinders, and blocks

- Lava seeps through the sides of the volcano

- Crater at summit contains vents

Then think aloud as you list the common features in the overlapping section of the circles. In Figure 6.8, features the volcanoes have in common include that both are types of volcanos, both have craters at the summit, and lava emerges from both. Next, consider the descriptors that are unique to cinder cones. Write them in the outer section of the circle labeled "Cinder Cones." Then, consider the qualities that are unique to composite volcanoes and record them in the outer portion of that circle. Note the similarities and differences as they are represented on the graphic organizer. Discuss the completed Venn diagram with your students.

3 **Guide:** Encourage students to work in pairs to complete Venn Diagrams. Read a short text and provide copies for students. Then ask the students to revisit the text to determine which two topics they might use in their Venn Diagrams. Discuss the topics. Next, invite students to list qualities or characteristics that are common to both topics. Discuss the common qualities or similarities. Encourage students to determine which qualities are unique to each topic and list them in the outer portion of each circle. Discuss the unique qualities (contrasts).

4 **Practice:** Encourage students to practice by reading a short text that presents a topic from two different perspectives and completing a Venn Diagram. Discuss students' completed diagrams.

5 **Reflect:** Invite students to reflect on how Venn Diagrams help us to think through text. Encourage students to reflect on how they can use Venn Diagrams in other content areas and in everyday life to compare and contrast or present two perspectives.

Figure 6.8 shows Derek and Marianne's Venn Diagram about volcanoes.

Making Connections
TO MULTIPLE LITERACIES

We can use ideas such as Mind and Alternative Mind Portraits to examine multiple perspectives, an aspect of critical literacy. When we examine text and determine which position is represented as more powerful and which is either missing or discounted, we move beyond the text to understand issues such as why the author wrote about a particular topic, wrote from a particular perspective, and chose to include some ideas about the topic and exclude others. This is especially important for us as teachers in the content areas, because authors and publishers determine which content is included and which perspectives are represented in textbooks. As an example, consider what you learned about Columbus from textbooks when you were in grade school and what you know to be the truth about Columbus now. ■

Teaching students how to use reading comprehension strategies to think their way through text has numerous benefits. In addition to helping students to become strategic readers and thinkers, it illuminates the value of questioning at multiple levels and using alternative modes of representation. Using the Guided Comprehension Model's five steps of explicit instruction to teach the strategies provides opportunities for students to engage in scaffolded learning, application, and reflection. In the next section, we move beyond how to explicitly teach strategies and discuss how we can work with other professionals to help our students reach their reading potentials.

Who Will Work with Us to Help Our Students Become Strategic Readers?

Students begin learning to read at a very early age. Throughout their education, they are taught by knowledgeable teachers who are well acquainted with concepts such as the constructivist perspective and the importance of prior knowledge. Students begin learning the reading comprehension strategies in the primary grades, in the hope that they will use them as necessary from that time forward. But, as Biancarosa and Snow (2006) remind us, there are 8 million struggling adolescent readers who have not had that experience. They are not using reading comprehension strategies at the middle school and high school levels.

So, although we teach upper grades, one of our goals is for our students to understand and use a repertoire of comprehension strategies that will help them think through the reading process. The good news is we are not alone in this effort. In addition to our fellow content area teachers, other professionals—such as reading specialists, literacy coaches, and administrators—are among those who can help ensure that our students know and use such strategies. Figure 6.9 features excerpts from the International Reading Association's Standards for Reading Professionals that describe how such professionals can contribute to students' knowledge of reading.

We should add one more category to the list of professionals who work with us to help our students comprehend to their greatest potential: English as a Second Language (ESL) teachers. These educators can help us to make connections to our students who are English learners. For more information about teaching English learners in the content areas and working with ESL teachers, see Chapter 9.

Making Connections | Thinking about Those Who Will Help Students Reach Their Reading Potential

■ Think about who taught you to read and who continued to support your reading in the content areas when you were in middle school and high school. Did the answer to part one of this question come more easily than your response to part two? It often happens that way, because many of us can focus on the one person we think taught us to read but find it difficult to remember if anyone supported our reading in later years. Now consider all those who are currently available to support students' reading in the content areas: reading teachers, reading specialists, literacy coaches, school administrators, and ESL teachers. Think about how you envision your role as a member of this team of professionals and how you can make the most valuable contribution.

■ Share your thoughts in small-group discussions.

FINAL THOUGHTS

When we teach our students a repertoire of comprehension strategies, they become active, strategic readers. These students can then use the strategies as needed to think through text. This results in greater understanding. It also accommodates Biancarosa and Snow's (2006) recommendation in *Reading Next* that we explicitly teach reading comprehension strategies at the middle school and high school levels.

In the next chapter, we extend our discussion to teaching and learning vocabulary. As we know, vocabulary is an essential component of comprehension. Chapter 7 features a number of practical, classroom-based ideas to help our students expand their knowledge of words.

FIGURE 6.9
IRA Standards for Reading Professionals: Excerpts from the Revised Role Definitions, 2007

The Classroom Teacher
Teaches at the early childhood, elementary, middle, or high school and/or adult levels. Develops children's reading and related language arts; includes content area teachers who integrate literacy instruction with subject learning.

The Reading Specialist
Works at the early childhood, elementary, middle, secondary, and/or adult levels. Fulfills a number of responsibilities and many have a specific focus that further defines their duties. For example, a reading specialist can serve as a teacher for students experiencing reading difficulties; as a literacy or reading coach; or as a supervisor or coordinator of reading/literacy. The reading specialist must be prepared to fulfill the duties of all three of these:

■ **A reading intervention teacher** is a reading specialist who provides intensive instruction to struggling readers. Such instruction may be provided either within or outside the students' classrooms.
■ **A literacy coach** is a reading specialist who focuses on providing professional development for teachers by providing them with the additional support needed to implement various instructional programs and practices. They provide essential leadership for the school's entire literacy program by helping create and supervise a long-term staff development process that supports both the development and implementation of the literacy program over months and years. These individuals need to have experiences that enable them to provide effective professional development for the teachers in their schools.
■ **A reading supervisor or reading coordinator** is a reading specialist who is responsible for developing, leading, and evaluating a school reading program, from kindergarten through grade 12. They may assume some of the same responsibilities as the literacy coach, but in addition have responsibilities that require them to work more with systematic change at the school level. These individuals need to have experiences that enable them to work effectively as administrators and to be able to develop and lead effective professional development programs.

The Administrator
■ Includes principals and superintendents. Recognizes and supports reading professionals as they plan, implement, and evaluate effective reading instruction.

Source: International Reading Association. Reproduced with permission.

Teaching Connections

APPLYING WHAT WE HAVE LEARNED

E-Links

Work with a partner and choose a website such as those listed below to locate text related to your content area. As you read, consciously use summarizing as a comprehension strategy. Note how often you informally summarize text to a given point. After reading, complete strategy-based ideas such as Bio-Pyramids or Narrative Pyramids and Paired Summarizing. (See the Appendix for graphic organizers.) Discuss with your partner how using these techniques helped you understand the text. Record your thoughts as a reflective entry in your portfolio.

EXAMPLE WEBSITES

Poets.org
http:www.poets.org

Profiles of Spanish-Speaking Countries
http://www.donquijote.org/tourist/profiles

Smithsonian's History Explorer (National Museum of American History)
http://historyexplorer.americanhistory.si.edu

The Time 100: The Most Important People of the Century (Leaders and Revolutionaries, Scientists and Thinkers, Heroes and Icons—and More)
http://www.time.com/time/time100/scientist/profile/wright.html

Accountable Talk

We know that being active, strategic readers benefits students' learning. Meet in small groups and discuss (1) how middle school and high school teachers can help students to become strategic readers and (2) how middle and high school teachers can embed strategy instruction in standards-based lessons. Record your ideas and share what you believe to be the best suggestions in our class discussion.

 ### Portfolio/Performance Opportunity

Work with a partner in your content area to develop a standards-based lesson plan that focuses on the following: (1) teaching course content and (2) using reading comprehension strategies to engage, guide, and extend student thinking (before, during, and after reading). Meet in small groups and teach your lesson to the group. Engage in peer feedback and revise the lesson plan as necessary. Reflect on your work and include your lesson plan in your portfolio.

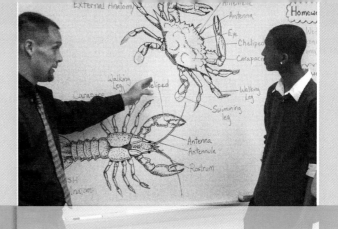

7

Chapter Overview

Teaching Vocabulary in the Content Areas

Our lives and the lives of our students are filled with words. We use words every day when we speak, write, read, and listen. We begin learning words when we are very young and continue to gain knowledge of them throughout our lives. Learning words is a lifelong pursuit, one in which we hope not only to participate, but also to engage our students.

Estimates of the number of words that students encounter in their reading at school range from 50,000 to 100,000 (Graves & Watts-Taffe, 2002). Researchers report that as students progress through school, their reading vocabulary increases by approximately 3,000 to 5,000 words each year. This results in a reading vocabulary of nearly 25,000 words by the eighth grade and more than 50,000 words by the end of high school (Graves & Watts-Taffe, 2002). Harris and Hodges (1995) describe this ever-growing knowledge of words and their meanings as *vocabulary development*. They note that vocabulary development also refers to the teaching–learning processes that lead to such growth.

Words fill our lives:

> They may seem simple like simple entities, but they are not. Their surface simplicity belies a deeper complexity. For example, they connect with experience and knowledge, and their meanings vary depending on the linguistic contexts in which they can be found. (Pearson, Hiebert, & Kamil, 2007, p. 286)

In this chapter, we learn about vocabulary, including how to teach it to our students. We begin by discussing the theoretical framework. Next, we study a variety of practical instructional approaches, including context clues, graphic organizers, and structural analysis. Then we use several strategy-related ideas to teach vocabulary in our content areas. Finally, we discuss several essential points that will guide our development of vocabulary lessons.

What Do We Know about Teaching Content Area Vocabulary?

The most important information we know about vocabulary can be easily summarized: If our students do not know the vocabulary, they will have difficulty comprehending what they are reading (Dixon-Krauss, 2001/2002; Duke, 2007; McLaughlin & Allen, 2002; National Reading Panel, 2000; Richek, 2005). This is especially true at levels of education beyond the middle grades (Rupley, Logan, & Nicholas, 1998/1999). As teachers, our goal is to help our students to continue to develop their vocabularies. We want them to know lots of words, understand many different concepts, use context clues, and have in-depth understandings (Brabham & Villaume, 2002).

Many of us can probably remember learning lists of words and their definitions and taking the dreaded Friday vocabulary quizzes. Such practices seemed to permeate our middle school and high school years. What makes this traditional practice seem misguided is that researchers now believe that studying words one at a time by writing definitions is not an effective way to learn vocabulary. As Blachowicz (2007) has noted, "Very few people learn from definitions. Definitions may refine our knowledge, but they do not give us our knowledge." Students need to do much more than write a word's definition to make the word part of their working vocabulary. They need to talk about words; feel comfortable using them when reading, speaking, and writing; and use them in a variety of contexts.

If we want our students to actively use content-related words, we need to motivate them to understand how words work. Graves and Watts-Taffe (2002) describe this process as "word consciousness —the awareness of and interest in learning and using new words and becoming more skillful and precise in word usage" (p. 144). This is an essential point: If we expect students to learn content area vocabulary, we need them to be interested—to be engaged in learning. We need to ensure that they are well motivated and help them see the connections between what they are learning and their everyday experiences. We need to remember that most of our students have had long vocabulary lists given to them since they were in the primary grades and that many are probably still working with such lists in their content area classrooms today. We need to make our enthusiasm for vocabulary evident to our students. We need to help them get excited about words and view vocabulary in new and engaging ways.

Making Connections | Thinking about Vocabulary

- Think about your vocabulary. Reflect on how it developed through the years. Consider two sources that you believe helped you to increase your knowledge of words and their meanings.

- Share your thoughts with others in small-group discussion.

Making Connections
TO MULTIPLE LITERACIES

Because it contributes to our understanding of what we read, vocabulary is an essential component of every literacy. For example, when we are discussing critical literacy, we must have an in-depth understanding of that term as well as those terms associated with reading from a critical stance— such as *alternative perspectives, juxtapositioning,* and *transformations.* When using information literacy and media literacy, we need to understand both those ideas and the other terms associated with them. Vocabulary is essential to our thinking and our understanding. ■

How Can We Integrate What We Know into Our Teaching?

Go to the Activities and Applications section under the topic *Developing Vocabulary, Concepts, and Fluency* in the MyEducationLab for your course and complete the activity entitled Assessing Content Vocabulary Knowledge to examine reasons students must understand content vocabulary to apply the concepts they are learning.

To integrate what we know about vocabulary into our teaching, ̶̶̶̶̶̶̶̶̶̶̶̶̶̶ ory into practice. Blachowicz and Fisher (2000) suggest four guide̶̶̶̶̶̶̶̶̶̶ that emerged from their review of the existing research. They no̶̶̶̶̶̶̶̶̶̶̶̶̶ ̶̶̶̶̶̶̶̶̶̶̶̶̶ should

- Be actively engaged in understanding words and related strategies.
- Personalize their vocabulary learning.
- Be immersed in words.
- Develop their vocabularies through repeated exposures from multiple sources of information.

Of course, these four guidelines have strong implications for us as teachers.

In order for our students to be actively engaged in understanding words and related strategies, we need to motivate them and teach them how to use vocabulary strategies. We can begin by helping our students to develop an interest in and make connections to our content areas, including the related vocabulary. We should also make sure that our students are well aware of our enthusiasm for learning. Insights from students' previous learning experiences are helpful as well. We can learn about our students' perceptions of their previous content learning by inviting them to write their Literacy Histories (see Chapter 1) and complete Content Inventories (see Chapter 8). We can also work to make our content areas appealing to the students by integrating creative and innovative practices as well as alternative modes of response, such as sketching.

When selecting vocabulary strategies to teach to our students, we can choose those that are interesting and work particularly well. We can also use a scaffolded approach when teaching such strategies. This means that we offer a great deal of support to our students when we begin teaching vocabulary strategies, but gradually decrease that level of support as students become more proficient in using the information we are teaching. For example, if we use the five-step Guided Comprehension explicit instruction process—explain, demonstrate, guide, practice, and reflect—we offer total support in the *explain* part of the process, as we provide the details of the strategy and how it works. When we *demonstrate*, we still offer a great deal of support, but we also use a think-aloud to share our thought processes with our students. Next, we *guide* students to work with partners as they attempt to use what we have just taught. In the *practice* part of the process, students use what we taught on their own. Finally, we and the students reflect on what we learned and how it will benefit our vocabulary development.

Making Connections
TO WRITING

Writing plays an important role in learning vocabulary. We use writing when we learn about words through strategies such as Semantic Maps and Concept of Definition Maps. We use the vocabulary we learn when we write for a variety of purposes, ranging from informal responses to long-term projects. Using the words in multiple formats and settings helps us to increase our vocabulary. ■

We know our students can learn vocabulary through explicit instruction and the use of context clues; but they can also learn vocabulary incidentally. When students learn new words and expand their understanding of words they already know by reading widely, having an extensive variety of experiences, engaging in discussion, and using technology, they are learning incidentally. As teachers, we can contribute to this incidental learning by creating informal opportunities to help students expand their vocabularies. For example, we can provide a rich context for learning, promote discussion, focus on multiple exposures to words, have a variety of reading materials available in the classroom, and use technology as an integral part of the teaching and learning process. Researchers acknowledge the importance of incidental word learning in students' general vocabulary development (Blachowicz, Fisher, Ogle, & Watts-Taffe, 2006).

Beyond opportunities for incidental learning, we can teach vocabulary through context clues and explicit instruction. Both of these approaches have been found to be effective, and research reports that using such strategies contributes to students' reading comprehension (Blachowicz & Fisher, 2000; National Reading Panel, 2000).

Making Connections
TO ENGLISH LEARNERS

When teaching vocabulary to English learners through explicit instruction, we can use pictures to scaffold students' learning. We should also encourage students to respond to the vocabulary words they are learning through alternative modes such as sketching. ■

Balancing Teaching And Context

When teaching vocabulary, explicit instruction and learning from context should be balanced. The instruction should be meaningful to students, include words from students' reading, and focus on a variety of strategies for determining the meanings of unfamiliar words. Two other important aspects of such teaching are making connections between the vocabulary and students' background knowledge and providing students with multiple exposures to words. In our study of approaches to teaching vocabulary, we will explore context clues, graphic organizers, structural analysis, and student self-selection.

**TEACHING IDEA**

CONTEXT CLUES. Context Clues help readers to become independent word learners. Readers use Context Clues to figure out the meaning of unknown words they encounter in text. For example, if we were to encounter the isolated word "pheffendorfer," we more than likely would not know what it means. If we encountered the word in context, however, we might easily determine its meaning. Consider the following scenario:

> *Before we started watching the movie at home, we decided to prepare some snacks. Bob poured the soda, while I put a popcorn packet in the <u>pheffendorfer</u> and waited for it to pop.*

At this point, we may guess that a pheffendorfer is a microwave oven, and in the context provided, we would be absolutely correct. In determining our response, we probably used the logic Context Clue. After reading the words surrounding the unknown word, we determined that the pheffendorfer provided a way to make popcorn. In our society, the appliance that usually performs this task is a microwave. So, even though "pheffendorfer" is not a real word, given the context, it means "microwave."

In our examination of "pheffendorfer," we used the logic clue. We often use more than one type of clue to determine a word's meaning. The types of Context Clues include the following:

Diameter

■ **DEFINITION CLUE:** connects the unknown word to a known word or words.

Example: Mitosis is a process in which a cell's nucleus replicates and divides in preparation for division of the cell.

■ **EXAMPLE/ILLUSTRATION CLUE:** provides a model or picture that shows the meaning of the word.

Example: The distance around a circle is its circumference, but, as seen in the figure, the diameter is the measure across the midsection of the circle.

■ **COMPARISON/CONTRAST CLUE:** provides information about something similar or something different from the unknown word.

Example: The square and the right triangle are both geometric figures, but the square has four interior right (90-degree) angles and the right triangle has only one.

■ LOGIC CLUE: provides a common-sense/contextual connection to the unknown word.

Example: When Tim collapsed from cardiac arrest, we grabbed the defibrillator and used it to restore the heart to a regular rhythm.

■ CAUSE/EFFECT CLUE: the reason/result relation allows the reader to predict the word's meaning.

Example: When the rain got heavy, it caused the car to hydroplane.

■ MOOD/TONE CLUE: description of the mood related to the word allows readers to predict the word's meaning.

Example: A feeling of despondency *overwhelmed him as he floated alone in the dark sea and watched the search helicopters fly away.*

To teach your students how to use Context Clues, follow these steps:

1 **Explain:** When we use Context Clues, we use the words surrounding the unknown word to try to determine the word's meaning. Then explain the eight types of Context Clues and provide examples of each.

2 **Demonstrate:** Use a read-aloud and a think-aloud to determine the meaning of an unfamiliar word in the text. The think-aloud should demonstrate the most effective clues based on the context of the sentence. Remember that readers often need to use more than one type of clue to determine the meaning of the unknown word. When the word's meaning has been determined, refine the meaning by using a dictionary.

3 **Guide:** Support students as they work with partners to find unknown words in the texts they are reading and use context clues to figure out the meanings. Monitor as students search for words, making suggestions as they use Context Clues to discover the meanings of unknown words. Visit the pages on which the words appear in context and discuss the students' suggested meanings. Discuss the type of Context Clues the students used and verify with a dictionary as needed.

4 **Practice:** Encourage students to read and use selected segments of text and use Context Clues to determine the meanings of unknown words.

5 **Reflect:** Encourage students to reflect on how Context Clues help us understand what we read. Discuss using Context Clues with students. Remind the students that if the context does not provide enough information, there are other strategies for figuring out the meaning of the unknown word.

Go to the Activities and Applications section under the topic *Developing Vocabulary, Concepts, and Fluency* in the MyEducationLab for your course and complete the activity entitled Intentional Vocabulary Instruction to consider the benefit of introducing new words in context.

TEACHING IDEA   GRAPHIC ORGANIZERS. Graphic organizers are visual representations of ideas. Using graphic organizers to teach vocabulary has several benefits. First, the visual design helps students to better remember the types of information associated with the term. Second, completing the organizers in a whole-class or small-group setting promotes discussion of the word or concept. Third, completed organizers contain information about the word that students can use to create oral or written summaries.

Semantic Maps, Semantic Question Maps, Concept of Definition Maps, and Semantic Feature Analysis Charts are graphic organizers that were designed to help students learn vocabulary. Of course, before using these graphics, we need to be able to complete them on our own.

Making Connections
TO ENGLISH LEARNERS

When using graphic organizers to teach vocabulary to English learners, number the sections of the organizer to help students focus on the point of learning or discussion. As an alternative, sections of the organizer can be highlighted in different colors. See Appendix A for copies of the graphic organizers discussed in this section. ■

SEMANTIC MAP. The Semantic Map (Johnson & Pearson, 1984) was developed to help students activate prior knowledge and organize knowledge about a specific topic. This type of map has a free form in that its design depends on students' responses. It is often used before reading and revisited during and after reading. For a step-by-step approach to teaching Semantic Maps, see Chapter 4.

We usually use Semantic Maps before students read the text to introduce concepts and assess students' background knowledge. For example, if we were about to teach a concept in mathematics, science, or history, we might use a Semantic Map to gain an understanding of what students know—what background knowledge they have—about that topic. Because all students contribute to the map, it is easy to discern which students have previous understanding of the topic and which do not. The results can provide us with a starting point for our teaching. We often revisit Semantic Maps after reading to add more information and create summaries based on the maps.

When students in a world history class focused on the term *World War II*, they developed the Semantic Map in Figure 7.1. In science class, students reviewed their understanding of the focus word *biology* as they prepared for a test. See Figure 7.2 for the map these students created. For an example of a Semantic Map based on geometry, see Chapter 4.

SEMANTIC QUESTION MAP. The Semantic Question Map (McLaughlin, 2003) is a variation on the Semantic Map, but its general design is fixed (see Appendix A for a reproducible organizer). The focus word is placed in an oval, and then several questions about it are raised. The questions, which may be provided by the teacher or generated by the students, are placed inside the ovals that extend from the oval containing the focus word.

We use Semantic Question Maps when we want students to focus on particular aspects of a topic. Rather than leaving the shape of the map to be determined by student responses, we provide the structure, which usually includes three or four questions. To teach your students how to use Semantic Question Maps, follow these steps:

1 **Explain:** Begin by explaining the strategy of Previewing and describing how to use a Semantic Question Map. For example, you might say, "Previewing is a comprehension strategy that includes activating background knowledge, setting purposes for reading, and predicting what will come next, based on what we have already read. Completing these Maps involves brainstorming responses to three or four questions about a selected topic. We

Go to the Activities and Applications section under the topic *Developing Vocabulary, Concepts, and Fluency* in the MyEducationLab for your course and complete the activity entitled Vocabulary and Content Area Learning to examine steps teachers can take to help English learners understand content specific vocabulary.

TEACHING IDEA

TEACHING IDEA

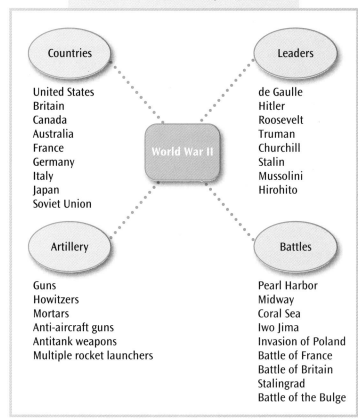

FIGURE 7.1 Semantic Map of World War II

World War II

Countries
United States
Britain
Canada
Australia
France
Germany
Italy
Japan
Soviet Union

Leaders
de Gaulle
Hitler
Roosevelt
Truman
Churchill
Stalin
Mussolini
Hirohito

Artillery
Guns
Howitzers
Mortars
Anti-aircraft guns
Antitank weapons
Multiple rocket launchers

Battles
Pearl Harbor
Midway
Coral Sea
Iwo Jima
Invasion of Poland
Battle of France
Battle of Britain
Stalingrad
Battle of the Bulge

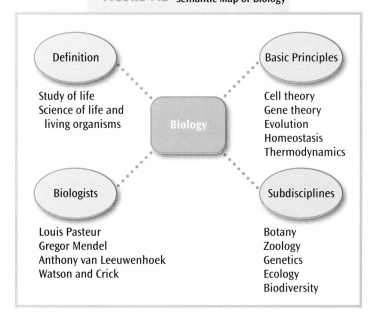

FIGURE 7.2 Semantic Map of Biology

Biology

Definition
Study of life
Science of life and
living organisms

Basic Principles
Cell theory
Gene theory
Evolution
Homeostasis
Thermodynamics

Biologists
Louis Pasteur
Gregor Mendel
Anthony van Leeuwenhoek
Watson and Crick

Subdisciplines
Botany
Zoology
Genetics
Ecology
Biodiversity

usually respond to the Semantic Question Map before reading a text, and revisit the map to verify our responses after reading."

2 **Demonstrate:** Begin the demonstration by choosing a focus word and writing it on a chart, chalkboard, or computer screen. Draw an oval around it. For example, in Figure 7.3, the focus word is *physics.* Then think aloud about that word. For example, you could say, "The focus word for this Semantic Question Map is 'physics,' so now I need to think of three or four questions about 'Physics' that need to be answered." Then you might say, "I have thought about the questions and I want them to relate to motion, velocity, acceleration, and speed. I think I will add these three questions to the map: *What are the rates that describe motion? In what ways can we describe relations such as velocity and acceleration? What is the difference between speed and velocity?*" Then write the questions on the map and use lines to attach the ovals containing the questions to the focus word. Next, offer a response to the first question. For example, you might say, "I know that speed is one of the rates that describes motion, so I am going to add *speed* under the first question." Next, ask students to brainstorm other rates that describe motion. If they suggest *velocity* and *acceleration*, add them underneath *speed* on the Semantic Question Map.

3 **Guide:** Guide students to work with partners to respond to the next two questions. In response to question 2, "In what ways can we describe relationships such as velocity and acceleration?", they might suggest *equations, tables,* and *graphs.* In response to question 3, "What is the difference between speed and velocity?", they might suggest that speed is *how fast an object moves* and velocity is *how fast AND in which direction an object moves.* Then read aloud the section of the text that addresses these topics and discuss it with the students. Make connections to the Semantic Question Map and confirm that the text verifies your responses.

4 **Practice:** Invite students to practice by responding individually to a Semantic Question Map about the next topic of study. Provide the Maps and ask students to write their responses, read the related text, and revise their answers as necessary. Then discuss the completed Semantic Question Maps.

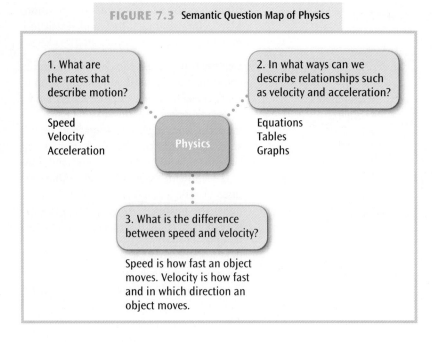

FIGURE 7.3 Semantic Question Map of Physics

1. What are the rates that describe motion?

Speed
Velocity
Acceleration

Physics

2. In what ways can we describe relationships such as velocity and acceleration?

Equations
Tables
Graphs

3. What is the difference between speed and velocity?

Speed is how fast an object moves. Velocity is how fast and in which direction an object moves.

5 Reflect: Reflect on how Semantic Question Maps are similar to Semantic Maps: Both help us preview the text, but the Semantic Question Maps raise specific issues. The Semantic Question Maps help to focus students' thinking. Also reflect on how we can use Semantic Question Maps when reading text in other content areas.

Semantic Question Maps help students to focus on responding to preset queries about the topic. Their responses provide information about their background knowledge and a starting point for teaching. After reading, we can revisit the Semantic Question Map and summarize the information. The questions also provide direction for that process.

TEACHING IDEA

CONCEPT OF DEFINITION MAP. The Concept of Definition Map (Schwartz & Raphael, 1985) is designed to help students construct meaning by making connections between their prior knowledge and new topics. It provides information such as a definition, a description, and examples. This graphic may be used before, during, and after reading. When the map is completed, the class should create a Concept of Definition Map Summary. When teaching summarizing, we usually ask students to extract important information from the text. Students, however, often struggle in determining which information is important. The completed Concept of Definition Map contains only important information. Therefore, creating a summary based on the Concept of Definition Map provides students with the opportunity to use the important information. In the process, students can learn that the important information includes the components of the Map: the definition, description, examples, and comparison.

To teach your students how to use Concept of Definition Maps, follow these steps:

1 Explain: Vocabulary helps us to understand what we read and the Concept of Definition Map is a graphic organizer that can help us to learn vocabulary.

2 Demonstrate: Use a think-aloud and a graphic organizer. Select or ask students to select a focus word to be explored. Write the focus word in the oval in the center of the Map. Think aloud to determine the broad category that best describes the word. Write the response in the "What is it?" box. Return to the focus word.

3 Guide: Guide students to work with partners to determine responses to the next question on the Concept of Definition Map: What's it like? Discuss the responses with the students and choose three to include on the map. Return to the focus word. Continue this process with the next question on the map: What are some examples? Return to the focus word. Then discuss possible comparisons for the focus word.

4 Practice: Encourage the students to read a related text and revisit and revise the Concept of Definition Map as necessary. Then invite the students to use the map to write Concept of Definition Map Summaries. Discuss the summaries.

5 Reflect: Encourage students to reflect on how Concept of Definition Maps help us to understand words and summarize our thinking. Discuss how we can use these maps in other content areas.

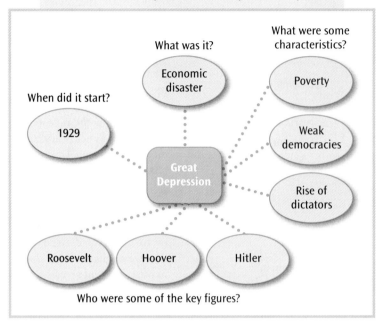

FIGURE 7.4 Concept of Definition Map of Great Depression

When did it start?

What was it?

What were some characteristics?

1929

Economic disaster

Poverty

Weak democracies

Great Depression

Rise of dictators

Roosevelt

Hoover

Hitler

Who were some of the key figures?

Note the following points:

- It is not always possible to determine a suitable comparison for the "A Comparison" section. If this is the case, eliminate that section of the graphic.

- Depending on the topic and the text being read, "What are some examples?" may not be the best question to ask in that section of the graphic. Changing the question to one that is more appropriate for the topic being studied is appropriate.

The Concept of Definition Map and Concept of Definition Map Summary shown in Figure 7.4 were created in a history class while studying the Great Depression.

A Concept of Definition Map about algebraic properties is featured in Figure 7.5. Notice that the comparison section is missing. As noted earlier, we can remove that section if there is no suitable comparison.

We can use the Concept of Definition Map for several purposes, including introducing a concept, sparking discussion, and summarizing. When a completed map is used as the basis of an oral or written summary, it is easier for students to summarize informational text. Instead of needing to extract essential information from the text, they simply use the information on the completed map. While using the Concept of Definition Map for this purpose, the students also learn what constitutes essential information from reading the categories on the map: What is it? How would you describe it? What are three examples? What is a comparison?

 **TEACHING IDEA** **SEMANTIC FEATURE ANALYSIS CHART.** The Semantic Feature Analysis Chart (Johnson & Pearson, 1984) is a graphic organizer that helps students make predictions about attributes related to specific words, sort by characteristics, and set a purpose for reading or researching. It is often used before and after reading informational text, but it can also be adapted for use with narrative or story text by replacing the categories with characters' names and listing attributes that characters may or may not possess. We can also cross-match a variety of genres in the category section with various attributes of those genres in the characteristics section.

To teach students how to use the Semantic Feature Analysis Chart, follow these steps:

1 **Explain:** Describe how the Semantic Feature Analysis Chart helps us to monitor our thinking and learn about words. Then explain how the chart matches categories and characteristics to provide information.

2 **Demonstrate:** Use a read-aloud and a think-aloud. Select a topic and some words or categories that relate to that topic. List the words or categories in the far left column of the Semantic Feature Analysis Chart. Choose characteristics that relate to one or more of the related words. List those across the top row of the chart. Share the Chart with the students. Make predictions about which categories will have the first characteristic. Place a plus sign (+) in the box if the characteristic fits the category; place a minus sign (−) in the box if the characteristic does not fit the category. Place a question mark (?) in the space provided if you are not sure of the response.

3 **Guide:** Guide students to work with partners in completing the chart, using the symbols you demonstrated. Then read a text that contains information about the categories and characteristics. Discuss the text and the charts with the students. Guide the students

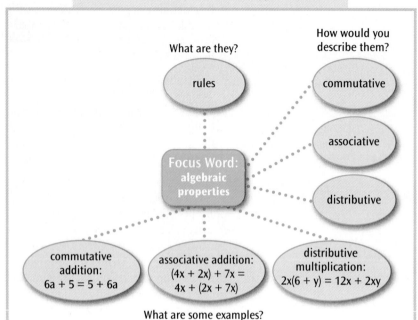

FIGURE 7.5 Concept of Definition Map of Derivatives

What are they?

How would you describe them?

rules

commutative

associative

Focus Word: algebraic properties

distributive

commutative addition:
6a + 5 = 5 + 6a

associative addition:
(4x + 2x) + 7x = 4x + (2x + 7x)

distributive multiplication:
2x(6 + y) = 12x + 2xy

What are some examples?

to revisit their Semantic Feature Analysis Charts and revise them as necessary.

4 **Practice:** Provide another Semantic Feature Analysis Chart and encourage students to complete it. Provide a related text for the students to read. Remind them to revise their charts as necessary based on what they read. Discuss the text and the revised charts.

5 **Reflect:** Encourage students to reflect on how Semantic Feature Analysis Charts help us to understand words and how we might use these charts in other content areas.

Students in science class used the Semantic Feature Analysis Chart featured in Figure 7.6 to analyze various life forms. As this example suggests, we use the Semantic Feature Analysis Chart when we want to compare and contrast the characteristics or qualities of multiple items or types of people. We use this chart before the students read to activate background knowledge and after they read to add information and/or draw conclusions.

Although research views graphic organizers as being highly effective in the teaching of vocabulary, there are other viable approaches. These techniques include structural analysis, which encourages the reader to examine small parts of a word to help determine its meaning.

Structural Analysis

When studying vocabulary, understanding the words and their meanings is our ultimate goal. Structural analysis contributes to that understanding. Knowing how to analyze a word's structure—its prefixes, roots, and suffixes—helps us to not only recognize the word, but also determine its meaning when we read.

Characteristics	Hair/fur	Lay eggs	Warm-blooded	Care for young	Live in water	Breathe air	Have gills
Categories							
Fish							
Birds							
Mammals							
Amphibians							
Reptiles							
Insects							
+ = yes			— = no			? = don't know	

FIGURE 7.6
Semantic Feature Analysis Chart

Prefixes, word roots, and suffixes are three types of word parts. *Pre* means "before" and *suf* means "after," so it makes sense that prefixes are added *before* the word root and suffixes are added *after* the root. Most words have at least one word root, and many have one or more prefix and suffix. Word roots are the main part of the word, so they are typically found after prefixes and before suffixes. Structural analysis refers to the process of examining each part of the word in an attempt to determine the word's meaning. The word root often provides the general meaning, while the prefixes and suffixes refine that meaning in that particular form of the word.

Knowing how to use structural analysis helps us determine words' meanings. For example, in the word "unhappiness," *happy* is the word root. We might define it as "joyful" or "glad", but when we add the prefix *un*, the word means the total opposite. When we add the suffix *ness*, the literal meaning of "unhappiness" becomes "the condition of not being happy." Similarly, *bio* is a word root that means "life"; *ology* is a suffix that means "study of." Therefore, *biology* is the "study of life." The better our students understand word roots, prefixes, and suffixes, the easier it will be for them to analyze the structure of words.

WORD ROOTS. The root is the main part of a word. There are usually many words derived from a single root. *Root mapping* provides an overview of a word root and the various words that are derived from it. In this technique, a root is selected to be the focus of the map. Then words containing that root are added at the end of branches that connect to the root. As the map is completed, it has the potential to continue growing, because as each new word is added, other words may branch from it. The following are examples of roots: *bio* (life), *chromo* (color), *psycho* (mind), *thermo* (heat), *zoo* (animal). A more extensive list of common word roots is presented in Figure 7.7.

FIGURE 7.7
Word Roots

Root	Meaning	Example
anthropo	*man*	anthropology
astro	*star*	astronaut
bio	*life*	biology
cardio	*heart*	cardiac
cede	*go*	precede
chromo	*color*	chromatology
demos	*people*	democracy
derma	*skin*	epidermis
dyna	*power*	dynamic
geo	*earth*	geology
helio	*sun*	heliocentric
hydro	*water*	hydroponics
hypno	*sleep*	hypnosis
ject	*throw*	eject
magni	*great, big*	magnify
man(u)	*hand*	manuscript
mono	*one*	monoplane
ortho	*straight*	orthodox
pod	*foot*	podiatrist
psycho	*mind*	psychology
pyro	*fire*	pyromania
script	*write*	manuscript
terra	*earth*	terrace
thermo	*heat*	thermometer
zoo	*animal*	zoology

PREFIXES. A prefix is a type of affix that involves adding a syllable or letter(s) to the beginning of a word to change its meaning or part of speech. According to *The Literacy Dictionary*, a prefix is "an affix attached before a base word or root, as *re-* in *re*print" (Harris & Hodges, 1995, p. 192). Working with prefixes helps students to understand the structure of words. The following are examples of prefixes: *ad-* (to, toward), *ante-* (before), *anti-* (against), *extra-* (beyond), *micro-* (small). A more detailed list of prefixes appears in Figure 7.8.

FIGURE 7.8
Prefixes

Prefix	Meaning	Example
ab-, abs-, a-	*from, away*	abstain
ad-	*to, toward*	addict
ambi-	*both*	ambidextrous
ante-	*before*	antecedent
anti-	*against*	antifreeze
auto-	*self*	autobiography
be-	*near, about*	beside
bene-	*well, good*	benefactor
bi-	*two*	bimonthly
cata-	*below*	catacomb
centi-	*hundred*	centimeter
circum-	*around*	circumnavigate
con-	*with*	concert
contra-	*against*	contraband
de-	*from, down*	depress
deci-	*ten*	decimeter
di-	*two*	diameter
dia-	*through*	diagram
dis-	*opposite*	disrespect
dys-	*bad*	dysfunctional
en-, em-	*cause to*	encode
epi-	*upon*	epidermis
ex-	*out, from*	excavate
extra-	*beyond*	extracurricular
for-	*off, to the uttermost*	forward
fore-	*before*	forecast
hetero-	*different*	heterogeneous
hyper-	*beyond, excess*	hyperactive
hypo-	*too little, under*	hypoactive
in-, il-, im-, ir-	*not*	immature
in-, im-	*in*	infringe
inter-	*between*	interstate
intra-	*within*	intramurals
intro-	*within*	introspection
juxta-	*near*	juxtapose
macro-	*large*	macrobiology
meta-	*beyond, denoting change*	metamorphosis
micro-	*small*	microbiology
mid-	*middle*	midway
milli-	*thousand*	millipede

mis-	*bad*	misbehave
mono-	*single*	monotone
nano-	*billion*	nanosecond
neo-	*new*	neoclassical
non-	*not, opposite from*	nonviolent
omni-	*all*	omnipotent
out-	*beyond, more than*	outlaw
over-	*too much*	overcompensate
pan-	*all*	panoramic
para-	*side by side, near*	paraphrase
per-	*throughout*	pervade
peri-	*all around*	periscope
poly-	*many*	polygon
post-	*after*	postpone
pre-	*before*	predetermine
pro-	*forward*	progress
prot-	*first*	prototype
re-	*again*	reappear
retro-	*back*	retrograde
semi-	*half, partly*	semicircle
sub-	*under*	submarine
super-	*more than*	supermarket
syn-, sym-	*together*	symbol
trans-	*across*	transatlantic
ultra-	*beyond, extremely*	ultraconservative
un-	*not*	unwilling
with-	*against*	withhold

SUFFIXES. A suffix is a type of affix that involves adding a syllable or group of letters to the end of the word to change its meaning or part of speech. Specifically, according to *The Literacy Dictionary*, a suffix is "an affix attached to the end of a base, root, or stem that changes the meaning or grammatical function of the word" (Harris & Hodges, 1995, p. 246). Working with suffixes helps students to understand the structure of words. The following are examples of suffixes: *-able* (can be done), *-un* (not), *-ic* (relating to), *-ist* (one who practices), *-ology* (study of). Figure 7.9 contains a more extensive list of suffixes.

Making Connections
TO STRUGGLING READERS

When teaching prefixes, suffixes, and roots that pertain to our content areas, we should work with other teachers to develop a list of word parts that will benefit students across the curriculum. Once the list has been created, we can display the affixes and roots in a "word wall" format that includes meanings and example words. We can also color-code the affixes and roots that appear in the sample words. ∎

Student Self-Selection

Using context clues, graphic organizers, and structural analysis will help students to develop their vocabularies, but using Vocabulary Bookmarks and the Vocabulary Self-Collection Strategy will

Suffix	Meaning	Example
-able, -ible	*can be done*	comfortable
-al, -ial	*relating to*	personal
-arium	*place of*	solarium
-ation, -ition, -ion, -tion	*act, process of*	animation
-dom	*quality/state*	freedom
-ed	*past tense for verbs*	voted
-en	*made of*	wooden
-er, est	*comparative*	harder
-er	*one who*	dancer
-ful	*full of*	hopeful
-ic	*relating to*	characteristic
-ile	*quality/state*	juvenile
-ing	*present participle*	hopping
-ism	*quality/state*	fanaticism
-ist	*one who practices*	zoologist
-ity, -ty	*state of*	infinity
-ive, -itive, -ative	*adjective form of a noun*	quantitative
-less	*without*	homeless
-ly	*characteristic of*	happily
-ment	*action or process*	excitement
-ness	*condition of*	sadness
-ology	*study of*	biology
-ous, -eous, -ious	*quality, state*	joyous
-s, -es	*more than one*	desks
-tion	*quality, state*	preservation
-ular	*relating to*	cellular
-y	*characterized by*	jumpy

FIGURE 7.9
Suffixes

help them take ownership of their learning. Both of these approaches invite students to select the vocabulary they would like to learn. This flexibility motivates students to choose meaningful, challenging words and promotes wonderfully rich discussion.

TEACHING IDEA

VOCABULARY BOOKMARK. Vocabulary Bookmarks (McLaughlin, 2003) are designed to motivate students to monitor their understanding and learn new words. When students use Vocabulary Bookmarks, they are able to choose a word from assigned class readings. This should be a word the student thinks the whole class needs to discuss.

When the student chooses such a word, she completes a Vocabulary Bookmark. The student writes three pieces of information on the Bookmark: (1) the word, (2) what she thinks the word means, and (3) the page number on which she found the word. Students enjoy choosing these vocabulary words, the resulting class discussion is rich and meaningful, and the whole class learns a wide variety of meaningful terms. During the class discussion, students introduce their words, explain what they think the word means, and tell the class where they found the word. Then they read the word in the context in which it appears and discuss the suggested meaning as well as their insights. A dictionary can be used after discussion to verify the meaning of the word. Finally, students discuss how they can use the new word and determine whether they want to add it to the word wall.

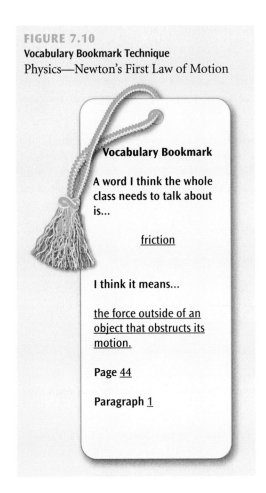

FIGURE 7.10
Vocabulary Bookmark Technique
Physics—Newton's First Law of Motion

Vocabulary Bookmark

A word I think the whole class needs to talk about is...

friction

I think it means...

the force outside of an object that obstructs its motion.

Page 44

Paragraph 1

To teach your students how to use Vocabulary Bookmark Technique, follow these steps:

1 Explain: Begin by explaining that the Vocabulary Bookmark Technique helps us monitor our understanding of text. When using Vocabulary Bookmarks, students choose a word they think the whole class should discuss. Then they write three pieces of information on the Vocabulary Bookmark: (1) the word, (2) what they think the word means, and (3) the page number on which they found the word. Explain that the words are then used during class discussions of the reading.

2 Demonstrate: Begin demonstrating by distributing the blackline for Vocabulary Bookmark Technique (see the Appendix for the graphic organizer). Introduce the text and demonstrate what monitoring is and how Vocabulary Bookmark Technique can help us monitor our understanding. Think aloud as you complete the Vocabulary Bookmark. For example, you might say:

> Our assigned reading for homework last night was about whales. While I was reading, I came across a word I think we should all discuss. It is *echolocation*. So, I am going to write *echolocation* on my Vocabulary Bookmark. I noticed it is on page 243, so I will write that in the space for the page number. Next, I am supposed to write what I think *echolocation* means. I think it means that whales can locate things using echos from sounds they make, so I am going to write that on the bookmark. Then I am going to write that I think dolphins and bats can also use *echolocation*.

Then demonstrate how to use the page number to find the word in context. Discuss the term with the students, and verify your thinking by checking a dictionary.

3 Guide: Guide students to work with partners to find a vocabulary word in the assigned reading that they think the whole class should discuss. For example, some of their choices might be *migration, intimidating, hierarchy*, and *invertebrate*. Ask students to record the page numbers on which the words appear and what they think each word means. Then discuss their word choices and the related information provided. While discussing words such as *hierarchy* and *invertebrate* for example, you might consult a dictionary to verify detailed meanings students suggest. Similarly, if it seems students' definitions of words are not clear, you might also consult a dictionary to clarify.

4 Practice: Encourage students to practice the Vocabulary Bookmark Technique by working individually to find words in the next section of the text. After they have completed the Bookmarks, discuss the words and verify their thinking by checking with a dictionary.

5 Reflect: Invite students to reflect on what they know about monitoring and how they can use the Vocabulary Bookmark Technique in other aspects of their content area learning.

Figure 7.10 features a Vocabulary Bookmark about friction completed in physics class. Vocabulary Bookmarking is one aspect of the Bookmark Technique, detailed in Chapter 4.

 **TEACHING IDEA** VOCABULARY SELF-COLLECTION STRATEGY. The Vocabulary Self-Collection Strategy (VSS) (Haggard, 1986) was created to encourage students' interest in vocabulary. Although it is most often used with informational text, this technique can also be used with literature.

To teach your students how to use VSS, follow these steps:

1 **Explain:** The VSS is a process that motivates us to learn about words we think are important. Explain that when we are reading, we select a word that we would like to learn more about, provide information about it, and nominate it for a place on the class vocabulary list.

2 **Demonstrate:** Model the VSS by reading a selection and choosing a word you would like to learn more about. Share the word with the class by writing it on the board, an overhead transparency, or a chart. Then discuss the word in context, including where it was found in the text, what you think the word means, and where you think it should be placed on the class vocabulary list.

3 **Guide:** Guide students to read a text and engage in VSS. Ask students to select words they would like to learn more about from a previously read text. You should also choose a word. Invite the students to share the words and the following information:

- The word in context
- Where it was found in the text
- What they think the word means
- Why they think the word should be on the class vocabulary list

Accept all nominations and record them on a chart, overhead, or chalkboard. Encourage more discussion about each word. Then narrow the list for study and refine the definitions.

4 **Practice:** Encourage students to record their final word lists and definitions in their vocabulary journals or content area notebook. Remember when planning lessons and assignments to include the words to reinforce meanings and use.

5 **Reflect:** Invite students to reflect on how selecting vocabulary words motivates us to learn and to think about how this process is different from being assigned long lists of vocabulary words to define. Then reflect on how we can use the VSS in other content areas.

Whether using Vocabulary Bookmarks or the VSS, students never seem to tire of self-selecting vocabulary. They choose wonderfully exciting and complex words and enthusiastically vie to report the details of their selections. Following discussions, they are quick to use *their* words in all modes of communication. Self-selecting vocabulary is a highly motivational, vocabulary-enriching strategy.

Making Connections
TO STUDY SKILLS

To help students study and remember vocabulary they have self-selected or learned through other methods, we can encourage them to create personal word walls or vocabulary cards. A personal word wall can be as simple as an alphabetical list of words and their meanings on a manila folder that the students can transport to classes and home or a list maintained electronically on students' computers. Vocabulary cards usually have the word printed on one side and the definition and sentence using the word on the other side. Maintaining these study aides electronically is often highly motivational for students. ◼

When Using These Ideas to Teach Vocabulary, What General Principles Should We Follow?

There are several general guidelines we can follow to ensure that our vocabulary instruction is effective:

1. *Our teaching should demonstrate that we have great interest in and excitement for vocabulary.* We know from experience that such enthusiasm is contagious and will motivate our students to expand their vocabularies.

2. *Our lessons should encourage students to make connections between their personal experiences and content area vocabulary.* For example, students may read about different legal cases that used DNA analyses to prove guilt or innocence before they encounter the detailed role of DNA in biology class.

3. *We should encourage students to understand that some words have multiple meanings in the content areas.* For example, students may know what the word "plot" means when they are reading a story, but they may not be aware of its meaning in mathematics when we "plot a point on a graph."

4. *Our teaching should incorporate multiple exposures to words, so students may become familiar with them and not view them as "words on a list" to be studied and forgotten, but rather as keys to engaging in higher-order thinking.*

5. *In our lessons, students should have opportunities to use content area vocabulary in multiple, meaningful ways.* This practice encourages students to take ownership of the vocabulary terms—to use them in conversation, in their writing, and in various performance projects.

6. *We should teach structural analysis as it relates to terms in our content area, so our students can learn how to analyze words they may encounter.*

7. *Our lessons should focus on **depth** rather than **coverage** of content area vocabulary.* This means that we should teach our students a reasonable number of terms in depth, rather than presenting a large number of words at a surface level. If we are required to teach a list of essential terms that appears to be somewhat extensive, we should consider using a vocabulary wall or having the students maintain electronic vocabulary notebooks to ensure that they have access to the words and their meanings as they engage in learning.

8. *We should use multiple texts in our teaching, so students will be aware of the multiple resources that address the topic they are studying.* Of course, these resources should include both print and electronic texts.

9. *Our lessons should reflect that although the vocabulary teaching ideas are effective, we may need to adapt them for our teaching.* For example, the Concept of Definition Map is a wonderfully effective graphic organizer, but we may want to use it to teach an idea that will not work well with the Concept of Definition Map's published format. For example, Figure 7.4 features a Concept of Definition Map about the Great Depression in which the teacher has kept the format of the Concept of Definition Map, but changed the labels on three of the categories. On the left side, where the original map asked for a comparison, this teacher asked when the Great Depression began. On the right side, where the map usually asks for three descriptive words, the teacher asked the students to list some of the characteristics of the Great Depression. Finally, at the bottom, where the original format asks for three examples, this history teacher asked the students to name some of the key players during the time of the Great Depression. In this example, the teacher adapted an effective teaching idea to the needs of his lesson, in which, of course, he was using a particular text.

10. *We should work with colleagues to ensure that we support students' use of vocabulary across the curriculum.*

FINAL THOUGHTS

As teachers, we have a lot to consider when we teach vocabulary. We want our students to increase their knowledge of words. We also want our students to actively engage with new vocabulary and use it freely when they read, write, speak, and listen.

In the end, it is important to remember that the most effective vocabulary instruction is the kind that improves comprehension. This relation or connection is especially important in the content areas, where the concepts students learn often become the basis for future learning. To accomplish this goal, our teaching must be motivational and our methods must be engaging.

Teaching Connections

APPLYING WHAT WE HAVE LEARNED

E-Links

Many websites provide lists of terms and definitions associated with the content areas. Examples are listed below. Visit two of these sites and complete the following tasks:

1. Note the website title and address. Reflect on all that you have learned about teaching vocabulary. Then critique the quality of the website's vocabulary list(s) and the suggestion(s) for teaching or learning it. Explain how you would teach such terms. Justify your response.
2. Choose 3 terms generally taught in your content area and demonstrate how you would use graphic organizers to teach them.

EXAMPLE WEBSITES
Languages
French Language
http://french.about.com/od/vocabulary/French_Vocabulary_Lessons_Lists.htm

Spanish Vocabulary
http://spanishvocabulary.ca

Mathematics
Mathword: Terms and Formulas from Beginning Algebra to Calculus
http://math.com/school/glossary/glossindex.html

Science
Science Academic Vocabulary—Biology I (also available for Chemistry, Physics, Ecology, and Anatomy/Physiology)
http://mnps.org/Page22565.aspx

Accountable Talk

As content area teachers of the 21st century, we have come a long way from the time when our learning consisted of writing long lists of vocabulary words and their definitions. Reflect on (1) how you will use more innovative practices, such as context clues, graphic organizers, structural analysis, and self-selection strategies in your subject area; and (2) how you will promote such teaching ideas among fellow faculty members, who may teach from a more traditional perspective. Share your thoughts in small groups.

 ## Portfolio/Performance Opportunity

When using the ideas presented in this chapter to teach vocabulary, we need to have models to share with our classes. Develop an electronic vocabulary resource file for your teaching by completing a model of each of the teaching ideas. Discuss your completed models in small groups. Provide feedback for peers and receive feedback for your work. Revise the models as necessary. Discuss how peer input influenced the final models. Email your completed project to your professor.

8

TEACHING IDEAS:

- ReQUEST • PAIRED QUESTIONING
- THICK AND THIN QUESTIONS • PATTERNED PARTNER READING • KWL AND KWLS
- INSERT (INTERACTIVE NOTATION SYSTEM TO EFFECTIVE READING AND THINKING)

Organizing for Teaching and Learning

Organizing for learning is an integral part of teaching. It demonstrates our understanding that teaching is about more than knowing the content. It involves a number of factors, including our understanding the concept of flexible grouping, our knowledge of multiple texts, ensuring that our students know and can use essential skills, and using a variety of methods to read texts.

Our organizational abilities greatly enrich our teaching. They help us to accommodate student needs and support learning in a variety of other ways. Our goal is to effectively structure our classrooms and our teaching so our students will be motivated to learn and be able to achieve to their greatest possible potentials. Questions we may have relating to organizing for teaching and learning include the following:

- What lesson plan format will we use?

- How can we differentiate instruction to accommodate students' needs?

- How can we group students for learning?

- How can we effectively use textbooks in the content areas?

- How can we teach students to generate questions?

- How can we teach students to recognize text patterns?

- How can students read text without engaging in round-robin reading?

- How can students learn to use textbook study strategies such as SQ4R?

In this chapter, we respond to each of these questions. We begin by discussing an effective lesson planning format. Then we focus on how we can adapt this format to differentiate instruction in the content areas. Next, we explore how to organize students in a variety of settings. Then we examine the use of textbooks in our teaching, and consider a variety of alternatives to students taking turns reading aloud in class. After that, we examine how to teach our students to generate questions and recognize text patterns. Finally, we focus on SQ4R, a study technique that students can use when reading content area texts independently.

What Lesson Planning Format Will We Use?

When creating lessons, we need to use a planning format that provides opportunities to address state standards, related lesson goals, authentic assessment, content, and multiple levels of student thinking. Although several different planning formats are used in our content areas, the one we will use integrates content and strategy use. In addition to the essential components, this lesson planning format provides opportunities for us to engage, guide, and extend student thinking.

As seen in Figure 8.1, we will need to include lesson goals and related state standards in our plans. Before reading, we will *engage* students' thinking by motivating our students, introducing the text, and encouraging students to activate their background knowledge, make connections, and set purposes for reading. During reading, we will *guide* student thinking by encouraging students to continue to make connections, self-question, monitor their understanding, visualize, summarize, and evaluate. After reading, we will help students to *extend* their student thinking by summarizing, evaluating, and discussing in the short term and applying what they have learned through inquiry-based projects in the long term. Discussion will permeate our lessons.

To engage students' thinking, we can use strategy-based teaching ideas such as Semantic Maps (Johnson & Pearson, 1984), Anticipation/Reaction Guides (Readence, Bean, & Baldwin, 2000), or Concept of Definition Maps (Schwartz & Raphael, 1985). When we guide students' thinking, we can engage students in using the Bookmark Technique (McLaughlin & Allen, 2002), KWL (Ogle, 1986), KWLS (Sippola, 1995), or Interactive Notation System to Effective Reading and Thinking (INSERT) (Vaughn, & Estes, 1986). To extend students' thinking, we can invite students to engage in summarizing techniques such as Summary Cubes (McLaughlin & Allen, 2002), Lyric Summaries (McLaughlin & Allen, 2002), or Bio-Pyramids (Macon, 1991). For examples of these strategy-based teaching ideas, see Chapters 4 through 6 and the Appendix. We can also encourage students to engage in inquiry-based projects (see Chapter 12), create alternative modes of representation (see Chapter 13), or participate in technology-based projects (see Chapter 11) to extend their thinking.

There are a number of ways in which we can adapt the lesson planning format of engaging, guiding, and extending student thinking to accommodate our students' needs. In the next section, we examine differentiated instruction, which provides for such adaptations.

How Can We Differentiate Instruction to Accommodate Students' Needs?

As teachers, we know that we have students of differing capabilities in our classes and we strive to help all students achieve to the best of their abilities. Differentiated instruction enables us to accommodate this diversity of student needs (Gibson & Hasbrouck, 2008; Tyner & Green, 2005).

FIGURE 8.1
Lesson Planning Format

I. Goals and Related State Standards
II. Bibliographic Information for Text(s) and Additional Materials
III. Engaging Students' Thinking (before reading)
IV. Guiding Students' Thinking (during reading)
V. Extending Students' Thinking (after reading)
VI. Assessments

To develop environments that promote differentiated instruction, Gibson and Hasbrouck (2008) suggest that we do the following:

- Embrace collaborative teaching and learning
- Use whole-class and small-group explicit strategy instruction
- Establish consistent routines and procedures
- Scaffold student learning
- Increase student engagement
- Teach students how to learn as well as what to learn
- Change the way teaching occurs

When we differentiate instruction, we create multiple pathways to learning. This practice supports our goal of helping students to perform to their maximum potential and motivates students to learn.

We can differentiate a number of instructional components to support students as they gain competence and confidence in learning. These include content—the information being taught; process—the way in which the information is taught; and product—how the students demonstrate their learning (Tomlinson, 1999). Details of each of these elements follow.

Differentiating Content

We can differentiate content by providing information about a topic or a group of related topics using a variety of sources. For example, there may be information in our textbook about the topic, but not all of our students may be able to read it. We can differentiate text by offering students alternative information sources such as informational articles, picture books, websites, video clips, or texts on tape or CD. These media would present the same or similar information in different ways and at different reading levels.

Differentiating Process

We can differentiate process by adapting our teaching methods. For example, we can preteach students who might be English learners or struggling readers; alternatively, we can teach these students in small groups, while other small groups work independently. We can also offer supports during teaching, such as including photos of essential vocabulary, numbering the components of graphic organizers, and providing students with opportunities to respond through multiple modalities such as sketching and labeling.

Differentiating Products

To differentiate products, we can provide a variety of ways for students to demonstrate what they have learned. For example, after learning about a new topic in a content area, some students might complete a research project requiring the use of multiple sources, some might write and illustrate form poems, and others might design informational posters. Students will show what they know through all three assessments, which vary in difficulty.

Making Connections
TO WRITING

When we differentiate instruction, we can use a variety of supports for student writing. For example, we can use photos or illustrations to support students' thinking as they write. We can also use paragraph frames (see Chapter 10) and study techniques such as text boxes and scaffolded outlines (see Chapter 10). ■

We can also use multiple grouping options when we differentiate instruction. In the next section we examine those possibilities.

How Can We Group Students for Learning?

Employing multiple instructional groupings helps us to accommodate student needs. There are several options for grouping students for learning, each of which is used for particular purposes. We call this practice *flexible grouping*, because the groups are not permanent and we have flexibility in using different kinds of groups at different points in our teaching. We can also use multiple grouping options within each lesson.

For group interactions to be effective, we need to align our reasons for grouping, the grouping formats we use, and materials we are using (Flood, Lapp, Flood, & Nagel, 1992). At this point the questions we may wish to explore about flexible grouping include the following:

- What are the possible grouping patterns?
- What are their purposes?
- When do we use them?
- What is our role in such groups?
- What are the students' roles?

Responses to these queries are provided in Figure 8.2. Details about each type of grouping follow.

Whole Group

All students are involved in this grouping option, which is used when we are teaching new information or any ideas that the whole class needs to learn. For example, if we were teaching mathematics and needed to introduce new information about different types of angles in geometry, we would use the whole-group format for our teaching. In this case, the teacher would be directly or explicitly teaching the information about angles; students would be participating and learning. If we were teaching new information and using the whole-group instructional pattern, however, we might also integrate other grouping patterns as the lesson progresses. For example, the teacher may at different points in the lesson ask students to draw a particular type of angle and then "turn to a partner" to share and explain the sketch. Similarly, we could integrate small groups by asking students to form them to practice drawing and discussing different kinds of angles. We can also use the whole-group option if we want to share a read-aloud with the class. (Learn more about read-alouds later in this chapter.)

Small Groups

Small groups may meet for several different purposes and often last about 20 minutes. As seen in Figure 8.2, the primary purposes of this grouping pattern are to preteach content, reteach the material, or reinforce learning. The focus of this kind of group will be students who did not have prior knowledge of the topic, did not demonstrate understanding after initial teaching, or seemed not to fully grasp the topic after it had been taught. For example, when teaching a new topic, we might survey the class and learn that most of the students already have some knowledge of the topic, but a few don't seem to have any knowledge of it. To ensure that the latter students gain initial understanding of the topic, we might meet with them in a small-group setting and preteach some information about the topic. Then, when we begin teaching the next level of the topic to the whole class, all of the students would be able to contribute to the discussion.

Enhancing students' learning is another reason we use small groups. The focus of this kind of small group might be students who are high-level thinkers and who easily become bored when learning is not consistently challenging or students who may have a great amount of knowledge about a particular topic we are teaching.

FIGURE 8.2
Content Area Grouping Options

Grouping	Purposes	When Used	Role(s) of Teacher	Role(s) of Students
Whole group	To teach new material	When everyone in the class needs to learn the material	Direct (explicit) instruction	Participating Learning
Small groups (approximately 5 students)	To preteach To reteach To reinforce learning	When some students need additional instruction or clarification	Guided instruction	Participating Clarifying Learning
	To enhance learning	When some students need to be challenged	Guided instruction	Participating Learning
Small Groups (3–5 students)	To work independently with peers	When the teacher is working with another small group	Monitoring students as they work	Participating Reinforcing Learning
Pairs/partners	To work in a guided context	During direct (explicit) instruction ("Work briefly with a partner" to apply . . . to discover)	Guided instruction	Participating Learning
	To work independently with peers	When the teacher is working with other students or the entire class is working in pairs	Monitoring students as they work	Participating Learning
Individuals	To work independently individually	When applying what has been learned or when reading silently	Monitoring students as they work	Engaging Learning

Another reason to use this type of organization is to invite students to work independently with peers in small groups while we are working with a particular group, such as English learners, advanced students, struggling readers, or special-needs students. For example, we might be involved in preteaching, reteaching, or enriching the learning of a small group of students, while the remaining students in the class also move into small groups for the purpose of working independently. The small groups may meet to continue to work cooperatively on a group project or as a discussion group. (For more information see the section about content area Discussion Circles.)

Making Connections
TO ENGLISH LEARNERS

Teaching in a small-group setting provides opportunities for us as teachers to work with students who may need extra support, such as English learners. While the other students work independently with peers in small groups, we can provide additional supports for students who are English learners by preteaching, teaching, or reteaching them in a small group. Examples of such supports include using visuals related to content vocabulary, offering students opportunities to respond through alternative modalities, providing a fluent oral language model, and encouraging students' learning by using scaffolded outlines. ■

Pairs or Partners

Students work with partners for a variety of reasons. First, students might work with partners as a grouping option. For example, everyone in the class might work with a partner to brainstorm what they know about a particular topic or to create a project, such as a content area alphabet book. Working with a partner can also occur within another organizational setting. For example, a teacher might be engaged in explicit instruction with the whole group, but, after teaching a concept, she might ask the students to "turn to a partner." This segment would be described as "guided instruction," because the teacher would guide the students through their task. In this situation, the teacher might offer a prompt, ask students to complete the next step in a strategy or process, or develop their application of an idea that was taught.

At other times, the students might work in pairs if the teacher is working with a small group and he invites the remainder of the class to work in pairs. In this setting, the teacher would not be able to walk around the room to directly monitor the partners' work, but the success of the pairs would be evident in their self-assessments as well as in the work they produced, which the teacher would review later in the day. Additionally, although the teacher would be busy teaching a pair or small group of students, the engagement of the pairs would be evident simply by quickly glancing around the room and listening to the low noise level.

As with small groups, the partner setting can accommodate the unique needs of English learners, advanced students, struggling readers, or special-needs students. For example, English learners can be partnered with English speakers who help provide a fluent language model, and struggling readers can be paired with students who have more background knowledge about the topic.

A paired setting also works well when students engage in peer assessment. In this case, students can exchange their work with partners, who would read it and provide feedback. In such situations, it is beneficial to ensure that the students understand that feedback should be constructive and generally involve providing a positive comment and a suggestion for improving the work.

Individuals

Students working individually is another option. For example, teachers might invite students to work individually to apply a concept that has already been taught and practiced with a partner. Students might also have some time in class to work on individual projects they may be creating. This is a good idea, because it allows us as teachers to observe how students engage in various steps of the project process. It also provides opportunities for students to ask us questions or to review their work to date. Of course, such occasions should conclude with the students developing new goals for the next step of their projects.

Making Connections | Thinking about Flexible Grouping

- Think about a theme or topic in your content area. Reflect on how you would use the various types of grouping to teach it. Be sure to focus on which students will be participating and why you think the option you selected is the most beneficial.
- Share your thoughts with others in small-group discussions.

How Can We Effectively Use Textbooks in the Content Areas?

Textbooks often serve as the foundation of content area instruction. For many teachers, they are the only texts used; for others, they are used in conjunction with a variety of other resources. In this section, we explore textbooks and examine how to select texts that are effective for our courses.

Content area textbooks are often used as the sole focus of instruction, but in today's educational contexts we have access to multiple text resources. We may choose to use a textbook, but we can easily supplement it with leveled texts, trade books, informational articles, websites, and DVDs. These supplemental types of text are rich sources of information and often have the ability to provide more up-to-date information than can be found in traditional textbooks.

Different levels of content area texts are available. From a reading perspective, texts are viewed as having three different levels. When texts are at the independent level, students can read them without any help. When texts are at the instructional level, students can read them with some help from the teacher. When texts are at the challenging level, students should not be asked to read them because attempting to do so could be a frustrating experience.

Using textbooks as the primary vehicle for instruction in content area learning has been a long-standing tradition. Textbooks designed for content area instruction can be traced as far back as the 1700s. The first geography text appeared in 1784, when Jedidiah Morse produced *Geography Made Easy* (McNergney & Herbert, 1998). As areas of study were added to school curricula, the use of texts to impart discipline-specific knowledge increased. Centuries later, textbooks continue to dominate content area instruction, with research suggesting that textbooks account for 75% to 90% of classroom instruction in the content areas (Palmer & Stewart, 1997; Tyson & Woodward, 1989) and that 95% of science teachers use a textbook 90% of the time. Despite these high percentages of use, textbooks often assume unrealistic levels of background knowledge (McKeown & Beck, 1993), cover a wide variety of topics at a surface level, fail to promote students' use of critical thinking (Morrow, Cunningham, & Murray-Olsen, 1994), and are written at levels that exceed students' reading abilities.

The readability level of textbooks should be a factor in their selection. We can determine approximate readability levels by using formulas, such as the Fry Readabilty Graph (1977), which consider length of text, length of sentences, and complexity of vocabulary. (To learn more about the Fry Readability Graph see school.discoveryeducation.com/schrockguide/fry/fry.html)

School districts may require their teachers to use textbooks, which we may or may not have a voice in selecting. If we are invited to review textbooks for our courses or to serve on a textbook selection committee, we should consider evaluating the texts based on elements such as the points presented in Figure 8.3.

Making Connections
TO MULTIPLE LITERACIES

What is included in or excluded from content area textbooks is decided by publishers. They also decide which voices are heard and which are silenced or discounted in texts. Consequently, the information that students learn from textbooks and the perspectives from which they are written are determined by those who publish the books. Decades ago, students would have been passive recipients of information, who were expected to believe that everything that appeared in textbooks was true. Today, critical literacy suggests that we comprehend text at deeper levels, question the author's message, examine the author's perspective, think about which perspectives may not be treated fairly, and take action to do what we can to ensure that all voices are heard. ■

Vardell, Hadaway, and Young (2006) suggest that we consider students' social and cultural backgrounds when selecting texts and planning instruction. This integration helps to create learning environments in which students feel engaged and successful. Holmes, Powell, Holmes, and Witt (2007) recommend using text that represents a variety of races and people to help students build awareness of and greater sensitivity toward one another.

As content area teachers, we need to do all we can to ensure that our students learn from multiple types and levels of text. This means that if we use a textbook, we should supplement it with a variety of resources. These sources should include, but not be limited to, informational articles from the Internet, newspapers, journals, magazines, primary sources, trade books, poetry, DVDs, leveled texts, and television segments.

1. Is the text well organized (contents, glossary, index, chapter structures)?

2. Is the text factually correct?

3. Is the text motivational?

4. What is the readability level of the text? For which grade was the textbook developed?

5. Does the textbook support state content standards? Is there evidence of standards-based learning?

6. Does the teacher's edition support teachers' use of a strategy-based lesson plan?

7. Is the content diverse?

8. Does the text require students to use skills and strategies?

9. Does the text integrate content literacy? Multiple literacies?

10. Does the text focus on meeting the needs of individual learners, such as English language learners, struggling readers, and special-needs students?

11. How are multiple types of assessment used throughout the text?

12. How are students asked to engage in higher-order thinking throughout the text?

13. How is technology integrated throughout the text? How are the students asked to use technology? Teachers?

14. Is a teacher's edition available? Are there special resources for English learners, struggling learners, and special needs students?

15. Are the charts, maps, graphs, tables, and illustrations accurate? Do they help to support students' thinking?

16. Are supplementary materials available (e.g., text on CD, leveled texts, videos)?

FIGURE 8.3
Questions to Consider When Evaluating a Content Area Textbook

How Can We Teach Students to Generate Questions?

The ability to generate questions is a skill that underpins many aspects of learning. Unfortunately, students more often think of themselves as those who answer questions than as those who ask questions. They are accustomed to responding to questions raised by teachers and textbooks, practices that have consistently been part of their learning experiences. They also view questions in terms of assessment and evaluation—items they respond to at the end of chapters and when taking tests—rather than as a learning skill.

We need to explicitly teach our students how to generate questions. We want them to understand that student-generated questions are an incredibly powerful tool for promoting student engagement, learning, and understanding (Busching & Slesinger, 1995). We want them to understand that questions are essential if we are to construct significant meaning. As Ciardiello notes, "To know how to question is to know how to become literate" (1998, p. 7).

Purposes of Questioning

When teaching students about questioning, we explain what questions are, discuss their purposes, and delineate their multiple levels. For example, we explain that there are many reasons for generating questions, including information seeking (Who was President in 1945?), connected understanding (How does the Holocaust relate to what we are learning about World War II?), psychological and moral reconstruction (What moral issues do you associate with the Holocaust and the Japanese American internment?), historical speculation (How would our world today be different if Hitler had never existed?), and imagination and research (If you had lived during that time, what contributions would you have made in the World War II era?). We also immerse students in topics from multiple perspectives by reading, writing, speaking, listening and viewing to foster their questioning abilities (Busching & Slesinger, 1995).

Memory Questions
    Signal words: who, what, where, when?
    Cognitive operations: naming, defining, identifying, designating

Convergent Thinking Questions
    Signal words: why, how, in what ways?
    Cognitive operations: explaining, stating relationships, comparing, and contrasting

Divergent Thinking Questions
    Signal words: imagine, suppose, predict, if/then
    Cognitive operations: predicting, hypothesizing, inferring, reconstructing

Evaluative Thinking Questions
    Signal words: defend, judge, justify/what do you think?
    Cognitive operations: valuing, judging, defending, justifying

FIGURE 8.4
Ciardiello's Levels of Questioning

Levels of Questioning

Ciardiello (1998) suggests that students generate questions at four levels: memory, convergent, divergent, and evaluative. As shown in Figure 8.4, he also provides signal words and describes cognitive (thinking) operations for each category. Figure 8.5 illustrates how Ciardiello's questioning levels are applicable across content areas.

When teaching students how to generate questions at multiple levels, we explain each question type and then model it. Next, students work with a partner in guided practice in a variety of settings. Finally, students engage in independent application and transfer. The effective teaching of skills, such as generating questions, creates links to reading comprehension strategies. For example, the skills of sequencing, noting details, making generalizations, and using text structure can be

Memory Level
    History: Who was the first President of the United States?
    Literature: Who is the author of the novel?
    Algebra: What are algebraic equations?
    Chemistry: What is the definition of liquid?
    French: What is the French word for bread?

Convergent Level
    History: How did the presidencies of Bill Clinton and George W. Bush differ?
    Literature: How are the novel *Jane Eyre* and the current production of the movie the same? How are they different?
    Algebra: How do the commutative property of multiplication and the distributive property differ?
    Chemistry: How do liquids and gases differ?
    French: How are French and English nouns similar? How are they different?

Divergent Level
    History: If you were President, what would your top three priorities be?
    Literature: Imagine that you were a character in the book. What would happen to you in a sequel to this novel?
    Algebra: Create an algebraic equation and predict what the solution will be.
    Chemistry: Oil-and-vinegar salad dressing contains two phases: an oil-rich liquid and a vinegar-rich liquid. What do you suppose will happen if you shake the bottle?
    French: Imagine you were one of the great French authors. Who would you be and what would you consider to be your greatest work? Please respond in French.

Evaluative Level
    History: Defend your position on paying taxes to the federal government.
    Literature: What is your opinion of the author? Justify your response.
    Algebra: Justify your prediction of the algebraic equation's solution.
    Chemistry: Why should students study chemistry? Defend your response.
    French: Why should students continue to learn French in today's global community? Justify your thinking.

FIGURE 8.5
Content Area Examples of Ciardiello's Four Levels of Questioning

FIGURE 8.6 Generating Questions: A Skill That Supports Comprehension Strategies

Comprehension Strategy	Informational Text	
	Example 1: World War II	**Example 2: Algebraic Equations**
Previewing	What do I already know about World War II?	What do I already know about algebraic equations?
Self-questioning	Why did World War II occur?	Why would I use an algebraic equation?
Making connections	What connections can I make between the text and the video we saw about World War II?	What connections can I make to the algebraic operations used in these equations?
Visualizing	How does my visualization of European concentration camps compare/contrast to the camps of the Japanese American internment?	How can my visualization of planning a party be expressed as an algebraic equation?
Knowing how words work	Which clues in the text can I use to figure out the word "draft"?	Which clues in the text can I use to figure out the word "polynomial"?
Monitoring	Does what I'm reading make sense? If not, what can I do to clarify my thinking?	Does what I am reading make sense? If not, what can I do to clarify my thinking?
Summarizing	What are the most important ideas in the text?	What is the most important information about algebraic equations?
Evaluating	Does the information presented support what I have learned from other sources?	Does the information in this section support what the author stated earlier in the chapter?

linked to summarizing, which is a comprehension strategy (Lipson, 2001). These and other skills, such as making inferences, distinguishing between important and less important ideas, and drawing conclusions, facilitate students' use of one or more comprehension strategies. The skill of generating questions, which underpins every comprehension strategy, is demonstrated in Figure 8.6, The figure features examples of questions at multiple levels using informational text.

Ideas for Teaching Question Generation

There are a variety of ways to teach students how to generate questions. ReQuest, Paired Questioning, and Thick and Thin Questions are three teaching ideas that work particularly well. Guidelines for teaching each of these strategies follow. The skills are presented here in order of "scaffolded" use. We begin with ReQuest, a process in which teachers and students actively engage. Next, we discuss Paired Questioning. The teacher does not have a role in this but the students work with partners. Finally, we explain Thick and Thin Questions; students may either work with a partner or generate questions individually when using this technique.

ReQUEST. When engaging in ReQuest (Manzo, 1969), students actively participate in the discussion of the text. After observing teacher modeling, students practice generating questions at multiple levels. Teachers and students also answer questions. This interaction provides opportunities to engage in the social construction of knowledge and learn the content.

When teaching ReQuest, follow these steps:

1 Explain: Focus on ReQuest as a type of *reciprocal questioning* that involves reading silently, generating questions at multiple levels, predicting, and discussing. Explain that the students and the teacher engage in ReQuest by reading silently and asking one another questions.

2 Demonstrate: Begin by introducing the text, and then invite students to participate in the demonstration. Join the students in reading a designated section of text (usually a few paragraphs) silently. Ask them to close their books when finished, while you ask them questions about the text they read. Comment on the quality of responses. Then close your book and encourage the students to ask you questions. Comment on the quality of the questions.

3 **Guide:** Guide students to engage in ReQuest by silently reading another section of text. Then question the students and encourage them to question you.

4 **Practice:** After students have read an appropriate amount of text, invite them to stop questioning and begin predicting. Provide prompts, such as "I think . . ." or "I wonder . . ." to encourage predictions. Then invite the students to read the remaining text silently. After the students have finished reading the text, facilitate a discussion based on the text and students' predictions.

5 **Reflect:** Encourage students to think about how ReQuest helps us to use reciprocal questioning and prediction to understand text. Discuss other content areas in which students could use ReQuest.

When engaging in ReQuest, we may find that students ask too many memory-level questions. If we teach Ciardiello's four levels of questioning before we teach ReQuest, students will be able to use the signal words to generate questions at all levels. Although memory-level questions are certainly important, we are also trying to encourage our students to think at higher levels. For example, if students are researching the biography of someone who is well respected in a particular content area—for example, Winston Churchill in history, Banneker in mathematics, Hemingway in literature, or Einstein in science—memory-level questions about where and when the person was born provide some background information. Nevertheless, we also want students to ask how that person's contribution to the field compared and contrasted to other contributions (convergent level), how the students could imagine themselves making such a contribution (divergent thinking), and how the students would defend or justify the person's contribution (evaluative level).

TEACHING IDEA

PAIRED QUESTIONING. In Paired Questioning (Vaughn & Estes, 1986), students engage in actively generating questions during reading. To teach Paired Questioning, follow these steps:

1 **Explain:** Explain that Paired Questioning involves students taking turns while generating text-related questions and responding to them. When the students have finished generating and responding to questions while reading segments of the text, one partner summarizes the important ideas in the text and the other agrees or disagrees and justifies his thinking.

2 **Demonstrate:** Arrange in advance to have a student volunteer be your partner during the demonstration. Introduce the text and demonstrate how you and your partner read the title or subtitle of a section of text, set the text aside, and then respond to the questions each of you generate. Remind students that asking questions about the title or subtitle helps the reader set purposes for reading. For example, if the title was *The Civil War* and the subtitle was *Causes of the Civil War*, the questions raised might be *What was the Civil War?* and *What were the causes of the Civil War?* Next, repeat this process, reading a section of text instead of the title or subtitle. After you and your partner have responded to the questions, discuss how generating questions as we read helps us to understand the text.

3 **Guide:** Invite students to work with a partner and a new section of text to engage in Paired Questioning, first with a subtitle and then with a section of text. Encourage discussion.

4 **Practice:** Invite students to finish reading the text by engaging in Paired Questioning. Stop periodically to discuss the text and the questions that have been raised. When the students have finished reading the text, invite one partner to share the important ideas in the text with the other. Then encourage the other partner to agree or disagree and justify her response.

5 **Reflect:** Invite students to share their thoughts about paired questioning, including how it can help us understand text.

**TEACHING IDEA**

THICK AND THIN QUESTIONS. Thick and Thin Questions (Lewin, 1998) encourages students to create questions pertaining to a text and helps students discern the depth of the questions they ask. Teachers often use sticky notes when teaching this technique. Smaller sticky notes are used to write thin questions (memory level) and noticeably larger notes are used to write thick questions (convergent, divergent, evaluative questions). We can also provide a blackline on which students can write Thick and Thin Questions (see Appendix A).

To teach Thick and Thin Questions, follow these steps:

1 **Explain:** Teach the students the difference between thick and thin questions. *Thick questions* deal with big pictures and large concepts. Answers to thick questions are involved, complex, and open ended (convergent, divergent, and evaluative questions). *Thin questions* deal with specific content. Answers to thin questions are short, close ended (memory-level questions), and usually clearly stated in the book.

2 **Demonstrate:** Model how to create thick and thin questions. Read a portion of text and think aloud about how to create a thick question and a thin question. Relate each type of question to Ciardiello's four levels of questioning. Discuss which signal words you used to create the questions and possible answers to them.

3 **Guide:** Guide students to work with partners to create Thick and Thin Questions as they read. Read another portion of text and prompt students with stems such as "Why . . ." or "What if . . ." for Thick Questions and "Who is . . ." and "Where . . ." for Thin Questions. Encourage students to respond to the questions their partners generate.

4 **Practice:** Invite students to work individually to generate Thick and Thin Questions as they continue to read the text. When they have finished reading the text, encourage students to share their questions with a partner, taking turns responding to them.

5 **Reflect:** Invite students to share their thoughts about Thick and Thin Questions and to describe how generating questions can help us understand text. Encourage the students to think about how they can use Thick and Thin Questions when reading in other content areas.

Generating questions is an essential skill. As Ciardiello notes, "Asking questions for the joy of discovery is the pathway to wandering and wondering" (2003, pp. 228–229). It is "wandering" in the sense of roaming or leisurely strolling through one's thoughts and reflections with no predetermined course to travel. The pathway is also filled with "wondering" in the sense of asking questions that express the object of curiosity or doubt. Ciardiello (2007) refers to this process as "question-finding" and notes that it strongly supports critical literacy (see Chapter 2) by helping students move beyond the surface message of text to actively question its deeper, more critical meanings.

Making Connections | Thinking about Generating Questions

■ Think about generating questions. Then choose a topic from your content area and use Ciardiello's signal words to develop one question at each level about that topic.

■ Share your thoughts with others in small-group discussions. Discuss how you will teach questioning to your students.

■ Save the questions you generated and use them as models when teaching your students about questioning.

How Can We Teach Students to Recognize Text Patterns?

Research tells us that students can find reading informational text challenging. Their knowledge of and experience with the text type and structure can influence the text's accessibility. For

Go to the Activities and Applications section under the topic *Text Structure* in the MyEducationLab for your course and complete the activity entitled Organization of Nonfiction to identify techniques teachers can use to guide their students to an understanding of text structures

example, many students have greater background knowledge of reading narrative text, which is generally based on characters, setting, problem, attempts to resolve the problem, and resolution. One reason they may find reading informational text more difficult is that they are not familiar with these text patterns (Dymock & Nicholson, 1999).

Researchers suggest that we should explicitly teach the informational text structure to our students (Pressley, 2002). Goldman and Rakestraw (2001) concur and note the following conclusions based on existing research on students' knowledge of text structure:

- Readers use their knowledge of structure in processing text.
- Knowledge of structural forms of text develops with experience with different genres, and is correlated with age and time in school.
- Making readers more aware of genre and text structure improves learning. (p. 321)

Research reports that if students know the text patterns and understand how to generate questions, they will improve their comprehension of text. The following five text patterns appear most prevalent in informational text. Descriptions and examples of each follow.

Description

This pattern focuses on characteristics, facts, and features related to a topic, person, event, or object.

EXAMPLE:

Apple has introduced the world's slimmest laptop, the MacBook Air. The density of the laptop measures between 0.4 centimeter and 1.9 centimeters. The 13.3-inch display is lit by an energy-saving LED display. Equipped with a built-in camera, the MacBook Air also comes with an Intel Core-2-Duo processor and either a 1.6- or 1.8-gigahertz chip. The MacBook Air has 2 gigabytes of memory, comes with an 80-gigabyte hard drive, and is pre-equipped for an 802.11n Wi-Fi connection. Because it is so slim, the laptop has no built-in DVD drive. Buyers can also opt for a solid-state hard drive and a flash drive without moving parts, making the computer more resistant to shocks and letting it run faster.

Sequence

This pattern relates steps in a process or the order in which things happened.

EXAMPLE:

First, Martin Luther King, Jr., delivered his "I Have a Dream" speech during the March on Washington for Jobs and Freedom. Next, he became the youngest man to be awarded the Nobel Peace Prize. Then he took the Civil Rights Movement north and moved his family into the Chicago slums to demonstrate support for the poor. Finally, in 1968, King was assassinated in Memphis, Tennessee, where he went to support striking garbage workers.

Comparison and Contrast

This pattern illuminates similarities (comparisons) and differences (contrasts).

EXAMPLE:

When we examine the issues that Democrats and Republicans are supporting in the Presidential election, we can see that there are some issues on which they are clearly divided and others where their goals are similar, but their approaches are different. An example of the former is that their positions differ on the war in Iraq. The Democrats are in favor of ending the war in Iraq, while the Republicans support the war and have developed strategies for victory. As an example of the latter, both the Democratic and Republican candidates support changes in health care, reform of immigration laws, and improvements in education. Of course, their policies to promote these changes differ, and in some cases, differ dramatically.

Cause and Effect

Go to the Activities and Applications section under the topic *Comprehension Strategies* in the MyEducationLab for your course and complete the activity entitled Text Structure and Comprehension to examine ways in which content area textbook structure affects student comprehension.

This pattern shows how events or ideas (effects) come to be because of certain other ideas, acts, or events (causes).

EXAMPLE:

A number of factors contributed to the start of the Civil War. Economic and social differences between the North and the South laid a foundation for the conflict when the South became a single-crop economy and the North became more industrialized and diverse. As the South became more dependent on slaves to work the cotton plantations, the North focused on city life, where people of many different cultures worked together. In addition, the issue of state versus federal rights was hotly contested. When the states felt they were no longer respected, several seceded. The slave versus nonslave issue was complicated by the growth of the country through the Louisiana Purchase and the Mexican War. Concerns about whether the additional states would permit slave-holding were hotly debated. The abolition movement grew as Northerners became more opposed to slavery and the Fugitive Slave Act was passed. Finally, when Abraham Lincoln was elected president, the South viewed him as antislavery and a supporter of Northern interests. Seven Southern states had already seceded when Lincoln took office.

Problem and Solution

This pattern showcases a difficulty (problem) and provides an example of how it can be resolved (solution).

EXAMPLE:

Violent tornadoes are destructive. They can reduce homes to rubble and are responsible for 70 percent of all tornado-related deaths. To combat the devastating effects of this type of severe weather, the National Weather Service recommends that people who live in areas prone to tornadoes develop a disaster plan. Such a plan includes learning the community's warning signal and evacuation plan, having frequent drills, paying attention to weather conditions, mapping severe storm movements, and preparing a kit of disaster supplies. The value of such plans was demonstrated this past week when a college was severely damaged by tornadoes. Several buildings were destroyed, but no lives were lost.

Signal words for each pattern are presented in Figure 8.7. These words often offer readers clues about which pattern is prevalent in a particular section of text.

Recognizing the text structure can help readers understand the type of information included in the text and predict the types of questions that may be raised about it. For example, if students are reading a biography and realize that the text pattern is sequential, questions may focus on what happened when. When reading a section of text in which the pattern is comparison/contrast, questions may focus on similarities and differences.

FIGURE 8.7
Signal Words Commonly Associated with Text Patterns

Description: above, below, behind, down, across, under, such as, appears to be

Sequence: first, second, third, then, next, finally, during, until, preceding, initially, following

Comparison/contrast: although, but, compared to, however, on the other hand, either . . . or, not only . . . but also, similarly, different from

Cause/effect: because, as a result, since, accordingly, for this reason, in order to, if . . . then, therefore, consequently, nevertheless

Problem/solution: because, cause, since, therefore, consequently, as a result, this led to . . ., solve, resolve, conclude

In the next section, we describe a variety of ways to help students read content area text more effectively. Our goal is to eliminate round-robin reading and encourage students to actively engage with text.

How Can Students Read Content Area Text Without Engaging in Round-Robin Reading?

Many of us grew up engaging in what we call *round-robin reading*. Unfortunately, many students are still engaging in this practice at their content area teachers' requests. One of our primary goals as teachers is to eliminate this dated method of reading from education.

As you may recall, round-robin reading involves students taking turns reading aloud. Generally, each student reads a paragraph or other short segment of text. This process has several negative outcomes. First, students are usually reading the text *cold*—which means they have not had time to read or make connections to the text before they read it aloud. This is often complicated by teachers who do not encourage students to activate their prior knowledge prior to reading. The second difficulty is that not all students are comfortable reading aloud—especially when they might be corrected by teachers and/or peers if they mispronounce a word or read in a less than fluent fashion. The third problem is that it is very easy for students to read their segment and then ignore the rest of the students' reading. As a consequence, many students may not be comprehending the text. Finally, we are trying to encourage students to become lifelong readers. Round-robin reading interferes with that goal, because it presents an unrealistic view of reading. There is no other time in their lives when our students will ever be asked to read one paragraph aloud in front of an audience. Consequently, round-robin reading is not a meaningful process.

Better, more meaningful ways to enable students to understand text include the following:

- Students reading aloud when they engage in Patterned Partner Reading
- Students reading silently using the Bookmark Technique, INSERT or KWLS
- Students listening to books on tape
- Students interacting with peers in Discussion Circles
- Teachers engaging in read-alouds of selected texts

Active participation in these techniques helps to engage students and encourage them to stay focused and monitor their reading.

Students Reading with a Partner

Students can read text aloud with a partner when they engage in Patterned Partner Reading. Using patterns contributes to students' purpose for reading.

 **PATTERNED PARTNER READING.** Patterned Partner Reading (McLaughlin & Allen, 2002) promotes strategic reading, while providing a structure for reading interactively with a partner. A popular alternative to round-robin reading, this technique is used when two students read a text or section of a text together. The partners generally take turns reading, but this approach differs from the traditional partner or buddy reading in that it provides a particular pattern to help both students stay focused, whether they are the reader or the listener. The following is a list of possible patterns in which students can engage while partner reading:

Read–Pause–Question: One student reads, the pair pauses, and the student that read asks the other student a question about the text.
Read–Pause–Make a Connection: One student reads, the pair pauses, and each student makes a connection to self, to text, or to the world.

Read–Pause–Bookmark: One student reads, the pair pauses, and the students use the Bookmark Technique to mark the following information, so they can share it with the class:

- Most interesting
- Most confusing
- A word the whole class needs to know
- A chart, map, illustration, or graph that helped the readers understand what they read

Read–Pause–Sketch and Share: One student reads, the pair pauses, and each student visualizes and sketches. Then the students share and discuss their sketches.

Read–Pause–Say Something: One student reads, the pair pauses, and each student "says something" that he found interesting or didn't know before reading.

Read–Pause–Summarize: One student reads, the pair pauses, and the other student summarizes the segment that was read.

Students Reading Silently

When students read silently, ideas such as Bookmark Technique, KWL/KWLS, and INSERT help the students to interact with text. Bookmark Technique, which is detailed in Chapter 4, provides purposes for reading and helps students to focus. While they are reading, the students complete four Bookmarks: (1) the most important section of the text, (2) a vocabulary word the whole class needs to discuss, (3) something the reader found confusing, and (4) an illustration, chart, map, or graph that helped the reader to understand what she read. KWL/KWLS requires that the students brainstorm, raise questions, and think about responses as they read. INSERT asks students to brainstorm and then insert several symbols as they read.

KWL AND KWLS. The KWL is a teaching idea that supports multiple reading comprehension strategies, including self-questioning, monitoring, and summarizing. Its purposes include activating students' prior knowledge about a topic, setting purposes for reading, and confirming, revising, or expanding original understandings of a topic. In the traditional form of KWL, developed by Donna Ogle in 1986, readers ask themselves, "What do I know?", "What do I want to know?", and "What have I learned?" In 1995, Sippola suggested that we add a fourth column to the KWL to create the KWLS. The fourth column accommodates the question, "What do I still want to know?" The final column of the KWLS encourages students to examine whether they have found answers to all of the questions they raised in response to "What do I need to know?" If students have not found responses to all of the questions they raised, they move the unanswered questions to the fourth column—or add new questions that may have arisen—and research responses to them. Graphic organizers for the KWL, KWLS, and the KWDL ("What I know," "What I want to know," "What I did," and "What I learned"), which is often used in science and mathematics—can be found in Appendix A. Guidelines for teaching the KWL and an example from a chemistry class can be found in Chapter 5. To teach your students how to use KWLS, follow these steps and encourage discussion throughout the process.

1. **Explain:** Explain that the KWLS supports the reading strategies of self-questioning, monitoring, and summarizing. Focus on the four steps involved in the KWLS: What I Know, What I Want to Know, and What I Learned, and What I Still Want to Know.

2. **Demonstrate:** Begin by introducing the topic and a short text. Share the KWLS graphic organizer with students (see the Appendix). Think aloud as you brainstorm what you know in the K column. Then move to the W column and list what you want to know. Discuss what you wrote in the K and W columns. Then read the text. After reading, record what you learned in the L column. Discuss what you learned with the class. Then revisit the K column to determine if what you knew was verified in the text and the W column to ensure

K What I Know	W What I Want to Know	L What I Learned	S What I Still Want to Know
Founded in 1949 as a coalition of social classes	What were the social classes?	The workers, the peasants, the petite bourgeoisie, and the national-capitalists	How were social classes determined?
Involvement in Korean War	Who were "the enemies of the state"?	War criminals, traitors, capitalists, counter-revolutionaries	Who decided who was an enemy of the state?
	What was the next transition?	Transition to socialism in 1953–1957	What did this involve?
	What were China's needs at this time?	Food, funds, technology, equipment and military weapons.	Where did China get the technology and the weapons?

FIGURE 8.8
KWLS about the People's Republic of China 1949–1957

that all of your questions were answered. Include any remaining questions from the W (What I Want to Know) column and any new questions about the topic in the S column of the KWLS. Find responses to the questions in the S column. When the KWLS is complete, discuss it with the students and use it to summarize the information on the chart.

3 **Guide:** Introduce a new text and guide students to work with a partner as each completes the K and W columns. Discuss the students' responses. Provide time for them to read the text and complete the L column. Discuss their responses. Then ask students to check the K and W columns to ensure that what they knew was verified by the text and that all of their questions were answered. Then invite students to list any questions remaining from the W column or any new questions that may have arisen in the S column. Encourage the pairs of students to respond to the questions in the S column and to summarize what they have learned.

4 **Practice:** Invite students to work on their own to complete a KWLS chart about another short text. Monitor as they complete each step, and discuss as noted earlier in the process. After the students have discussed the completed K, W, and L columns, encourage them to revisit the K and L columns as noted earlier. Invite them to add and respond to questions in the S column. Finally, invite students to share an oral summary of what they learned with a partner.

5 **Reflect:** Invite students to think about how the KWLS helps us comprehend by providing opportunities to self-question, monitor, and summarize text.

Figure 8.8 features an excerpt from a KWLS about the People's Republic of China.

 **TEACHING IDEA** INSERT (INTERACTIVE NOTATION SYSTEM TO EFFECTIVE READING AND THINKING). The INSERT method was developed to encourage students to become active readers. When using this technique, students insert a number of different symbols into the text. INSERT provides students with opportunities to reflect about what they know and encourages them to make some decisions about the ideas expressed in the text. It is important to note that we have adapted INSERT for our students' use. Our approach requires the reader to insert fewer symbols than the original version.

To teach students how to use INSERT, see the guidelines presented in Chapter 5. For examples of completed student INSERT Bookmarks, about the Louisiana Purchase, see Chapter 5. For examples of INSERT Bookmarks about marine life zones, see Figure 8.9.

1 **Explain:** Begin by explaining that INSERT helps us to self-question, monitor, and summarize as we read. Focus on how INSERT begins with readers brainstorming a list of what

FIGURE 8.9 INSERT Bookmarks about Marine Life Zones from Tarbuck, E.J., & Lutgens, F.K. (2006). *Earth Science.* Needham, MA: Pearson.

they know about the topic, reading the text, and inserting four symbols as they read. Introduce the four symbols to be inserted into the text and explain what each means:

- Place a check mark (✓) in the margin if the information in the text verifies what is on their brainstormed list.
- Place a plus sign (+) in the margin if the information is new to them—that is, not on their list.
- Place a minus sign (−) in the margin if the information contradicts or disproves information on the brainstormed list.
- Place a question mark (?) in the margin if there is something in the text that is confusing.

Explain that if the students are completing the INSERT Bookmarks, they will write information on each Bookmark, rather than in the margin of the text. Share the INSERT Bookmarks with the students and use them throughout the remainder of the lesson.

2 Demonstrate: Introduce a short text and think aloud as you brainstorm what you know about the topic. Write your brainstormed list on the board, on an overhead transparency, or on a computer. Then read the text and complete an INSERT Bookmark each time you insert a notation. For example, in Figure 8.8, when David Bishop wanted to indicate that he read something that confirmed what he had brainstormed, he wrote the page and paragraph numbers and indicated what was confirmed on the ✓ (check symbol) Bookmark. When he encountered information that was new to him, he wrote on the + (plus symbol) Bookmark. When he read something that did not support what appeared on his brainstormed list, he wrote it on the − (minus symbol) Bookmark. When he read something that confused him, he wrote it on the ? (question mark symbol) Bookmark.

After you have finished reading, discuss the notations you inserted and explain how they related to your brainstormed list. Then summarize the text.

3 **Guide:** Introduce another short text and invite students to work with a partner to brainstorm what they know about the topic. Then encourage the students to complete the INSERT Bookmarks, indicating when the text supported what they had brainstormed, when the text contained new information, when the text disconfirmed something that appeared on the brainstormed list, and when text information was found to be confusing. After the students complete the Bookmarks, invite them to discuss their responses and summarize the text.

4 **Practice:** Encourage students to work on their own to complete the INSERT Method. Introduce another short text and encourage the students to brainstorm what they know. Then monitor them, assisting as needed, as they read the text and complete the INSERT Bookmarks. Encourage the students to discuss their completed Bookmarks and summarize the text.

5 **Reflect:** Invite students to reflect on how using INSERT helps us to self-question, monitor, and summarize as we read. Encourage students to think abut other situations in which they can use the INSERT Method.

For more ideas to help students interact with text, see Chapters 4 through 6 and the Appendix.

In the following example, David Bishop, a high school history student, used INSERT while reading about the Louisiana Purchase. He began by brainstorming what he knew about the historic event before he began to read. David's brainstormed list included the following five statements:

1. The United States wanted the right to use the Mississippi River for shipping.
2. The United States purchased Louisiana.
3. The land was bought from France.
4. The land was bought for $15 million.
5. Napoleon, Monroe, and Livingston negotiated the deal.

After brainstorming what he already knew, David read the section about the Louisiana Purchase in his history textbook. As he read, he completed the INSERT Bookmarks (McLaughlin & Allen, 2002) shown in Figure 8.8.

Students Reading for Discussion Circles

Students can read on their own and share their insights, questions, and interpretations of texts in Discussion Circles. These small groups, which are similar to Literature Circles, provide students with an opportunity to discuss texts with peers in rich and meaningful ways. In our content area classes, we can use informational articles, sections of text, or theme-related novels as the focus of our Discussion Circles. Also, although Discussion Circles usually include just the students in our classrooms, we can arrange to have online Discussion Circles with students anywhere in the world.

To facilitate students' use of Discussion Circles, we need to explicitly teach the concept and engage in active demonstration. It is also important to review various aspects of cooperative learning before the students meet in their groups. Understanding that each person's opinion has value is an important idea to revisit.

The following guidelines facilitate the use of Discussion Circles:

1. Groups are temporary and are based on the texts students choose to read.
2. Each group may read a different text or all groups may read the same text.
3. Students take active roles in reading and discussing the texts.
4. Students' personal interpretations drive the discussion. There is not a list of questions to be answered, but rather a focus on students' inquiries, connections, and interpretations.
5. Groups meet regularly, according to predetermined schedules.
6. Students decide on topics for discussions and lead the conversations.
7. Sharing ideas in this format helps the students to broaden their interpretations and gain new perspectives from the other members of the group.
8. The teacher acts as a facilitator, not as an instructor or discussion leader.
9. Teachers assess students by observing conversations within groups and engaging students in self-assessment.

The time spent in Discussion Circles varies based on the length of the text, but usually 20 minutes is sufficient. It is important to allow enough time for each group's conversation to evolve on its own.

Some teachers prefer to use assigned roles and responsibilities as a way to guide the conversations. Roles adapted from their use in Literature Circles (Daniels, 1994) include the following:

- *Discussion Leader:* takes on the leadership of the group and guides the discussion. Responsibilities include choosing topics for discussion, generating questions, convening the meeting, and facilitating contributions from all members.
- *Passage Selector:* helps students revisit the text. Responsibilities include selecting memorable or important sections of the text and reading them aloud.
- *Connector:* guides students to make connections with the text. Responsibilities include sharing text–self, text–text, and text–world connections and encouraging others to do the same.
- *Illustrator:* creates a drawing or other symbolic response to text. Responsibilities include making the visual response and using it to encourage others to contribute to the conversation.
- *Word Finder:* selects one or two words from the reading that the whole class needs to discuss. Responsibilities include finding the words, noting where they are located in the text, and proposing definitions based on their use in context.

Students alternate roles each time a circle meets, so that eventually every student has a chance to take each role. Starting with clearly defined roles and then relaxing or relinquishing them as the students gain competence in Discussion Circles appears to be especially effective.

Books and Chapters on Compact Disc

Providing students with access to books and text chapters on compact discs or tapes is another way that students can learn what the text contains without engaging in round-robin reading. This approach simply requires that we or volunteer students record ourselves as we read a chapter or other segment of text. Students can then listen to the tapes or CDs individually or in pairs.

Making Connections
TO STRUGGLING READERS

Providing alternatives to round-robin reading is helpful for all students, but especially for students who struggle to read. Engaging struggling readers in Patterned Partner Reading, reading along with a tape or CD, reading leveled text, or reading in preparation for Discussion Circles and providing appropriate supports can increase student performance and motivation as well as self-esteem. Providing these students with alternative ways to respond to their reading is also beneficial. ■

Teacher Read-Alouds

Read-alouds play an important role in content area teaching and learning. They are used in the early grades and continue right through high school. As Albright (2002) notes, read-alouds and discussion engage adolescents, enrich content knowledge, and stimulate higher-order thinking.

When reading aloud to our content area classes, we may choose to read theme-related picture books or novel segments, but our options do not end there. We may also read excerpts from informational articles in magazines or newspapers, poetry, or various types of text from the Internet. It is important to remember that teacher read-alouds should include class discussions.

We begin this section by providing a rationale for using read-alouds in the content areas. Next, we explore how trade books can enhance our teaching. Finally, we discuss the role of informational articles in the read-aloud process.

RATIONALE. The rationale for using read-alouds in the content areas is multifaceted. They provide motivation; engage prior knowledge; furnish background information; introduce key concepts; can be used to teach strategies; incorporate a variety of genres, including biography and poetry; promote inquiry; and encourage students to view topics from different perspectives. Reading aloud also improves listening skills, builds vocabulary, aids reading comprehension, and positively influences students' attitudes toward reading (Fisher, Flood, Lapp, & Frey, 2004; Santoro, Chard, Howard, & Baker, 2008). Purposes for reading aloud in the content areas include stimulating interest in a topic, initiating discussions, posing dilemmas, stimulating debates, posing questions for research, and making interdisciplinary connections.

Teacher read-alouds can be narrative or informational text and include, but are not limited to, trade books, informational articles, poetry, lyrics, and primary sources, such as letters. For example, when teaching about DNA in biology, we can read articles about the role DNA plays in today's court cases. When studying about the Civil War, we can read aloud letters and examine photographs that family members sent home during the conflict. When studying great works of literature, we can read aloud a segment of the author's work. In mathematics, we can read aloud segments of biographies of famous mathematicians or informational articles about mathematics in everyday life. In foreign language classes, we can read aloud segments of poetry from a particular culture or informational articles written in that language.

TRADE BOOKS. Researchers who promote using trade books, such as picture books and novels, in the content areas report that these read-alouds expand students' knowledge base (Freeman & Person, 1998) and help them to develop richer understandings (Savage, 1998). They also explore topics in depth, enhance critical thinking, and help students to make connections to everyday life.

Trade books address a wide variety of content area topics. The diverse nature of such books is evident in the following examples in which content area topics are linked to particular trade book titles:

- If the Holocaust is the topic being studied, reading a segment from *The Diary of Anne Frank* will offer students a succinct understanding of her life, while selections from *I Never Saw Another Butterfly* will offer the perspectives of numerous Jewish children who were held in concentration camps during World War II.

- If Marie Curie or radium is the topic of study, consider reading aloud a section of *Something Out of Nothing: Marie Curie and Radium,* a text that chronicles the scientist's life.

- Another effective pairing uses *Baseball Saved Us* and excerpts from the novel *Snow Falling on Cedars* when the topic is the Japanese American internment during World War II.

- If any type of mathematics is the topic, we can share Jon Scieszka's *Math Curse,* a humorous look at mathematics for students of all ages. In science, read Scieszka's *Science Verse.*

- When teaching about African American contributions to our society, read *Martin's Big Words* or *Talkin' about Bessie* (Coleman).

For a more extensive list of trade books recommended for use as read-alouds in the content areas, see Figure 8.10.

INFORMATIONAL ARTICLES. Informational or factual articles are rich alternatives to traditional textbooks because the author's voice and point of view are obvious, making them more readable and more interesting. The high quality of pictures and graphics that accompany

FIGURE 8.10
Examples of Trade Books to Use as Content Area Read-Alouds

Bunting, E. (1998). *So far from the sea.* New York: Clarion Books.

Frank, A. (1993). *Anne Frank: The diary of a young girl.* New York: Bantam Books.

Frazier, C. (1997). *Cold mountain.* New York: Atlantic Monthy Press.

Gibson, K. B. (2005). *The life and times of Catherine the Great.* Hockessin, DE: Mitchell Lane.

Gunderson, J. (2007). *Sacagawea: Journey into the west.* Mankato, MN: Capstone Press.

Guterson, D. (1994). *Snow falling on cedars.* New York: Harcourt.

Jacobs, F. (1992). *The Tainos: The people who welcomed Columbus.* New York: G. P. Putnam's Sons.

Keating, F. (2006). *Theodore.* New York: Simon and Schuster.

King, D.C. (2006). *Charles Darwin.* New York: DK Children.

McClafferty, C. K. (2006). *Something out of nothing: Marie Curie and radium.* New York: Farrar, Straus, Giroux.

McCollough, D. (2001). *John Adams.* New York: Simon & Schuster.

Mochizuki, K. (1995). *Baseball saved us.* New York: Lee and Low Books.

O'Connor, B. (2002). *Leonardo Da Vinci: Renaissance genius.* Minneapolis, MN: Carolrhoda Books.

Rappaport, D. (2001). *Martin's big words.* New York: Hyperion.

Scieszka, J. (1995). *Math curse.* New York: Viking.

Scieszka, J. (2004). *Science verse.* New York: Viking.

Volavkova, H. (1993). *I never saw another butterfly: Children's drawings and poems from Terezin Concentration Camp, 1942–1944.* New York: Schocken.

Whiting, J. (2006). *Aristotle.* Hockessin, DE: Mitchell Lane.

Wilkinson, P. (2007). *Gandhi: The young protester who founded a nation.* Washington, DC: National Geographic Children's Books.

Yolen, J. (1992). *Encounter.* New York: Harcourt Brace Jovanovich.

these selections add to the information they present and heighten their appeal to students. Informational articles are also more up-to-date in their coverage of topics than textbooks could ever be.

When selecting articles, we should remember to choose those that feature vivid descriptions and promote inquiry. Choosing articles that are reasonably short is also important. If we find longer articles that complement topics we are teaching, we can read selected segments of them. For example, we may choose to read the opening section and invite students to finish reading the article with a partner. Short, pertinent selections can be integrated seamlessly into the flow of our content area lessons. Sources of read-aloud articles include magazines and newspapers as well as a wide variety of websites such as Biography.com and Discovery.com.

Reading aloud can have many positive outcomes for students. For example, it may increase students' comprehension, enrich their vocabulary, help them become better writers, and motivate them to read on their own (Blessing, 2005).

How Can Students Learn to Use Textbook Study Strategies such as SQ4R?

We have already discussed the importance of students being able to generate questions and recognize text patterns while they are reading. We know it is essential for students to have background knowledge, to use a variety of reading comprehension strategies, and to discuss the meaning they construct. Textbook study strategies such as Survey, Question, Read, Record, Recite, and Reflect (SQ4R) can also help students when they are reading informational text independently.

SQ4R (Robinson, 1946) is a textbook reading study strategy that incorporates several of the strategies introduced in Chapter 4. It also accommodates learning styles by integrating multiple modes of learning. When using this study technique, students survey, question, read, record, recite, and reflect about the text. A detailed description of the process follows.

Step 1: Survey

Before you read, preview the text, activate prior knowledge, and make connections. When surveying, consider these suggestions:

- Read the text outline (title, headings, and subheadings) and the captions that accompany pictures, charts, graphs, or maps.
- Preview the introductory and concluding paragraphs.
- Read the summary.
- Review text-provided or teacher-created questions.

Step 2: Question

While you are reading, generate questions to help you think through the text and set purposes for reading; consider how to respond to text-provided or teacher-created questions. When questioning, consider these suggestions:

- Turn the title, headings, and subheadings into questions.
- Consider the questions provided in the text or by the teacher.

Note: If you believe you learn better by recording ideas while studying, you may wish to write the questions you are considering. This variation on the SQ4R study technique is called SQW4R.

Step 3: Read

Use the purpose questions you developed for each section to set purposes for reading. Read to respond to those questions. While reading, consider these suggestions:

- Set times to read and schedule regular breaks.
- Use your comprehension strategies as you read. If possible, use ideas such as Bookmark Technique or INSERT to help monitor your understanding.
- Think about possible responses to the questions you raised.

Step 4: Record

Recording information in writing, by taking notes or completing a text outline, can help to ingrain the ideas in our memory. When recording, consider these suggestions:

- Put the information in your own words to ensure understanding.
- Record information clearly, so that the written records can be used for review later.
- Record information after reading a section of text. (When we engage in writing or highlighting as we read, we often emphasize too much information.)
- Use marginal notes as another way to emphasize ideas.

Step 5: Recite

Reciting—saying and listening to information—helps us to remember it. When reciting, consider these suggestions:

- Recite aloud the major concepts of the section using your own words.
- Ask and answer questions relating to key terminology and important facts aloud.
- Study with a partner and orally explain the information to each other.

Step 6: Reflect

Reflecting helps us to remember information and become more self-aware of our learning. When reflecting, consider these suggestions:

- Make connections between new information you have learned and what you already knew.
- Think about how you can effectively use the new information.
- Review the information often to retain it.

SQ4R is an effective textbook reading strategy that includes strategies such as previewing, making connections, questioning, monitoring, and summarizing. It also incorporates reflection. Although SQ4R is only one of several textbook reading strategies, it is often viewed as the most effective.

FINAL THOUGHTS

Organizing for learning is an essential part of our teaching. Knowing how to group students, teaching them how to generate questions, understanding the roles of textbooks in teaching, and using alternatives to round-robin reading are everyday practices for us as teachers. The more we know about organizing for learning, the more likely our students are to be highly motivated, engaged learners who participate in high-quality, meaningful instruction.

In the next chapter, we investigate writing in the content areas. We explore the differences between informal and formal writing, and explain how we can integrate both in our content area teaching.

Teaching Connections

E-Links

Work with a partner and visit a website that features standards-based lesson plans for your content area. Imagine that you are using that lesson to teach your students. Then consider how you could differentiate (1) the content, (2) the process, and (3) the product for English learners and special-needs students. For example, how would you group students for instruction? How could students use their ability to generate questions in the lesson? Will you choose more than one text? How will students show what they know and can do?

Discuss the possibilities in each category with your partner and record your thinking as a reflective entry in your portfolio.

EXAMPLE LESSON PLAN WEBSITES

Read–Write–Think: Literature, Content Areas
www.readwritethink.org

Teachnology: Lesson Plans—Math, Science, Social Studies
http://www.teach-nology.com/teachers/lesson_plans/math/

Accountable Talk

Think about the topics addressed in this chapter—lesson planning, grouping, skills instruction, alternatives to round-robin reading, and more—and explain how you will use them to create a foundation for your teaching. Focus on specific examples. Then share your ideas in a small group of students who are studying your discipline. Work together to complete a graphic organizer that represents your ideas. When your conversations in the small groups conclude, discuss this issue across subject areas.

Portfolio/Performance Opportunity

As noted early in this chapter, textbook selection is a component of teaching. So, for your performance opportunity, you will work with a partner to complete a special project: the content area textbook evaluation. After the content area textbook evaluation is explained and modeled, you and your partner will complete one together. See the Evaluation of a Content Area Textbook form on the next page for details.

During this project, you and your partner will evaluate a discipline-specific content area textbook that you have brought to class. While evaluating the textbook, you will engage in several steps. First, you will review the questions included in the Evaluation of a Content Area Textbook form. Next, you and your partner will examine the textbook and respond to the questions that have been raised. When you have finished examining the text and responding to the questions, you and your partner will share what you have learned with another pair of students who are examining a text from the same discipline. You should then engage in a general class discussion about textbooks, including how teachers can use the textbook selection process to help them evaluate texts for their teaching. Finally, you will create a portfolio entry in which you summarize the information you learned about the text you examined and reflect on what you have learned about textbook selection.

Directions:

1. Work with a partner to evaluate a content area textbook.

2. Both of you should record your responses on separate copies of the Evaluation of a Content Area Textbook form.

3. When you and your partner have finished completing your forms and you have shared what you have learned with others, work on your own to write a summary of the information you recorded on your form and, based on what you have learned, explain whether you would use this textbook in your teaching. Justify your thinking.

4. When you have completed this project, remember to put your completed form and your "Summary and Explanation" into your portfolio.

Text Title: _____

Text Series: _____

Publisher: _____

Copyright Year: _____

Cost: _____

Authors: _____

_____

_____

In reviewing the textbook, your question is **Are the following qualities present in the text you are examining?** If your response is "yes," provide an example of it from the text along with the page number on which the example is located. If your answer is "no," explain whether you would be able to teach effectively if this quality were not present in the textbook.

1. Is the text well organized (contents, glossary, index, chapter structures)?

2. Is the text factually correct? (Review pages at the beginning, middle, and end of the text to determine if they are factually correct. Include examples of factual text from each page you review.)

3. Is the text motivational? (Is it the kind of text that you think would motivate students at that grade level to learn? Is it colorful? Does it have pictures? Does it include graphics? If you were a student, would you want to use this book?)

4. What is the readability level of the text? For which grade was the textbook developed?

5. Does the textbook support state content standards? Is there evidence of standards-based learning? (Does the text include state standards? Does the textbook indicate which standards the content addresses? What are three examples of standards that are included?)

6. Does the teacher's edition support teachers' use of a strategy-based lesson plan? (Does the text promote using a lesson format similar to the one we have learned—engaging, guiding, and extending student thinking? If so, provide examples.)

7. Is the content diverse? (Is there evidence of multiculturalism in the text? Are people with special needs represented? Are genders treated equally in the text?)

8. Does the text require students to use skills and strategies? [Skill examples would include generating questions and recognizing text patterns. Strategy examples would include previewing (Semantic Maps), monitoring (Bookmark Technique, Pattern Partner Reading); making connections (Connection Stems); knowing how words work (Concept of Definition Maps); summarizing (Lyric Summary, Concept of Definition Map Summary, Bio-Pyramid); and evaluating (Discussion Web).]

9. Does the text integrate content literacy? (Does it encourage reading, writing, speaking, listening, and viewing across the curriculum?) Multiple Literacies?

10. Does the text focus on meeting the needs of individual learners? (e.g., English language learners, students who struggle to read, special-needs students)?

11. Are multiple types of assessment used throughout the text (e.g., chapter questions, projects, research, tests, teacher observation)?

12. Are students asked to engage in higher-order thinking throughout the text?

13. How is technology represented throughout the text? How are the students asked to use technology? Teachers?

14. Is a teacher's edition available? Are there special resources for English learners, struggling learners, students with special needs?

15. Are the charts, maps, graphs, tables, and illustrations accurate? Do they help to support students' thinking?

16. Are supplementary materials available (e.g., text on CD, leveled texts, videos)?

Evaluation of a Content Area Textbook

9

 TEACHING IDEAS:

• THINK-ALOUD • SEMANTIC QUESTION MAP • CONNECTION STEMS • SKETCH AND LABEL CONNECTIONS • PURPOSE QUESTIONS • BOOKMARK TECHNIQUE • CONCEPT OF DEFINITION MAP • INTERNET-RELATED PROJECTS

Teaching Culturally and Linguistically Diverse Students

As teachers in the 21st century, we find ourselves living in a time in which English learners are the fastest-growing portion of the U.S. population (Young & Hadaway, 2006). With more than 400 languages spoken in U.S. schools (Hadaway & Young, 2006), we are teaching increasingly high numbers of culturally and linguistically diverse students. "These students offer a rich resource of diversity that can enhance classroom dynamics" (Drucker, 2003, p. 22). Some are immigrants; others are U.S. citizens growing up in contexts in which English is not commonly spoken.

English learners are students who speak one or more languages and are learning English (Opitz & Harding-DeKarn, 2007). Pilgreen (2006) reminds us:

> Language is what enables students to communicate, language is what makes collaboration possible, and using language is a way of transmitting and negotiating knowledge. But language is precisely the barrier that English learners face when they sit in the classroom. (p. 41)

We want to help the English learners in our classes to move past the language barrier and learn content. To help our students learn how to use language more effectively, we will need to learn more about how to teach them (Fitzgerald & Graves, 2004/2005; Young & Hadaway, 2006).

That is why the focus of this chapter is teaching English learners. We begin by examining what we need to do to prepare to teach English learners at the middle and high school levels. Next, we explore the general instructional strategies that help us to teach these students. Then we discuss how we can teach reading comprehension strategies. After that, we examine ideas for teaching academic and functional vocabulary to English learners. Finally, we discuss some guidelines we can follow when teaching English learners.

How Can We Prepare to Teach English Learners?

Go to the Activities and Applications section under the topic *Diversity, Culture, and Literacy* in the MyEducationLab for your course and complete the activity entitled Cultural and Language Experiences to examine ways teachers can create a supportive environment for English learners.

Imagine how challenging it would be for us to learn about our content areas in a language we did not know. This is the challenge English learners face—except they are not just learning one content area, they are learning an entire grade's schedule of classes. As teachers, our goal is to do all we can to help these students be successful. Dong (2004/2005) reports that "Research in second-language acquisition has shown that adapting classroom discussion, textbook reading, and written activities to the language proficiencies of English language learners triggers English language acquisition in subject matter classrooms" (p. 14). Our challenge is to make this goal a reality.

Researchers report that the most important feature of English learners is their diversity (Peregoy & Boyle, 2005; Short & Echevarria, 2005). English learners have diverse backgrounds, languages, and educational experiences. Some are literate in their first languages; others are not. Some have had successful school experiences; others have had little schooling. Perkins-Gough (2007) describes the diversity of English language learners (ELLs) in this way:

Adolescent ELLs differ from native English-speaking students in the dual challenge they face: They must learn to speak, read, and write in English and master complex academic content at the same time. Aside from this common characteristic, however, adolescent ELLs come to the classroom with widely diverse education backgrounds and socioeconomic circumstances. Some are recent immigrants who received effective schooling in their countries of origin, are literate in their native language, and have excellent content knowledge even though they lack English skills. Others came to the United States as refugees fleeing violence, have attended school only intermittently or not at all, and lack basic literacy skills. Some are undocumented, which can affect both their socioeconomic status and, in some states, their postsecondary education opportunities. The largest group of adolescent ELLs (57 percent) was born in the United States but has not developed academic literacy in English for various reasons, such as high mobility. (pp. 90–91)

Researchers tell us that appropriate professional development can help prepare us to teach English learners content and literacy skills (Short & Echevarria, 2004/2005). They suggest that we begin by accepting students from diverse cultural and linguistic backgrounds as capable learners. Figure 9.1 features a glossary of terms related to teaching English learners to help us get started.

To further promote our understanding of these students, researchers suggest that we do what is described in the following sections (Peregoy & Boyle, 2005; Short & Echevarria, 2004/2005; Villegas & Lucas, 2007).

Understand How Students Construct Meaning

As we learned in Chapter 1, constructivism is the process through which students create meaning. It involves the students using their background knowledge to make sense of the new information they are reading. The meaning that is constructed is personal, because each person's background knowledge is different. This is a crucial point for English learners. They may have a great deal of background knowledge in their first language, but it may differ significantly from the background knowledge of native English speakers. For example, there may be structural differences between English and their first language. In English, adjectives often come before nouns; in other languages, adjectives may come after the nouns.

Background knowledge is an essential ingredient in the construction of meaning. The more background knowledge we have, the better we can comprehend. Background knowledge is essential for all readers, but it is particularly important for English learners because it interacts with language proficiency during reading to alleviate comprehension difficulties (Aguilar, Fu, & Jago,

FIGURE 9.1
Glossary of Terms
Related to Teaching
English Learners

Comprehensible content Clear and understandable text. Teachers use a variety of methods to help make the text comprehensible for students.

Comprehensible input Language that students hear or read that is understandable enough for their brains to acquire and process (Krashen, 1982).

Culturally and linguistically responsive teachers Educators who take time to become knowledgeable about and open to students' cultures.

English as a Second Language (ESL) Term commonly used to refer to classes or programs in which English learners are taught.

English learners Students who are learning English in addition to their native language.

L1 Abbreviation that refers to a student's first or native language.

Native language A student's first language.

Scaffolded teaching and learning Providing varying degrees of support throughout the learning process from initial instruction to independent application.

Sheltered instruction Teaching content to English learners "in strategic ways that make the concepts comprehensible while promoting the students' academic language development" (Short & Echevarria, 2004/2005, p. 10).

2007). When teaching English learners, our goals concerning background knowledge are twofold: We need to ensure (1) that our students have background knowledge about a variety of topics and (2) that they are able to activate it. There are many different ways to assess whether students have and can activate background knowledge about a topic. These methods include discussion, engaging in informal writing, and completing activities such as Admit Slips and Tickets Out (see Chapter 10).

Using examples that relate to students' lives helps students build bridges between what they already know and what they are learning. Once again, it is important to remember the diversity of English learners. Knowledge acquired in their cultures may differ from that of native English speakers.

As culturally and linguistically responsive teachers, we need to help students make connections between what they already know and what they need to learn. Imagine the extent and type of background knowledge students might have if we were teaching about immigration in one of our courses. Students whose native language is English may have some background knowledge about immigration, particularly since immigration is a national political issue. By comparison, English learners may have much more to contribute to such a discussion, because they may have recently gone through the immigration process. Examples of books that can be used as read-alouds to facilitate discussions about immigration are listed in Figure 9.2. For more information about read-alouds and a more general list of books to read aloud in the content areas, see Chapter 8.

FIGURE 9.2
Read-Aloud
Books about
Immigration

Blohm, J. M., & Lapinsky, T. (2006). *Kids like me: Voices of the immigrant experience.* Boston, MA: Intercultural Press.

Bode, J. (1991). *New kids in town: Oral histories of immigrant teens.* New York: Scholastic.

Gallo, D. R. (Ed.) (2007). *First crossing: Stories of teen immigrants.* Somerville, MA: Candlewick Press.

Knight, M. B. (1993). *Who belongs here?* Gardiner, ME: Tilbury House.

Lai, H. M., Lim, G., & Yung, J. (1999). *Island: Poetry and history of Chinese immigrants on Angel Island, 1910–1940.* Seattle, WA: University of Washington Press.

Motomura, H. (2006). *Americans in waiting: The lost story of immigration and citizenship in the United States.* New York: Oxford University Press.

Making Connections
TO ENGLISH LEARNERS

Sharing a short text or a picture book through a teacher read-aloud contributes to student motivation and background knowledge. Teacher read-alouds, which are detailed in Chapter 8, are especially helpful to English learners because they eliminate the need for the students to read the text, provide information that supports the topic being studied, and promote discussion. In addition, read-alouds are often accompanied by photographs or illustrations that scaffold the students' understanding of language. ■

Learn about Students' Lives and Appreciate Their Cultures

As teachers, we need to know about our students' families, immigration histories, previous educational experiences, and information such as students' strengths, interests, and attitudes toward school. We can obtain this information in many ways, including learning about our students' backgrounds through conversations with them and their families. We can also use peer interviews, in which native English speakers and English learners can exchange information. Figure 9.3 features questions that can be used during peer interviews. Finally, we can integrate information about students' lives in class assignments and projects.

The information we gather will inform our teaching. For example, throughout this book, we have talked about ideas such as student-centered learning and discussion as natural components of teaching and learning. They are part of our culture, but there are other cultures in which teaching is very lecture based; in those classrooms, discussion and *sharing* ideas do not have an active role. In fact, there are languages in which the word "sharing" does not exist. If we learn that is the case for any of our students, we can incorporate that knowledge into our teaching and offer support as our students gradually become accustomed to student-centered learning and grow more comfortable with sharing their ideas through discussion.

Possess and Promote Positive Views about Diversity

When we are culturally responsive, we view ourselves and our students as participants in a learning community. We set high standards for all students and we inspire our students to gain confidence, participate in rigorous curriculums, use strategies to monitor their learning, strive to meet high standards, and contribute their personal and cultural backgrounds as resources for class learning. To accomplish these goals, we need to understand both ourselves and our students.

FIGURE 9.3
Peer Interview
Questions

Family
1. Please tell me about your family. Share photos, if possible.
2. When did your family come to the United States? What country did you come from? (Provide a world map, so both students can show the countries from which their families immigrated.)

Education
1. What do you like most about school? Why do you like it?
2. What was school like in the country in which you used to live?

Special Interests
1. How do you use technology in your life (computers, cell phones, digital cameras)? (Have a computer available.)
2. Do you like music? What is your favorite band? (Have CDs available.)
3. Do you watch television? What is your favorite television program?
4. What do you like to do when we are not in school?

We need to create ways to support English learners' abilities to learn content and acquire a new language. To do so, we will need to use supports such as welcoming the students' first languages into our classrooms, ensuring the prominence of vocabulary study, using cooperative learning, and incorporating culturally relevant materials into our lessons.

Work Collaboratively with Colleagues to Provide Support for English Learners

When we teach English learners, we can join or organize support teams. For example, schools often have ESL teachers whose focus is teaching the English language to students who are not native speakers. Developing positive relationships with these teachers can be helpful. This is especially true when we integrate students' native languages into our classes as a scaffold and when we need to know how much scaffolding particular students may need. Other members of such a support team may include, but are not limited to, literacy coaches and upper-grade students, as well as community volunteers, who speak students' first languages. When we partner with those who speak students' native languages, we can use those languages to help English learners access our curricula. Villegas and Lucas (2007) suggest that providing materials in students' native languages, such as informational articles, text adaptations, leveled text, or textbooks, can help them build background knowledge.

Making Connections | **Thinking about Working with Other Professionals**

■ Think about the value of working with a team of professionals to support students who are English learners. Reflect on how being a team member might enrich your teaching. Consider what you perceive to be the positive and negative points of such collaborative efforts. Focus on specific examples.

■ Share your thoughts with others in small-group discussions.

Understanding learning from a constructivist perspective, learning about our students' lives and appreciating their cultures, and having and promoting positive views about diversity will provide a sound foundation for teaching English learners. Of course, accomplishing each of these tasks should not be solely a personal effort or a team effort, but rather one in which entire school districts and communities engage.

Making Connections | **Thinking about English Learners**

■ Most of us are familiar with the phrase, "It takes a village to raise a child." Let's apply this idea to teaching English learners. It takes a community to make resources available to English learners, to teach them, and to provide them with full access to the community in which they and their families live. Consider how school administrators, community members, business leaders, and regional families can help these students reach their maximum potential. Focus on specific ideas. Then reflect on what you and fellow faculty members can do to enrich English learners' education.

■ Share your thoughts with others in small-group discussions.

What General Instructional Techniques Can We Use to Support Our Teaching of English Learners?

When we have established a solid foundation for teaching English learners, we will need to think about general approaches to instruction. We know that language acquisition involves the interplay of many factors (Hadaway & Young, 2006), and we want English learners to experience success in our content area courses. Researchers suggest that English learners need opportunities to gain knowledge, feel successful, acquire strategies, monitor learning, and be motivated to practice (Koskinen, Blum, Bisson, Phillips, Creamer, & Baker, 1999). In this section, we focus on general teaching techniques that will help ensure their success. These include scaffolded teaching and learning, sheltered instruction, and accessible text, among others.

Scaffolded Teaching and Learning

When we scaffold learning, we use supports to help students gain knowledge. For example, when we teach reading comprehension strategies, we provide the necessary supports, by explaining and modeling the strategies. This may include using think-alouds that provide a model for active thinking during the reading process.

TEACHING IDEA

Go to the Activities and Applications section under the topic *Comprehension Strategies* in the MyEducationLab for your course and complete the activity entitled Think Alouds to Model Comprehension to examine why this strategy can be effective with English learners.

THINK-ALOUD. Think-Alouds (Davey, 1983) help us to understand what we are reading. To teach your students how to use think-alouds, follow these steps:

1 **Explain:** Select a passage to read aloud to the students. The passage should require some strategic thinking to clarify understandings. Explain that we use Think-Alouds to model strategic behaviors and thoughts as we engage in the reading process. That is, we use Think-Alouds to help ourselves focus on strategically thinking our way through text. Then introduce the text.

2 **Demonstrate:** Before reading, demonstrate your connections to the text by thinking aloud. To make text-self connections, use prompts such as "I have a connection to this because . . ." and "This reminds me of . . ." To make text–text connections, use prompts such as "I read about this in an article and it said . . ." or "I read about this on the Internet and it said . . ." As you read, think aloud to demonstrate other reading comprehension strategies, including monitoring, visualizing, and summarizing. The following examples show how you might think aloud while using reading strategies.

- Monitoring—ensuring that what we have read made sense: "I read this section about mitosis, but it does not make sense to me. I am going to go back and read it more slowly."
- Visualizing—making mental pictures while reading: "When I read about mitosis and meiosis, I pictured how they were different in my mind. I am going to sketch my visualization so I can share what I am seeing in my mind with you."
- Summarizing—synthesizing important ideas: "This part of the chapter is about meiosis. I know that I will be writing a summary about it when I finish reading, so I am going to take notes about the definition of meiosis, because I think that is important information to include in the summary."

3 **Guide:** After demonstrating the Think-Aloud several times, invite the English learners to practice with native English-speaking partners.

4 **Practice:** After sufficient practice, encourage students to try Think-Alouds on their own using text in which they have interest and about which they have background knowledge.

5 **Reflect:** Invite students to reflect on how thinking aloud helps them to focus on what they are reading. Encourage them to think about how they can use Think-Alouds in other subject areas.

Next, students can work with a partner as they attempt new tasks—in this case, using new strategies. Finally, students can apply the strategies independently. Throughout this process, we are gradually releasing responsibility for learning to the students, who learn about the strategies from the teacher, try them with a partner, and then try them on their own. There are a number of scaffolds we can use when teaching English learners, including using the student's native language.

Sheltered Instruction

Sheltered instruction involves teaching content to English learners "in strategic ways that make the concepts comprehensible while promoting the students' academic language development" (Short & Echevarria, 2004/2005, p. 10). One method for teaching sheltered instruction is to use the Sheltered Instruction Observation Protocol (SIOP). The SIOP Model is a "scientifically validated model of sheltered instruction designed to make grade-level academic content understandable for English learners while at the same time developing their English language" (Echevarria, Vogt, & Short, 2008, p. 246). The SIOP Model is a lesson planning and delivery system; the SIOP protocol is an instrument used to observe, rate, and provide feedback on lessons (Echevarria et al., 2008).

The following sheltered instruction techniques are recommended by a number of researchers (Genesee, 1999; Short & Echevarria, 2004/2005; Peregoy & Boyle, 2005). We can use these methods in our teaching.

USING COOPERATIVE LEARNING. Engaging English learners in cooperative learning supports them in a variety of ways. For example, students in the group who speak English can provide fluent language models. They can also listen to and support the English learners as they communicate their thoughts. In addition, learning in a peer setting is often motivational for students. Because valuing the ideas of others is a basic premise of cooperative learning, all students have opportunities to successfully participate in the learning process.

MAKING CONNECTIONS TO STUDENT EXPERIENCES. Students construct meaning by making connections between their background knowledge and experiences and the information that they are learning. The more background knowledge the students have, the better they comprehend. We also know that if students don't have background knowledge of or experiences with a topic, we can provide information in several ways, including through read-alouds, discussion, and sharing visuals.

USING SLOWER SPEECH AND FEWER IDIOMATIC EXPRESSIONS. As teachers, we should ensure that we not speak too quickly when teaching English learners so we can be fluent English language models and help students understand what we are saying. We should also try to avoid the use of idiomatic expressions, because they do not translate literally. Examples of idiomatic expressions include the following phrases:

- Actions speak louder than words
- Against the clock
- Dot all the i's and cross all the t's
- Lose face
- Take a raincheck
- Think outside the box
- Time flies
- Two heads are better than one

USING VISUAL SUPPORTS AND DEMONSTRATIONS WITH VERBAL INSTRUCTION. When we use visual supports such as pictures and demonstrations, we provide additional cues for English learners. For example, showing pictures of fruits and vegetables or the actual fruits may make it easier for English learners to understand the concept of nutritious foods. Demonstrating how to search for information about a topic on the Internet, in addition to providing directions, may help students to better understand how they should search.

USING ADAPTED TEXT AND SUPPLEMENTARY MATERIALS. When we paraphrase text, provide text on CD or tape, or make leveled text available, we support English learners' comprehension of text. Paraphrasing allows us to present the text in a less complex format.

Accessible Text

When teaching English learners, we must ensure that our students have accessible text—text they can read. This often means that we need to adapt texts and provide study aids. In this section, we examine several ways to help make text more accessible to our students. Examples include scaffolded outlines, study guides, rewritten texts, texts on tape or CD, and leveled texts. When reading about these processes, consider the benefits of working with English as a Second Language (ESL) teachers and fellow content area teachers.

SCAFFOLDED OUTLINES. Scaffolded outlines provide an opportunity for students to take limited notes. In a scaffolded outline, we provide part of the outline and students add to it. Students then use the outline to support their understanding of the content. Having a topic-based outline that uses key words and simplified language helps English learners comprehend.

The best way to introduce these outlines to English learners is to scaffold the process—beginning by providing a great deal of support and very gradually encouraging the learner to take more responsibility. For example, we would begin by providing outlines that are essentially complete. Over time, we would provide increasingly less information and require the students to add more. For example, when studying "the active sun" in earth science, a section of an outline we might usually provide for students would differ from a scaffolded outline that we would create for English learners. Figure 9.4 shows parallel sections of a traditional outline and a scaffolded outline with supports for English learners. The outlines are based on a section of text titled "The Active Sun" in Tarbuck and Lutgens' *Earth Science* (Prentice Hall, 2006).

STUDY GUIDES. Creating study guides in which we use simple language, key vocabulary, simple sentences, and meaningful questions is another way we can help English learners understand what they read. When structuring these guides, it is important to note the structure of the text for which the guide will be used. For example, many content area texts have subheadings, so study guides for those texts should have the same subheadings. Other texts have subheadings and a variety of tables and figures. If that is the case, we can create guides that loosely parallel the structure of the pages students will be reading. This consistency will help English learners to make connections between the information in the guide and the information that appears in the text. In addition, numbering each section of the page may help English learners to locate the area to which the teacher or partner may be referring.

Figure 9.5 shows an excerpt from a study guide for chemistry. The section to which the guide applies is primarily print (text), but does include one figure.

REWRITTEN TEXT. We can also rewrite text in simple sentences, focusing on text frames, the main idea, and supporting details. This approach works particularly well if we can share the task with peers. For example, if we teach chemistry and two other teachers teach the same course and use the same text, then each teacher can take responsibility for rewriting designated chapters. Copies of the rewritten text can be kept in three-ring notebooks that allow students to easily add or delete information.

FIGURE 9.4
Traditional and Scaffolded Outline Examples: Earth Science— "The Active Sun"

Traditional Outline Example	Scaffolded Outline Example
I. The active sun	1. Why is the sun described as "active"? (page 687)
A. Sunspots	2. What are sunspots? See Figure 15. (page 687)
B. Prominences	3. What are prominences? See Figure 16. (page 688)
C. Solar flares	4. What are solar flares? (page 688)
	• How do they impact solar wind?
	• What are auroras? What else are they called?
	• What happens following a strong solar flare? See Figure 17.

FIGURE 9.5
Excerpt from a
Study Guide for
Matter and
Measurement: The
Study of Chemistry

Chemistry: The Central Science (2008)

Making Connections to What We Know (Activating Background Knowledge)

We may think we do not know anything about chemistry, but we can see chemistry in our lives every day. The authors of our textbook tell us that when we light a match, that is chemistry. When drugs are developed to cure diseases, that is chemistry. So, even though we may not have studied chemistry before, we see it happening every day.

Chemistry is the study of properties of materials and the changes that materials undergo. Chemistry is how leaves change color in the fall and how batteries generate electricity. Chemistry is how our bodies use food. Chemistry is how our world works.

Key Vocabulary

1. What is matter? **Matter is the physical material of the universe.** It is anything that has mass and occupies space. Houses have mass and occupy space. Cars have mass and occupy space. Even our textbook has mass and occupies space.

2. What is a property? **A property is any trait or characteristic that allows us to know that one type of matter is different from another.**

3. What are atoms? **Atoms are the smallest building blocks of matter.**

4. What are molecules? **Two or more atoms can combine to form molecules.** (See Figure 1.1.)

5. Sketch molecular models of oxygen, water, and carbon dioxide. (See Figure 1.1.)

The **white spheres** represent **hydrogen.** When you sketch a hydrogen molecule, write an **H** on it.

The **dark gray spheres** represent **carbon.** When you sketch a carbon molecule, write a **C** on it.

The **red spheres** represent **oxygen.** When you sketch an oxygen molecule, write an **O** on it.

1. **Oxygen Molecular Model**

2. **Water Molecular Model**

3. **Carbon Dioxide Molecular Model**

TEXT ON TAPE OR CDS IN ENGLISH AND IN NATIVE LANGUAGES. Having texts on tape or CDs can support English learners in gaining knowledge of content and developing fluency as they read along. Having simultaneous access to the written text and the oral reading will provide students with opportunities to see, to listen, and to read along to improve their fluency. To enrich this process, invite students to work with partners who are fluent, native English speakers. Texts in native languages provide support and help students to learn content. Some publishers also provide texts in languages other than English and sectional summaries on CD-ROM. Miller and Levine's *Biology* (Prentice-Hall, 2008) is an example of a text for which such materials are available. Working with other teachers and with students who have already completed the course can also facilitate the development of a text on tape or CD library.

Go to the Activities and Applications section under the topic *Developing Vocabulary, Concepts, and Fluency* in the MyEducationLab for your course and complete the activity entitled Vocabulary and Content Area Learning to examine why it is helpful to work with English learners on content-specific vocabulary.

LEVELED TEXTS. We can also use texts about the topic being studied that have readability levels lower than that of the course textbook. English learners can read these texts while the other students are reading more complex texts, such as the course textbook. The information would focus on the same topic, but the leveled texts would be easier to read. These texts can be used to support English learners as they read about the topic in everyday settings, or they can be the texts that English learners read when the class engages in Discussion circles. (To learn more about Discussion Circles, see Chapter 8.) In the latter case, each student in the group would read a different title, and share the book they had read with the group. For the English learner, the book would be selected from leveled text.

All of these techniques will help us successfully face the challenges of planning instruction for this highly diverse group of learners. Of course, throughout our teaching, we also need to encourage English learners to use multiple modes of response, including speaking, writing, sketching, dramatizing, and music. For example, when students engage in the Say Something, they respond orally (see Chapter 5). When they complete a Scaffolded Outline, they respond in writing (see page 145). Sketching is a mode of response students use when they create Sketch and Label Connections (see Chapter 6) or complete adapted versions of teaching ideas such as the Bookmark Technique (see Chapter 5). To engage in activities such as Dinner Party and Living Newspaper Theatre (see Chapter 12), students dramatize. To respond through singing, students can create Lyric Summaries or participate in Rapping for Review (see Chapter 13).

Making Connections
TO STRUGGLING READERS

Although the scaffolding techniques discussed in this chapter are designed to benefit English learners, many of them also support the learning experiences of struggling readers. For example, struggling readers would benefit from the use of multiple modes of response, adapted graphic organizers, scaffolded outlines, and leveled texts. ■

Engaging, Guiding, and Extending Student Thinking

When teaching English learners, it is important that we use a structured approach. The SIOP Lesson Plan Design Template 1 provides a research-based lesson design for sheltered instruction (Echevarria et al., 2008, p. 230). In the SIOP Lesson Plan, there is a section labeled "Lesson Sequence", in which we can use the classic three-part lesson plan commonly known as *before*, *during*, and *after reading* that we use throughout this text. Viewing the stages of this plan as *engaging*, *guiding*, and *extending* student thinking helps us to make connections between our planning and our view of reading as a thinking process. This lesson format also provides the perfect opportunity to focus on reading comprehension strategies. Roit (2006) supports this approach and notes, "Teaching reading comprehension creates the perfect environment for English learners to not only learn how to derive meaning from text but also to learn how to talk about text and about what they are learning" (p. 80).

Each section of this plan has particular purposes. Figure 9.6 shows examples of what we can do during each stage.

As noted in the figure, *before* reading, we engage students' thinking by motivating them and helping them to make connections to their background knowledge. *During* reading, we provide a variety of ways to guide students' thinking by helping them monitor their understanding. *After* reading, we encourage students to engage in summarizing and completing a variety of projects to extend their thinking. Discussion permeates the plan. Details of each stage follow.

Engaging	Guiding	Extending
Activating or building background knowledge (read-alouds, films, photos, websites)	Teacher read-aloud of short section of text	Making connections to life experiences
Making text–self connections	Reading along with text on CD	Summarizing
Providing text overviews or scaffolded outlines	Patterned Partner Reading	Informal writing
Explaining directions	Cross-age reading experiences	Alternative modes of response
Developing purpose questions	Using purpose questions to guide reading	Inquiry-based projects/rubrics Discussion
Preteaching vocabulary and essential concepts	Bookmark Technique	
Obtaining assistance from native language speakers	Adapting text/accessible text	
Discussion	Discussion	
	Sketching	
	Informal writing	

FIGURE 9.6
Engaging, Guiding, and Extending Student Thinking

Engaging Students' Thinking (Before Reading)

Before reading, we engage students' thinking. Roit (2006) notes that motivation is key to reading comprehension for English learners. We motivate our students to read in a variety of different ways, including sharing pictures, visiting a website, or engaging in a read-aloud. We want to ensure that our students have background knowledge. If they don't have background knowledge, we engage in preteaching to provide it. We help them to activate this knowledge through discussion or use of a comprehension strategy. We also help students to set purposes for reading. Reading comprehension strategies, key vocabulary concepts, and discussion are prevalent in this stage.

If we know that the English learners in our classes do not have any background knowledge about a particular topic or strategy, we can preteach them. This involves a brief period of time away from the rest of the class in which we can (1) explain a concept we will be teaching later that day or (2) explain and demonstrate a graphic organizer the rest of the class already knows how to use. In the first case, preteaching content will help the students to feel more comfortable as they recognize related terminology while learning about the topic with the class. In the second case, preteaching the graphic organizer will help the English learners to feel comfortable using it with other class members. When we teach English learners about graphic organizers, we often number the sections of the organizer, so students can attend to them more readily. We can also simplify their structure if the model is too complex.

In the *before reading* stage of the lesson, there are many different ways to engage English learners (see Chapters 4 and 7). Two possibilities are discussed next.

TEACHING IDEA

SEMANTIC QUESTION MAP. Using a Semantic Question Map (McLaughlin, 2003) instead of the more common Semantic Map helps to focus students' thinking on predetermined questions and set purposes for reading. As presented in Figure 9.7, the components of the Semantic Question Map are determined before the students begin working with the map. The students' task is to contribute responses to the four questions that have been posed. This structure helps to focus student thinking, as do the numbers that appear before each question and in the corresponding numbered spaces where students can write their responses. In the traditional Semantic Map, responses are less structured and categories emerge from students' responses.

The Semantic Question Map featured in Figure 9.7 was used in a science class learning about the world environment. It provides examples of predetermined questions about the rainforests,

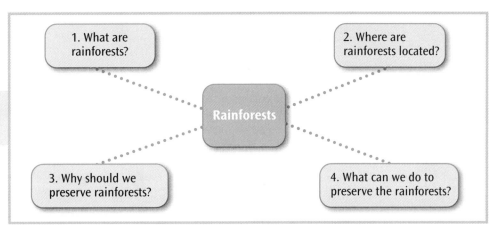

FIGURE 9.7
Semantic Question Map about Rainforests

which were one aspect of the discussion. This was an especially good choice of topic, because asking about the locations of rainforests may invite English learners to refer to their native lands.

For more information about the Semantic Question Map and the more traditional Semantic Map, see Chapters 4 and 7.

 **CONNECTION STEMS AND SKETCH AND LABEL CONNECTIONS.** We can teach our students how to make text–self connections, text–text connections, and text–world connections (Harvey & Goudvis, 2000) to help them activate their background knowledge. See Chapter 4 for detailed descriptions of these teaching ideas and teaching examples; see Figure 4.10 for an example of Sketch and Label Visualizations. We can adapt the process of making connections for English learners by focusing on connections to their lives and changing the mode of response from only oral to sketch and label, followed by sharing with a peer.

Guiding Students' Thinking (During Reading)

During reading, we help to guide students' thinking, as they interact with text, construct meaning, and share ideas. Reading comprehension strategies, individual/partner perceptions, and discussion are evident in this stage.

TEACHING IDEA **PURPOSE QUESTIONS.** To help students focus on particular sections of text, we can use Purpose Questions. These are easily constructed by turning text subheadings into questions to help guide students' reading. For example, in a geometry chapter about triangles, a subheading might read "Right Triangles." Our purpose question might be, "What are right triangles?" or "How do right triangles differ from other triangles?" English learners would then read to find the answer to that question. When they find it, they could sketch a right triangle to show that they understand what it is.

TEACHING IDEA **BOOKMARK TECHNIQUE.** We use Bookmark Technique (McLaughlin, 2003) to help students set purposes for and monitor their reading. There are four types of Bookmarks, each of which seeks particular information. Bookmark 1 asks students what they thought was most interesting. Bookmark 2 asks them to find and attempt to define a vocabulary word they think everyone needs to learn. The third Bookmark asks students to share something they found confusing. The fourth Bookmark asks them to explain a chart, map, graph, or illustration that helped them to understand what they have read. We can adapt the Bookmark Technique by numbering the sections of the Bookmarks, simplifying the language, and offering students the option of sketching some of the responses instead of writing them. Figure 9.8 shows both the original Vocabulary Bookmark and a Bookmark adapted for use with English learners. For details about how to teach the Bookmark Technique and related student examples, see Chapters 5 and 8. For reproducible organizers, see the Appendix.

FIGURE 9.8
Bookmark Technique

Extending Students' Thinking (After Reading)

When students have finished reading the text, we help them to clarify their understandings and extend their thinking across the curriculum and beyond the classroom. This is also a time when we can reteach concepts students may not have thoroughly understood.

In this *after reading* stage of the lesson, there are a variety of ways to encourage English learners to extend their thinking. Two examples are discussed next.

 **CONCEPT OF DEFINITION MAP.** As we learned in Chapter 7, one of the easiest ways to learn how to summarize informational text is to write a summary based on a completed Concept of Definition Map (Schwartz & Raphael, 1985). See Chapters 7 and 10 for detailed information about and examples of the Concept of Definition Map Summary. Modifications we can make to this graphic organizer include numbering each section so that English learners can attend to sections as we refer to them, and providing the option of sketching in the sections labeled "Comparison" and "What are three examples?" Other ideas that help students summarize using alternative modes of response include Sketch to Stretch (see Chapter 6) and Lyric Summaries (see Chapter 13).

 **INTERNET-RELATED PROJECTS.** Students engage with computers in school for a variety of purposes—from searching for information to participating in school projects that involve communicating with the global education community. Computers offer a number of

supports for English learners. These include colored photos and graphics, access to a variety of sources, and opportunities to read about topics at text levels that may not be as challenging as the levels of class textbooks. As teachers, we can scaffold students' use of computers as an information source by bookmarking class-related websites, preparing scaffolded outlines for selected sites, and providing opportunities for students to engage in projects that we can scaffold. Internet Project (Leu, 2001) and Internet Workshop (Leu, 2002), are two examples of high-interest Internet projects in which students can engage. The first can be used with classrooms around the world, which may allow students who speak the English learner's native language to participate. The second is an individual research project that involves raising a question, using the Internet to seek responses, and analyzing the information. For details about and examples of these projects, see Chapter 11. For other inquiry-based projects, see Chapter 12.

Making Connections
TO MULTIPLE LITERACIES

When English learners use the Internet to participate in projects in which they generate search questions, locate information, synthesize the information, and communicate it to others, they are engaging in informational literacy (Leu, Kinzer, Coiro, & Cammack, 2004). Depending on their previous experiences, English learners may need to learn how to use, or require extra support when using, the Internet to engage in information literacy across the curriculum. This is a need that may be addressed through collaboration with other content area teachers, ESL teachers, computer specialists, and school administrators. ■

The engaging, guiding, and extending students' thinking (before, during, and after) lesson structure contributes to the context for learning. It helps students to make connections to text and provides a variety of ways in which students can express their ideas. Haag and Williams (2004) support this thinking and remind us to encourage English learners to use these alternative formats to demonstrate what they know and can do. They also suggest that we should listen carefully to English learners' responses.

Figure 9.9 features a biology lesson plan that was created using the engaging–guiding–extending students' thinking format. Note how the teacher integrated supports for English learners throughout the lesson plan. The Pennsylvania State Standards are listed as the related standards in Part 1.

Making Connections
TO WRITING

Student writing is an integral part of the biology lesson shown in Figure 9.9. It is important to note that we can support English learners' writing in a variety of ways—for example, by providing illustrations and creating a word wall with photos that focuses on the current topic of study. We can also . scaffold students' learning of summary writing (see Chapter 10). ■

Aguilar, Fu, and Jabo (2007) note that in addition to well-structured lessons, we need to provide English learners with time to actually use the language. Offering access to a variety of texts, opportunities for choice, time for informal writing, fluent reading models, and social interaction with native English speakers will motivate students to become active language learners. Throughout these opportunities, we want our students to experience comprehensible text—language that students hear or read that is understandable enough for their brains to acquire and process (Krashen, 1982).

FIGURE 9.9   Biology Lesson Plan with Supports for English Learners

Content Area Reading Lesson Plan

Text: Chapter 3, "The Biosphere"; Section 3-2, "Energy Flow" in Miller, K. R., & Levine, S. J. (2008). *Biology.* Upper Saddle River, NJ: Prentice Hall.

I. Goals and Related Standards

Students will

- Use a Semantic Question Map. Standards: learning to read independently; quality of speaking and listening.
- Discuss. Standards: read, analyze and interpret text.
- Use Bookmark Technique. Standards: learning to read independently.
- Describe and discuss ecological pyramids. Standards: explain the structure and functional similarities and differences found among living things (biological sciences).
- Create six-slide PowerPoint presentations. Standards: learning to read independently; types and quality of writing, speaking, and listening; utilize computer software (technology).
- English Language Proficiency Standard 4: English language learners communicate information, ideas, and concepts necessary for academic success in the content area of science. Grade level Cluster: 9–12.

II. Engaging Students' Thinking

I will begin the lesson by reviewing what we have learned about food chains, food webs, and their trophic levels.* Then I will discuss *pyramids* with the students to help them activate their background knowledge about them. Next, I will explain the Semantic Question Map and model how it works. I will explain to the students that the focus words for the Map will be the *ecological pyramid.*

I will begin completing the Map by thinking aloud. I will ask myself, "What is it?" I will respond by saying, "An ecological pyramid is a diagram in a pyramid shape that shows the relative amounts of energy or matter contained within each trophic level in a food chain or food web." Then I will write my response on the Semantic Question Map.

Next, I will invite the students to work with a partner to explain the definition of *ecological pyramid* to each other and sketch the pyramid. I will monitor students' discussion and assist as necessary.

Then I will invite the students to help me respond to the remaining questions. When responding to question 2, we might say, "An energy pyramid shows that organisms pass on only small amounts of energy to the next level because they use much of the energy they store for respiration (breathing), movement, and reproduction." In response to question 3, we might say, "A biomass pyramid represents the amount of potential food available for each trophic level in an ecosystem." In response to question 4, we might say, "A pyramid of numbers refers to the number of individual organisms at each trophic level." When the Map is completed, we will discuss it and create a summary of the Semantic Question Map.

III. Guiding Students' Thinking

I will begin by introducing the section of the text on Ecological Pyramids. Next, we will make connections from the text to our completed Semantic Question Map. Then I will explain to the students that they will be using Patterned Partner Reading, using the pattern Read–Pause–Sketch-Share, to read the text.* I will explain that they will have 20 minutes to complete the reading. I will monitor as students engage in Patterned Partner Reading and assist as necessary. When the reading is completed, we will discuss what the students have read and the illustrations that appear as supports in that section of the chapter.

IV. Extending Students' Thinking

Students will extend their thinking by forming small groups and creating six-slide PowerPoint* presentations about ecological pyramids or a previously studied topic such as producers, consumers, and feeding relationships. Each group will address a different topic and share its presentation with the class. Before the students begin this project, I will provide them with a checklist to ensure that they include all of the necessary elements and present their work in a professional manner.

V. Assessment

I will

- Observe students as they contribute to the Semantic Question Map.
- Observe students' discussion to monitor participation and understanding.
- Observe students as they engage in Patterned Partner Reading and express their understandings through their sketches.
- Observe students as they work cooperatively in small groups.
- Use a checklist to assess students' PowerPoint presentations.

*I will meet with the English learner students to preteach the concepts in the section of text about ecological pyramids. I will use the illustrations of the various pyramids as visual supports. Preteaching using the text illustrations will provide the students with background knowledge about the topic before they participate in the lesson.

*I will pair students so that English learners will read with a more capable and fluent reader. I chose to use the Read–Pause–Sketch–Share) Pattern so English learners would be able to engage in sketching as an alternative mode of response.

*I will group students to ensure that English learners are supported. If needed, I will preteach English learners to create PowerPoint presentations.

Making Connections | Thinking about English Learners

■ Reflect on the need to provide English learners with opportunities to use the language. Consider what you can do to help these students become active language learners in your content area. Think about specific examples.

■ Share your thoughts with others in small-group discussions.

How Can We Teach Vocabulary to English Learners?

Discussions about teaching vocabulary to English learners generally focus on two types of language: functional and academic. Dong (2004/2005) notes that we should teach academic, discipline-specific language systematically and pay close attention to the functional use of language in our classrooms.

Teaching Academic Vocabulary

Gersten and Baker (2002) suggest the following guidelines for selecting and teaching academic vocabulary to English learners:

■ *Limit the number of new vocabulary words introduced in a lesson.* This is now a widely accepted idea in the teaching of vocabulary. Although some of us can recall times when teachers assigned twenty or more new words at the start of each chapter, today we are more likely to focus on five or six. These are generally terms that are critical to students' understanding of the material in the chapter.

■ *Teach the words in a variety of ways and ensure multiple exposures.* In the past, students were often told to look up words in a dictionary. Now, however, we teach terms in several different ways. For example, we might use (1) graphic organizers such as the Concept of Definition Map or Semantic Question Map; (2) the Vocabulary Bookmark from Bookmark Technique; (3) Context Clues; (4) Narrow Reading; and (5) teacher read-alouds to help students learn particular terms.

■ *Select words that convey key concepts, are widely used in content, and have meaning to the students' lives.* Although this practice specifically refers to words that are essential for students' understanding of our disciplines, words that are relevant across content areas would also be included. It is especially motivational if the terms students are learning relate to their lives. This link helps students to see beyond the classroom to their need to use the terms in their everyday lives.

■ *Use visuals such as graphic organizers to help students process and integrate word knowledge.* Using graphic organizers helps English learners remember the various aspects of a concept by identifying the information with a particular section of the graphic. Although this is certainly helpful, our teaching should not stop there. We need to move beyond promoting students' initial understanding of terms to ensure that the words become part of their speaking and writing vocabularies.

When teaching vocabulary to English learners, Echevarria and Graves (1998) suggest that we define words with the support of pictures, demonstrations, and examples familiar to students. Nagy (1988) proposes that we relate the words to familiar concepts, integrate new words by building prior knowledge, process words using new vocabulary to describe reality, and promote oral language development and listening comprehension. Dong (2004/2005) notes that extensive real-life examples help create a rich context in which students discover meaning for themselves.

Narrow reading and read-alouds are two effective methods for helping English learners to expand their vocabularies. Narrow reading focuses on students selecting texts from collections that either teachers or students and teachers have organized. Teachers select the texts they will use when reading aloud to the class. Details of these two techniques follow.

NARROW READING. Schmitt and Carter (2000) suggest that we engage students in narrow reading, which supports vocabulary acquisition. With this approach, students read authentic texts about a particular topic from many different sources. This helps the words to become part of the students' vocabularies. For example, students could read articles about global warming found in newspapers, in magazines, or on the Internet. Although the articles would come from different sources and would be written by different authors, they would feature common vocabulary. This would offer students multiple exposures to a variety of terms related to global warming.

READ-ALOUDS. Reading aloud to students every day promotes language development and vocabulary acquisition. We can read a wide variety of materials, ranging from theme-related picture books to articles found on the Internet, and from poetry to ongoing segments of theme-related biographies or novels. When we read aloud, students are free to relax and construct personal meaning. When reading aloud to English learners, it is a good idea to stop periodically to ensure understanding. Teaching ideas such as Photographs of the Mind (Keene & Zimmerman, 1997), and "Say Something" (Short, Harste, & Burke, 1996) work well when we are reading aloud to students.

- *Photographs of the Mind* is a simple graphic organizer that has four sections in which students can sketch their ideas in response to what teachers read. When we read aloud, we predetermine four stopping points—usually three during the reading of the text and one at the end. When we stop, students quickly sketch what they are thinking at that time. Then they share and discuss their sketches with their peers. This practice is especially beneficial because it offers students an opportunity to use sketching as an alternative mode of response. (See Chapter 5.)

- *Say Something* involves each student commenting to a peer when we stop at predetermined points. They literally Say Something to each other after short segments of the text are read. The exchanges are often supported by prompts such as "I did not know that . . ." or "I was surprised to learn that . . ." (see Chapter 5.)

Both Photographs of the Mind and Say Something create comfortable contexts for English learners because the students are only sharing their responses—either sketched or oral—with a peer. For details about these and other teaching ideas, see Chapters 4, 5, 6, and 7. (For more detailed information about using read-alouds in the content areas, see Chapter 8.)

When teaching vocabulary to English learners, Beck, McKeown, and Kucan (2002) suggest that we select an appropriate number of words for students to learn and create activities that provide multiple, diverse ways for students to practice. Approaches such as those listed next help us to scaffold and encourage students' learning of vocabulary:

- Provide numerous opportunities to say and write new words.
- Use word maps and word walls.
- Create sentence walls as a visual language scaffold (Carrier & Tatum, 2006).
- Use pictures or short video segments associated with keywords.
- Provide opportunities to practice language in an environment in which students feel safe.
- Encourage students to use their familiarity with the language of technology.
- Use the vocabulary during class.

Functional Vocabulary

When thinking about what functional terms we need to teach to English learners, it is a good idea to meet with other content area teachers as well as the English as a Second Language (ESL) teachers in our school. Together, we can brainstorm a meaningful list of functional vocabulary terms that our English learners will use across the curriculum. For example, we will all want the students to understand words such as *summary* and *concept*. We will also want the students to learn text pattern words such as *cause and effect, comparison and contrast*, and *problem and solution* and words that help us generate questions at multiple levels, including *imagine, predict*, and *justify*. (For more information about teaching text patterns and signal words for generating questions, see Chapter 8.) The ESL teachers can make suggestions about developing the list of functional vocabulary terms as well as ideas about how to teach them—especially about creating links from students' native languages to English. Learning a common list of functional terms will help our students to make connections across the curriculum. These terms can then be featured on word walls within each classroom.

When focusing on functional language, Dong (2004/2005) suggests we should promote English learners' participation. We can do this by checking on students' understanding during discussions ("What we are saying is . . ."), summarizing periodically ("The main point of our discussion is . . ."), and defining and discussing key vocabulary ("This means . . .").

Researchers note that poor vocabulary is a major cause of reading comprehension problems for English learners (Carlo et al., 2004). It is especially important that we help these students learn both functional and academic vocabulary. We can partner with other teachers to select functional vocabulary on which we will place a shared focus. We can also agree to teach students academic terms that extend beyond our discipline. Finally, we can ensure that we provide a wide range of authentic opportunities for students to use academic and functional vocabulary, teach a variety of effective vocabulary study techniques, and ensure that students learn words through a variety of modes, including seeing, hearing, and sketching.

When Using These Ideas for Teaching English Learners, What General Principles Should We Follow?

There are several general guidelines we can follow to help ensure that our teaching of English learners is effective:

1. We should teach from a culturally responsive perspective and establish high standards for English learners.
2. We should welcome diversity and teach all students from a constructivist perspective.
3. Working with peers, students, and families to learn about our students' cultural and linguistic backgrounds will help us to gain greater understanding of our students.
4. We need to scaffold teaching and learning to offer ongoing support for our English learners.
5. Sheltered instruction supports content learning.
6. Teaching English learners through explicit models, such as SIOP, provides structure for students' learning.
7. We should work with school administrators, peers, and current and former students to ensure that our English learners have accessible text—in a variety of formats.
8. Working with peers and students can help us provide the necessary supports for English learners in content classes.
9. Supporting English learners to ensure they are comfortable responding orally, in writing, and in other modes is essential.
10. Our teaching should reflect that we have in-depth knowledge of our content area and in-depth understanding of English learners.

FINAL THOUGHTS

Because the English learner population is ever-increasing, it is essential that we continue to learn all we can about how to teach these students effectively. From individual students' backgrounds to appropriate teaching methods and ways to adapt text, there is much we need to know. As Dong (2004/2005) notes, "Our classes are becoming increasingly linguistically and culturally diverse. It is imperative that subject-matter teachers sensitize their instruction to ELLs' backgrounds and needs and teach content knowledge through language" (p. 19).

In the next chapter, we explore writing in the content areas. We discuss a variety of purposes for writing and a number of engaging writing activities.

Teaching Connections

APPLYING WHAT WE HAVE LEARNED

E-Links

In Chapter 3, we learned about the role of state standards when planning instruction. Many states also have Language Proficiency Standards for English Learners. Visit the website for the Department of Education in the state in which you teach or plan to teach. Access the state's Language Proficiency Standards for English Learners. Consider how English learners in your classes can meet these standards. Examine a lesson plan that you have already written and think about how you can include the standards in that lesson. Discuss your ideas with a partner.

EXAMPLES OF WEBSITES FOR STATE LANGUAGE PROFICIENCY STANDARDS FOR ENGLISH LEARNERS

Guidelines for Implementing English Language Proficiency Standards in Iowa
www.iowa.gov/educate/archived/content/view/683/898

Pennsylvania Language Proficiency Standards for English Language Learners PreK–12
www.pde.state.pa.us/esl/lib/esl/Standards_Document_%28June_2007%29.doc

Accountable Talk

English learners are the fastest-growing student population in the United States. Reflect on what that trend means to you as a teacher. Consider how you will accommodate English learners' needs in your teaching. Focus on specific examples, including accessing textbooks, learning vocabulary, and using multiple modes of response. Think about how you can effectively prepare supports for these students. Discuss your thoughts with a partner.

 ### Portfolio/Performance Opportunity

Develop a lesson plan that shows how you would teach English learners using the "engaging, guiding, and extending students' thinking" format.

Meet in small groups with others within your academic discipline. Discuss your lessons, focusing on the instructional and text adaptations you made for English learners. Adapt your lesson for teaching during your field experience. Include it in your portfolio.

TEACHING IDEAS:

• CONTENT AREA INVENTORY • CONTENT HISTORY • QUICKWRITES • ADMIT SLIPS • JOURNALS • DIALOGUE JOURNALS— PROMPTED AND UNPROMPTED • DOUBLE-ENTRY JOURNALS (LEARNING LOGS) • INVESTIGATIVE JOURNALS • WRITTEN CONVERSATIONS • TICKETS OUT • WRITE AND SKETCH IN MATH AND SCIENCE • BE A MATH OR SCIENCE AUTHOR • PARAGRAPH FRAMES • STRUCTURED NOTE TAKING • TEXT BOXES • EYEWITNESS ACCOUNT • DESCRIPTIVE TIMELINE • FIRST-PERSON EXPERIENCES • INQUIRING MINDS • LETTERS • ORAL HISTORY PROJECT • POETRY • STUDENT-AUTHORED ALPHABET BOOKS • TRANSMEDIATIONS • TRAVELOGUES

Writing in the Content Areas

At the beginning of this text, we learned that reading is a thinking process. Reif (2007) describes writing in the same way. Writing in the content areas is students' thinking in print. It enhances their learning and provides insights into how they think. It is not an add-on or something we use on rare occasions. Writing plays a dynamic, ongoing role in our teaching (Romano, 2007).

According to Tierney and Pearson (1983), reading and writing are inextricably linked—they cannot be separated. Brandenburg (2002) notes that learning integrates writing and reading to enhance students' comprehension. Duke and Pearson (2002) report that students who engage in writing in the content areas comprehend better than students who do not. Gammill (2006) agrees, noting, "Those teachers who do include writing components document more student involvement in their own learning and greater gains on test scores" (p. 754).

In this chapter, we explore writing in the content areas. We begin by presenting a rationale for writing in such contexts. Then we examine writing from two perspectives: informal and formal. Next, we investigate a variety of ideas for engaging our students in each type of writing. Following that, we discuss how to assess informal and formal writing. Finally, we consider the general principles we should follow when integrating writing into our content areas.

What Is "Writing to Learn"?

Like reading, writing is a constructivist process (Tierney & Pearson, 1983). Writers construct meaning when they make connections between prior knowledge and new information and then think through how they can best communicate their message. Research reports that writing promotes critical thinking, problem solving, and reading comprehension. Langer and Applebee (1985) see writing as helping students to make connections among what they read, what they understand, and what they think. Researchers agree that writing helps students to become better communicators and, consequently, better learners (Gammill, 2006).

According to Knipper and Duggan (2006), "Writing to learn helps students think about content and find the words to explain what they comprehend, reflect on how they understand the content, and consider what their own processes of learning involve" (p. 469). It engages students, encourages self-questioning, and deepens understanding, which leads to more student-centered classrooms and better test scores (Gammill, 2006; Knipper & Duggan, 2006). It also helps students to become active learners who reflect and think critically about content (Gammill, 2006).

Writing to learn requires that students question at higher thinking levels, analyze what they have learned, and synthesize their thoughts. This process allows us, as teachers, to gain insights into students' thinking processes as well as the products they create. Because it permeates our teaching, technology plays a prominent role in writing to learn. For more detailed information about the role of technology in writing, see Chapter 11.

In the following sections we investigate two types of writing: informal and formal. Informal writing naturally occurs in classroom situations when students write a short response to an open-ended question or create a journal entry. Informal writing is draft-stage writing. Formal writing is associated with long-term projects such as research papers or inquiry-based projects. These products are usually evaluated through the use of scoring guides called rubrics.

How Can We Use Informal Writing in Our Content Area Teaching?

Informal writing occurs in our classrooms every day. This is the type of writing in which students engage when they share their thoughts about content areas, discuss their prior experiences, respond to what they are learning, use reading comprehension strategies, and employ study skills. Figure 10.1 provides an overview of the desired student outcomes as well as corresponding types of informal writing.

Informal writing can usually be completed relatively quickly. For example, students often complete Tickets Out in five minutes at the end of class, and journal entries are often written in fewer than ten minutes. Of course, these times are approximations. We need to be aware of students' abilities and needs when estimating the amount of time they will need to engage in informal writing.

In the following sections, we explore how we can use informal writing in the content areas. We discuss the purposes of informal writing, including students sharing their thoughts about the content areas, the prior knowledge they may have, the ways they respond to learning, and the role of writing in reading strategy use. Then we describe examples of the writing activities that support each purpose.

Discovering Students' Prior Experiences with and Beliefs about Content Areas

To learn what students think about our content areas or about their previous experiences in our content areas, we can consider inviting students to create Content Inventories and Content Histories. These informal writing tasks are especially informative at the start of a course.

 **CONTENT AREA INVENTORY.** In Content Area Inventories, students record their thoughts about content-related topics. Content Area Inventories promote reflection and provide students with an opportunity to express their feelings about a content area they are studying.

To share information about previous experiences in this content area:
- Content histories
- Content inventories

To reveal the nature and depth of students' background knowledge:
- Quickwrites
- Admit slips

To communicate what students have learned and what they think about what they have learned:
- Dialogue journals (prompted and unprompted)
- Double-entry journals (learning logs)
- Investigative journals
- Written conversations
- Tickets out

To create and solve problems:
- Math problems/solutions
- Science experiments/outcomes

To use study skills:
- Paragraph frames
- Structured note taking
- Text boxes

To write summaries:
- Concept of Definition Maps
- Questions into Paragraphs (QuIP)
- Writing summaries independently

FIGURE 10.1
Student Learning Outcomes and Types of Informal Writing

Figure 10.2 contains a World Language Inventory that can be adapted for all subject areas. Richard completed this one when he was studying Spanish.

TEACHING IDEA

CONTENT HISTORY. A content history details a person's development in a particular content area from earliest memory to present day. Inviting students to contemplate their previous experiences in a content area has numerous benefits. For students, it promotes reflection,

FIGURE 10.2
Richard's World-Language Inventory: Spanish

1. **The best thing about the language I am studying is . . .** the culture. Spain has beautiful beaches and great guitar music. It has fascinating traditions like running with the bulls.

2. **The worst thing about the language I am studying is . . .** learning all the new vocabulary words and how to use them correctly when writing.

3. **One way that I use this language outside of school is . . .** at work. Sometimes people speak only Spanish and I can tell them what they owe for their purchase in Spanish.

4. **My favorite part of language class is . . .** speaking Spanish with my friends.

5. **In language class, I like to work in groups to . . .** practice my Spanish. I feel more confident speaking in a small group than in front of the class.

6. **In language class, I like to work . . .** alone to read and comprehend text. Working alone helps me concentrate better.

7. **When I speak the language I am studying, I feel . . .** accomplished. It makes me feel proud to know I can use what I have learned.

8. **My language journal helps me to . . .** keep track of my learning. It helps me know what I need to work on.

9. **When I am using this language, I am really proud of . . .** the way I have learned to understand and use it on my own.

10. **One thing about this language I wish I knew more about is . . .** how to speak with a better accent.

FIGURE 10.3
Mathematics History
Prompts

These prompts are offered to help you create your math history. A math history details a person's mathematical development from earliest memory to present day. Please note that these prompts are intended only to stimulate your thinking. You should feel free to include any information you would like to make your history viable.

1. What is your earliest math memory?

2. Can you recall how or if you used numbers before you entered school?

3. Can you recall any specific experiences from your math education in elementary school? Middle school? High school?

4. Do you remember any person or activity that helped you learn about math?

5. Do you recall any ways you used math outside of school in your elementary, middle, or high school years?

6. Did you enjoy math class at any particular grade level? Why? Why not?

7. Do you feel comfortable using math now? Why? Why not?

8. If you could change one thing about your experiences with math, what would it be? How would you change it?

9. If you could offer advice to students just beginning to study math, what would it be?

10. What are two ways you think you'll use math after you graduate from school?

FIGURE 10.3 Mathematics History Prompts

helps make connections between past and present-day experiences, and cultivates self-understanding. For teachers, it provides insights into students' previous learning experiences that can be used to foster motivation and inform planning. Figure 10.3 features prompts to facilitate this process in mathematics. The prompts are easily adaptable to all content areas. Figure 10.4 shows Lisa's Mathematics History, in which she shares memories from her engagement with math over the years.

Learning What Prior Knowledge Students Have

To learn what background knowledge our students already have about a topic, we often engage in discussion or complete a Semantic Map (see Chapters 4 and 7), but Quickwrites and Admit

FIGURE 10.4
Lisa's Mathematics
History

My earliest math memory is playing "Heigh Ho! The Cherry O" game with my mother. It was one of my favorite games. In this game, the goal was to have the most cherries in your bucket. It taught preschoolers basic math. At home, my parents tried to make math fun. In school, however, I was never a good math student. In elementary school, the teachers always did timed problems. I could do the work, but I just couldn't do the work as fast as the teacher wanted it done. The goal was to see how many problems I could solve in a minute; unfortunately for me that wasn't many.

In middle school, we began learning algebra. I did well mostly due to the fact that my best friend took algebra with me and helped me along the way. In geometry, I was on my own, and I had a terrible teacher. He didn't seem to care whether we understood the problems. He just kept moving along. I was frustrated and couldn't wait for the class to end. I had this teacher two years in a row and didn't do well either time. I think the teacher really hindered my learning and made me fear math all the more. I am the kind of student who needs practice and he just moved on too quickly for me to keep up. He also made me feel dumb when I couldn't solve an equation and that kept me from asking questions that I really should have asked.

In high school, I had my best friend tutor me and I did better in math. I was able to ask her questions I feared that the teacher would laugh at. I have come to realize now that there is no stupid question. I am sure that there were other students just as lost as I was in those math classes. If I could give any advice to my younger self, I would say that it's okay to ask questions and admit when you need help. I'd also say that even though there are some terrible teachers, you shouldn't let one bad experience ruin a whole subject area. You never know what next year will bring. I am still not the world's greatest math student, but when I put my mind to it, I can do it.

When I finish high school, I will use math every day to ensure that I am being paid correctly. I will also use math to calculate my investments and do my taxes.

Slips also provide this information. Neither of these techniques requires more than five minutes of the students' time. We may or may not choose to ask students to include their names on the Quickwrites and Admit Slips, depending on our reason for using them. For example, if we want to know about the general prior knowledge of the entire class, we may not require student names. Conversely, if we want to know what prior knowledge each individual student has, we may require student names.

QUICKWRITES. This informal writing technique requires very little time and provides an effective way to learn what students know about a particular topic. In this reflective activity, students write what they know about a given topic. Depending on when this type of writing takes place, it can provide insight into students' prior knowledge, monitor students' understanding, or summarize what students have learned. This information can help us to determine a starting point for our teaching, assess student learning, and inform future planning. Once the purpose has been set, we should provide the students with a specified period of time—generally three to five minutes; offer them a topic or prompt about what they have just learned or what they know about a related topic; and ask them to write in response to the prompt for the specified amount of time. Figure 10.5 shows an example of a quickwrite about aqueducts.

ADMIT SLIPS. When completing this informal writing measure, students reflect on what they know about a particular topic. Students can write their responses on a graphic organizer (see the Appendix) or on an index card. On the first side, students write what they already know about a topic; on the second side, they write a question they have about that topic. Students need about five minutes to complete their Admit Slips.

This activity is called Admit Slips because teachers collect the slips before formally beginning class. It takes just a few minutes to read the Admit Slips. We should collect them with side one facing up. That way, we can quickly read all of the responses about what students know about the topic. As we read, we should be careful to set aside any responses that may need clarification. Then we can turn all of the Admit Slips over and read the questions students have about the topic. As we read, we should set aside questions that we think we will need to respond to in the next class. This is often just four or five questions, because several questions may be similar. Reading the slips will take only about five minutes.

Admit Slips can be used to assess prior knowledge when we are preparing to teach about a topic or assess student understanding of a topic as we teach it. In the first case, we can use what we learn from the Admit Slips (1) to assess how much—if any—prior knowledge the students already possess and (2) to determine the starting point for our teaching. In the latter case, we can use the information to understand how student learning is progressing. Figure 10.6 shows an Admit Slip that Shaquil wrote about triangles in his geometry class.

Gaining Insights into Students' Thoughts about Content

To learn what our students know about what we have been teaching or what they think about what we have been teaching, we can consider using journals, written conversations, or Tickets Out. These informal writing techniques provide insights into students' thinking about the content being taught.

JOURNALS. Traditional or electronic journals can be maintained in all content areas. Journals offer students a means to use writing to summarize, respond to, or extend their thinking

FIGURE 10.5
Quickwrite about Aqueducts

Prompt: What do you know about aqueducts?

Quickwrite: Aqueducts carry water from one place to another. One of the most famous aqueducts was in Rome. It had underground pipes that carried water all over the city. You can still see the remains of the aqueducts today.

FIGURE 10.6
Shaquil's Admit Slip

I know what triangles are and that there are different kinds. I know that an equilateral triangle has equal sides. My questions are, "What are the other kinds of triangles and how are they different?"

about what they have read. Three types of journals frequently used in the content areas are dialogue, double entry, and investigative.

Journals have many positive outcomes. Students can use them to dialogue with us concerning their thoughts about a particular issue. They can summarize and comment on their thinking as they engage in course-related tasks such as conducting experiments. They can also use journals as a place to record their thoughts about topics for future research or other content investigations. Although journals can be used beneficially in a variety of ways, students often lose interest if journals are overused. For example, when keeping dialogue journals, students may view them as more motivational if used once or twice a week rather than every day.

TEACHING IDEA

DIALOGUE JOURNALS—PROMPTED AND UNPROMPTED. We can dialogue—converse in writing about a variety of topics—with our students in this type of journal. Students can also dialogue with peers. These entries may be prompted or unprompted.

Gordon and Macinnis (1993) suggest that when using prompts, we ask direct questions about learning, such as "What was the Renaissance?" "How do we form the future tense in Spanish?" "What are semiconductors?" or "What is a rhombus?" When using unprompted responses, students can write their reactions to learning, analyze their thinking, attempt to define new topics, or raise questions about what they have learned. Our responses validate students' ideas, offer new information, and/or pose new questions.

Figure 10.7 features mathematics journal prompts that can be adapted for all content areas. Figure 10.8 shows examples of Mary Ann's responses to selected math prompts. Figure 10.9 features an unprompted excerpt from a dialogue journal written by Jason and his English teacher while he was reading *Lord of the Flies*.

When students are creating journal responses, they may self-select a topic to write about or they may respond to a prompt. Prompts may be particularly effective when introducing the concept of math journals or if you need specific feedback from the students. The following example prompts may be used as presented or adapted to facilitate such journal use.

1. Explain what you know about_____(a particular math concept).

2. (A) Create, solve, and explain a math problem using a math concept we studied in class this week. (B) Describe how you used technology to facilitate your work.

3. Explain how you could use_____ (fractions, algebraic equations, geometry, and so on) in another class or outside of school.

4. Use the newspaper to find an example of how a business in our community uses math. Respond to the article in your journal, citing the math concept(s) used and your thoughts on other ways math might benefit the company.

5. Create an acrostic poem about a particular math concept.

6. What are_____ (fractions, decimals, algebraic equations, geometric principles, and so on)?

7. Write questions about something in math you are having difficulty understanding or write questions about something we haven't studied yet that you would like to know about.

8. Draw a mathematician. How might he or she be employed in our community?

9. Describe a mathematically talented character from a book or television series.

10. Create a math problem based on a concept we are studying and explain how you would solve it.

FIGURE 10.7

Mathematics Journal Prompts

1. **Explain what you know about area.**

Area is the space an object takes up. For example, if I were going to carpet a room, I would need to know the area of the room to buy the correct amount of carpet.

5. **Create an acrostic poem about a particular math concept.**

Angles

Angles are two rays that share the same endpoint.

Names for angles are right, obtuse, and acute.

Get the size of an angle by measuring degrees.

Let's use a protractor to create an angle.

Endpoint is called a vertex.

Supplementary angles have degree measurements that equal 180 degrees.

7. **Write questions about something in math you have difficulty understanding or write questions about something we haven't studied yet that you would like to know about.**

When solving an algebraic equation, I would like to know where to begin the equation. Do I start with the equation in the parentheses or do I start with the equation outside the parentheses?

FIGURE 10.8
Examples of Responses to Selected Math Prompts

TEACHING IDEA   **DOUBLE-ENTRY JOURNALS (LEARNING LOGS).** Double-Entry Journals, also known as learning logs, help us to monitor students' reading outside of class, promote reflection, and provide solid foundations for student interaction, class discussion, and conferencing. There are several ways to format double-entry journals; we should choose the approaches that best accommodate our students.

For example, we may choose to use the double-entry journal blackline that is available in the Appendix. The blackline is divided down the center. To the left of the divider line, students write summary statements or note important ideas from a chapter they have read. To the right of the divider line, students write their reflections or questions about the information they recorded on the left. Lealya's double-entry journal in this format is presented in Figure 10.10.

Making Connections
TO ENGLISH LEARNERS

When English learners use this Double-Entry Journal graphic organizer, we can structure it to include space for student sketching and include numbers to label spaces and provide focus points for students. For example, the Double-Entry Journal could be formatted as a Triple-Entry Journal that has three columns: Notes, Sketches, and Reflections/Questions. ■

FIGURE 10.9
Unprompted Dialogue Journal Excerpt

Student

I read the first chapter of *Lord of the Flies* and learned that the story is about a group of school boys who crash land on a deserted island. The boys create their own form of government because there are no adults on the island. Ralph is elected leader, and Jack is elected head of the hunters.

I do have one question about what I have read so far. The book talks about a scar on the island. I am confused about what that is.

Teacher

You seem to have a good understanding of what happens in Chapter 1. The scar on the island is a long trail that was created by the plane crash. I am looking forward to your thoughts about the next chapter.

FIGURE 10.10 Excerpt from Lealya's Double-Entry Journal: Three Civilizations in the Americas

Notes	Reflections and Questions
Civilization is an advanced culture in which people have developed cities, science, and industries.	I wonder how our civilization compares to those of the Mayas, Aztecs, and Incas.
Mayas lived in Mexico and Central America. Their greatest period was from 300 A.D. to 900 A.D.	I wonder if ruins of the Mayan civilization still exist.
The Mayas developed a government and a written language. They created the most accurate calendar known until modern times.	I wonder how the Mayan calendar differed from the one we use.
The Aztecs built Tenochtitlan in central Mexico. It was built on an island and they raised crops on floating platforms.	The Aztecs were inventive. I'd never think of planting crops on platforms that float.
By the early 1500s, the Aztecs had built an advanced civilization including cities, pyramids, and temples in Mexico.	
The Incas lived in South America. They were great engineers who built Forts, roads, and aqueducts.	
The Incas built using stones that carefully fit together.	I have seen some of the structures the Incas built. The way the stones fit together reminded me of the Pyramids.

In another approach to Double-Entry Journals, the first entry contains a summary of a chapter or informational article, and the second features students' reflections on what they have read. (See the Appendix for this blackline.) Figure 10.11 provides an excerpt from Lucia's "Summary and Reflection" Double-Entry Journal.

 INVESTIGATIVE JOURNALS. Content area students maintain Investigative Journals to record ideas about topics they have interest in investigating at a future time or ideas about ongoing research. These journals promote inquiry, reflection, and critical thinking. Encourage students to begin their journal entries with the phrase "I wonder." Once ideas are recorded, students' "wonderings" can serve as the basis for written conversations or peer discussions. For example, students may be listening to other students or to a teacher present information to the class. If a topic in which they have interest is addressed, they would record an "I Wonder . . ." Statement about it in their Investigative Journals. Later, when selecting research topics of their own, students can review their Investigative Journals and revisit the topics in which they expressed interest. Figure 10.12 features an excerpt from Connor's Investigative Journal in biology.

 WRITTEN CONVERSATIONS. Written Conversations offer an effective format for students to share their wonderings with peers. In this process, a student selects an "I wonder" section of his investigative journal and shares it in a Written Conversation with another class member. That student then reacts to the original idea and raises any questions he has, and the correspondence continues. This process both promotes student interaction and encourages reflection. Because it is a Written Conversation, it can occur without disturbing the rest of the class. The completed conversation then becomes the basis of further inquiry for the student who originated the dialogue. The "conversation" can be kept either in the investigative journal or in a class portfolio.

 **TICKETS OUT.** This informal writing measure asks students to reflect on what they have learned and share two types of information: (1) What is the most important thing they

Summary

This article is about people during the time of the American Revolution. People who lived in our country at that time did not want to pay taxes to England when they had no say in the government. It was taxation without representation that motivated people to throw tea in the Boston Harbor. This event is now known as the Boston Tea Party.

The article also discusses leaders of importance in revolutionary times. George Washington and John Adams were two of the most important people in that category. George Washington was said to be indispensable in the war effort because he was such a well-respected leader. John Adams was described as a champion of independence. He was a diplomat who later served as Vice-President and President of the United States.

In 1776, the Declaration of Independence was approved by the Second Continental Congress. This document officially broke ties with England, although King George III wasn't willing to let that happen without a fight. It was not an easy war, but when Washington crossed the Delaware and won two battles in New Jersey, the people began to see the war as one the United States could win. The Treaty of Paris officially ended the war in 1783.

Reflection

This was a good article to read before we start studying the Revolutionary Era. As I read, I could make connections to events like the Boston Tea Party and to people such as George Washington and John Adams.

While reading, I was struck by the role individual citizens played in Revolutionary times. I thought about the townspeople who tossed the tea into Boston Harbor and those who fought in the military. These were everyday people doing what they could to help their lives by stopping taxation without representation and fighting for freedom.

Learning more about George Washington and John Adams helped me to see them not only as leaders, but also as citizens who greatly valued freedom. When I read that Washington and Adams were elected President and Vice-President by the Electoral College, I was surprised, but I was also able to make connections to how we vote today. I investigated the Electoral College on the Internet (www.archives.gov). I learned that during Washington's and Adams' first election, there were electors from 10 states. There were electors from 15 states in the election for their second term. In both cases, Washington had the highest amount of votes, followed by Adams.

FIGURE 10.11

An Excerpt from Lucia's "Summary and Reflection": Double-Entry Journal

learned during class that day? and (2) What questions do they have about what they learned that day? The student's response to what she has learned that day is usually recorded on the front of the graphic organizer, and any questions she may have are written on the back. The students need only about five minutes to complete their tickets.

This type of writing is called Tickets Out, because we collect the tickets as we stand at the door at the end of class. When the students hand us their tickets, they are able to leave the classroom. After the students have left, it takes just a few minutes to read their tickets. We collect the tickets with side one facing up, so we can quickly read all of the responses about the most important thing the students learned. As we read, we should be careful to set aside any responses that may need clarification. Then we can turn over the class tickets and read the questions students have about their learning. As we read these, we should set aside questions that we think we need to respond to in a whole-group setting. This is often just four or five questions, because several of them may be similar. Reading the tickets will only take about five minutes. The next day, we can begin class by clarifying any necessary information and responding to the students' questions.

FIGURE 10.12

Excerpt from Connor's Investigative Journal

In today's Press Conference, Kevin talked about DNA and people having DNA tests to find out if they might get heart disease or other illnesses. I would like to know more about this topic, so I might research it. I am wondering why people would want to know if they might get a disease when there isn't anything they can do to stop it. I am also wondering if these processes are private. I'm thinking about what would happen if an employer discovered that someone who works there might get heart disease, Alzheimer's disease, or some other serious disease.

FIGURE 10.13
Everene's Ticket Out

The most important think I learned today is:
The most important thing I learned today is the difference between inflation causing an economic slowdown and what a recession is.

One question I have is:
Is there any way to predict if a slowdown in the economy means that a recession is coming? If there is, are there ways to predict when the recession will happen?

This technique provides good transition from class to class, offers insights into students' learning, and lets students know that we value their thinking. (See Appendix C for a graphic organizer for Tickets Out.) In Figure 10.13, Everene shows how she completed her ticket in economics class.

Learning How Well Students Use Writing to Create and Solve Problems

To learn how well students use informal writing to create or solve problems, we may want to try some forms of informal writing that are used in mathematics and science to record problem creation and problem-solving efforts. Examples of these include Write and Sketch and Be a Math (or Science) Author.

WRITE AND SKETCH IN MATH AND SCIENCE. This type of informal writing allows students to use both language and symbols to make their thinking about problem solving or conducting experiments visible to themselves and others. For example, in math a problem is posed. Students read or listen to the problem and paraphrase it. Then they record their thinking about how to solve the problem on a paper that has been divided in half vertically. On the left side of the paper, students sketch a picture to show how they solved a problem or completed an experiment. On the right side of the paper, students use words to describe how they solved or completed it.

BE A MATH OR SCIENCE AUTHOR. When students create their own math problems or science experiments, they become more interested and engaged. Designing written problems or experiments is an effective way to tap into students' personal experiences and bridge the gap between existing and new knowledge. In addition, practice in interpreting problems or experiments invented by peers helps students better interpret more formal information presented in textbooks or by teachers. When engaging in the Be a Math or Science Author technique, students create problems to be solved by classmates. Problem topics may be left open to the imagination of the students, or may be directed by a topic currently being studied in math class.

Helping Students Engage in Note Taking and Using Study Skills

To help our students use writing when using note taking and study skills, we can scaffold their learning by using Paragraph Frames, Text Boxes, and Structured Note taking.

PARAGRAPH FRAMES. When engaging in informal writing, students need to be able to write good summary paragraphs. If our students are new to writing in the content areas or if their content area writing is not strong, Paragraph Frames will help to scaffold their paragraph summary writing experiences. Scaffolding means that as teachers, we begin the process by providing a great deal of support and we gradually withdraw it over time. As our support dwindles, the students take on more and more responsibility until, in this case, they are writing paragraph summaries without using the frames. Paragraph Frames complement the text pattern (see Chapter 8) the students are reading. For example, if students are reading a section of the text that uses the comparison and contrast structure, they will focus on the similarities and differences in their paragraph.

This is the example of the comparison/contrast text pattern that was included in Chapter 8:

> *When we examine the issues that Democrats and Republicans are supporting in the Presidential election, we can see that there are some issues on which they are clearly divided and others where their goals are similar, but their approaches are different. An example of the former is that their positions differ on the war in Iraq. The Democrats are in favor of ending the war in Iraq, while the Republicans support the war and have developed strategies for victory. As an example of the latter, both the Democratic and Republican candidates support changes in health care, reforming immigration, and improving education. Of course, their policies to promote these changes differ, and in some cases, differ dramatically.*

Figure 10.14 features a comparison/contrast paragraph frame that students can use to write a one-paragraph summary as well as the summary itself. For Paragraph Frames based on the other informational text patterns, see Appendix C.

STRUCTURED NOTE TAKING. This informal writing technique provides a visual framework or organizer for students to use as they take notes. The visual framework looks like the layout of the page. This helps students to take notes more efficiently. Some frameworks focus only on text, while others include illustrations, charts, and graphs. Students can use the completed organizers when studying for tests. To ensure that students are proficient in note taking, we can scaffold students' learning. For example, when providing the graphic organizer the first time, we might complete most of the information, leaving just a few sections for students to complete. The next time we share the organizer, we would complete half of the information and ask the students to complete more sections. We should continue this process until we are not providing any details on the organizer and the students are completing all of the note-taking sections. Figure 10.15 features Jose's completed Structured Note Taking about the stages of food processing in biology class. Notice that the rectangles represent where text appears on the page and the oval represents an illustration.

To use Structured Note Taking in an alternative format, students can draw a line about two inches from the left margin of their notebook paper. Then, as they read or listen to the teacher, they record key words and phrases to the left of the line and details to the right. When they finish reading or listening, students use their notes to write a brief summary at the bottom of the page.

TEXT BOXES. Topping and McManus (2002) suggest that we can also use Text Boxes to promote successful note taking. In this approach, the design of the Text Boxes mirrors the

---

FIGURE 10.14
Comparison/Contrast
Paragraph Frame and
Paragraph

Comparison/Contrast Paragraph Frame

_____ and _____ agree on some topics and disagree on others. They both support _____ (comparison/similarities), but they differ on _____ _____ (contrast/differences).

The completed paragraph frame would read as follows:

<u>Democrats</u> and <u>Republicans</u> agree on some topics and disagree on others. They both support <u>health care, reforming immigration, and improving education</u> (comparisons/similarities), but they differ on <u>their positions about the war</u> (contrast/difference).

FIGURE 10.15
Structured Note
Taking in Biology

Food processing—four stages:

1. Ingestion—the act of eating

2. Digestion—breaking food down into molecules small enough to be absorbed

3. Absorption—cells lining digestive tract absorb products of digestion (amino acids and simple sugars)

4. Elimination—undigested materials pass

Chemical digestion—breakdown from polymers to monomers:

1. Protein to amino acid (protein-digesting enzymes)

2. Polysaccharide and disaccharide to monosaccharide (carbohydrate-digesting enzymes)

3. Nucleic acid to nucleotide (nucleic acid–digesting enzymes)

4. Fat to glycerol, fatty acid (fat-digesting enzymes)

Illustration of Cat's Digestive Process

The illustration of the cat's digestive system showed how a cat ingests food and what happens as the food is digested. It also showed how nutrient cells are absorbed in the cat's body and, finally, how the food is eliminated. The illustration showed how the processes happen inside a cat.

paragraphs, diagrams, and photos on a particular page of text. This is similar to the format used in Structured Note Taking, but the techniques differ significantly. Each Text Box contains *two* columns. The first column contains students' notes about important facts, much like in Structured Note Taking. The second column contains students' reflections about the text and any questions they may have about what they have read. The information required is similar to one of the options for creating double-entry journals, but the format is different.

Text Boxes help students to monitor their reading by focusing on text structure and important facts, as well as information provided by illustrations, charts, maps, and graphs. Todd's example of the Text Boxes he created while reading about the Rosetta Stone, including his reflections and questions, can be seen in Figure 10.16.

Scaffolding Students' Summary Writing

We usually teach our students to write summaries by pulling out the important facts in the text. So, if our students summarize a story, they include the narrative text pattern elements: the characters, setting, problem, attempts to resolve the problem, and resolution. As we learned in Chapter 8, however, informational text has several different patterns, so determining what the important facts are in this type of text can be more challenging.

We can eliminate this challenge if we scaffold our students' summary writing. We can support the class as members engage in completing a Concept of Definition Map. Then we can provide our total support as students write summaries based on the completed Concept of Definition Map (see Chapter 7). All of the information that appears on the map is essential, so when writing summaries students can use the categories as well as the responses.

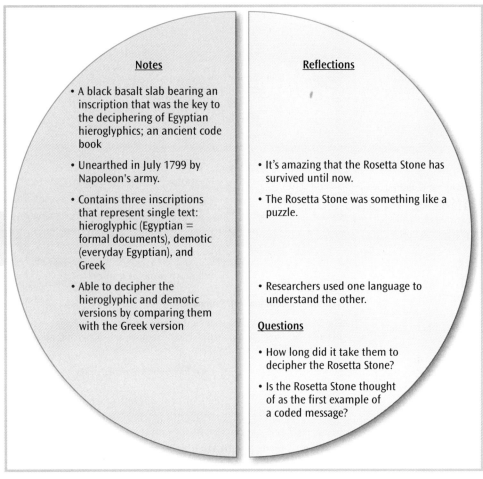

FIGURE 10.16

Text Boxes:
The Rosetta Stone

Notes

- A black basalt slab bearing an inscription that was the key to the deciphering of Egyptian hieroglyphics; an ancient code book

- Unearthed in July 1799 by Napoleon's army.

- Contains three inscriptions that represent single text: hieroglyphic (Egyptian = formal documents), demotic (everyday Egyptian), and Greek

- Able to decipher the hieroglyphic and demotic versions by comparing them with the Greek version

Reflections

- It's amazing that the Rosetta Stone has survived until now.

- The Rosetta Stone was something like a puzzle.

- Researchers used one language to understand the other.

Questions

- How long did it take them to decipher the Rosetta Stone?

- Is the Rosetta Stone thought of as the first example of a coded message?

Consider Maria's completed Concept of Definition Map and Summary about the presidency of the United States, shown in Figure 10.17. All of the information in the summary appears in the completed map, so there is no need for students to determine which information may be important.

The resulting summary is brief, but includes all of the essential information. Teaching our students to write summaries using Concept of Definition Maps provides the necessary information to write a summary and also reminds students that the important information includes facts such as "What is it?", "How would you describe it?", "What are some examples?", and "What is a comparison?" Of course, as noted in Chapter 7, we can change the "What are some examples?" question to accommodate the text we are reading and we can choose to eliminate the comparison.

If we begin teaching summary writing with the Concept of Definition Map, we can then move on to teaching Questions into Paragraphs (QuIP), which will allow students to extend their thinking about a topic. When students use QuIP, we are still providing some teacher support, but we are gradually releasing responsibility to the students. We support student learning by teaching them how to use QuIP and the accompanying graphic organizer. Students then take responsibility for selecting a topic, generating three research questions, and using two different sources to respond to the questions. When the graphic organizer is complete, the students use the information to write a summary paragraph. Once again, we are not asking students to "pull out important facts." Students already provided the important facts when they completed the QuIP graphic organizer. Figure 10.18 features Ben's completed QuIP graphic organizer about hurricanes, as well as the paragraph he wrote based on his questions and responses.

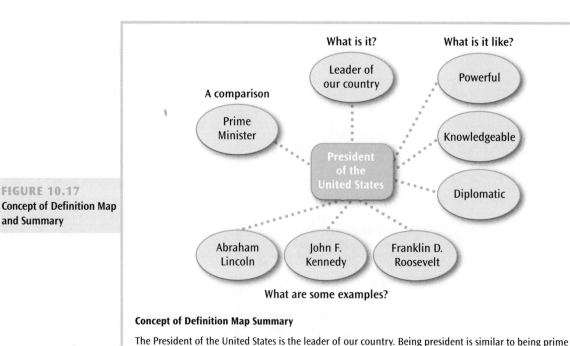

FIGURE 10.17
Concept of Definition Map and Summary

Concept of Definition Map Summary

The President of the United States is the leader of our country. Being president is similar to being prime minister. The President is powerful, knowledgeable, and diplomatic. Abraham Lincoln, John F. Kennedy, and Franklin D. Roosevelt were Presidents of the United States.

After students have used Concept of Definition Maps and QuIP to write summaries several times, we can begin teaching other techniques for summary writing. These include Lyric Summaries (see Chapter 13), Biopyramid and Narrative Pyramid (see Chapter 6 and the Appendix), and form poems such as Acrostics and Definition Poems (see Chapter 13). After learning and practicing these summary techniques, students should be able to use them to write summaries independently.

FIGURE 10.18 **QuIP Research Grid: Hurricanes**

Questions	Answers	
	Source A: *Earth Science*, Tarbuck and Lutgens	**Source B:** www.nhc.noaa.gov
1. What are hurricanes?	Hurricanes are whirling tropical cyclones that produce winds of at least 74 miles per hour.	A hurricane is an intense tropical weather system with a well-defined circulation and *sustained* winds of 74 miles per hour (64 knots) or higher.
2. How do hurricanes develop?	A hurricane is a heat engine that is fueled by the energy given off when huge quantities of water vapor condense.	Hurricanes are products of a tropical ocean and a warm, moist atmosphere. They are powered by heat from the sea.
3. How are hurricanes classified?	The intensity of a hurricane is determined according to the *Saffir–Simpson Hurricane Scale*. It ranges from category 1, least powerful, to category 5, most powerful.	The *Saffir–Simpson Hurricane Scale* is a 1 to 5 rating based on the hurricane's sustained wind speed. This scale estimates potential property damage. Category 3 and higher/hurricanes are considered major. Katrina was a category 3.

QuIP Paragraph

Hurricanes are severe tropical weather systems that are usually described as whirling cyclones having sustained winds of 74 miles per hour or more. Hurricanes are powered by heat given off when massive quantities of water vapor condense. They often develop over tropical seas. The power of hurricanes is determined according to the *Saffir–Simpson Hurricane Scale*. The scale estimates property damage by designating hurricanes in categories from 1 (least powerful) to 5 (most powerful). Hurricanes in category 3 or higher are considered most dangerous. Katrina is an example of a category 3 hurricane.

Making Connections
TO STRUGGLING READERS

Scaffolding students' learning is especially important when we are teaching struggling learners. Using a completed Concept of Definition Map or QuIP offers support for these students when they engage in summary writing. Struggling students can use the graphic organizers, while other students may be able to write summaries independently. In the end, all of the students will write summaries. ■

There are many different ways for students to engage in informal writing. As teachers, our key tasks are to teach these ideas and demonstrate our enthusiasm for writing, so students can feel good about their writing and use it freely throughout the content areas.

How Can We Assess Informal Writing?

To assess our students' informal writing, we usually offer praise and suggestions based on the content. It is important to remember that we do not evaluate or grade informal writing because it is a draft and students have not had the opportunity to revise and edit. For more information about assessing informal writing, see Chapter 14.

How Can We Use Formal Writing in Our Content Area Teaching?

Formal writing is most often associated with long-term, performance-based projects. These projects are usually evaluated with rubrics. (For more information about rubrics, see Chapter 14.) Naturally, the types of projects we use depend on the content area we teach. Reasons for using formal writing in the content areas as well as suggested projects follow.

Persuasive Writing

When we want to learn our students' positions on particular topics, we need to provide them with ways to engage in persuasive writing. Students in the content areas can engage in this mode of writing in a variety of ways, including the following:

■ Persuasive essays
■ Newspaper editorials

- Political speeches (e.g., stem cell research, health care, the economy)
- Position statements
- Reviews of books, films, music, or websites
- Photo or illustration analysis
- Political cartoon analysis

When thinking about how our students can engage in this mode of writing, we can consider the following possibilities:

- Science students can argue their positions about Pluto being a planet.
- Mathematics students can write reviews of websites for their subject area.
- World-language students can write position statements about why that language should continue to be practiced when so much of the world is communicating in English.
- History students can write newspaper editorials about the impact of the past on present-day events.
- English students can write persuasive essays about their favorite authors.
- Science students can inquire about additional planets or life on Mars by studying photos of outer space.
- Mathematics students can create political cartoons about the state of the world as it relates to mathematics.
- World-language students can analyze the cultures of countries where the language they are studying is spoken by examining photos from different points in history.
- History students can analyze political perspectives by reviewing political cartoons.
- English students can speculate on the role of literature in a culture by analyzing photos and political cartoons of the period.

Inquiry-Based Writing

To determine how well our students can use writing to engage in inquiry-based learning, creative thinking, and research, we need to provide access to these types of projects. We should include projects such as the following on a list of possibilities and encourage student self-selection. Because these are examples of formal writing, we should also ensure that students have the project rubrics before they begin.

 **EYEWITNESS ACCOUNT.** In-depth research is essential for this project, which puts the writer in the moment. Excellent examples of published Eyewitness Accounts can be found in *The Century* by Peter Jennings and Todd Brewster (1998). In one of them, Mabel Griep, an eyewitness to the Wright brothers' first flight, details her experience. Of course, our students cannot be eyewitnesses to such events, but they can research and use this format to communicate their findings.

 **DESCRIPTIVE TIMELINE.** Chronological order is required in this project that extends the traditional timeline to a more detailed descriptive version. This encourages students to associate the sequence of dates with details about particular developments.

 **FIRST-PERSON EXPERIENCES.** In this inquiry-based project, individual students select a course-related topic, research it, and choose the mode in which they will present their findings. For details about First-Person Experiences and excerpts from students' projects, see Chapter 12.

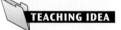 **INQUIRING MINDS.** This is a small-group, inquiry-based research project in which students work with others who have interest in particular topics. For details about Inquiring Minds, see Chapter 12.

 **LETTERS.** The power of using letters to communicate, to inform, and to persuade is well represented in recently published books. David McCullough's *John Adams* (2001) is based on letters exchanged between John and Abigail Adams, and Andrew Carroll's multiple volumes, including *War Letters: Extraordinary Correspondence from American Wars* (2001), feature authentic, soldier-authored letters. Students can choose to respond to these letters or use letter writing as a format when completing an inquiry-based project.

 **ORAL HISTORY PROJECT.** In this project, students choose a person to honor and document his life history in a variety of modes. For more details about the Oral History Project (Dickinson, Hyler, Reilly, & Romano, 2006), see Chapter 12.

 **POETRY.** This is an often-forgotten creative mode of communicating information. To learn about a variety of poetry formats and read student-authored poems, see Chapter 13.

 **STUDENT-AUTHORED ALPHABET BOOKS.** This project can be completed by individual students; alternatively, students can each contribute a page to a class book. For details about Student-Authored Alphabet Books, see Chapter 13.

 **TRANSMEDIATIONS.** When students create Transmediations, they change the medium of the original work. For example, a poem might be transmediated into a picture book, a novel might become a poem, or song lyrics might become a story. For more information about this project, see Chapter 13.

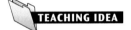 **TRAVELOGUES.** When students engage in this project, they chronicle their virtual visits to countries that may be the origin of the language they are studying, the setting for a novel they are reading, or the location of a historic event. Travelogues can be formatted in many ways, including as a travel journal, a PowerPoint presentation, or a video.

When contemplating how our students can engage in inquiry-based writing, consider the following:

- Science students can write Eyewitness Accounts of significant scientific discoveries.
- Mathematics students can take on the identities of famous mathematicians when creating First-Person Experiences.
- World-language students can write in the language they are studying and create Travelogues through countries that speak that language.
- History students can engage in small-group research projects about multiple aspects of an historic event in Inquiring Minds.
- English students can create Descriptive Timelines of various periods of literature.

Making Connections
TO MULTIPLE LITERACIES

When students engage in formal writing, they should be able to use information literacy to use the Internet to develop important questions, locate information, synthesize the information to answer their questions, and communicate the information to others. ■

Making Connections | Thinking about Formal Writing in the Content Areas

- Reflect on how you can incorporate formal writing into your content area. Describe the connections you can make between two formal writing activities and your subject area. Reflect on how you would motivate your students to engage in these activities.
- Share your thoughts with others in small-group discussions.

How Can We Evaluate Formal Writing?

We evaluate students' formal writing because it is usually a long-term project with multiple opportunities for revising and editing. We discuss information about how students use the writing process in formal writing in the next section.

To evaluate students' formal writing, we usually use rubrics or scoring guides. They include the criteria we will use to evaluate the project. We need to ensure that the students have copies of the rubric and are familiar with it before they begin their work. Knowing what they need to do to complete the project successfully helps to provide direction for students as they research and write. For more detailed information about evaluating writing and the use of rubrics, including sample scoring guides, see Chapter 14.

When students engage in formal writing, they often use the writing process. This recursive process enables them to evolve their writing from their initial thoughts to the rubric-evaluated final copy. In the next section, we describe the writing process and consider how students can use it in the content areas.

How Can We Use the Writing Process in the Content Areas?

Although much of the writing in which our students engage is draft level, more formal writing requires them to revise and edit their work. The writing process provides guidelines to help students advance their ideas from draft stage to final copy. In this section, we discuss the writing process and consider how students can use it when writing in the content areas.

Students generally begin learning about the writing process when they are in the primary grades. By the time they reach middle school or high school, they have had many years of practice writing in this format. The writing process consists of several stages, including drafting, revising, editing, and publishing (final copy). For our purposes, we will add "making connections" as a first step. Figure 10.19 presents an overview of the stages for using the writing process in the content areas.

In the first stage, students select a topic and make connections between their topic and their prior knowledge. They also review the project rubric, think about their audience, develop questions to guide their writing, locate meaningful references, and develop a format for sharing the information. For example, if students in a mathematics class were investigating famous mathematicians, a student might ask himself, "Which mathematician interests me the most?"

Let's imagine that he chose Benjamin Banneker. During the *making connections* stage, he would also ask himself the following questions:

- What did I learn from reviewing the rubric? What am I required to do in this project?
- What do I already know about Benjamin Banneker?
- Who is the audience for this research?
- What do I want to know about Banneker? Which questions can I generate to guide my writing?
- What resources can I use to get the information I need?
- What format can I use that will allow me to present the information about Banneker in the most effective and engaging way?

FIGURE 10.19
The Writing Process in the Content Areas

I. Making connections
II. Drafting
III. Revising
IV. Editing
V. Publishing

Go to the Activities and Applications section under the topic *Writing* in the MyEducation-Lab for your course and complete the activity entitled Peer Editing to describe ways to group students for peer editing sessions.

In the *drafting* stage, students write their ideas. Informal writing such as journal entries, open-ended responses, and reading strategy applications stops at this stage, but formal writing such as research papers and projects continues through all stages of the writing process.

During the *revising* stage, students adapt or change the content based on suggestions offered by peers, teachers, or modifications in their own thinking. Peer revision, which is often used during this stage, involves students reading and commenting on the content of each other's writing. Peer revision can take place through peer conferencing or peers can provide written comments. Either way, it is important to teach students how to engage in peer revision. For example, students often offer one positive comment and one suggestion. In the case of the student researching Benjamin Banneker, the peer revisor might say:

- "I didn't know very much about Banneker until I read your paper. You did a good job of finding out information about him." (positive comment)
- "My idea is that you not use Banneker's name so often. Maybe you could use *he* or *this mathematician* instead." (suggestion)

In the *editing* stage, students focus on grammar and formatting. They can use a checklist or engage in a quick conference based on the checklist. Editing checklists often include the items featured in Figure 10.20. Students use such checklists to make sure that they have used correct grammar and formatting in their writing. For example, in this stage, the student researching Benjamin Banneker might decide to combine some simple sentences into compound or complex ones. He might also choose to use fewer quotations by paraphrasing some of the information.

Making Connections
TO ENGLISH LEARNERS

When English learners engage in peer revising or editing, we should partner them with students who speak English clearly at a comfortable rate. We should also ensure that the partners discuss their comments and suggestions to promote understanding. ■

In the *publishing* stage, students review what they have written, proofread carefully, and make final changes. After the students' writing has been through the publishing stage, it is submitted to the teacher to be evaluated using the rubric that was distributed at the start of the project.

We should note that although we have presented a series of stages, the writing process is recursive—not linear. This means that although there are several stages in the process, students do not just advance their writing from one stage to the next. For example, in the case of the student researching Benjamin Banneker, after suggestions for revision had been made, he would have reverted to the draft stage to revise the content of his writing.

FIGURE 10.20
Editing Checklist

1. Did the writer use complete sentences?
2. Do the sentences begin with capital letters and end with periods?
3. Is the other punctuation appropriate—apostrophe use, comma use?
4. Is the paper written in the active voice?
5. Is there subject–verb agreement?
6. Did the writer use correct verb tenses?
7. Are the paragraphs indented?
8. Are there simple, compound, and complex sentences?
9. Are tired words used—said, nice, good?
10. Do the pronouns correctly reference the people or items to which they refer?

Whether informal or formal in nature, writing is a mainstay in the content areas. Students can use informal writing to communicate their ideas every day and formal writing to demonstrate what they have learned over time. In the next section, we explore the general principles we should follow when integrating writing in the content areas.

When Integrating Writing in the Content Areas, What General Principles Should We Follow?

There are several general guidelines we can follow to ensure that our use of writing in the content areas is effective:

1. *We should integrate both informal and formal writing in our content area teaching.* Writing is not an add-on; it is a natural part of teaching and learning. As such, it should occur in everyday settings as well as in the form of long-term projects.

2. *Our teaching should encourage students to make connections between their previous writing experience and content area writing.* For example, most of our students—if not all—will have learned the writing process during their elementary school years. If this is the case, our students will probably have had better writing experiences than we did during our K–12 years. Although we may enjoy writing now, many of us grew up with "red ink syndrome." This occurred when teachers who were reading our writing covered our work with "red ink" negative comments and crossed out sections of our papers. We were usually told only what was wrong with our writing and we were not provided with opportunities to revise. Our students' experiences with the writing process, which includes positive comments, suggestions for improvement, and opportunities to revise and edit, probably differ greatly from the writing experiences most of us had.

3. *When asking our students to engage in informal writing, we should remember not to evaluate or grade the students' writing.* Informal writing is a draft. We should comment only on its content.

4. *When inviting our students to engage in formal writing, we should distribute the rubric we will be using when the assignment is introduced.* Rubrics provide content and format criteria for students, and they should have this information from the very beginning of the assignment. (See Chapter 14 for more information about rubrics.)

5. *Our lessons should focus on **depth** rather than **coverage** of content area writing.* We don't need to use every idea to incorporate writing in the content areas. Rather, we need to choose topics and methods that are particularly meaningful.

6. *Our teaching should reflect our understanding that informal and formal writing enhance learning in the content areas and that both can be adapted to accommodate our students' needs.*

7. *When we invite our students to write in the content areas, we should demonstrate our enthusiasm for writing.* As Murray (2007) reminds us, teachers need to be writers. Our students need to know that we have positive feelings about writing. Although it involves a certain amount of risk taking on our part, sharing examples of our informal and formal writing will help our students see us as writers. We know from experience that our enthusiasm will motivate our students.

Making Connections | Thinking about Our Writing

■ Think about yourself as a writer. Reflect on your K–12 writing experiences. Consider the following types of teachers you had: (1) teachers who did a great job of incorporating writing into their content areas; (2) teachers who did not include writing in their content areas; and (3) teachers who provided only negative comments about writing in the content areas. Think about what has changed over the years and how you will use your previous writing experiences to develop writing in your content area.

■ Share your thoughts with others in small-group discussions.

FINAL THOUGHTS

Writing offers us insights into students' thinking and promotes communication in all content areas. It also enables students to share their knowledge, reveal their interests, contemplate connections, and engage in inquiry.

In the next chapter, we learn about technology in the content areas. We make connections to the literacies discussed in Chapter 2 and focus on how to integrate technology into teaching and learning.

Teaching Connections
APPLYING WHAT WE HAVE LEARNED

E-Links

We know that writing is a natural component of teaching and learning in the content areas. We also know that writing is another aspect of our teaching that relates to state standards. Consider the writing standards in the state in which you teach as well as state-assessment-based writing rubrics. Then (1) explain how you plan to address the standards in your teaching and (2) how you can use the state writing rubric to help students meet the criteria on which their state assessment writing sample will be evaluated.

SAMPLE WEBSITES

For examples of e-links to state standards, see Figure 3.7. For examples of state writing rubrics, access the following websites:

Delaware State Writing Rubric
http://www.doe.k12.de.us/aab/files/GeneralRubricforWriting.pdf

Michigan Merit Exam (MME) Persuasive Writing Rubric Grade 11 (This assessment is evaluated separately for writing and for content.)
http://www.michigan.gov/documents/mde/MME_Persuasive_Writing_Rubric_174205_7.pdf

Pennsylvania State Writing Rubric—11th Grade PSSA Persuasive Writing Rubric
http://www.stsd.org/shs/staff/rj/Student%20Resources/
PSSA%20PERSUASIVE%20RUBRIC%202006.doc

Accountable Talk

Meet in discipline-specific small groups to discuss how you plan to integrate informal and formal writing in your content area teaching. Consider the following issues: (1) how you will make connections between writing and your content area; (2) how you will motivate your students to use writing to learn; and (3) how you will promote writing in the content areas among fellow faculty members who teach from more traditional perspectives.

 ### Portfolio/Performance Opportunity

Choose a lesson plan you have already completed, and integrate informal writing into it. Then choose a formal writing project that could be meaningfully introduced at the conclusion of that lesson. Complete the informal writing activities and the formal writing project that you add to the lesson, and save them as models to be used in your future teaching. Share and discuss your revised plan and models with peers who teach your content area.

11

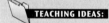

TEACHING IDEAS:

• INTERNET WORKSHOP • INTERNET PROJECT • INTERNET INQUIRY • WEBQUESTS

Using Technology in the Content Areas

Information and communication technologies provide exciting new ways to teach and learn. These technologies are ever-changing and, as new ones emerge, we must keep pace to ensure that we can provide our students with access to innovative practices. The possibilities for integrating technology into our teaching seem unlimited. We can use graphing calculators in mathematics to convert equations to graphic representations, and we can use calculator-based "laboratories"—hand-held devices that enable students to collect data, in science (Davis, 1997). We can take digital photos and compose digital movies in all of our classes (Brass, 2008). We can podcast Discussion Circles in any area of the curriculum. And, of course, we can use the Internet—perhaps our greatest technology—for extensive purposes throughout the content areas.

Researchers report that we are living in a technological revolution. Tierney (2008) observes that "the advent of digital spaces, especially the advent of hypertext, represents a revolution in communication of a magnitude exceeding the printing press" (p. 262). Leu, Coiro, Castek, Hartman, Henry, and Reinking (2008) agree, noting that the Internet has been adopted more quickly than any other technology for reading, writing, or communicating. These findings are corroborated by the fact that more than a billion people are already reading information online (de Argaez, 2006).

In this chapter, we explore the role of technology in the content areas. We begin by examining a rationale for using technology in our teaching. Next, we compare and contrast reading online and reading offline. Finally, we discuss a variety of Internet strategies and projects we can use in our content area classes.

How Does Using Technology in the Content Areas Enrich Our Teaching?

Technology permeates education, and incorporating it into our content area teaching provides a variety of benefits. These range from immediacy of response to increased socialization in learning. The benefits of using technology include the following:

- Making topics more real.
- Linking disciplines.
- Promoting collaboration.
- Lending immediacy to inquiry and data sharing.
- Promoting higher-level thinking.
- Deepening students' understanding of research.
- Helping students learn that content areas involve questions, not answers.
- Promoting inquiry.
- Encouraging learning in a social context.
- Promoting discussion at multiple levels (adapted from Lonergan, 1997; Mike, 1996).

Although a variety of technologies complement our teaching, we use the Internet most frequently for this purpose. Castek, Bevans-Mangelson, and Goldstone (2006) believe this approach is beneficial to our students. They note, "Providing opportunities for students to use the Internet at school helps them develop literacy skills that are important for their future participation in a digital world. Using computers increases students' motivation to read, write, and learn" (p. 715). Researchers report that many of our students also use the Internet at home. More than 90% of the adolescent students in the United States who have access to the Internet at home use this technology to do homework (Pew Internet & American Life Project, 2001). Mike (1996) notes that the Internet offers users "a natural blend of communication and information retrieval functions incorporated within a framework that literally encompasses the world" (p. 4). Figure 11.1 presents a glossary of Internet-specific terms that we frequently encounter in our teaching.

Making Connections
TO ENGLISH LEARNERS

Before inviting an English learner to participate in a technology-based project, use an informal assessment, such as an interest inventory or discussion, to learn about the student's previous experience using technology. The student may have a great deal of prior knowledge or very little. Knowing the degree of experience with technology will inform the teacher's understanding of whether the student needs support when using technology or will be able to complete the project on her own. ■

Making Connections | Thinking about Technology

- Consider technology-infused teaching. What do you think are the greatest challenges we, as teachers, face when trying to incorporate technology in our courses? The greatest benefits? Focus on specific examples.
- Share your thoughts with others in small-group discussions.

Blog (web log) An Internet journal that has dated entries. It provides opportunities for responses between the author and the readers. A blogosphere is the virtual community of blog writers and readers and the texts they create.

Discussion board An online venue for posting a comment or question that others can read and respond to over time. Those who respond do not need to be online at the same time as the person who posted the question. If one person *posts* a question and five others respond, those six *posts* form a *thread*.

Hypertext Digital print that allows for a variety of reading options in a single text. It contains hyperlinks that readers can click on to access other texts.

Key word search A search engine query (question) that contains carefully selected words to enable users to reach specific information.

FIGURE 11.1

Glossary of Selected Internet Terms

New literacies The new skills, strategies, and dispositions that are required to successfully identify important questions, locate information, engage in critical evaluation, synthesize information, and communicate on the Internet.

Networked classroom The context in which teachers and students use the Internet for educational purposes.

Networked culture A geographical community connected to its members by the Internet.

Podcast A way to receive broadcasts through the Internet using an automatic *feed* in a process called *subscribing*. Podcast episodes can consist of audio files, video files, or documents, or any combination of the three.

Real time A descriptor for live interactions that occur online.

Search engine An online program that indexes the contents of registered websites and provides lists of responses to search queries.

WebQuest A scaffolded, inquiry-oriented activity in which motivated students use specific Web resources to investigate an open-ended question.

Wiki A collection of text that multiple users can revise and edit freely online. The wiki, which was inspired by the Hawaiian word for "quick," is a unique means of group communication because it allows not only the content to be revised and edited, but also the organization of the contributions.

How Are Reading Online and Reading Offline Similar? How Are They Different?

When the Internet first emerged as a popular technology, it was generally accepted that reading offline skills and strategies were all that were required for successful online reading. Since then, however, researchers have determined that online readers need skills and strategies beyond those traditionally learned in school (Coiro, Knobel, Lankshear, & Leu, 2008). In this section, we explore the similarities and differences that exist between offline and online reading, particularly in terms of the nature of reading, the types of text encountered, and the appropriate skills and strategies.

Nature

Just like reading offline, reading online is constructivist in nature. Rather than having information transmitted into the learner by the Internet, knowledge is constructed by each individual. Students actively create meaning based on their personal paths to inquiry and discovery (El-Hindi, 1998; Schmar-Dobler, 2003). This approach is supported by researchers' beliefs that online reading comprehension is a problem-based, inquiry-focused process (Coiro et al., 2008; Leu, Kinzer, Coiro, & Cammack, 2004).

Text

Text is a critical factor in both offline and online reading. In Chapter 1, we discussed the expanding notion of text. In Chapter 2, we learned about the role of text in critical literacy. Now we compare and contrast offline and online text. Although they share several similarities, they also have marked differences. In Figure 11.2, which is presented in a Venn Diagram format, the overlapping circles in

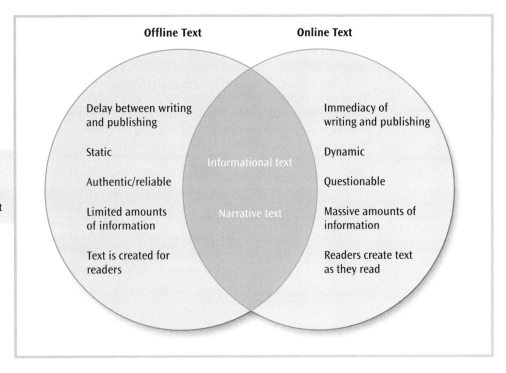

FIGURE 11.2
Comparing and Contrasting Offline and Online Content Area Text

the center feature the similarities. The information contained in the outer circles shows what is unique to offline and online reading, For example, we can see that narrative and informational text are common to both offline and online reading. We can also see that they differ in terms of immediacy of access and nature (Gilster, 1997), as well as in terms of the amount of information they provide.

Kamil and Lane (1998) report that reading on the Internet can be demanding. For example, although the Internet's bright colors, animation, audio, and video may be viewed as motivational by some users, they may be viewed as visually distracting by others. Kamil and Lane further note that the Internet provides access to massive amounts of text, which may be challenging to navigate.

Traditional print text is usually viewed as accurate and reliable, but anyone can post information on the Internet, whether it is accurate or not. For this reason, we must constantly question who has created a website and for what purpose.

Coiro and Dobler (2007) report that both offline and online reading involve purpose, task, and context, but only online reading features self-directed text construction. When reading online, self-directed text is constructed as readers navigate personal paths through massive amounts of information, creating their personal versions of the online texts they read. In essence, several students could be researching the same question online, but because of choices they make about key words, search engines, and site selection, each would construct unique, self-directed text. In contrast, although students reading traditional offline texts would also construct meaning as they read, they would not be constructing text.

Skills and Strategies

As we learned in Chapter 2, the nature of literacy and learning changes as new technologies emerge. A prime example of this can be seen in the increasing popularity of the Internet. In addition to an awareness of the variations in text found on the Internet, a variety of reading comprehension skills are required to navigate Internet-based text (Coiro & Dobler, 2007). As Coiro (2003) notes, "The Internet provides new text formats, new purposes for reading, and new ways to interact with information that can confuse and overwhelm people taught to extract meaning from only conventional print" (p. 458). The skills and strategies we use when reading online build upon those we use when reading offline (Coiro, 2003; Leu, 2000).

Researchers suggest that when we think about what we need to know and be able to do to use the Internet efficiently, we are focusing on what researchers refer to as *new literacies*. The term has several different meanings. We will focus on "new literacies" as the new skills, strategies, and dispositions that are required to successfully identify important questions, locate information, engage in critical evaluation, synthesize information, and communicate on the Internet (Castek et al., 2006; Leu et al., 2004). Kist (2000, 2002) suggests that students in new literacy classrooms construct meaning, understand different symbol systems, use creative forms of expression and representation, and evaluate and communicate information from multiple media. He further notes that such contexts are highly motivational.

Making Connections | Thinking about Technology as Motivation

- Consider the motivational nature of technology. Think specifically about how you can use technology to motivate students to learn in your content area. Focus on specific examples.
- Share your thoughts with others in small-group discussions.

When our students use the Internet for course-related projects, they generally follow these steps:

1. Select a topic of interest.
2. Generate a research question.
3. Think about key words.
4. Question search engines.
5. Evaluate the multiple sources provided by the search engine.
6. Synthesize information relevant to the research question.
7. Choose a mode to represent/communicate the findings.

While reading this list, we may notice that it is somewhat similar to the steps in a more traditional research process. The major difference, of course, is that rather than using reference books in the library, students research topics online. That distinction has implications for both reading and researching.

The good news is that when researching online, students use the traditional reading skills and strategies we have been learning to teach throughout this text. However, when using the Internet, students also need to be able to (1) identify important questions, (2) locate information, (3) evaluate information, (4) synthesize the information relevant to the question, and (5) communicate the answers to others (Leu et al., 2004, p. 1570; Leu, Zawilinski, Castek, Banerjee, Housand, Liu, & O'Neil, 2007). Bell (2001) reminds us that such skills are most productive when they are taught explicitly.

IDENTIFY IMPORTANT QUESTIONS.   When we read online, we are usually seeking to answer a question or to solve a problem. This may be a key difference between online and offline reading (Leu et al., 2007). Of course, although our reading of traditional text doesn't necessarily begin with a question, questioning does play a vital role in offline reading. As we learned in Chapter 8, generating questions is an important offline reading skill; as we learned in Chapter 4, self-questioning is an important offline reading comprehension strategy. Our students' abilities to generate questions at a variety of levels and to self-question while reading offline strongly support this aspect of online reading.

In addition to developing an important question to direct our research, Burke (2002) suggests that when planning to access the Internet, we should consider the questions featured in Figure 11.3. Burke proposes that questioning should begin before we approach the Internet, continue as we search for information, and persist even when the search has concluded.

LOCATE INFORMATION.   Leu et al. (2007) suggest there are at least four types of skills associated with locating information on the Internet: (1) knowing how to use a search

FIGURE 11.3
Questions to Raise When Using the Internet (Burke, 2002)

Before Using the Internet

- What is my goal?
- What kind of information do I need?
- What kinds of sources will provide that kind of information?
- How will I use the information?
- What are some key words that will help me locate the information?

During Use of the Internet

- Who is responsible for the website?
- What information is provided about the authors?
- When was it last updated?
- Who is the intended audience?
- Is the website clearly organized?
- Do the illustrations, charts, maps, graphs, and videos provide/clarify essential information?
- Is the information presented factually correct?

After Using the Internet

- How will I choose to communicate what I have learned?

engine effectively, (2) reading search engine results, (3) reading a webpage, and (4) making inferences when selecting a link at one site in an effort to find information at another site. Of course, all of these steps are dependent on the first skill: knowing how to use a search engine effectively.

When searching for information on the Internet, students are often content to type in a word or phrase and await the results. As teachers, we can help students make their searches more effective. For example, we can use search engine math—that is, simplified Boolean searching—to obtain more focused results. Ideas for using key words and symbols such as plus signs, minus signs, and quotation marks to search more effectively are presented in Figure 11.4.

FIGURE 11.4
Search Engine Math

Guidelines for Using Search Engine Math (Simplified Boolean Search)

To focus your search on a specific topic, follow these guidelines:

1. Put a *plus sign* (+) in front of words that *must* be present on the webpage.

2. Put a *minus sign* (−) in front of a word to tell the search engine to *subtract* pages that contain that particular word.

3. A plus sign (+) is equivalent to the Boolean search term AND.

4. A minus sign (−) is equivalent to the Boolean search term NOT.

5. Avoid using a "−" term as the first term in your query. For example, if you are searching for information on horses and want to exclude information about ranches, write the query as "horses −ranches" rather than as "−ranches horses."

6. Use the minus sign (−) carefully. If you exclude topics with minus signs, you may also exclude pages that contain information about the topics you are trying to locate.

7. Plus and minus terms can be combined with quotation marks to focus searches.

8. There cannot be any space between the relevant sign and the word to which it refers. For example, write +"Pluto", not + " Pluto".

Source: Pandia Goalgetter Search Tutorial on Search Engine Math (http://www.pandia.com/goalgetter/10.html).

We can also teach our students to use search engines such as NetTrekker (http://www
.nettrekker.com/) to locate quality educational information. An award-winning educational
search engine that is aligned with state standards, NetTrekker connects users to educator-
approved sites that are organized by subject area and readability levels. It also provides supports
such as read-alouds and customized content for English learners. NetTrekker is frequently used
by teachers, students, and parents of K–12 students.

Using informational search tools such as search engine math and NetTrekker not only saves
time, but also helps the researcher to locate focused, quality, relevant information. We should
note that the process of locating text contributes to the text that Internet readers construct as
they read.

CRITICALLY EVALUATING INFORMATION. According to Coiro (2007) at least five different
types of evaluation occur online:

- Evaluating understanding: Does it make sense to me?
- Evaluating relevancy: Does it meet my needs? Does it help me respond to my question?
- Evaluating accuracy: Can I verify it with another reliable source?
- Evaluating reliability: Can I trust it?
- Evaluating bias: How does the author shape it? Whose perspective is represented?

Although evaluation is especially important on the Internet, where anyone can post any
type of information, we do engage in evaluating when reading offline. Evaluating is an essential factor in both reading and critical literacy. In the former, we evaluate elements such as the
consistency of the author's message. In the latter, we question sources, authors' intent, and other
issues (see Chapter 2). We should also note the importance of knowing how to generate questions at multiple levels when evaluating text (see Chapter 8).

SYNTHESIZING INFORMATION. As online readers seek answers to questions, they synthesize
or integrate information in two ways (Leu et al., 2007). They pull relevant information from
a variety of sources and combine it in terms of its relevance to the topic. Imagine that the
research question was "What caused the Civil War?" Results of an Internet search would
likely provide information about several issues that contributed to the Civil War. Students
would then synthesize this information by organizing what they learned from different sites
by topic. For example, there were economic causes of the Civil War, so students would
synthesize or blend the information about that cause from all of the websites they choose to
access. Synthesizing online text also means that students, "actively construct the texts that
they read through the choices they make about which sites to visit, which links to follow,
whom to communicate with, and whose messages to read as they seek answers to the
questions that direct their online reading" (Leu, et al. 2007, p. 48).

COMMUNICATING INFORMATION. After students synthesize information, they need to choose
a way to communicate their findings. They may choose to use discussion, a PowerPoint
presentation, or art forms such as dramatization or music to share what they have learned
(see Chapter 13). Other options include blogs, wikis, discussion boards, and phone and video
conferencing (Leu, et al. 2008).

Making Connections
TO WRITING

Writing plays a critical role in our use of technology. We use it—with immediacy—to communicate
through e-mail and share ideas in blogs and wikis. As Leu (2000) has noted, we are living in a global
society in which writing will become even more important than it is today. ■

How Can We Use Technology as a Natural Part of Teaching and Learning?

When we use technology in our teaching, we need to be aware of how to incorporate it seamlessly in meaningful ways. In this section, we share general ideas about how to do that. Next, we discuss specific Internet-based strategies including Internet Workshop, Internet Project, Internet Inquiry, and WebQuests. Then we discuss how to use podcasts, blogs, and wikis as resources to facilitate such projects.

Guidelines for Integrating Technology

Richardson (2004) suggests that we consider the following factors when designing content lessons that incorporate technology:

1. *Think broadly.* Technology involves more than the Internet. Consider using presentation software, digital photography, e-mail, threaded discussions, podcasts, and wikibooks.
2. *Use an appropriate form of technology.* Consider the students, the materials you have to work with, the level of complexity, and the amount of preparation needed.
3. *Always have a backup plan.* Locate more than one website, in case the site is taken down before you teach the lesson. When using a digital camera, have an extra power extension and an extra battery at hand. If you need to transfer software or data, store it in two different ways (e.g., memory stick, CD).
4. *Incorporate technology as seamlessly as possible.* Technology is the means, not the content of the lesson. It should enhance the lesson, not overwhelm it. (p. 15)

Figure 11.5 features some examples of Internet resources we can use for teaching in the content areas.

 **TEACHING IDEA**

INTERNET WORKSHOP. Internet Workshop (Leu, 2002) is especially useful for introducing students to sites for an upcoming unit and developing background knowledge. During such a workshop, students can work individually, in collaboration with classmates, or in conjunction with international peers.

The workshop format is flexible, but it usually involves the following steps:

1. *Locate a central site, or several sites,* on the Internet with content related to a classroom unit of instruction and set a bookmark for the location(s). This limits random surfing on the Internet and helps ensure student safety on the Internet.
2. *Develop an activity related to class learning goals* that requires students to use the site(s). Internet Workshop works well before learning to help students build background knowledge, and during learning to enrich individual and class knowledge of the topic.
3. *Encourage students to record information in an electronic journal.* While students are using the Internet, we should be monitoring their work. Questions that might guide our observations include these:

■ Did the student easily access the site?
■ Is the student focused on the task?

FIGURE 11.5
Internet Teaching
Resources for the
Content Areas

Annenberg Media Learner.Org
http://www.learner.org

Art at the Getty (J. Paul Getty Museum)
http://www.getty.edu

The History Channel
http://www.history.com

Language Learning Center
http://depts.washington.edu/llc/main/links/world.php

The Learning Page: Especially for Teachers (Library of Congress)
http://memory.loc.gov/learn

Mathworld
http://mathworld.wolfram.com/BolzaProblem.html

NASA's Online Interactive Projects
http://www.quest.arc.nasa.gov
(Students participate in scientific research.)

National Geographic Society Home Page
http://www.nationalgeographic.com

PBS
http://www.pbs.org

Smithsonian Museums
http://www.si.edu

Remember.Org: A Cybrary of the Holocaust
http://www.remember.org

> ■ Does the student seem to be gathering quality information that will contribute to the class learning goals?
> ■ If students are working in groups, are all members making valuable contributions?

4. *Hold periodic workshop sessions,* so students can share their work, raise questions, reveal new insights, and discuss the skills needed to function effectively online.

Internet Workshop is an effective way to help expand students' understanding of the topic being studied. For example, if we are beginning to teach a unit or topic about which students have little or no background knowledge, we can use Internet Workshop to increase their knowledge before reading text chapters or engaging in more formal projects. We can also use Internet Workshop when students are creating projects or after learning to extend their thinking.

The following is an example of how we can use Internet Workshop in literature class:

> **Literature Internet Workshop:** *Imagine that we are planning to begin teaching our students about Native American authors, but students have little or no background knowledge about the topic. We can research and locate several websites that offer quality information, bookmark the sites, and engage students in Internet Workshop. If necessary, we can also teach mini-lessons on topics ranging from ways to locate quality websites to the lives and publications of Native American authors. Students can then use the websites to gather information and report it to the class. During workshop sessions, they can also engage in conferencing, peer review, or idea exchanges.*

We can also use the Internet Workshop format when students are creating Internet Projects, undertaking Internet Inquiry, and engaging in WebQuests. This provides the students with regular access to mini-lessons as well as opportunities for sharing and peer feedback.

TEACHING IDEA | **INTERNET PROJECT.** Internet Project (Leu, 2001) is a collaborative learning experience between two or more classrooms that takes place over the Internet. Internet projects may be either website-based or engaged in spontaneously.

Website Projects are coordinated through a website developed by the originator. They are usually precisely defined and include clear directions for participation. Because of their precise nature, website projects are sometimes more limited in scope and learning potential.

Spontaneous Projects include the following steps:

1. *Develop a collaborative project.* Be sure to include a summary of the project, a clear list of learning goals, expectations for the collaborating classrooms, and a projected timeline from beginning to completion.
2. *Post the project description and timeline on the Internet* several months in advance to seek collaborative class partners.
3. *Arrange collaboration details with teachers* of other classes who agree to participate.
4. *Exchange information* with your collaborating classrooms. Encourage discussion between and among classes as the project progresses.
5. *Complete the project.* Celebrate with the collaborating classrooms.

As teachers, we can engage our classes in Internet Projects that have been created by other teachers or experts in the field, such as those on the GLOBE Program and NASA Quest websites. In addition, we can create Internet Projects that provide opportunities for our students to interact with students throughout the United States or around the world. In the following example, we present specific steps to follow when creating an Internet Project.

When developing Internet Projects, we should choose a specific topic and post the following types of information on the Internet:

1. **Project title:** Choose a title that clearly relates to what the students will do. For example, if students will study African cultures, an appropriate title might be "Exploring Africa."
2. **Project summary:** Describe the project and its expected outcomes. For example, if our Internet Project is "Exploring Africa," we might summarize the project in this way:

   In *Exploring Africa,* students from the United States will investigate African culture, history, and geography. The project will be created collaboratively with other classes throughout the world. The components of the project will be discussed through e-mails, and each class will assume responsibility for a particular section. The components of the project will then be fused into a digital movie and shared with all participants.

3. **Dates:** Provide the dates on which the Internet project will begin and end.
4. **Ages:** List the student ages that would be appropriate for the project. Ages generally work better than grade levels, because many countries have school structures that differ from the U.S. system.
5. **Curriculum areas:** Indicate the subject areas involved in the Internet Project. For example, if the project is "Exploring Africa," areas such as the arts, history, language, and technology might be included.
6. **Types of technology:** Describe the types of technology that will be used. For example, in "Exploring Africa," the list might include audio files and CDs, student-created websites, e-mail, wikis, video clips, DVDs, and discussion forums.
7. **Types of collaboration:** Describe the nature of the collaboration. For example, in "Exploring Africa," the types of collaboration in which students engage might include information exchange, electronic publishing, intercultural exchange, peer feedback, and virtual meetings.
8. **Project registration:** Register the Internet Project online several months in advance, so other classes can access information about it. **Internet Projects Registry** (http://www.gsn.org/GSH/pr/) is the original clearinghouse for collaborative projects from around the world. This site features projects hosted by the Global SchoolNet Foundation, other well-respected organizations, and teachers around the globe.

INTERNET INQUIRY. When students engage in Internet Inquiry (Leu & Kinzer, 1999; Leu & Leu, 1999) they use online sources to conduct research. During this discovery-based process, students identify important questions and then gather information as they seek answers to those questions. Internet Inquiry is a student-centered activity in which students choose the issues they explore and take responsibility for completing the research. Students can work individually or in groups organized by interest.

Internet Inquiry includes five phases of student participation:

1. Generate research questions about a theme or topics being studied.
2. Search for responses to the research questions on the Internet.
3. Analyze the information found online.
4. Choose a mode to present the findings.
5. Share the results with the whole class.

For example, if we were planning to engage our students in Internet Inquiry about famous scientists, we might follow these guidelines:

INTERNET INQUIRY: FAMOUS SCIENTISTS

1. Create an Internet Inquiry about biographies of famous scientists.
2. Invite students to select a person to research from a list of possibilities.
3. Share and explain the rubric that will be used to evaluate Internet Inquiry.
4. Encourage students to choose how they will present the biographical information they locate about the person they chose.
5. Encourage students to generate questions to direct their research.

Example questions for a student who has chosen to investigate Albert Einstein:

- What scientific discoveries did Einstein make?
- What is Einstein's general theory of relativity?
- What role did Einstein play in the creation of the atomic bomb?

6. Monitor students' progress as they gather and analyze information.
7. Invite students to participate in periodic conferencing or workshops to ask questions, engage in peer review, and share ideas about the projects they are developing.
8. Use the rubric to evaluate students' Internet Inquiry projects.

Examples of how Internet Inquiry can be used in mathematics, history, and literature include the following:

- Mathematics Internet Inquiry: Students investigate famous women mathematicians.
- History Internet Inquiry: Students investigate the Spanish–American War.
- Literature Internet Inquiry: Students investigate the lives and achievements of F. Scott Fitzgerald and Ernest Hemingway.

Go to the Activities and Applications section under the topic *Technology* in the MyEducationLab for your course and complete the activity entitled Wireless WebQuests to explain ways in which WebQuests can enhance instruction in content area literacies.

TEACHING IDEA   WEBQUESTS. WebQuests are inquiry-oriented online tools for learning that are based on the teachers' preselected Internet resources (Dodge, 1995). There are six components to a WebQuest:

1. Introduction (activate background knowledge and motivate)
2. Task (formal description of what needs to be done)
3. Process (steps to accomplish the text)
4. Resources (list of bookmarked websites and other materials that will be used)
5. Evaluation (rubric)
6. Conclusion (summary and reflection).

March (2003/2004) notes that WebQuests are scaffolded and involve authentic tasks that respond to an open-ended question. Engaging in WebQuests helps students develop online expertise, promotes group participation, and cultivates critical thinking. To explore WebQuests such as *Genes: The Building Blocks of Life,* in which genetics-related issues are explored; *Artwork in Central Park: A WebQuest Integrating Geometry and Art,* in which students create art; and many others, visit the website entitled "Index of /academics/education/projects/webquests" (http://oncampus.richmond.edu/academics/education/projects/webquests).

Tools to Facilitate Online Learning: Podcasts, Blogs, and Wikis

Podcasts, blogs, and wikis are three technology tools that students can use to facilitate communication with their peers and with us during projects and other learning experiences. In the following section, we describe each and provide details about its use.

PODCASTS. Podcasting is a way to receive broadcasts through the Internet using an automatic *feed* in a process called *subscribing*. Podcast episodes can consist of audio files, video files, or documents, or any combination of the three. Kajder (2007) offers a classroom example. She notes that teachers can use podcasts to electronically review student conversations in Literature or Discussion Circles. For example, each small group can use an iPod paired with an iTalk microphone to digitally record their discussions and provide their teacher with access to their conversations. To learn more about podcasts, visit the Education Podcast Network at www.epnweb.org.

BLOGS. Blogs (more formally, "web logs") are websites that "allow individuals to create personal webpages of text, pictures, graphics, videos, and other multimedia with the same ease as creating a word processing document" (Boling, Castek, Zawilinski, Barton, & Nierlich, 2008, p. 504). According to Oravec (2002), blogs are similar to online journals. The format allows authors (known as "bloggers") to work individually or in teams, engage in personal expression, and interact with others who comment on their blogs.

There are numerous ways to use blogs in content area teaching. They include the following options (adapted from edublogs.org):

- Post materials and resources.
- Hold online discussions.
- Create a class publication.
- Replace your newsletter.
- Get your students blogging.
- Share your lesson plans.
- Integrate multimedia of all descriptions.
- Organize.
- Get feedback.
- Create a fully functional website.

To examine sites that promote blogging, visit Edublogs at edublogs.org or Word Press at wordpress.org.

WIKIS. As noted in Figure 11.1, *wiki* is the Hawaiian word for "quick." Wikis allow a number of people to freely revise and edit text online. Content area students can use wikis for a variety of purposes, including revising and editing small-group research projects and class-authored books.

Making Connections | Thinking about Technology

- Consider specific ways in which you could use podcasts, blogs, and wikis when teaching in your content area.
- Share your thoughts with others in small-group discussions.

Using technology in the content areas seems to have endless possibilities. The following list of ideas is designed to help us think about specific ways in which it can be integrated into our teaching. Students can:

- Become authors on the Web and share their self-authored poems and stories with other students.

- Collaborate with other students on a worldwide basis on Internet projects
- Conduct online Discussion Circles.
- Use web-based bookmarking (Forbes, 2004).
- Refine a search.
- Evaluate online sources in several ways, including learning who constructed the site and for what purposes, and comparing and contrasting the information posted on several sites.
- E-mail and chat with peers around the world.
- Experience virtual field trips ranging from a tour of the White House (www.whitehouse.gov) to a tour of the Egyptian pyramids (www.pbs.org/wgbh/nova/pyramid).
- Create virtual field trips.
- Use webcam sites on which they view exactly what is happening at the time—for example on safari (www.africam.com) or at the Eiffel Tower (www.abcparislive.com).
- Collaborate with other classes to publish electronic newspapers or literary magazines.
- Use digital photography to represent their thinking.
- Create a class website or create personal websites.
- Communicate with students who are native language speakers and practice speaking the language.
- Collect data about environmental issues.
- Compare and contrast historical events in the area in which students live with those in areas in which other students live (Mike, 1996).
- Create a network of classes to explore ecological issues.

There are myriad ways to integrate technology into our teaching—not as an add-on, but as a natural and beneficial component of teaching and learning. Encouraging our students to use technology to learn will motivate them and extend their understandings.

 Making Connections
TO MULTIPLE LITERACIES

As Leu (2000) has reported, students write just as much in the age of technology as their counterparts did when curriculums were more traditionally based. This is especially true when students use information literacy to research. We need to ensure that our students know how to use the Internet as a research source and that they understand how to use informal and formal writing to record their thinking about these sites. For more information about these types of writing, see Chapter 10. ■

FINAL THOUGHTS

There is no doubt that technology has made, and will continue to make, important contributions to teaching and learning. It is certain that the future holds even greater possibilities. Clearly, traditional teaching and the technologies of the future will continue to be integrated. As Means (2000/2001) has observed:

> Schools that incorporate the technology of the future can offer the best combination of traditional face-to-face instruction—role modeling, socialization, and morale building—and projected benefits of learning with new technologies: increased participation in systems of distributed learning that engage broader communities, learning-enhancing representations of concepts and data, a restructuring of teaching and learning roles, and more meaningful assessment practices. (p. 61)

In the next chapter, we examine inquiry-based learning, a topic in which technology plays a significant role. Although inquiry can be traced back to early Greece, it has not always been valued in education. In Chapter 12, we explore it from a 21st century perspective.

Teaching Connections

APPLYING WHAT WE HAVE LEARNED

E-Links

The International Society for Technology in Education (ISTE) has developed National Educational Technology Standards and Performance Indicators for Students. Numerous Departments of Education have adapted these standards for use at the state level.

1. Review the ISTE Standards.
   (a) Consider how you plan to address selected standards in your teaching. Make specific connections between content and technology projects such as Internet Inquiry, Internet Project, Internet Workshop, or WebQuests. Record your thinking in a reflective portfolio entry.
   (b) Develop a standards-based lesson that integrates content and technology, including the use of resources such as podcasts, blogs, and wikis. Include your lesson in your portfolio as a resource for future teaching.

EXAMPLE WEBSITES

To review the National Educational Technology Standards and Performance Indicators for Students, visit this site:
http://www.iste.org/Content/NavigationMenu/NETS/ForStudents/2007Standards/NETS_for_Students_2007_Standards.pdf

Accountable Talk

Technology is an important facet of today's teaching. Meet in discipline-specific small groups to discuss how you will integrate technology into your teaching in your content area. Consider (1) what kind of technology access your students will need, (2) how you will motivate your students to participate in technology-based learning, and (3) how you will teach your students the skills needed to read online.

 ### Portfolio/Performance Opportunity

The Content Area Resource Anthology (CARA) is a project that is designed to align online resources with a variety of inquiry-based, creative teaching ideas. See Figure 11.6 for specifics of the project and Figure 11.7 for the CARA rubric. Create a CARA based on a specific topic related to your content area. The topic should be one you expect to teach, and one in which you have personal interest. (See Appendix F for sample excerpts from a CARA.) Include your CARA in your portfolio.

The Content Area Resource Anthology (CARA) is an Internet-based compilation of instructional resources that you can use in your teaching. Begin by selecting a topic that you would like to investigate—one that you believe will enhance your teaching and deepen students' understanding. After you discuss the topic with your professor, begin your investigation. The following guidelines will facilitate that process.

   I. **Contents Page:** List each segment of the CARA and its corresponding starting page.

  II. **Reflective Introduction:** Express your ideas about the topic, why you selected it, and how you think it will benefit your teaching.

 III. **Poems:** Use the Internet to locate 3 topic-related poems. Include copies of the poems, APA references, and brief summaries in your CARA. Then describe a creative and innovative teaching idea for each poem. (See your notes and this text's chapters on technology, inquiry-based learning, and alternative modes of representation.)

 IV. **Books (3 picture books, one chapter book):** Use the Internet, the library, and bookstores to locate 3 topic-related picture books and a chapter book. Include APA references and brief summaries of the books. Then describe a creative and innovative teaching idea you would use for each book. (See your notes and this text's chapters on technology, inquiry-based learning, and alternative modes of representation.)

  V. **Informational Articles:** Use the Internet to locate 3 topic-related informational articles that are either short enough to be used as read-alouds or have segments that can effectively be used as read-alouds. Include copies of the articles, APA references, and brief summaries. Then describe a creative and innovative teaching idea you would use for each. (See your notes and the section on read-alouds in Chapter 8.)

 VI. **Websites:** Use the Internet to locate 3 topic-related websites. Include APA references and brief summaries of the sites. Then describe a creative and innovative teaching idea you would use for each website. (See your notes and this text's chapters on technology, inquiry-based learning, and alternative modes of representation.)

VII. **Videos, DVDs, and CD-ROMs:** Use the Internet to locate 2 topic-related videos, DVDs, or CD-ROMs. Include APA references and brief summaries. Then describe a creative and innovative teaching idea you would use for each. (See your notes and this text's chapters on technology, inquiry-based learning, and alternative modes of representation.)

FIGURE 11.6
Content Area Resource Anthology

FIGURE 11.7 Content Area Resource Anthology Rubric

Reflection	4	3	2	1
Connections to topic	4	3	2	1
Teaching ideas	4	3	2	1
Differentiated instruction	4	3	2	1
Display of dispositions	4	3	2	1
Use of technology	4	3	2	1
Professional appearance	4	3	2	1

4: Excellent reflection demonstrating depth of reasoning. Outstanding connections to the CARA topic. In-depth, resourceful use of a wide range of creative and innovative teaching ideas, methods, instructional grouping practices (whole class, small groups, pairs, individual, and computer based), and curriculum materials, including types and levels of text, technology-based information, and nonprint materials for students at differing stages of development and cultural and linguistic backgrounds. Differentiated instruction demonstrates exceptional knowledge of students' abilities, interests, and cultural and linguistic backgrounds. A wide variety of texts (books, articles, technology-based texts, and nonprint material) reflecting students' interests, cultures, and linguistic backgrounds are selected, reviewed, and used. Risk taking is evident. Advanced dispositions related to content area reading are displayed. Fully developed and detailed use of technology. Totally professional in appearance (design, presentation, APA format).

3: Thorough reflection demonstrating sound reasoning. Detailed connections to the CARA topic. Integration of a variety of creative and innovative teaching ideas, methods, grouping practices (whole class, small groups, pairs, individual, and computer based), and curriculum materials, including types and levels of text, technology-based information, and nonprint materials for learners at different stages of development and cultural and linguistic backgrounds. Differentiated instruction demonstrates thorough understanding of students' abilities, interests, and cultural and linguistic backgrounds. A variety of texts (books, articles, technology-based texts, and nonprint material) reflecting students' interests, cultures, and linguistic backgrounds are selected, reviewed, and used. Proficient dispositions related to content area reading are displayed. Appropriate use of technology. The paper is professional in appearance (design, presentation, APA format).

2: Adequate reflection demonstrates reasoning. Connections to the CARA topic are somewhat consistent. Teaching ideas, methods, grouping practices (whole class, small groups, pairs, individual, and computer based), curriculum materials, including types and levels of text, technology-based information, and nonprint materials for learners at different stages of development and cultural and linguistic backgrounds lack variety and creative and innovative perspectives. Differentiated instruction demonstrates adequate knowledge of students' abilities, interests, and cultural and linguistic backgrounds. A limited variety of texts (books, articles, technology-based texts, and nonprint material) reflecting students' interests, cultures, and linguistic backgrounds are selected, reviewed, and used. Developing dispositions related to content area reading are displayed. Limited use of technology. Lacking elements of professional appearance (design, presentation, use of APA format).

1: Inadequate reflection—lacks depth and logical reasoning. Connections to the CARA topic are nonexistent or illogical. Teaching ideas, methods, grouping practices (whole class, small groups, pairs, individual, and computer based), curriculum materials, including types and levels of text, technology-based information, and nonprint materials for learners at different stages of development and cultural and linguistic backgrounds are not creative or innovative. Differentiated instruction demonstrates insufficient knowledge of students' abilities, interests, and cultural and linguistic backgrounds. Texts (books, articles, technology-based texts, and nonprint material) have little or no variety and do not reflect students' interests, cultures, and linguistic backgrounds are selected, reviewed, and used. Unacceptable dispositions related to content area reading are displayed. Inadequate use of technology. Less than professional in appearance (design, presentation, APA format).

12

Inquiry: Key to Critical and Creative Thinking in the Content Areas

For many of us, content area learning experiences were passive situations in which we either copied information from the board or took notes while a teacher lectured. These activities were, of course, routinely interrupted by a written quiz or test. There were few opportunities for student interaction, and the questions raised came from either the teacher or the text. Clearly, opportunities for inquiry in these contexts were extremely limited. Bruce and Bishop (2002) acknowledge that such practices remain common:

> Traditional curricula in most countries have emphasized a delivery of content approach. Knowledge is assumed to exist or be encoded within texts. The role of the teacher is to manage the delivery of this knowledge, and the role of the learner is to absorb as much as possible. More specifically, students are expected to master certain basic learning skills such as solving problems, remembering textbooks, following directions, working alone, and "covering" the curriculum.

These teaching and learning practices were not adequate in the past, and they are not adequate now. Today we and our students need to be thinkers—critical thinkers who know how to raise meaningful questions, and creative thinkers who see multiple ways to engage in problem solving. Such thinkers see the world as their text. For these thinkers, classrooms are transitioning from the more traditional model to a student-centered paradigm that provides a solid foundation for inquiry-based learning.

In this chapter, we discuss the theory that underpins inquiry-based learning and present content area activities that promote inquiry in a variety of contexts. We begin by defining inquiry-based learning and linking it to constructivism. Next, we explain two types of inquiry: problem-based and project-based learning. We explore a variety of inquiry-based activities in each category, provide guidelines for engaging in them, and present student examples. Finally, we discuss how to assess and evaluate inquiry-based projects.

What Is Inquiry-Based Learning?

Inquiry-based learning (IBL) is a project-oriented teaching method that is constructivist in nature (Eick & Reed, 2002). It is a process in which students ask questions that lead to new understandings, which in turn lead to new questions (Flint & Bomer, 2002). Short and Burke (1996) suggest that inquiry should be viewed as a framework for learning, a context in which students are encouraged to understand at deeper levels.

Although inquiry-based learning can be traced back to Socrates, its most recent emergence is linked to the constructivist movement, which suggests that students link what is new to what is known to construct personal meaning. In constructivism, problem-solving approaches, project-based learning, and many other variations on the theme, inquiry is a student-centered process (UICU, 2008). Taking this active role in learning implies that students possess the skills needed to seek resolutions to issues, as new knowledge is constructed ("Concept to Classroom," 2008). Principles that guide the teacher's role in constructivism include emphasizing students' responsibility for learning and promoting connections between what students learn and the world in which they live.

Inquiry-based learning is viewed as a cyclical process that includes five steps: question, investigate, create, discuss, and reflect. This process begins with curiosity and reflection, which lead to question generation. This is followed by an investigation. When the research is complete, the student creates a solution or product. The creation is then presented and discussed. This leads to more reflection, which in turn leads to more questions—and the process begins anew. During this recursive inquiry process, the student makes a variety of decisions, including selecting a topic, generating questions, determining research methods, choosing resources, and deciding on a mode of presentation.

Making Connections
TO MULTIPLE LITERACIES

When students engage in inquiry-based learning, they use multiple literacies including content literacies, adolescent literacy, and critical literacy. In addition, students need to have a good understanding of information literacy to complete inquiry-based tasks. They need to be able to ask good research questions, conduct a viable search, use a variety of quality sources, understand the information they locate, synthesize what they learn, and communicate their findings. Before engaging students in inquiry-based learning, we should use discussion or an informal assessment such as Tickets Out to ensure that all of our students are comfortable using information literacy. ■·

As noted in Figure 12.1, a number of motivational factors—including student self-selection of topics, accommodation of students' learning styles, and self-assessment and reflection—characterize inquiry-based learning. In addition, performance assessment provides students with opportunities to show what they know and can do through multiple modes. Inquiry-based learning also provides opportunities for students to use their strength modalities.

Inquiry-based learning benefits students in a variety of ways. It promotes collaborative learning and encourages students to understand at deeper levels. In the process, students become

Student centered	Self-selection of topics and research methods
Risk-taking context	Student ownership/responsibility for learning
Critical and creative thinking	Accommodation of students' learning styles
Research and exploration	Cross-curricular understandings
Social nature of learning	Self-assessment and reflection
Multiple modes of communication	Performance assessment
Learning at deeper levels	Teacher as facilitator

FIGURE 12.1
Factors That Characterize Inquiry-Based Learning

active, motivated participants. They generate questions and access and gather information. They engage in critical and creative thinking, and they analyze and synthesize information. They become problem solvers and understand questioning as a cyclical process.

Making Connections | **Thinking about Inquiry-Based Learning**

■ Teachers often recall their best teachers as those who engaged in inquiry-based learning. Reflect on your educational experiences. Did inquiry play a role? Contemplate how you would integrate inquiry into the curriculum you teach.

■ Share your reasoning with a partner and then join your partner in developing arguments to justify including inquiry-based learning in middle school and high school curriculums.

Making Connections
TO STRUGGLING READERS

When engaging struggling readers in inquiry-based learning, we can begin by reviewing Ciardiello's question generation techniques (see Chapter 8) and encourage use of presentation modes that accommodate students' differing learning styles. For example, some students might prefer to create a PowerPoint slideshow, use an electronic picture book format, or present what they have learned through songs or dramatizations. It is important that students choose a presentation mode that works well for them and that we, as teachers offer as much support as possible by scaffolding learning, arranging cross-age experiences, and ensuring students have a variety of accessible sources. ■

Which Instructional Techniques Promote Inquiry?

There are a variety of ways to integrate inquiry into content area teaching and learning. In this section, we address two frequently used approaches: problem-based and project-based learning. These methods naturally embed critical and creative thinking in inquiry-based experiences.

Problem-Based Learning

Problem-based learning challenges students to work collaboratively to reason their way to solutions of real-world problems. The problems are designed to motivate students to learn. The students work together and think critically and creatively to create solutions. As Checkley (1997) notes:

Problem-Based Learning is an instructional method that uses a real world problem as the context for an in-depth investigation of core content. The problems that students tackle are ill-structured; they include just enough information to suggest how students should proceed with an investigation, but never enough information to enable students to solve the problem without further inquiry. (p. 3)

Problem-based learning is generally characterized by four stages:

1. *Engaging students.* We motivate students by sharing general ideas about the problem-based scenario. We also leave gaps in the information. Students use questioning to fill in those gaps. This engages student interest in the problem-solving process.
2. *Inquiry and investigation.* Once students know some general information, they generate questions based upon it. Then they try to reason their way through the responses offered or derived from research.
3. *Solution products.* The products of problem-based learning are generally reasoned explanations. Students develop these solutions based on the information originally provided, responses to the questions they generated, and subsequent reasoning and additional questions.
4. *Debriefing.* This stage takes place after a solution has been proposed. Students revisit the clues derived from the responses, analyze the subsequent questions they generated, and discuss the paths each traveled to the solution.

These stages are linked because each progressive level builds a foundation for the subsequent phase (Stepien & Gallagher, 1997). Students become better problem solvers through problem-based learning because they refine their reasoning abilities, collaboration skills, and persistence as they engage in self-directed searches for solutions (Checkley, 1997).

GUIDELINES FOR STUDENTS ENGAGING IN PROBLEM-BASED LEARNING. When teaching this inquiry-based method to students, we can begin by explaining and demonstrating the process while emphasizing the importance of inquiry and reasoning. We can also share the following general guidelines, which provide direction for students engaging in problem-based learning:

1. *Understand the problem.* Listen carefully as your teacher explains what is known about the problem. Prepare to use your knowledge, skills, and other information as the solution progresses. Review the project rubric.
2. *Determine what you need to know.* Discuss what is known about the problem in small groups and brainstorm how it might be resolved. Revisit the rubric as necessary.
3. *Use collaborative skills when working in groups.* List each group member's strengths and consider how each might contribute to the solution.
4. *Communicate effectively.* Write the problem in your own words and revise as necessary throughout the process. Focus on meaningful questions and logical reasoning.
5. *Support thinking with evidence and sound reasoning.* List and discuss possible solutions. Write the group's solution and justify group members' thinking. Reflect on the reasoning process in which you engaged.

These guidelines provide support for students as they engage in problem-based learning and begin to structure problems on their own. As noted in these suggestions, questioning, collaboration, and reasoning are at the heart of this inquiry-based process.

Dramatized problem-based learning and Ripped from the Headlines: Real-Life Investigations are two examples of problem-based learning. In the former approach, students gather clues by interacting with those who have the problem; in the latter case, students work together to identify and resolve news-based problems.

**TEACHING IDEA**   DRAMATIZED PROBLEM-BASED LEARNING. In dramatized problem-based learning, students use inquiry to identify the problem and work toward resolution, while interacting with

people integrally involved in the problem (Stepien & Gallagher, 1997). The following scenario offers an example of dramatized problem-based learning:

> Ask students to imagine that the classroom is actually their home. After a knock is heard on the door, students begin to respond to it. Before they open the door, the students begin brainstorming about what awaits them when the door is opened. Students ask questions of the visitors before opening the door. After the questions are raised and answered, the students choose to open the door. At this point, students know what the problem is. In this case, students determined that the problem was set in the 1850s and the people at the door were runaway slaves. The students chose to open the door and admit the visitors to their home.
>
> After the visitors have entered, students engage in conversation with them. As the scenario progresses, students learn that the runaway slaves were destined for a stop on the Underground Railroad when they noticed fugitive slave catchers, who would capture them and force them to return to their owners, near that house. To avoid apprehension, they journeyed on in the darkness to the students' door.
>
> At this point the students focused their questions on what they believed they needed to know to resolve the problem. They worked collaboratively and communicated with one another and with the runaway slaves. The students knew that letting the runaway slaves into their home was just the beginning. They reasoned that the real problem was how to hide the runaway slaves and avoid breaking the law.

In this scenario, once all the information was discovered, the students realized that they must confront the situation and find a solution to the problem. This matter was, of course, complicated by the fact that it was illegal to hide runaway slaves in some states in the 1850s. This led to a number of fact-finding activities, including students' researching the issue using library and Internet sources, reviewing a journal kept by one of the runaway slaves, determining what they learned about the Underground Railroad that could help them resolve the problem, reading newspaper articles from the nineteenth century, and holding roundtable discussions about particular facts involved in the decision-making process. The inquiry-based process continued until the students came to a consensus of opinion about whether to hide the visitors in their home. After listing and debating possible solutions, the students decided to hide the runaway slaves in their home, find another home connected to the Underground Railroad, and send representatives there to determine how best to get the slaves back on the path to freedom.

 **TEACHING IDEA** **RIPPED FROM THE HEADLINES: REAL-LIFE INVESTIGATIONS.** Ripped from the Headlines is a long-term inquiry-based investigation that is often cross-curricular in nature. When using Ripped from the Headlines, teachers and students select an intriguing problem-based story from a news source as the basis for inquiry. Students clearly define the problem, and then they work to solve it. They decide which classes will investigate which aspect of the problem. They generate questions and use multiple research sources to gain and report information that will be used in the resolution of the case. Students brainstorm the types of information they need to know to make informed decisions and decide which research sources they will use. They meet regularly in workshop sessions, determine a solution to the problem, and often dramatize the outcome. In Ripped from the Headlines, the stories are always current, the basic information about the problem comes directly from a news source, and all of the known facts are released to the students at the start of the investigation.

The following application of this strategy was developed by Debi Stinner and her colleagues in the Bangor School District, Bangor, Pennsylvania. It focuses on integrating physics, history, and reading/language arts.

In this multiple-phase cross-curricular unit, students follow the events of an actual bus and train crash from reports of its occurrence to its closure in the judicial system. The unit incorporates reading/language arts, physics, and history classes and lasts for a period of approximately four weeks. All students work together, but each discipline does have some specific tasks. For example, physics students research the speed and impact of the train and bus, and history students investigate the state and town's train-crossing laws. The students' ultimate task is to decide who is responsible for the accident. Students clearly define the problem and research information about the accident through newspapers and the Internet. They carefully examine this information and participate in discussions with guest speakers, who include a defense attorney and a district attorney. Students also view the film *Twelve Angry Men*. As time progresses, the students develop courtroom evidence such as aerial scale drawings of the accident scene and calculations concerning momentum, stopping distance, speed, and force of impact.

The students then decide who they think caused the accident. They have determined that there are a variety of possibilities including the following:

- The bus driver, for not realizing the back of the bus was over the tracks
- The train engineer, for speeding
- The bus company, for improperly training substitute bus drivers
- The highway department, for widening the highway and not checking the timing on the trip switch
- The town council for insisting the highway be widened on the side toward the tracks

Next, the students participate in a mock trial. Prior to starting the unit, students have studied the judicial system, the roles it encompasses, and appropriate courtroom procedures. Students portray all roles including judge, jurors, prosecuting and defense attorneys, witnesses, and bailiff. Over the next several days, members of the court do a variety of things, including the following:

- Witnesses prepare their statements by researching their role and the comments they made in the newspaper articles.
- Lawyers prepare their cases, including interviewing the witnesses.
- Lawyers are provided with the National Transportation Safety Board report of the accident.
- The judge reviews the rules of the courtroom.
- The jurors review literature about types of evidence.

Then the actual trial takes place. After the verdict has been determined, members of the court engage in reflection about the roles they played. For example, the judge may ponder how she influenced the outcome of the trial and explain whether she agrees or disagrees with the verdict. Members of the jury may document why they felt the defendant was guilty or innocent. The lawyers may describe what the basis of their case was, who they think won or lost, and what they would do differently if the trial could be held again.

Ripped from the Headlines: Real-Life Investigations enhances students' learning and motivates them in a number of ways. First, it requires students to read the newspaper—a primary information source for our society. While students may have already been reading newspapers for sports, comics, advertisements, or advice columns, this activity helps them connect to actual news stories and raise their own questions. Students become attuned to the print medium and often continue reading the news after the project is complete, frequently suggesting topics for future investigations. In addition, the integrated nature of Ripped from the Headlines helps students see connections between and among subject areas. Further, students interact not only with classmates and teachers, but also with community members whose professions are linked to the topic of investigation. Finally, dramatizing the event accommodates individual learning styles and offers students an alternative way to demonstrate what they have learned.

Students are motivated to engage in problem-based learning because they find the real-life topics interesting and because they can contribute to the problem-solving process as independent thinkers. Students take an active role, raise questions, apply content area knowledge, use multiple sources, work cooperatively with others, and engage in decision making—all skills they will use throughout their lives.

Problem-based learning provides opportunities for students to take ownership of their learning, gain insights into their reasoning processes, and work with others to develop common understandings. In the next section, we focus on project-based learning, another type of inquiry-based experience.

Project-Based Learning

Project-based learning is a dynamic process that encourages students to learn at deeper levels. Students develop confidence in their ability to communicate, learn, and research when engaging in this project-centered approach. They create knowledge based on questions they have raised and information they have gathered. They can also choose to respond in modes that accommodate their learning styles.

Project-based learning generally involves long-term projects. After making several choices, students engage in inquiry about a self-selected topic. They research that topic using a variety of methods, including reference books and websites. The task usually ends in the creation of a product or performance that reflects what the students know and how they can use what they have learned.

GUIDELINES FOR STUDENTS ENGAGING IN PROJECT-BASED LEARNING. When teaching this type of inquiry-based learning to our students, we can begin by explaining how it works and encouraging students to make connections to previous knowledge and experiences. Then we can demonstrate it, emphasizing the critical roles that questioning and reasoning play. We can also share the following general guidelines, which provide direction for students engaging in project-based learning:

1. *Select an inquiry focus.* Choose a content-related topic to be the focus of your investigation. Be prepared to justify your choice. Review the project rubric.
2. *Consider what you want to know about the topic and develop a research plan.* Create meaningful questions and consider how you will navigate your route to responses, knowing that those questions may lead to other questions.
3. *Choose a presentation format.* Consider a variety of possibilities and choose one that accommodates your learning style preferences.
4. *Use multiple sources to research your topic.* Remember to include each in your list of references. Revisit the project rubric periodically to ensure you are addressing all of the criteria.
5. *Participate in class inquiry workshop sessions.* Discuss a variety of topics, including your research plan, questions, sources, and progress with peers. Provide feedback to others. Consider feedback you receive and revise your plan as necessary.
6. *Schedule progress conferences.* Meet with the teacher at least twice during the planning stages and after that as needed. Consider feedback and revise as necessary.
7. *Engage in self-evaluation by completing the project rubric.* Consider the outcome and revise as necessary.
8. *Practice and present the inquiry-based investigation.* Reflect on the inquiry processes in which you engaged.

These guidelines provide support and direction for students as they engage in project-based learning. As noted in these general suggestions, questioning, researching, revising, and reasoning play important roles in this inquiry-based process. Examples of project-based learning featured in this section include individual projects as well as small-group endeavors.

FIRST-PERSON EXPERIENCES. In First-Person Experiences, students assume the identities of people who played an active role in the event or time period they have chosen to investigate. This inquiry-based project is based on three student-directed decisions. First, students determine the topic they want to research and which person they will become to report their research. Second, they choose the format through which they will share their investigation. Third, they determine the information sources and inquiry techniques they will use to conduct their investigation.

Books, articles, newspapers, public documents, DVDs, interviews, correspondence, and the Internet are some of the information sources students have accessed when creating First-Person Experiences. Research techniques have included personal interviews, surveys, library and Internet searches, experiments, letters of inquiry, field trips, and e-mail. Figure 12.2 shows some of the formats students have chosen to use when presenting First-Person Experiences.

When teaching students how to create First-Person Experiences, we should explain and model the process, emphasizing the critical roles of student choice, reasoning, and

FIGURE 12.2

Examples of Formats for Presenting First-Person Experiences

Advertising campaigns	Alphabet books	Correspondence
Diaries	Digital films	Dramatizations
Historical documents	Interviews	Inventions
Journal entries	Messages in bottles	Newspaper articles
Personal narratives	Photo histories	Poetry
Radio scripts	Song lyrics	Travel brochures

planning. We should also share the following general guidelines, which provide direction for students:

1. Review the project rubric.
2. Choose the person that will be the focus of your First-Person Experience.
3. Discuss your choice and describe what you expect to learn from your research.
4. Create viable research questions.
5. Consider the sources you will use to research your topic.
6. Determine how you will present your First-Person Experience.
7. Meet in workshop sessions to review the project rubric, compile your information, discuss your progress, and plan your presentation.
8. When the research is complete, ensure that all of the important information and appropriate references are included in the presentation. Review the rubric. Practice the presentation.
9. Engage in self-evaluation by completing the project rubric. Revise as necessary.
10. Present your First-Person Experience.

The following is an excerpt from a First-Person Experience created in biology class. In this presentation, Yvonne Stoffey communicates what she learned about Robert Hooke, a scientist who discovered the cell, through a series of letters. She chose this mode of presentation because she learned that throughout his life Hooke had corresponded with Grace, a woman he loved but never married.

September, 1665

Dearest Grace,

This is perhaps the greatest day in my entire scientific career. I was looking through an instrument called a microscope. I was examining various objects and trying to figure out how the microscope can be helpful in applications to different aspects of sciences. I took a piece of cork and placed it under the scope. Alas! There were many small compartments. After studying them closer, I concluded they were pores. I also believe that they are passages to carry liquids for the plant's growth, and I am trying to locate the valves that must obviously be present.

I continued my investigation and examined materials from the mineral, vegetable, and animal kingdoms. I realized that they all consisted of the same tiny "cells." This is the term my fellow researchers and I have decided to label these small compartments. The cells have various shapes and sizes. I drew diagrams of my discovery. My work will now be published in a book I have written entitled Micrographia.

I miss you and wish you could be here to share these exciting times.

Robert

Students are motivated to create First-Person Experiences because they can self-select the topics and communicate factual information in creative ways. This inquiry-based process requires students to think in depth about their research topics and helps them feel as if they are participants in the times and events they are investigating.

First-Person Experiences offer students opportunities to present research in different modes. The Rest of the Story, another inquiry-based technique, encourages them to think more deeply about people and events about which they already have superficial knowledge.

THE REST OF THE STORY. Most of us can clearly recall particular facts we learned in science or social studies, such as lists of inventors and their inventions or explorers and their discoveries. Alexander Graham Bell is a great example. For most of us, his name was on an inventors list as the person who created the telephone. But what is The Rest of the Story? Did you know that Bell was very dedicated to helping the deaf and was, in fact, a mentor to Helen Keller? Did you know that he served as president of the National Geographic Society? Did you know that he filed his patent for the telephone hours before another man filed a similar patent? Did you know that Bell was very interested in airplanes and worked with a group that flew a plane they had developed in Canada in 1909? This is the type of information revealed when students choose to research The Rest of the Story.

The Rest of the Story is an inquiry-based investigation that encourages the researcher to go beyond the basic facts generally known about a person, discovery, invention, or event in content area study. When engaging in this project, students locate information by using reference books and websites as resources. Technology also plays a role in the way students choose to format their investigations to share them with the class; they often elect to design a home page or create software. CDs and DVDs are other popular formatting selections. When using DVDs, students may report their research as a news story or choose to dramatize the results of their investigation (for more information about drama in the content areas, see Chapter 13).

The following example of The Rest of the Story about Albert Einstein was researched by science student Sue Matol:

> Most people know that Albert Einstein is considered one of the greatest scientific minds the world has ever known. He is the physicist who discovered the theory of relativity. People quickly associate him with $E = mc^2$ because the formula is so closely linked to his name. Einstein's genius is legendary, but there is much more to know about him. The following is an excerpt from the Rest of the Story.
>
> Did you know that Einstein did not speak until he was four years old? Or that despite his high IQ, he failed his initial entrance exam to Zurich Polytechnic? Albert's favorite pastime was sailing, which he considered "the sport which demands the least energy." In 1905 Albert Einstein wrote his famous "Special Theory of Relativity" paper. It was published in a scientific journal that same year, but it took many years for Einstein's ideas to gain general acceptance. In fact, his theory was not verified by actual experiment until 25 years later. Einstein won the Nobel Prize for Physics and he was asked to be the president of Israel, but he declined.
>
> After his death, a pathologist removed Einstein's brain and preserved it for future study, hoping to one day learn the secret of Einstein's genius. Because Einstein feared his gravesite would attract curiosity seekers, he was cremated and his ashes were scattered over a river in New Jersey. In the year 2000, Time magazine named Einstein the "Person of the Century."

Students are motivated to engage in The Rest of the Story, because they are interested in learning more about people they know about only in passing. The research itself is motivational because students are interested in what they can learn and share that their classmates may not know. It is like successfully putting together the rest of a life puzzle.

When researching the rest of the story, students use their curiosity to learn more about a person's life. In Press Conference (another inquiry-based project), students use inquiry to learn more about topics—often current events—of interest to them. Then they present the information orally.

PRESS CONFERENCE. Press Conference is an inquiry-based activity that promotes oral communication. It is based on student interest in a particular content-related topic. Students peruse newspapers, magazines, or the Internet to find articles of interest to themselves and their peers. When they find a topic that intrigues them, they discuss it with their teacher and then begin their research.

Because a Press Conference lasts only a few minutes, it is the type of inquiry-based activity that each student might present once each marking period. To support students'

FIGURE 12.3 QuIP Research Grid: Tsunamis

Questions	Answers	
	Source A: The Tsunamis Story http://www.tsunami.noaa.gov/	**Source B: Tsunami** http://encarta.msn.com/encyclopedia_761559898/Tsunami.html
1. What are tsunamis?	Tsunami is a Japanese word, represented by two characters: tsu, meaning, "harbor", and nami meaning, "wave".	Tsunami is a Japanese word meaning "harbor wave," used as the scientific term for a class of abnormal sea wave that can cause catastrophic damage when it hits a coastline.
2. What causes tsunamis?	Tsunamis are caused by any large, abrupt disturbance of the sea-surface, such as earthquakes.	Tsunamis can be generated by an undersea earthquake, an undersea landslide, the eruption of an undersea volcano, or by the force of an asteroid crashing into the ocean. The most frequent cause of tsunamis is an undersea earthquake.
3. How dangerous are tsunamis?	Since 1850 alone, tsunamis have been responsible for the deaths of more than 420,000 lives and billions of dollars of damage.	The worst tsunami disaster in history occurred in December 2004 when a tsunami that struck the coasts of 14 countries from Southeast Asia to northeastern Africa caused the deaths of 250,000 people.
4. How do tsunami warning systems work?	Since 1946, the tsunami warning system has provided warnings of potential tsunami danger in the pacific basin by monitoring earthquake activity and the passage of tsunami waves at tide gauges. But there is no instrument that accurately predicts the impact of a tsunami at a particular coastal location.	The Pacific Marine Environmental Laboratory developed the first reliable scientific instrument for detecting tsunamis and quickly alerting scientists when a tsunami occurs. The instrument, known as a tsunameter, is anchored on the ocean floor and measures changes in water pressure when a tsunami passes above. The early warning system is known as the Deep-ocean Assessment and Reporting of Tsunamis (DART).
5. What can people do to survive tsunamis	Listen to the tsunami warning system.	Listen to reports from DART.

preparation for Press Conference, teachers can encourage them to use an extended Questions into Paragraphs (QuIP) organizer to structure their research questions and responses. We can extend the QuIP to include five questions or three sources, or both. For example, the QuIP about tsunamis featured in Figure 12.3 has been extended by adding two additional research questions.

When preparing for Press Conference, students consult a minimum of two research sources. After reading the information they have searched, focusing on its essential points, synthesizing it, raising additional questions, and reflecting on personal insights, each student shares the information through an informal presentation to the class. Then members of the audience raise questions—just as if they were participating in an actual press conference. If the presenter cannot answer the question, he joins the questioner in researching a response and reporting back to the class.

To assess Press Conference, we can use a checklist that provides direction for students as they engage in this inquiry-based activity. Students can also use the checklist as a self-assessment after they have completed their Press Conference. Figure 12.4 features an example of such a checklist.

Press Conferences usually focus on content-related developments or current events. Students are motivated to engage in Press Conferences because they can choose the topics and engage in self-directed research.

Making Connections
TO ENGLISH LEARNERS

When English learners research and present Press Conferences, teachers can support them in several ways. To begin, students might choose a topic that relates to countries where their native language is spoken. Then they might choose to present the information with a native English speaker, with each partner reporting the research sentence by sentence first in one language, then in the other—a format similar to echo reading. Students can also choose to use a PowerPoint slideshow or record the Press Conference with a peer for presentation to the class. The presenter(s) could then become the press secretaries and ask preplanned questions. English learners can also use the Questions into Paragraphs graphic organizer when planning the presentation. To facilitate the organizer's use, we can color-code the various sections. The important point is that the English learners feel confident engaging in oral presentations that focus on self-selected content area topics. ■

Press Conference Checklist

The student

_____   Chose a topic.

_____   Conferenced with the teacher.

_____   Used the Questions into Paragraphs (QuIP) organizer.

_____   Developed at least 3 quality research questions.

_____   Conducted a viable search for sources.

_____   Used at least 2 quality sources.

_____   Demonstrated knowledge of the topic.

_____   Presented Press Conference effectively.

Student's comments:

_____

_____

_____

Teacher's comments:

_____

_____

_____

Name _____   Date _____

FIGURE 12.4
Press Conference Checklist

Making Connections | Thinking about Press Conferences

- Peruse current newspapers and websites to locate a topic that relates to your content area. Research the topic, complete a QuIP, and prepare a 3-minute Press Conference.

- Present your Press Conference to a partner. Save your research and completed QuIP as examples for when you teach Press Conference to your students.

Although students preparing Press Conferences work on their own when selecting topics and completing their research, they do have opportunities to conference with the teacher and workshop their ideas with peers. In Inquiring Minds, our next inquiry-based project, students work in small groups organized by topics of interest.

 **TEACHING IDEA**

INQUIRING MINDS. Inquiring Minds is an inquiry-based, small-group research activity based on student-selected content area topics. When using Inquiring Minds, students form small groups based on their topic choices. The small groups brainstorm three to five questions about their topic that the group members would like to be able to answer through their research. This sets a purpose and offers direction to their investigation. Group members list their topic and the questions on a piece of chart paper. Each group in the class uses a different color marker to record this information.

After all groups have completed their questions, the charts are posted around the room. Each group then engages in a gallery walk, moving together from posted list to posted list reviewing the topics and questions each of the other groups has proposed. Each group in the class then adds any questions its members may have to the posted lists. Each group's contributions can either be labeled (e.g., "Group 3") or be indicated through the use of different colored markers. This allows the students who originated the list to see which groups made inquiries about their topics. It also provides a way to contact the contributors if any of the questions is unclear.

Next, the posted list about each topic is returned to the group that created it. At this point, the list contains both the original questions and the queries that have been added by other research groups. The group members then discuss the questions that have been proposed by their peers and seek clarification as necessary. This process helps the original group to broaden the scope of its research and creates great interest among those who added questions when the research is reported. They have interest in the results of all of the research, but they are especially motivated to learn how groups responded to the questions they raised. Figure 12.5 features a final research question list for Group 2 from a history class studying the American Presidents.

When teaching students how to engage in Inquiring Minds, we should explain and model the process, emphasizing the critical roles that reasoning, collaboration, and planning play in this project. We should also share the following general guidelines, which provide direction for students engaging in Inquiring Minds. To begin, students make a list of three research topics in which

FIGURE 12.5
Group 2's Original
Research Question List
and Final Research
Question List

Group 2: Abraham Lincoln

Research Questions

1. What is known about Abraham Lincoln's early life?

2. How did Lincoln become interested in public service?

3. Why did Lincoln decide to write the Emancipation Proclamation? What was the message of this document?

4. How did Lincoln serve his country before becoming President? (Group 1)

5. Describe Lincoln's beliefs about our country at the end of the Civil War. (Group 3)

6. Compare and contrast the messages of Lincoln's first inaugural address and his second. (Group 5)

they have interest. Next, we review their lists and organize the students into groups of 4 or 5 members who have interest in researching the same topic. Then the students follow these guidelines:

1. Meet as a group and review the project rubric.
2. Discuss the group-selected topic and determine what the members would like to learn from researching it. Write the topic at the top of the chart paper provided.
3. Discuss how the group will share its research—PowerPoint slideshow, dramatization, alphabet book, and so on.
4. Create 3 to 5 research questions and write them on the chart paper using the color markers provided.
5. When the questions are complete, post the chart paper on the wall.
6. As a group, visit each posted list. Read the topic and the proposed research questions. Discuss these queries as a group. Then add one or two questions the group would like to have researched concerning the topic of each list. Be sure to label the questions your group adds with the group's number.
7. When all groups have visited all of the research lists, remove your group's list from the wall and discuss any additional questions with group members. Consider whether the questions would enhance the research goals and whether any of the questions can be combined. If necessary, contact the group that proposed the question for clarification.
8. Discuss how the group members will conduct the research. Develop a schedule to meet the Inquiring Minds project due date.
9. Meet in workshop sessions to review the project rubric, compile information, discuss progress, and plan the presentation.
10. When the research is complete, ensure that all of the important information is included in the presentation. Review the rubric. Practice the presentation.
11. Engage in self-evaluation by completing the rubric. Encourage all group members to share their completed rubrics. Discuss and revise the project as necessary.
12. Join the group in presenting Inquiring Minds.

Students are motivated to engage in Inquiring Minds because it is a student-centered activity. Group members enjoy working with peers who have expressed interest in researching the same topic and making the essential decisions about the project. They also take ownership of learning as they use the project rubric as a guide to research, workshop, plan, and present what they have learned.

The Oral History Project is another technique that captures students' interest. In this inquiry-based project, students choose an individual they know as the focus of their inquiry. The Oral History Project works because everyone has a life story to tell.

 **TEACHING IDEA** **ORAL HISTORY PROJECT.** The Oral History Project is a long-term process in which students research the personal histories of other individuals (Dickson, Heyler, Reilly, & Romano, 2006). It is an authentic experience that often includes working with members of previous generations. This helps students to make connections to the past—times that they themselves did not experience—while researching another person's life story. During the project, students actively engage in interviewing the person they have selected and develop a presentation that will include research, artifacts, a feature article, a personal memoir, and a photograph.

When the project is complete, it is given to the person it is designed to honor during a class celebration. The Oral History Project has been purposefully designed to meet academic standards for reading, writing, speaking, and listening, as well as those related to information literacy and historical understanding. Formatting of oral histories can vary from traditional tri-folds to more creative methods. Figure 12.6 shows the completed history of Kevin Michael Gallagher.

Students find this project to be highly motivational for a number of reasons. First, the students choose the person they will honor in the oral history project. Next, even though they have a project outline and rubric to follow, the students are in charge of contacting the person, conducting the interview, and making the project work. Third, the students work with primary sources, which they often find more exciting than using secondary sources.

FIGURE 12.6
An Oral History Project

When students engage in inquiry-based learning, they create meaningful questions, use strategies, communicate effectively, think critically and creatively, and use technology. Detailed descriptions of resources students can use to facilitate these processes can be found in chapters throughout this text.

Making Connections
TO WRITING

Although students can use many creative ways to present what they learn through inquiry-based learning, writing is often part of the process and the product. For example, as they engage in the process of researching topics, students use writing to take notes and synthesize information about the inquiry-based topics. They also use writing when they choose to present what they have learned through writing-based products such as diary pages, PowerPoint slides, Inquiring Minds, and the Oral History Project. ■

How Can We Effectively Assess and Evaluate Inquiry-Based Learning?

When students engage in inquiry-based learning, they demonstrate what they know and can do. In most cases, we can assess how students engage in the process and evaluate the product they create.

To assess or gather information about how students engage in the process, we can use observation and a checklist. For example, if students were creating a First-Person Experience, we might include the items featured on the checklist in Figure 12.7. Then we could indicate that students have demonstrated each factor by placing a check mark in front of each statement.

Observation Checklist: First-Person Experience

The student

1. _____   Self-selected content-related topic to research.
2. _____   Determined which person to become.
3. _____   Selected, accessed, and used relevant information sources.
4. _____   Sought feedback from several peers during workshop sessions.
5. _____   Used feedback to revise project.
6. _____   Chose a meaningful format for presenting information.
7. _____   Presented First-Person Experience effectively

Comments on student performance:

_____

_____

_____

_____

_____

Name _____ Date _____

FIGURE 12.7
**Observation Checklist:
First-Person Experience**

We often use a checklist in conjunction with a rubric or scoring guide. We can use the checklist to assess students during the process and use the rubric to evaluate the final First-Person Experience. Rubrics, which are detailed in Chapter 14, are provided before students begin a project. This affords students the opportunity to view the rubric as a performance guide: In other words, they understand what they need to do to achieve at various levels.

Rubrics generally have multiple criteria, each of which is described at multiple levels. For example, a rubric for The Rest of the Story would include research sources. The sources would then be described at each level of the rubric. As seen in Figure 12.8, the research sources at the highest level (4.0) would be described as *outstanding* and at the lowest level (1.0) as *inadequate*. When creating rubrics, it is important to use language that clearly indicates the differences between and among performance levels.

FIGURE 12.8
First-Person
Experience Rubric

4.0 Made excellent decisions concerning topic selection. Used outstanding sources. Demonstrated exceptional knowledge of information literacy. Included excellent information. Demonstrated outstanding critical and creative thinking. Chose a superb presentation format. Used the workshop format to greatest benefit. Collaborated extremely well with others. Excellent reference list. Outstanding presentation.

3.0 Made very good decisions about topic selection. Used high-quality sources. Demonstrated proficient knowledge of information literacy. Included in-depth information. Demonstrated high levels of critical and creative thinking. Chose a very good presentation format. Used the workshop format to great benefit. Collaborated very well with others. Detailed reference list. Skillful presentation.

2.0 Made appropriate decisions concerning topic selection. Used satisfactory sources. Demonstrated adequate knowledge of information literacy. Included essential information. Demonstrated critical and creative thinking. Chose a viable presentation format. Used the workshop format to benefit. Collaborated with others. Sufficient reference list. Adequate presentation.

1.0 Made poor decisions about topic selection. Used inadequate sources. Demonstrated insufficient knowledge of information literacy. Included insufficient essential information. Demonstrated little critical and creative thinking. Chose a poor presentation format. Used the workshop format to little benefit. Did not collaborate well with others. Inadequate reference list. Poor presentation.

Comments: _____

_____

When we use a rubric to evaluate student work, it is essential that we provide it to the students when the project is first introduced. We should discuss the rubric at that point, noting that it provides a clear picture of what needs to be included and the quality of work it requires. For more detailed information about rubrics and further examples, see Chapter 14.

FINAL THOUGHTS

Inquiry-based learning experiences foster creativity, variety, and innovation. They also motivate and engage students. Inquiry-focused classrooms become places where ideas are born, valued, and nurtured. Students become problem seekers as well as problem solvers. Inquiry-based experiences and the resulting critical and creative thinking serve as the foundation of dynamic teaching and learning. These are, without question, the direct antithesis of the "read the chapter and answer the questions" contexts in which many students experience content area instruction. Rather, they are the classrooms of the 21st century in which teachers, students, and texts come together as active participants in learning communities.

In the next chapter, we discuss alternative representations of thinking. These modes provide students with a variety of ways to express their ideas and be creative in the process.

Teaching Connections
APPLYING WHAT WE HAVE LEARNED

E-Links

Consider how you will integrate project-based learning into your teaching. Then choose a topic related to your content area and develop an annotated list of 10 websites your students can use when engaging in inquiry-based learning. Share your choices with peers in small group discussions.

Use websites such as these to complete your project:

History: *The American Civil War Homepage*
http://sunsite.utk.edu/civil-war/warweb.html

Mathematics: *Biographies of Women Mathematicians*
http://www.agnesscott.edu/lriddle/women/alpha.htm

Biology: *The Biology Project*
http://www.biology.arizona.edu/

Accountable Talk

Inquiry is at the center of all learning. Think about the role inquiry has played in your learning process, and then reflect on how you might integrate it into your teaching. In particular, consider how you might teach your students to think from an inquiry-based perspective. Discuss your thoughts with others who teach in your content area. Include a summary of the discussion and your thoughts as a reflective entry in your portfolio.

Portfolio/Performance Opportunity

Meet with peers in a small group and discuss how you can integrate the inquiry-based activities presented in this chapter into your teaching. Then (1) choose one of the project-based activities presented in this chapter, (2) select websites related to your content area to support your task, (3) choose a mode of presentation, and (4) complete the project. Share your completed project with peers and discuss your reflections on learning through inquiry. Include the completed project in your portfolio.

13

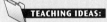
Poetry, Drama, Music, and Art: Alternative Representations of Thinking

In our teaching, traditional spoken and written responses may be the most common, but they are not the only modes of representation to which we and our students have access. Poetry, drama, music, and art permeate all subjects of content area study and may provide more meaningful and more creative ways for students to represent their ideas. These modes of representation, which are also known as symbol systems, can be used independently or in conjunction with other modes.

Elliot Eisner (1997) speaks about forms of representation as accommodating "the possibilities of the human mind." He notes:

> Each product humans create embodies the forms of thinking that led to its realization, each of them provides testimony to what humans can achieve, each one represents a silent but eloquent statement concerning the scope and possibilities of the human mind, and each one comes into being through the use of one or more forms of representation. (p. 350)

Eisner and others see forms of representation as culture based (Eisner, 1997; Greene, 1997; Salomon, 1997). Eisner (1993) also reminds us that using multiple modes of representation encourages students to construct meanings that they otherwise may not create. Understanding poses challenges to learners; using alternative modes of representation provides unique ways of expressing their understanding.

In this chapter, we provide information about the use of alternative modes of representation in content area study. We begin by presenting a rationale for using multiple modes of presentation. Next, we examine poetry, drama, music, and art individually. In each of these sections, we discuss rationales for using the formats, student motivation, teaching ideas, student examples, and assessment possibilities.

Why Should We Use Multiple Modes of Representation?

The goal of our teaching is student understanding, but our definition of understanding reaches beyond the usual comprehension of text. Mansilla and Gardner (1997) suggest that we consider understanding as "both the ability to use knowledge and the ability to engage in disciplinary modes of thinking" (p. 386). Eisner (1997) extends this thinking by proposing five principles that support our understanding of forms of representation:

1. The form we use to represent our ideas influences the processes and products of thinking.
2. Different forms of representation nurture different thinking skills.
3. The form of representation we choose influences what we are able to represent as well as what we are able to see.
4. Forms of representation can be combined to offer students a greater array of resources.
5. Each form can be used in different ways, each of which requires different skills and forms of thinking.

When we contemplate the prospect of students representing their content area thinking through a variety of modes, we should consider the possibilities provided by poetry, drama, music, and art. In poetry, students can share their thoughts by phrasing and organizing them in creative ways. In drama, students can use dialogue and actions to represent their thoughts. In music, students can represent their thoughts by writing song lyrics or by selecting instrumental music to support their thinking. Finally, in art, students can create transmediations, sketch, sculpt, paint, make collages, or integrate modes of representation by creating projects such as self-authored electronic books.

In the sections that follow we focus on poetry, drama, music, and art as modes students can use to represent their thoughts. These methods provide a variety of options beyond those commonly used in content area classrooms.

How Can We Teach Our Students to Use Poetry as a Mode of Representation?

Reading poetry offers a way to motivate students and help them acquire background knowledge. As teachers, it provides us with a means to capture students' attention, establish a focus, and encourage discussion. Using poetry as a mode of representation supports and enriches students' learning in the content areas. It also helps students to think critically and extend their understanding.

Using poetry in the content areas has benefits for both teachers and students. As noted in Figure 13.1, poetry offers us a variety of ways to motivate and encourage student learning in the content areas. Poetry also accommodates students' needs. As noted in Figure 13.2, it provides them with opportunities to engage in learning, use higher-level thinking, and communicate in alternative modes.

Poetry stimulates the use of mental imagery and critical thinking. Within that context, science and math concepts can more easily be visualized, social issues can be discussed or debated, people or events of historical significance can be made authentic, alternative viewpoints can be explored, and connections between personal experiences and new concepts can be made.

FIGURE 13.1

The Benefits of Using
Poetry to Teach in the
Content Areas

Teachers can use poetry for the following purposes:

- Motivating student learning
- Activating prior knowledge
- Providing prior knowledge
- Encouraging students to create personal meaning
- Encouraging students to engage socially
- Offering a different perspective
- Encouraging students to take an aesthetic stance
- Enriching and extending students' thinking
- Assessing student learning
- Providing an alternative mode to represent thinking

Using poetry as a form of representation expands the students' role from readers to authors and engages them in deeper thinking processes. It also offers multiple opportunities for student choice: They may self-select their writing topics; write in response to something they've read or reflect on personal content-related experiences; choose from a variety of formats to express their ideas; write collaboratively or individually; and express perspectives ranging from humorous observations to serious contemplations.

We can use discussion or simple informal measures such as quickwrites to determine what our students' past experiences with poetry have been. We can dispel misconceptions about poetry before teaching students how to use it to represent their thoughts. Among the most frequently encountered—and mistaken—beliefs are that poetry always needs to rhyme, poems have only one interpretation, and poetry is boring. Discussing these issues openly assures students that poetry has many formats, is open to personal interpretation, and is content related.

To assess the form poems in this section, we can use observation, use checklists that address components of the poems and students' work habits, or read and comment on the poems. These modes of representation are informal, so we should not use rubrics to evaluate them. For more information about formal and informal assessment, see Chapter 14.

The following examples of form poems are appropriate for all content areas. We will need to explain and demonstrate the poetry formats, but because the formats guide students' thinking, they often feel comfortable writing form poems relatively quickly. Encouraging students to begin by working with a partner provides additional support during their initial endeavors.

 **TEACHING IDEA**

ACROSTIC POEMS. Using Acrostic Poems as forms of representation is motivational for students, because they have knowledge about the topic before they write. Acrostics are the easiest of the form poems to write and, consequently, serve as a good way to introduce content area students to using poetry to represent their thinking. This type of poem can be used for several purposes in the content areas. For example, students can use this format to share background knowledge about a topic, provide insights into their thinking, or summarize

FIGURE 13.2

The Benefits of Using
Poetry to Learn in the
Content Areas

Students can use poetry for the following purposes:

- Experiencing an alternative way of learning
- Developing communication skills, including active listening
- Thinking critically and creatively
- Summarizing their thinking
- Gaining new perspectives
- Exploring personal interpretations in social settings
- Visualizing abstract or challenging concepts
- Communicating in alternative modes

what they have learned. This form poem is appropriate for students at most grade levels, including those in middle and high school.

After explaining and demonstrating the format, we can invite students to use their first names to write Acrostics about themselves. This is a fun activity, because the students definitely have background knowledge of the subjects. Encouraging students to share their ideas with partners provides additional support.

When writing Acrostic Poems, students vertically write the word or phrase that is the focus of their poem. Then they use each letter of the word or phrase to start a line of the poem that refers to or describes the topic. This is an example John McGraw created to represent his thoughts about himself while learning about Acrostics in chemistry class:

Junior

Overworked

Happy

Never satisfied

Students can also use Acrostics to provide summaries about their content areas. Stephen Inghrim did just that when he wrote this Acrostic about geometry:

Graphs of points on a Cartesian plane

Endless calculations of areas

Oblique and right, obtuse and acute

Measures of angles

Endpoints, midpoints, bisectors

Three-dimensional or perhaps only two

Rectangles, squares, and circles abound

You are the mathematics of shapes

Once students have learned how to use this format, writing Acrostics takes only a portion of a class period. During the writing process, we should be available to support students as needed. When the Acrostics are completed, students should have the opportunity to share them in small groups. If they have written about their content area, they can also contribute their poems to a class book of Acrostic poems.

When creating Acrostics, the content of the poem is determined by the topic. When writing Cinquains, another type of form poetry, the content is also determined by the topic, but the number and types of words required in each line are determined by the format.

TEACHING IDEA

CINQUAINS. The Cinquain (pronounced "sin-kane") is another poetry format that can be used by middle and high school students to represent ideas in the content areas. The format of this 5-line poem focuses on a word and its synonym—a word that has the same meaning. (For a reproducible copy of the Cinquain poem format, see Appendix A.)

As when teaching all new ideas, we can begin by explaining how a Cinquain works and encouraging students to make connections. Then we can demonstrate the Cinquain by writing one. Students are motivated to use this format to represent their thoughts because following the Cinquain format is similar to completing a puzzle. Students may self-select topics, but they need to ensure that the topic they choose also has a synonym. When teaching students how to write Cinquains, it is a good idea to begin by completing the first line (the topic) and the last line (the synonym). Then write the remaining lines, which provide details about the topic. Encouraging students to write their first Cinquain with partners enables students to share ideas and provide support. When the Cinquains are completed, students can share them in small groups.

In the following example, Javier Martinez shares the Cinquain about Martin Luther King, Jr., in his American history class. Notice that the Cinquain format features a description of the words required directly below each line.

King
One-word noun

powerful intelligent
Two adjectives describing line 1

marching reasoning uniting
"Ing" words telling actions of line 1

inspirational civil rights defender
Four-word phrase describing a feeling related to line 1

leader
One-word synonym or reference to line 1

Once students are familiar with writing Cinquains, creating them should take only part of a class period. We can use Cinquains to make comparisons and to summarize ideas. When writing diamantes, the next poem format we will explore, we focus on antonyms instead of synonyms.

DIAMANTES. The Diamante is a poetry format in the shape of a diamond that encourages the writer to contrast a topic and its antonym or opposite. These 7-line poems can be used in all content areas. The first three and a half lines address the original word; the remaining three and a half lines address the antonym. The change in topic, which reveals a noticeable contrast, occurs midway through line 4. (For a reproducible copy of the Diamante poem format, see Appendix A.)

After explaining the diamante format and encouraging students to make connections to it, we can demonstrate how to write Diamantes. We also encourage students to work with partners to write their first Diamante. We might suggest that the partners begin by writing the first line (the topic) and the last line (its opposite). This approach will help ensure that the topic they choose has a viable antonym. As teachers, we should be available to support students as needed as they write. When the Diamantes are completed, students can share their poem with another pair or in small groups.

In the following example, Beth Gress shares a Diamante about peace and war that she created after learning about World War II in history class.

Peace
Subject—one noun

Quiet Agreeable
Two adjectives describing the subject

Calming Nurturing Inspiring
Three participles ("ing" words) telling about the subject

Contentment Freedom Conflict Weapons
Four nouns: first two relate to subject; last two relate to the opposite

Crushing Storming Debilitating
Three participles ("ing" words) telling about the opposite

Harmful Dangerous
Two adjectives describing the opposite

War
Opposite of subject—one noun

We can encourage middle school and high school students to use Diamantes to summarize ideas about contrasting topics. Once students know how to write Diamantes, they should need only a portion of a class period to complete them. We can assess students' Diamantes by reading and commenting on them or by using an observational checklist. (For more information about assessment, see Chapter 14.)

Students can also use definition poems to represent their thoughts. These poems focus on our providing characteristics or details about the topic, rather than the antonyms required when writing diamantes.

 **DEFINITION POEMS.** Definition Poems provide a format for us to represent our ideas about a particular topic, including nine specific descriptors. The format, which can be used by middle and high school students, is easy to follow and concludes in an exclamation about the topic. (For a reproducible copy of the definition poem format, see the Appendix.)

We can begin teaching Definition Poems by explaining what they are and inviting students to make connections. Then we can write a poem to demonstrate how the format works. When students are comfortable with the format, we should encourage them to write a Definition Poem with a partner. As teachers, we should be available to provide support as needed when students are writing. When the poems are completed, students can share them in small groups.

In the following examples, Louis Pacchioli and Ken Gilbride share their Definition Poems about chemistry and history.

WHAT IS CHEMISTRY?

The central science

The study of all matter and all changes of matter

What our bodies do to survive

What industries do to make our lives easier

What industries may do to make our lives more dangerous

Research that helps to find cures for diseases

Baking cookies, shooting off fireworks, and burning wood in a fireplace

The only way plants can make their own food

The reason why you were able to drive your car today

That is chemistry!

WHAT IS HISTORY?

An attempt to explain past events

Where your ancestors came from

An exceptional tool used to help guide your future

What life was like long ago

The evolution of music, sports, and entertainment

A journey through many cultures

The key to understanding our world today

Not to be forgotten

The greatest story ever told

That is history!

We can use Definition Poems in all content areas to summarize or review what we know about a topic. Students often find this format motivational because it is open ended and they have control over the content. The format can easily be converted to a Biography Poem by changing the first and last lines. For example, the first line might say, "Who was George Washington?" and the last line could say, "That is who George Washington was!"

In the final type of poetry format, students have the opportunity to create Repeated-Phrase Collaborative Poems. These are class- or group-authored poems that have a unique structure.

TEACHING IDEA

REPEATED-PHRASE COLLABORATIVE POEMS. Repeated-Phrase Collaborative Poems are usually written by students working together in small groups. After reading a text chapter or a content-related novel, the students choose three passages of one to three lines that they found especially meaningful or powerful. Then they work in small groups, organizing the passages to evoke a mood. Next, they create the repeated phrase and insert it after each of the passages. For example, when writing about the Great Depression in the United States, the repeated phrase might be "We will survive." That phrase would appear after each passage. Repeated-Phrase Collaborative Poems rely on students' understanding of what they have read, their passage selections, the way they organize the ideas, and the repeated phrase.

The following is an excerpt from a Repeated-Phrase Collaborative Poem about Albert Einstein that was written by high school students in physics class. Prior to writing the poem, the students engaged in Discussion Circles (see Chapter 8). As a circle activity, six groups of students (approximately 5 students per group) read different chapters from *Einstein: His Life and Universe* (Isaacson, 2007) as well as a variety of articles about Einstein. As one of their extending activities, each group chose three passages (quotations or ideas) to share with the class through a Repeated-Phrase Poem. After organizing the passages about Einstein, the class created the repeated phrase. Here is an excerpt from the class's Repeated-Phrase Collaborative Poem:

ALBERT EINSTEIN

You can learn a lot of good things from me that no one else can offer you.

He had the greatest mind of the 20th century.

He to whom emotion is a stranger, who can no longer wonder and stand rapt in awe is as good as dead, a snuffed-out candle.

He had the greatest mind of the 20th century.

Logic will get you from A to B. Imagination will take you everywhere.

He had the greatest mind of the 20th century.

The only source of knowledge is experience.

He had the greatest mind of the 20th century.

We cannot solve our problems with the same thinking we used when we created them.

He had the greatest mind of the 20th century.

The important thing is not to stop questioning.

Middle and high school students find Repeated-Phrase Collaborative Poems to be motivational because the format provides them with opportunities to represent their shared thinking. Students can also use this format to demonstrate their understanding of multiple perspectives. To assess Repeated-Phrase Collaborative Poems, we can use a group observational checklist, such as the one shown in Figure 13.3.

Poetry provides an array of means for content area students to represent their thinking. These alternative modes of representation provide rich and stimulating ways for students to share their thoughts.

Making Connections | Thinking about Poetry in the Content Areas

■ Reflect on your content area and choose one or more topics. Then use three different form poems to represent your thinking about the topic(s) you selected.

■ Share and discuss your poems with a partner. Save the poems and use them as models for when you teach your students how to use poetry to represent their thinking.

Checklist for Repeated-Phrase Collaborative Poems

Group Members

1. _____ Selected a topic to address in the poem.
2. _____ Discussed the quotations from which selections would be made.
3. _____ Brainstormed, discussed, and chose a repeated phrase.
4. _____ Selected the quotations to include in the poem.
5. _____ Created a reference list.
6. _____ Formatted the poem correctly.
7. _____ Worked well together.
8. _____ Respected one another's ideas.

Group Comments:

_____
_____
_____
_____

Teacher Comments:

_____
_____
_____
_____

Names:_____   Date _____

FIGURE 13.3
Checklist for Repeated-Phrase Collaborative Poems

Making Connections
TO WRITING

The process of using multiple modes of representation often includes some form of writing. For example, students can represent their ideas through poetry, song lyrics, and electronic books. To effectively use many of these modes of representation, students need to know how to write in both informational and creative ways. From the simple act of summarizing to completing a project in which writing is a rubric criterion, students need to be able to effectively communicate their thoughts through writing. For more details about teaching writing in the content areas, see Chapter 10. ■

How Can We Teach Our Students to Use Drama as a Mode of Representation?

When we engage in drama, we use dialogue and actions to represent our thinking. Drama promotes active learning and accommodates a variety of learning styles. Students are motivated to engage in drama activities because they offer opportunities to interact with peers and to share thinking in unique ways.

Expressing ideas through drama can help students organize and clarify information. Such activities also enhance social and cognitive development and contribute to the development of learning communities (Wagner & Barnett, 1998).

Making Connections
TO ENGLISH LEARNERS

Working with peers and revisiting information during active learning can help scaffold learning and language acquisition for English learners (Richard-Amato, 1988). Representing ideas through drama also helps lessen the anxiety that English learners may experience when encountering new content, because students work in small groups and make choices about how ideas will be represented. Engaging in drama is motivational for English learners, and we should strive to ensure that it is included periodically as an option for representing students' ideas. ■

Drama helps students develop their strengths and foster their talents (Wagner & Barnett, 1998). Students who may be reluctant to speak out during content discussions can put aside their concerns and become a historic figure, an inventor, or a great mathematician during active learning.

Drama activities do not require large amounts of instructional time or theater expertise on our part. They do require that we plan appropriately, develop worthwhile applications, and use authentic assessments. (To learn more about assessment, see Chapter 14.) In this section, we discuss several drama activities that are appropriate for middle and high school students. Some require less than a class period and can be assessed informally. Others are more long range in nature and should be evaluated through the use of a rubric.

TEACHING IDEA   DINNER PARTY. Dinner Party (Vogt, 2000) is a small-group drama activity that works well for middle and high school students in all content areas. When planning, the class raises questions about guests from the content area they are studying who might attend a dinner party. For example, if the class were studying English literature, the question might be, "Imagine you could have a dinner party for eight British authors or poets whom we have studied. Who would you invite? Why would you select them? What would be the seating arrangement of the guests at your table, and why would you place them in that order? What do you think the guests would talk about during dinner? Include specific references to the authors' lives and works in your response." This creative approach to assessing students' knowledge of English literature can serve as a springboard for dramatic play.

The purpose of the Dinner Party is for students to represent their thinking by assuming personas, such as those of authors or poets, historical figures, scientists, artists, or musicians. For example, Alexander the Great might be engaged in conversation with General George Patton and Hannibal, arguing the finer points of military strategies. Scripts can be written, but improvisation is often more interesting and fun. Of course, its success depends on the students' content knowledge. During each Dinner Party, specific content must be included, and the guests must respond to one another as realistically and accurately as possible. It is important to stress that in-depth knowledge of the figures' lives, accomplishments, flaws, and works must be used to inform the "performance."

To engage students in Dinner Party, we should begin by explaining how this activity works and inviting students to make connections. Then we can demonstrate the process and share a project rubric. (For information about how to create rubrics, see Chapter 14.) We can also suggest they follow these guidelines when participating in Dinner Party :

1. Meet with a small group (approximately 6 students) that has interest in researching and dramatizing the question. Review the project rubric.
2. Decide who will attend the Dinner Party, what the participants might contribute to the conversation, and who will research and assume each role.
3. Develop a schedule to plan, research, and dramatize the Dinner Party.
4. Sign the schedule for the date you will present your Dinner Party.
5. Meet in workshop sessions to exchange ideas, review the rubric, and provide feedback periodically during the research process.
6. Practice Dinner Party, provide feedback to the group, and revise as necessary.
7. Invite the class to observe as you engage in your Dinner Party.

Dinner Party is an example of a long-range project that should be evaluated by using a rubric. Middle and high school students may need three to four weeks to prepare for this project, depending on the number of guests that will attend and how much time will be available for small-group meetings and class workshop sessions.

Students are highly motivated to engage in Dinner Party, because they are actively involved in every stage of production. They choose the topic, develop a plan, decide which research sources to use, and use drama to represent their thinking.

MEETING OF THE MINDS. Meeting of the Minds (Richard-Amato, 1998), a small-group drama activity, can be used in all content areas. In this active learning method, participants, who are usually well known in history, science, mathematics, or literature, are interviewed by a "host."

To begin, we can explain Meeting of the Minds and invite students to make connections. Then we can demonstrate the activity. When students are comfortable using the format, they can meet in small groups to engage in Meeting of the Minds. To begin, students take on the roles of individuals who have distinctly different viewpoints about a topic. The host is another student who directs questions to the participants, with the intent of pitting participants against one another in a debate about a particular topic. An interesting variation is an interview between a historical figure and a modern-day celebrity or expert with considerable knowledge of the same topic.

For example, in one world history class that was studying the 16th century and Henry VIII, students engaged in a discussion of the role of women. After additional reading and research, students participated in Meeting of the Minds. One student became Henry VIII, while another assumed the role of Anne Boleyn, the wife he executed in 1536. A third student served as the "host of the show," questioning the King and Queen about women's rights within the context of England in the early 1500s. Two more students entered the conversation as Eleanor Roosevelt and Hillary Clinton. Together, the women confronted Henry VIII about not only his beliefs, but also his methods for eliminating those who fell into his disfavor. The team enacting this Meeting of the Minds conducted in-depth research as they took on the identities involved.

Like the other drama activities, Meeting of the Minds can be used in science and mathematics as well as in history or literature. For example, the famous astronomer and physicist Galileo was imprisoned during the Inquisition because of his belief that the sun was at the center of the universe. Archimedes, the Greek mathematician, engineer, and physicist, also discovered the principle of buoyancy. The brilliant physicist and astronomer Stephen Hawking is a quadriplegic (he has amyotrophic lateral sclerosis, better known as "Lou Gehrig's disease") who has overcome more challenges as he explores the universe than most of us can imagine. The vivid tapestries of these lives provide enriching opportunities for students to represent their lives and beliefs in active learning.

Students are motivated to participate in Meeting of the Minds, because they can self-select the topic and view it from different perspectives. As teachers, we can use either a checklist or a rubric to assess or evaluate this project. (For more information about assessment and evaluation, see Chapter 14.)

LIVING NEWSPAPER THEATER.   The Living Newspaper Theater (Morrison & Chilcoat, 1998), a government-subsidized presentation of major current issues in a dramatic forum, was created in the 1930s. Its purpose was to educate the citizenry about socioeconomic problems of the times through drama. This same type of structure can be used in middle school and high school classrooms today.

To begin teaching the Living Newspaper Theater, we should explain how the process works and demonstrate it for students. Next, students can work in groups to select a historical topic of interest and research it. The topic should focus on some sociological, economic, or political issue, such as child labor laws, the role of women in the workforce, or economic and educational disparity. Students use what they have learned during the course of their research to write a script for a 15- to 20-minute dramatization involving people associated with the researched topic. The scripts should include an explanation of the problem (e.g., child labor in factories at the beginning of the 20th century), development of the problem (e.g., the government's role in protecting child laborers), and a solution to the problem (e.g., implementing legislation forbidding child labor despite protests from manufacturers). Students discuss and act out their scripts, revising their work as necessary. After sufficient rehearsal, each group presents its dramatization for the class. This includes involving class members in discussion about the problem and possible solutions.

In Living Newspaper Theater, authenticity is essential. Researching a topic from differing perspectives and including accurate facts are integral to the success of the project. The Living Newspaper Theater presents students with multiple challenges—researching, analyzing, designing, and presenting a dramatization of historical events, experiences, and lives. This project is designed to help students consider how their thinking informs their current experiences.

SNAPSHOTS OF HISTORY.   In the mid-1800s, theatrical tableaux were frequently used to celebrate a striking historical scene such as the signing of the Declaration of Independence. Snapshots of History (Shurtz, 1998) combines theatrical tableaux and imaginative writing about historical events. We can begin by explaining and demonstrating how to create a tableau, a scene with groups of people who remain silent and motionless in appropriate postures. Then the students select a photograph or painting of an historical event that includes a fairly large group of people and make copies for all participants.

Begin creating the tableau by adding a few students at a time until approximately half the class is involved. Then, repeat this process with the other half of the class. Explain that students will make a "talking tableau" by adding dialogue that would lead up to the moment represented in the original picture. Rehearse what the figures might have been talking about prior to the scene being captured in the photo or painting. When we give the cue, "Begin," the scene comes alive. It continues to evolve until we say, "Freeze." At this point, the scene becomes the tableau. The other half of the class also practices until everyone understands the process

Next, divide the entire class into three to four groups. Let each group select a historical painting or photograph to depict. Then each class member should choose one person in the picture to represent. Next, each student writes a first-person narrative from the perspective of the person within the picture. These narratives are shared with other group members prior to creating the group's final tableaux. The members rehearse both their "frozen" and "talking" tableaux, prior to presenting the event for class members.

Drama enables students of all ages to personally experience the thoughts, motives, conflicts, ambitions, and emotions of other people. It can represent student thinking and encourage students to view content knowledge not as a series of abstract concepts, but rather as personally constructed understandings.

How Can We Teach Our Students to Use Music as a Mode of Representation?

Music is a mode of representation that provides a fun and creative way for students to express their thinking. Most of the teaching ideas related to music focus on either working with partners or working in small-group settings. These activities range from students performing songs for which they have written lyrics to rap songs they've created to review content.

LYRIC SUMMARIES. Students create Lyric Summaries (McLaughlin & Allen 2009) after learning and focusing on the topic of discussion or a unit of study. In this small-group activity (approximately 5 students per group), students meet and quickly brainstorm lists of what they perceive to be the most important information they have learned; then they use that information to write a Lyric Summary. First, the group members select a song that they all know. Students often choose television theme songs, classic children's songs, holiday songs, or current, popular songs. The selected song becomes the music for their Lyric Summary, and students use their list of important facts to write a summary as new lyrics to the song. Finally, the group sings its Lyric Summary for the class.

This is a great exercise in cooperative learning and a fun experience. Students remember the important facts because they are included in the lyrics they have written.

The following excerpt is from a Lyric Summary that students created about Edgar Allan Poe's short story, "The Tell-Tale Heart." They chose to write their Lyric Summary to the tune of the theme song from *The Addams Family*.

> *The young man and the old man*
> *As neighbors living they can,*
> *They didn't have a problem,*
> *Until the young man saw his eye.*
> *The eye was weird and creepy,*
> *It made him feel so freaky,*
> *He had to kill the old man,*
> *He was so very scared.*
> *Thumpety-thump-click, click,*
> *Thumpety-thump-click, click,*

Of course, in the theme from *The Addams Family*, the "click, click" phrases are not words to be read, but rather the sounds made when the performing students snap their fingers.

Lyric Summaries can be written and performed by students in all content areas. The song selections vary, but students always seem to enjoy singing their summaries. Lyric Summaries also help students to review essential facts about content area topics.

RAPPING FOR REVIEW. In this activity, students write rap songs to represent their thoughts about the content they have studied. Rapping for Review works best as an after-learning, small-group activity. (Each group should have approximately 5 members.) As teachers, we can create an extensive list of topics related to the content most recently studied and ask each group to choose a topic from the list or create one of its own. Then the group members focus on the most essential information connected to their topic and create a rap about it. Of course, the only way to share the rap is for each group to "rap" it to the class.

Rapping for Review is an engaging way to represent students' thinking and review content before an examination. The following is an excerpt from a rap created by a group of students in biology class:

THE BIO RAP

Lots of people think mitosis and meiosis are one and the same

But each of these bio-terms has its own game.

Mitosis results in the production of two

Genetically identical diploid cells

While meiosis produces four—not two—

Genetically different haploid cells.

They might look similar but they are different three ways.

Mitosis produces two cells; meiosis four.

Mitosis produces genetically identical; meiosis genetically different.

Mitosis produces diploid; meiosis produces haploid.

Now no one is thinking these terms are the same

Everybody knows each has its own game.

Rapping for Review is a motivational, small-group activity. Students will need at least half a class period to write their raps. To assess this activity, we can use an observation checklist. like the one shown in Figure 13.4.

How Can We Teach Our Students to Use Art as a Mode of Representation?

From sketching to painting to transmediating, art offers students many different options for sharing their ideas. In this section, we discuss four artistic modes students can use to represent their thinking.

IN MY MIND'S EYE. When working on this project, students represent their ideas through digital photography or movies. They choose a content-related topic, conference with us about their project, and then begin photographing or filming their ideas. As with other projects, students meet occasionally in workshop sessions to discuss the projects, share their progress, and review the project checklist or rubric.

When completing this project, students begin by choosing content-related topics. For example, mathematics students might select "geometry in everyday life" as a topic. Then they would outline the goals of their project. Next, they would digitally photograph or film everything from billboards to stop signs as examples of the use of geometry in the community. The students can also choose to narrate their presentations and integrate background music before sharing them with the class.

Students find In My Mind's Eye to be highly motivational, because they can self-select the topic and design a project to meet their goals. Middle and high school students also seem to enjoy representing their thinking in these digital formats.

 *Making Connections*

Multiple literacies can both inspire thinking that can be represented in alternative modes and provide modes through which students may choose to represent their ideas. For example, if students read from a critical perspective, they can question the author's intent and why he chose to include some information and discount or ignore other ideas. To represent their thinking, students might create alternative texts or juxtaposition texts, photos, films, or sketches. If the topic the students were studying was the Boston Massacre, they might choose to represent their ideas by juxtapositioning sketches of the encounter from both military and civilian perspectives. ■

Checklist for Rapping for Review

Group Members

1. _____ Selected a recently studied content topic to review.

2. _____ Determined which information they would need.

3. _____ Used multiple sources to learn essential facts about the topic.

4. _____ Collaborated well.

5. _____ Used feedback to revise the rap.

6. _____ Effectively shared the rap.

Group Comments:

_____

_____

_____

_____

Teacher Comments:

_____

_____

_____

_____

Names:_____ Date _____

FIGURE 13.4
Checklist for Rapping
for Review

TEACHING IDEA STUDENT-CREATED ELECTRONIC PICTURE BOOKS. Creating electronic picture books offers students opportunities to blend knowledge and creativity. The resulting project provides students with an alternative mode to represent their thinking and a variety of ways to format their content area research. The electronic nature of these books conserves paper and printer ink, while enabling students' to import illustrations and use LCD projectors to project the books when they are ready to be shared.

To teach students how to use an electronic book format, we can explain and demonstrate the process. We should also provide copies of the rubric we will use to evaluate the electronic books before the project begins. Figure 13.5 features an example of such a scoring guide, which focuses on criteria such as creativity, information, and technology use. The rubric can be adapted for use with particular types of books, such as biographies, fact/fiction, or alphabet.

Rubric for Student-Authored Electronic Books

Creativity	4 _____	3 _____	2 _____	1 _____
Quality of information	4 _____	3 _____	2 _____	1 _____
Content area connections	4 _____	3 _____	2 _____	1 _____
Relation of illustrations to text	4 _____	3 _____	2 _____	1 _____
Use of technology	4 _____	3 _____	2 _____	1 _____
Professional appearance	4 _____	3 _____	2 _____	1 _____

4 Outstanding creativity is evident. Excellent-quality information. Exceptional content area connections. Excellent relation of illustrations to text. Fully developed use of technology. Totally professional in appearance (e.g., format, conventions of writing, design, text, illustrations, and references).

3 In-depth creativity is evident. High-quality information is consistently used. Proficient content area connections. Skillful relation of illustrations to text. Consistent use of various types of technology. Very professional in appearance (e.g., format, conventions of writing, design, text, illustrations, and references).

2 Creativity is evident. Quality of information is adequate. Consistent connections to the content area. Illustrations and text are related. Use of technology is evident. Professional appearance (e.g., format, conventions of writing, design, text, illustrations, and references).

1 Creativity is lacking. Quality of information is inadequate. Inconsistent connections to the content. Illustration and text relations are inappropriate. Poor use of technology. Less than professional in appearance (e.g., format, conventions of writing, design, text, illustrations, and references).

Student Comments:_____
_____
_____

Teacher Comments:_____
_____
_____

FIGURE 13.5
Rubric for Student-Authored Electronic Books

Two types of electronic picture books that middle and high school students often use to represent their thinking are alphabet and informational books. Descriptions of each follow.

TEACHING IDEA

ELECTRONIC ALPHABET BOOKS. Alphabet picture books are currently enjoying a renaissance in the content areas. Books that were once characterized by "A is for apple, B is for boy" have emerged in recent years as themed volumes filled with in-depth research designed to inform students of all ages. *Jazz A-B-Z: An ABC Collection of Jazz Portraits* (Marsalis, 2005), *The Battle Alphabet Book* (Pallotta, 2004), *G Is for Googol: A Math Alphabet* (Schwartz, 1998), and *Q Is for Quark: A Science Alphabet Book* (Schwartz, 2001) are just a few examples of such published works.

Content area students can create alphabet books to share information about topics they choose to investigate. This format also affords opportunities for students to creatively illustrate their research. They learn early in the experience that although everyone may not be a gifted artist, everyone can be creative. The result is books that are informative, visually appealing, and inexpensive. Figure 13.6 features selected pages from *A Geometry Alphabet Book,* which was created by Stephen Ingram.

When they are creating alphabet books, students need to provide information about 26 aspects of a self-selected topic. These books also challenge students to develop illustrations that complement each topic discussed in the text. This activity incorporates student choice, research, writing, creativity, and technology and may be extended to other genres, including biography.

STUDENT-AUTHORED ELECTRONIC INFORMATIONAL BOOKS. Students can also create other types of books as alternative representations of their thinking. For example, they might investigate an aspect of the content they are studying and choose to report what they have learned in a self-authored book as opposed to a more traditional report.

While picture books were once enjoyed only by very young children, they are now widely used at all levels of education to stimulate students' engagement with the learning process. As a result, students often choose to create picture books to report their research. The books are then shared with classmates to stimulate their interest in the book's topic. They may also become part of the classroom library or be shared with younger learners.

Creating a picture book presents a number of challenges for the students. First, they must select a content-related topic for the book and research it. Second, they need to convey the essential elements of their research topic in a multiple-page narrative. Third, students need to develop illustrations to support the text. Fourth, the story they write needs to be creative and motivational, yet logical and informative. Students also need to choose the book style that best complements their story. Shape books, accordion books, pop-up books, television scrolls, and computer-animated books are among the styles most frequently selected. Finally, students need to use the appropriate conventions of writing. A rubric detailing these elements should be shared with students before the research project begins.

As mentioned earlier, students may use a variety of book formats to share their content knowledge, including shape books, accordion books, and slotted books, as well as PowerPoint files. In past projects, students have addressed topics ranging from outer space to Egyptian mummies. Examples of books they have created include the following: *John and Wayne's Excellent Outer Space Adventure, Geometry Is All Around Us, Man on the Moon,* and *Medieval Times.*

TRANSMEDIATIONS. Within a constructivist perspective, "teachers invite students to search for understanding, appreciate uncertainty, and inquire responsibly" (Brooks & Brooks, 1993, p. 6). These teaching practices help students internalize and shape new information, enabling them to make connections between what they know and what they are learning (McLaughlin & Allen, 2009; Wagner & Barnett, 1998). Understandings are further expanded through a process identified as transmediation (Harste, Burke, & Short, 1988; Hoyt, 1992). During this process, students transfer information and knowledge from one communication system to another.

When creating transmediations, students choose ideas in an existing medium and change its representation to another medium. For example, students might choose to take a poem and turn it into a picture book or they might choose song lyrics and turn them into a work of art. Maya Angelou's *Life Doesn't Frighten Me,* illustrated with the paintings of Jean-Michel Basquiat, is an example of a published transmediation. Angelou originally wrote "Life Doesn't Frighten Me" as a poem in 1978, but it was later published as text for a picture book illustrated by Basquiat.

Middle and high school students are motivated to create transmediations because they can self-select topics and choose the medium in which they will work. They also do not need to worry about content, because they are working with existing works (e.g., poems, song lyrics, paintings). Examples of excerpts from a transmediation created by a student can be found in the Appendix.

FIGURE 13.6 Excerpts from *A Geometry Alphabet Book*

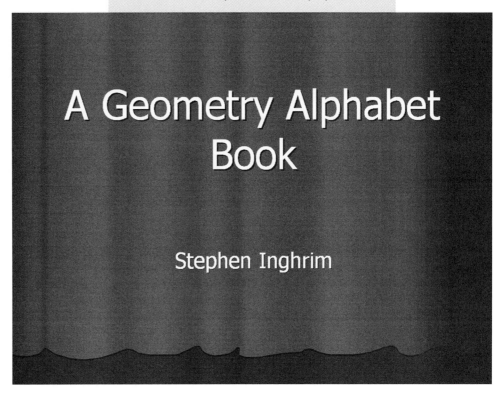

FIGURE 13.6 *Continued*

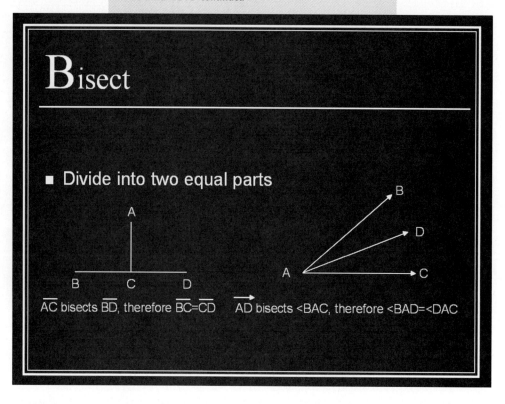

Making Connections
TO STRUGGLING READERS

Providing opportunities for students to represent their thinking in alternative modes often makes it possible for struggling students to show what they know and can do in ways that are more compatible with their learning styles. For example, when creating transmediations, struggling students may choose to read a poem, song lyrics, or a news article and change the original medium to a work of art. Having the option of creating a performance that does not involve writing may alleviate anxiety for students who may be less than confident about their writing abilities. ■

We and our students know that we are not all artists, but we can all express ourselves in artistic ways. Infusing art into our teaching encourages students to express their understandings in that mode of representation.

FINAL THOUGHTS

Our ultimate goal in teaching students multiple modes of representation is to ensure that they have the best possible means of communicating their thoughts. Each of us is an individual, capable of expressing thoughts in a variety of ways. Multiple forms of representation celebrate our unique natures and encourage us to share our ideas in the most meaningful ways. As Eisner (1997) has noted,

> Schools that cultivate the differences among us while escalating the mean for performance in each of these forms of representation provide for the richness of the full orchestra. We do better as a culture when we are not all violinists—even brilliant ones. (p. 352)

Teaching students to represent their thoughts in a variety of ways broadens their communication possibilities and strengthens their understanding. It also helps to engage their thinking and accommodate their learning styles.

In the next chapter, we discuss meaningful classroom assessment. We examine informal and formal assessments and explore how to use assessment and evaluation in our teaching.

Teaching Connections
APPLYING WHAT WE HAVE LEARNED

E-Links

Consider how you will integrate alternative forms of representation into your teaching. Meet with a small group of teachers from your content area and plan how each of you will help your students use music, drama, and art to represent their thinking. Each group member will (1) choose a topic; (2) select a specific mode of representation (e.g., Rapping for Review, Dinner Party, Transmediations); (3) develop an annotated list of at least 3 quality online sources; and (4) describe how he would use these sources to help represent his thinking. Provide feedback to each group member. Save the resources for use in your teaching.

EXAMPLE WEBSITES

Use websites such as these to complete the project:

Modern American Poetry
http://www.english.uiuc.edu/maps/poets.htm

Coolmath Algebra
http://www.coolmath.com/algebra/Algebra1/index.html#Algebra_1:_Absolute_Value_
Inequalities

Cells Alive!
http://www.cellsalive.com/pen.htm

Accountable Talk

Consider the modes of representation you use most commonly and reflect on why you do
so. Then consider a mode that you do not commonly employ. Reflect on how you might use
this mode to expand representations of your thinking, using a specific project as an example. Record your thoughts as a reflective entry in your portfolio and share them in small-
group discussion.

Portfolio/Performance Opportunity

Meet with your peers in a small group and discuss what you consider to be students' most
common modes of representation in your area of study. Think about how you would integrate other modes into your teaching, and focus on a discipline-specific project you think
could work well in at least two different modes. Complete the project in both modes. Share
your work with the class by briefly discussing the project you chose. Include your work in
your portfolio.

14

Course-Based Assessment, Evaluation, and Reporting

According to Peter Johnston (1997), teachers must become assessment experts. Johnston reminds us that assessment is a natural component of our teaching. We need to know how to assess student learning—to gather information that demonstrates what our students know and can do. We also need to evaluate the products that our students create. To do this, we often develop criteria that students can use as a guide when creating their presentations. This leads us to a distinction between two essential terms: assessment and evaluation. *Assessment* is the gathering and synthesizing of information concerning students' learning (Ferrara & McTighe, 1992). *Evaluation* is making judgments about students' learning (Ferrara & McTighe, 1992).

In this chapter, we explore assessment and evaluation as they apply to all content areas. We begin by examining the theoretical framework of assessment, including a glossary of assessment-related terms. Next, we describe formative (informal) and summative (formal) assessments and observe how they can be integrated into various disciplines. Then we study issues of organization and management. After that, we examine rubrics and innovations in reporting student progress. Finally, we discuss the implementation of assessment and evaluation in today's classrooms, including the importance of administrative support and ongoing professional development.

What Is the Current Thinking about Assessment?

Developments in assessment and evaluation indicate that we have made great strides since assessment was viewed from the perspective of the banking model of education (Freire, 1970). In that theory, teachers were seen as educators depositing knowledge into students' minds, often without any interaction or discussion. In such times, students returned the information to the teachers through written tests. We learned from the banking model that learning was not sustained – but rather information was "deposited," studied for a test, and then often forgotten. In addition, learning was viewed as a passive activity, lacking interaction and student ownership. It also often resulted in contrasts between students. ("I got a B, but my friend got an A.")

Today we strive to encourage students to be all that they can be—to reach their maximum potential. This approach results in a focus on the progress of each individual student, which may be best documented through the use of a developmental continuum ("This is what I knew when I started the course; this is how much progress I have made since then."), rather than with the more traditional "what grade I received versus what grade my friend received" mindset.

As 21st century content area teachers, we are striving to move away from the teacher/text-dominated classroom and to transition to a time of student-generated ideas, self-selection, critical thinking, creativity, interaction, and personal construction of meaning. In such contexts, authentic content area tasks assimilate real-world experiences, provide a purpose for learning, and encourage students to take ownership of their educational experiences. The paradigm is shifting from a teacher-centered approach to student-centered learning, and from a more traditional view of literacy to multiple literacy perspectives. These transformations are leading to a deeper understanding of content and changes in assessment and evaluation practices.

As a result of this changing paradigm, assessment has been undergoing a major reformation. Practices have been shifting from the traditional "read the book and answer the question" method to a more performance-based "show what you can do with what you have learned" approach. The thinking that has emerged is dynamic, authentic, reflective, and standards based. It accommodates students' diverse learning styles by providing opportunities to respond through a variety of modes, including speaking, writing, sketching, dramatizing, and singing.

As with most core issues in education, there are distinctive terms associated with contemporary assessment practices. Figure 14.1 features the terms that are critical to understanding current assessment processes and the related concepts presented in this chapter.

Theoretical underpinnings for current literacy assessment practices have emerged from a variety of sources, including schema-based learning development, constructivism, social negotiation and the zone of proximal development, and reflective practice (McLaughlin & Vogt, 1996). A discussion of each of these terms follows.

Schema-based learning development suggests that learning takes place when new information is integrated with what is already known (Anderson, 1994). In this process, it is important that students have as much background knowledge as possible to make connections to the new information they are learning.

Constructivists believe that students create knowledge socially by linking what is new to what is already known. Consequently, what is learned cannot be separated from the context in which it is learned. The learners' goals are essential to this construction of knowledge (Cambourne, 2002; McLaughlin & Vogt, 1996).

Vygotsky's (1987) work serves as the foundation for social negotiation and the zone of proximal development. These concepts support student learning that is scaffolded by more experienced people and that promotes social interaction. The zone of proximal development represents the level at which a student is capable of working when he has the assistance and support of others. For example, Vygotsky (1987) believed that students are capable of working at a higher level (instructional level) if they have the assistance of a "more knowledgeable other"—in this case, a teacher or more knowledgeable peer.

Teachers who engage in reflective practice learn to teach and improve their teaching through ongoing reflection about their practices and their students. As a result of these reflections, teachers

FIGURE 14.1
Assessment
Terminology

Anchor performances Examples of different levels of student performances that are evaluated using the same checklist or rubric. Anchor performances represent evaluation possibilities and also provide a standard to help teachers evaluate students' work fairly.

Assessment The gathering and synthesizing of information concerning students' learning (Ferrara & McTighe, 1992).

Authentic assessment The process of engaging students in tasks that are grounded in instruction, are personally meaningful, and take place in real-life contexts (McLaughlin & Kennedy, 1993).

Baseline measures Assessments of what students know about a topic or concept at the beginning of a course. A baseline measure for each course goal is collected within the first few weeks of the start of the course.

Benchmarks Grade-level indicators of students' progress toward achieving the goals or standards.

Developmental continuum A range that shows student progress over time and that is often used as an alternative to the traditional (numeric or letter grade) reporting system.

Evaluation The process of making judgments about students' learning (Ferrara & McTighe, 1992). Its result is usually reported through grading.

Exhibitions Demonstrations that embody multiple performance requirements that are developed over an extended period of time. These are typically multimedia in nature and may involve writing a paper, making an oral presentation, building a model, creating computer graphics, and responding spontaneously to questions. They may be individual or collaborative and are often used as culminating activities (Willis, 1996).

Formative assessment Informal assessment measures, such as attitude and interest surveys, content area histories, strategy applications, and teacher observations, which occur during everyday learning.

Grading. See *Evaluation*.

Performance assessment A type of assessment that requires students to demonstrate what they know.

Portfolio assessment A goal-based, multidimensional collection of student performances that demonstrates effort, progress, and achievement over time.

Reporting A method for sharing evaluations of student learning. Such information is usually reported through grading and formatted as a report card or report of student progress.

Rubrics Scoring guides/criteria designed to describe progressive levels of performance.

Summative assessment Formal assessment measures, such as projects, research papers, and teacher-designed tests, which often are accompanied by rubrics and are completed after learning.

FIGURE 14.1
Assessment
Terminology

develop understandings and insights that can lead to better ways of teaching that more effectively accommodate students' needs (Schon, 1987).

To visualize how these theories support our teaching, consider the following scenario:

Elizabeth Watkins is teaching algebraic equations to her students in mathematics. Through discussion at the end of the previous class, she learned that this would be a new concept for her students, so she decided to teach it in a whole-class setting. Elizabeth begins by *motivating* her students to learn this new concept. Next, she *explains* what algebraic equations are and *activates students' background knowledge by making connections* to concepts they have previously studied. She notes that as they solve algebraic equations, students will be using several mathematical operations they already know. Then she *invites the students to share their connections*. This process results in a brief class discussion. Next, Elizabeth uses the chalkboard to *demonstrate* how algebraic equations work. She completes her first example herself, *thinking aloud* as she works. A brief class discussion follows. In her *second demonstration* of how algebraic equations work, Elizabeth *pauses occasionally to ask her students to turn to a partner and provide ideas to help solve* various aspects of the equation. This process is also followed by a brief discussion. Next, she shares an algebraic equation and invites her *students to work with partners to solve it*. When the students have finished, the class discusses the responses. Finally, Elizabeth shares another equation, which *students solve individually*, and the *whole class discusses* various aspects of the equation. During the last two steps—partner and individual equation solving—Elizabeth is monitoring students' work by walking around the room, *informally observing students as they work and responding to questions when asked. Discussion* follows these segments.

In addition to illustrating how theory underpins our teaching, this scenario shows how assessment occurs as a natural part of teaching and learning. During this lesson, the teacher had numerous opportunities to observe how well students contributed to discussion, how well they solved the algebraic equations, and how well they worked with others. In other words, she had multiple opportunities to engage in dynamic, authentic assessment. We explore these terms in detail in the sections that follow.

Making Connections | Visualizing Teaching and Assessing in Your Classroom

■ Reflect on the scenario involving teacher Elizabeth Watkins, and then visualize how theory supports your teaching. Sketch what you see in the mental picture you created and list a few descriptive phrases that represent what is happening in your sketch.

■ Share your sketches and thoughts with others through small-group discussions.

Assessment Is Dynamic

Dynamic assessment presents a natural, viable, and continuous means for teachers to learn about what students know and can do. It occurs every day and provides in-depth information about students and the learning process. Dynamic assessment is an authentic alternative to traditional, static assessments that require students to choose the correct response, or those that focus on the product to summatively assess student knowledge. Assessment is dynamic when it is inter-active, ongoing, and focused on process. It is distinctive because it documents the responsive-ness of the learner, offering not a snapshot but an ongoing video view of student performance. It demonstrates that assessment is not an educational add-on, but rather a natural, continuous component of teaching and learning (McLaughlin, 1995). Dynamic assessment also offers a more authentic expression of current cognitive-developmental theory than traditional standard-ized procedures do (Lidz, 1995).

Dynamic assessment is characteristic of the types of measures often compiled to show growth over time in portfolio assessment (Tierney, 1998; Valencia, 1998. In her work, Valencia (1998) notes that in addition to being authentic, multifaceted, and reflective, assessment should be a continuous, ongoing process that chronicles development: This is the key difference between assessing the product and assessing the process of learning over time. Tierney (1998) concurs, reporting that the integration of assessment with teaching and learning entails the dynamic/ongo-ing use of assessment practices as well as assessment tailored to classroom life.

From a theoretical perspective, Vygotsky's thinking reflects the essence of dynamic assess-ment: elements of social transaction and discourse, contextual embeddedness, and creation of a zone of proximal development (Lidz, 1995, p. 149). In addition, Vygotsky's work tells us that assessment practices that focus entirely on the student's unaided performance fail to tap important information that can be identified by analyzing the dynamic nature of the student responding with adults or more capable peers (Minnick, 1987).

Because assessment has a dynamic nature, it is viewed not as an event, but rather as a natural, ongoing, purposeful component of teaching and learning. As Brooks and Brooks (1993) note:

> In a constructivist setting, assessment of student learning is done naturally within the context of lessons and activities. Teachers analyze student products and exhibitions as bench-marks and garner information for using in developing future activities and informing ongo-ing practice. (p. 122)

Making Connections
TO MULTIPLE LITERACIES

Just as assessment is a natural, dynamic component of teaching and learning, it is a natural, dynamic component of all literacies—even though we may learn some literacies in ways that differ from the traditional approach. For example, when we engage in information literacy, we can assess students' abilities to select meaningful research topics and determine unique research paths. In media literacy, we can assess students' abilities to interpret and comprehend messages represented in alternative modes and use a variety of media to support their thinking. Assessment—both formative and summative—permeates all literacies. ■

Assessment Is Authentic

Authentic tasks are those that are grounded in instruction, personally meaningful, and situated in real-world experiences (Clinchy, 1995; Hiebert, 1994; McLaughlin, 1995) According to Hosking (2000), "The term *authentic assessment* conveys an expectation that students are actively engaged in applying knowledge and competencies in some relevant situation."

Afflerbach (2002) notes that it is "how the materials and procedures connect with the curriculum, how information is used, and what the assessment demands from the students that signify an assessment as authentic" (p. 37). Examples of authentic assessments in the content areas include strategy applications (see Chapters 4, 5, 6, and 7), student writing (see Chapter 10), and performance assessments (see Chapters 12 and 13, as well as later sections of this chapter).

Assessment Is Reflective

Reflection encourages student ownership of learning and affirms that student thinking is valued (McLaughlin & Vogt, 1998). Reflection is also a component of constructivism. Brooks and Brooks (1993) note that from a constructivist perspective, learning is understood as a process that incorporates concrete experience, collaborative discourse, and reflection. The results of reflection lead us to "ask better questions, break out of fruitless routines, make unexpected connections, and experiment with fresh ideas" (Brandt, 1991).

Because there is shared responsibility for learning, the assessment process is reflective for both students and teachers (Leahy, Lyon, Thompson, & Wiliam, 2005). The reflection in which both engage serves as an informal assessment of teaching and learning. Reflection provides teachers with the opportunity to review what they taught, how they taught it, and how well the lesson worked with a particular group of students. This process, in turn, leads to analysis that informs future lesson planning. Reflection also provides students with the opportunity to examine their thinking, which leads to personal goal setting—a valuable life skill. Douillard (2002) summarizes the importance of reflection in students' learning by noting, "Reflective activities in the classroom help make thinking more visible, enabling students to learn from one another and to gain greater insights into their own thinking and learning processes" (p. 93).

TEACHER REFLECTION. As educators, we know reflection is a natural part of teaching, and we engage in it daily. For example, when planning our lessons, we reflect on our students' abilities and think about how to accommodate them. After teaching, we reflect on what worked well in the lesson and what we might change if we taught the lesson again.

As teachers, we can also reflect on student performance. This type of reflection enables us to confirm student progress, question process and understanding, discover strengths and needs, and support revision and personal goal setting. Our knowledge and the classroom environment are critical factors in this process. We need to know how to ask meaningful questions, understand how the teaching and learning process works, and determine how to keep students motivated as they engage in revision and personal goal setting.

STUDENT SELF-REFLECTION.   Students can also reflect effectively. Engaging in self-reflection encourages them to contemplate what they are doing, why they are doing it, how they are doing it, what contributed to its success, and what they would do differently to improve it next time. This process involves self-assessment and leads to individual goal setting. Students reflect on both the processes and the products of learning. Topics of student self-reflection include progress in meeting a standard, connections between academic work and other life experiences, their view of learning as a process, and what they do and do not understand.

Student self-reflection, self-assessment, and goal setting have several positive outcomes. These processes

- Help students to take ownership of their learning, which leads to greater interest in and commitment to their learning goals.

- Offer students access to what they have learned, which helps them to come to understand what they know.

- Provide students with information about how they are progressing, which contributes to motivation and helps them to understand how they learn best.

PEER REFLECTION.   Peer reflection supports the collaborative nature of learning and demonstrates that the work in which students engage is valued. Suggestions from peers can affirm students' ideas, raise questions, and guide revision.

Students can also engage in peer assessment and evaluation. In such cases, peers use checklists or rubrics to assess or evaluate one another's work, before it is submitted to the teacher. Following peer evaluations, students would have another opportunity to revise their work before presenting the final version to the teacher.

Making Connections | Thinking about Reflection

- Think about when you became reflective about your learning. Do you recall the circumstances? For example, were you working on a project? Were you working alone or with others? Share your experiences in small groups.

- To help your students become more reflective about their work, consider modeling the following activity. (1) Tell the students about a hobby or special interest you have. (2) Describe how well it went the last time you engaged in it. (3) Share one thing you could do to improve it the next time you do it. Share your responses with a partner.

- After modeling this process, invite students to reflect on a hobby or special interest they have and respond to the same three questions. Then encourage them to share their thoughts with a peer. After they have had a few minutes to share, encourage them to apply the three questions to an aspect of their learning. For example, they could question, "How well did I do on my last project?" "How well did my last experiment work?" Then they can share one thing they can do to improve it the next time they do it. This leads the students into personal goal setting.

- Talk with a partner about the value of student reflection and how you can help your students to use reflection as they learn in your content area.

Assessment Is Standards Based

Because a majority of academic disciplines and virtually all states have developed educational standards, current lesson plans and assessments are standards-based. This is viewed as a positive development because, as Schmoker and Marzano (1999) observe, "The success of any organization is contingent upon clear, commonly defined goals" (p. 17). (For more information about standards-based instruction, see Chapter 3.)

Assessment Has Multiple Response Formats

Accommodating students' strength modalities is an essential element of assessment. For some students, that strength may best be exhibited through writing; for others, the best mode of expression may be discussion; for some, it may be dramatization; and for still others, it may be projects. It is, therefore, important to offer a variety of assessment choices to accommodate students' individual needs. The activities presented throughout this text provide opportunities to assess student progress through a variety of modes, including speaking, writing, dramatizing, digital pictures and film, music, and artistic representations.

Making Connections | Thinking about Assessment and Evaluation

■ Reflect on assessment and evaluation. In what ways have these processes changed since you were a high school student? In what ways do you perceive these developments to be positive? Negative?

■ Share your thoughts with others in small-group discussions.

How Can We Use Assessment Effectively in Our Teaching?

When thinking about the roles assessment will play in our teaching, we should begin by creating a classroom assessment plan that has a sound theoretical foundation. The plan should address the different types of assessments we use. For example, formative assessments are informal and occur naturally in everyday teaching and learning experiences. They include teacher observation, students' strategy use, and students' informal writing. In contrast, summative assessments are more formal measures, such as projects or research papers that occur over longer periods of time. In this section, we discuss developing a classroom assessment plan, as well as formative and summative assessments.

Developing a Classroom Assessment Plan

Before organizing and implementing classroom assessments, we need to develop a classroom assessment plan. This plan should include our assessment philosophy, delineate its organization and valued components, and provide a foundation that serves as a springboard for all of the assessments we create. The plan should also incorporate clear, connected purposes for teaching, learning, and assessing. The following guidelines facilitate creating such plans.
Assessments should:

1. *Relate to standards-based curriculums and instructional goals.* Basically, this means we should assess what we teach. Generally, standards-based curricula, instruction, and assessment are inextricably linked.
2. *Provide opportunities to examine both process and product.* Although we are very interested in what our students know and how they can use what they have learned, we are equally interested in understanding their thinking processes—their critical and creative reasoning as well as their communicative abilities. For example, we value our students' completed research projects, but we equally value how the students gathered the information, organized their ideas, and chose a mode of presentation.
3. *Have clear purposes.* Assessment results should provide purpose-related information. For example, we can ask students to complete a quickwrite—an informal writing task in which students take just a few minutes to write everything they know about a topic—to determine what they know about a topic before we teach it. We can also observe to monitor students' progress or give a test to assess students' knowledge at the end of a unit of study.

4. *Demonstrate a clear match between the task and the intended student outcome.* What we are assessing should be clearly aligned with what the students will learn and be able to do after the learning experience. For example, we may ask students to create and solve problems to assess their understanding of algebraic equations and the way in which they function.

5. *Have clear evaluation criteria.* These criteria are often formatted as checklists or rubrics. Checklists and rubrics should be shared with and explained to students before the assessment begins. This practice helps to provide direction for students' work. When students see the completed checklists or rubrics, they know what they did well and what needs improvement, which in turn leads to personal goal setting. Of course, in the case of informal assessment, written or oral comments are used to provide the necessary feedback.

6. *Include multiple measures to provide feedback on student growth and substantive data for making informed decisions about subsequent teaching, student learning, and future planning.* We learn very early on in our teaching preparation to never make judgments based on one assessment. Having multiple measures provides us with more information about the students and their learning experiences over time.

7. *Generate reflection and personal goal setting* (Herman, Ashbacher, & Winters, 1992; McLaughlin, 1995). Reflecting on a completed assessment or examining a completed rubric encourages students to think about what they did well and what they could do to improve their performance next time. Their personal goals focus on what they can do to improve. For example, if a student is reading a completed rubric for a project and the teacher notes that the student's research did not include enough sources or that the student did not use quality sources, the student might set personal goals to include enough sources or to be sure to use quality sources the next time.

Making Connections
TO STRUGGLING READERS

Examining the processes in which students engage is especially important when we are teaching struggling learners. Multiple pathways to learning exist, and observing the processes in which students engage can provide insights into their thinking. This assessment can, in turn, provide opportunities for us to offer additional support. For example, if students are engaging in research, then examining the process might provide insights into the nature of the research questions or students' ability to use information literacy to research a topic. In response, we could offer additional support ourselves, suggest that the student partner with a peer, or propose that the student choose a mode of response that more strongly supports her learning style. ∎

Creating an assessment plan provides us with a set of beliefs we can use as a guide as we integrate formative and summative measures into our teaching. It also reminds us that assessment is an active process for both students and teachers.

Formative and Summative Assessments

As teachers, we use both formative and summative assessment to help us understand what our students know and can do. Each of these types of assessment has particular characteristics, ranging from how often students engage in them to their informal and formal natures.

For example, formative assessment is ongoing, classroom based, and informal. Summative assessment usually occurs at definitive times, such as the end of a chapter, a theme, or marking period; it is a more formal type of assessment. McTighe and O'Connor (2005) distinguish between these two types of assessments by viewing formative assessment as a means of improving learning and summative assessment as a way to provide reliable information about what has been achieved.

Shephard (2005) notes that formative assessment is a collaborative process in which how to improve learning is negotiated between teacher and student. Weber (1999) proposes that formative assessments suggest future steps for teaching and learning. Such steps might result from observations that allow us to determine how well a student contributed to a class discussion or informal writing that documents whether a student is able to apply a particular skill or strategy. Formative assessment not only reinforces how students learn and what students know, but also identifies what needs to be clarified. In addition, Stiggins and DuFour (2009) suggest that formative assessment can be used for purposes, such as determining student understanding, informing and improving instructional practice, motivating students by building their confidence, and promoting continuous improvement processes.

Making Connections
TO ENGLISH LEARNERS

We can monitor all students' progress through formative assessments, but this type of assessment is especially valuable in the case of English learners. We often provide these students with additional support, and observing their progress through formative assessments provides us with ongoing insight into their thinking and abilities. This helps us to understand whether the supports were helpful or whether they should be changed. The resulting information informs our future lesson planning. ■

In contrast, summative assessment usually occurs at the end of a unit or lesson. It is designed to measure students' skills and knowledge related to the unit of study. Summative assessment addresses final outcomes, and usually involves evaluation or grading (Weber, 1999). Figure 14.2 details the differences between formative and summative assessments.

Classroom Examples of Formative Assessment

Examples of formative assessments include observation, reflection, informal writing, student-constructed responses, problem solving, and comprehension strategy use. (For more information about using comprehension strategies in the content areas, see Chapters 4, 5, and 6, as well as the Appendix.) The following formative assessments are among those that can be used in all content areas.

FIGURE 14.2
Characteristics of Formative and Summative Assessment

Formative	Summative
Occurs daily	Occurs at the end of a theme or chapter
Measures current learning goals	Measures learning goals over time
Is a dynamic process	Is a final product
Assesses current learning	Assesses what has been taught over a period of time
Offers immediate feedback	Offers periodic feedback
Measures one set of experiences	Includes multiple sets of experiences
Is less formal	Is more formal
Provides information about individual student goals in various settings	Provides information about group learning in one setting
Documents individual student progress	Provides for comparison/contrast of students' performances
Suggests ideas for future teaching and learning	Judges students' knowledge of unit of study; work is evaluated
Feedback is provided	Rubrics are used

OBSERVATION. Observations are informal assessments that allow us as teachers to capture the essence of a live performance by watching students as they engage in a task. These informal assessments are purposeful and offer evidence of student motivation, communication, interaction, risk taking, collaboration, and critical and creative thinking.

One way to organize and manage observations is to use a clipboard. One sticky note or mailing label is attached to the clipboard for each student in the class. When a student is observed, the teacher's notes are recorded on the sticky note or mailing label, dated, removed from the clipboard, and placed on a sheet of paper either in the student's portfolio or in an observation folder. The names of students who have not yet been observed remain on the clipboard. When all students have been observed, the sticky notes or mailing labels are replenished. As students are observed multiple times, the sticky notes or mailing labels are placed chronologically on the designated sheet in either a portfolio or an observation folder. This method of recording information offers a running history of observations throughout a marking period and, eventually, throughout the year. Such observations help teachers remember specific attributes of student performance and provide informal assessment information for student evaluation.

There is no magic number of observations that should be completed each day. Starting slowly, using the clipboard method, is a good way to begin. After all students have been observed once or twice, teachers generally find a comfort level with this process.

It is important to remember that every observation should have a purpose. For examples of the types of information we can learn through observations, see Figure 14.3. It features sample observation prompts to use when students are working both individually and in cooperative settings.

To understand how we can use the observation prompts, consider the following scenario in which a student is conducting a dissection in biology class.

Cody Baker is about to dissect a frog in a laboratory section of his biology class. His teacher has prepared individual trays for the students, each of which contains a dead frog and a scalpel. Cody has his biology textbook open to the page on which the dissection process is described. His task is to dissect the frog and label its parts. While observing Cody performing the dissection, his teacher, Karen Gress, is using a clipboard to hold her anecdotal notes. As he begins the initial cut, she observes, "Cody is confident as he begins to cut the frog. He seems very familiar with the process, which means he is well prepared for today's lab task. When the incisions are complete, he carefully removes and labels each organ/segment of the frog."

Of course, Ms. Gress was not able to stay with Cody through the entire process, because she had other students to observe. Nevertheless, we learn several important things from what

FIGURE 14.3
Observation Prompts

Prompts for Observing Students Working Individually

- Does the student demonstrate interest in learning?
- How does the student interact with the course materials?
- Does the student utilize background knowledge when exploring the subject area?
- How does the student use new information?
- Does the student appear to be a risk taker?
- Does the student readily share ideas?
- Does the student relate new concepts to previously learned information?
- Does the student link his learning to his life experiences?
- Does the student engage in critical and creative thinking?

Prompts for Observing Students Working in Cooperative Settings

- Does the student focus on the group task?
- Does the student participate in group discussions?
- Does the student actively contribute to the group activity?
- Does the student respect the ideas of others in the group?
- Does the student demonstrate curiosity?
- Does the student apply content area concepts to the group activity?
- Does the student communicate ideas effectively?
- Does the student engage in critical and creative thinking?

she did see and record: Cody is confident, well prepared, and successful. Ms. Gress will date her observation and place it in Cody's assessment folder, which she keeps in her desk. As the marking period progresses, she will add other observations to the file. At the end of the marking period, she will review her anecdotal notes and use them to help her determine Cody's course grade/evaluation.

After Ms. Gress observed Cody, she spent some time watching Eugene Wilson dissect his frog. In her observational notes, she recorded, "Eugene was hesitant while dissecting the frog. He kept referring to his text and didn't seem to know what to do next. Although he was successful with this task, it was clear he was not very well prepared. It was also clear that he had not paid close attention when I had explained and demonstrated how to dissect a frog in our previous class." From her anecdotal notes, we learn that Eugene was not very well prepared and may not have paid close attention to the demonstration, but he did manage to complete the task.

As you can imagine, when reviewing these notes at the end of the marking period, Cody's work might enhance his course grade, while Eugene's might not. From a teaching perspective, Ms. Gress might consider what she could have done to ensure that all students had read the text as preparation for the dissection. She might also reflect on what she could have done to ensure that all students were attentive during her explanation and demonstration of the dissection.

INFORMAL WRITING. As teachers, we can use informal writing to encourage reflection, provide a means of documenting students' reasoning, and promote inquiry. Examples of informal writing include content area histories, content inventories, journal entries, freewrites, quickwrites, Admit Slips, and Tickets Out. For detailed descriptions of these types of informal writing, see Chapter 10.

When students write content histories, complete inventories, maintain journals, or create freewrites or quickwrites, we need to remember that these informal assessments involve writing at the draft stage. Communication of ideas is the ultimate goal with this type of writing. For this reason, we should not evaluate such writing or expect the level of correct spelling or grammar that would appear in more formal work, which the students would have time to revise. We can, however, model conventional spelling and grammar in our written responses. From an assessment perspective, informal writing helps us to monitor student understanding and provides direction for future lesson planning.

STUDENT-CONSTRUCTED RESPONSES, PROBLEM SOLVING, AND STRATEGY USE. Student-constructed responses, problem solving, and strategy use are additional informal ways in which students demonstrate their knowledge. Each of these informal tasks helps students understand that their thinking has value. They also increase our understanding of students' thinking processes and provide opportunities for formative assessment.

STUDENT-CONSTRUCTED RESPONSES:

Student-constructed responses require students to create their answer rather than select it from a variety of choices. This type of response, which answers an open-ended question, offers more insight into student thinking than formats such as multiple-choice or matching. For example, when Mrs. Curry, a geometry teacher, asked her students, "How do equilateral and scalene triangles differ?" Meredith replied, "In an *equilateral triangle* all of the sides are equal, but in a *scalene triangle* none of the sides are equal."

PROBLEM SOLVING:

Problem solving, which is applicable in all content areas, provides rich information about students' thinking and enables students to view learning as a process involving multiple possibilities. When problem solving, students often use multiple strategies to discover a variety of approaches to the problem and its solution. For example, when his science class was studying endangered species, Mr. Watkins asked pairs of students what people could do to solve the problem of endangered species. Nate and Rueben consulted several sources and suggested the following:

> We think there are three things people could do to help save endangered species: They could conserve habitats, share the environment, and be an active voice in the community and beyond. They could begin by making sure that people create places where endangered species can live and be safe. Then they could build birdhouses or plant trees. They could also recycle garbage and reuse shopping bags. Finally, they could join organizations that raise money and support awareness of endangered species.

We can learn from these students' response that they knew how to access information about endangered species and that they were able to develop a three-part solution to the problem. Through observation, we would also be able to determine how well the students worked together.

STRATEGY USE:

Many of the strategies for critical and creative thinking featured throughout this book also serve as informal assessments. The Concept of Definition Map, KWLS, and Lyric Summary are examples. After we explain and demonstrate a strategy, students practice and apply it. We can easily assess how well students can use the strategy by asking them to apply it in a particular context (For more information about these strategies, see Chapters 4, 5, and 6, applications throughout this text, and the Appendix.). In the following Concept of Definition Map, we can assess that the students who completed this map had knowledge of the Japanese American internment during World War II. They also knew how to use the graphic organizer and how to write a summary.

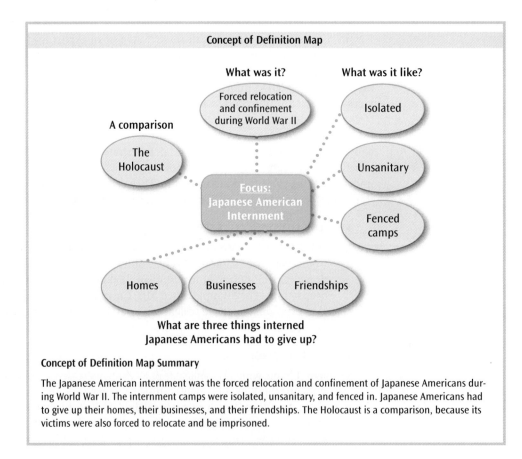

Concept of Definition Map

What was it? — Forced relocation and confinement during World War II

What was it like? — Isolated — Unsanitary — Fenced camps

A comparison — The Holocaust

Focus: Japanese American Internment

What are three things interned Japanese Americans had to give up? — Homes — Businesses — Friendships

Concept of Definition Map Summary

The Japanese American internment was the forced relocation and confinement of Japanese Americans during World War II. The internment camps were isolated, unsanitary, and fenced in. Japanese Americans had to give up their homes, their businesses, and their friendships. The Holocaust is a comparison, because its victims were also forced to relocate and be imprisoned.

Classroom Examples of Summative Assessment

As noted earlier, summative assessments are usually more complex and take a longer period of time to complete. In this section, we discuss examples of summative assessments, including some performance-based assessments (exhibitions and inquiry-based projects, group projects, research, and debate) and teacher-designed or textbook-related tests. These assessments are usually evaluated. Performance assessments are evaluated by using rubrics, or scoring guides, which we should share with the students before the assessment begins. Teacher- or textbook series-designed tests usually designate a certain number of points for each question or section.

PERFORMANCE ASSESSMENTS. Performance assessments incorporate motivation, content knowledge, thinking processes, and authentic tasks. This type of assessment has quite a long history in education (Madaus & O'Dwyer, 1999). Its latest renaissance can be traced to a number of factors.

The first, and perhaps most important, is the depth and variety of information that performances offer. Traditional measures such as multiple-choice questions simply do not provide the types of information needed to fully understand student learning (Haertel, 1999). When students engage in performances, they can demonstrate what they know. This process offers insight into students' knowledge of content and their thinking. (What did the students perceive the issue to be? What were their thoughts on the problem—on the solution? Why did they approach it in the way they did?) The choices students make when completing performance assessments help us to better understand that there are multiple approaches to learning.

The second factor is the performance assessment's connection to life experiences. The vast majority of professions are assessed through performance (e.g., physicians, chefs, teachers, construction workers, mechanics). Using similar assessments in our schools prepares students for experiences beyond the classroom. They come to understand that although they need to know the content, they must also be able to apply it.

The third factor is that performance assessments can accommodate students' individual needs, including learning styles, because performances provide opportunities for students to make choices to accommodate their strengths.

Finally, context is a factor when discussing performance assessment. These assessments are situated in response-centered classrooms that are characterized by motivation, high expectations for all learners, risk taking, self-selection, student ownership of learning, and cooperative and collaborative tasks. Examples include group investigations, exhibitions, and inquiry-based projects.

GROUP INVESTIGATIONS/PROJECTS:

When engaging in group investigations or projects, students "work together on a complex problem that requires planning, research, internal discussion, and group presentation" (Arter, 1996, p. 3). Projects offer students opportunities to demonstrate their knowledge while engaging in risk taking, creativity, and authentic experiences. As with all performances, evaluative criteria are shared with the students before the investigations or projects begin. For example, Debi Stinner and her colleagues created an interdisciplinary group investigation entitled "Mystery in Room 3." This culminating project for a unit integrating science and literature focused on forensic chemistry, the mystery genre, and descriptive writing. Students undertook the roles of detective, pathologist, and crime scene reporter. In addition, they analyzed and synthesized clues to develop a theory to solve the mystery. Assessment was based on students' participation, collaboration, lab reports, and writing. A rubric, created by teachers with student input, which included criteria for evaluating the accuracy of the information presented, the logical order of events, the mechanics of writing, creativity, and the solution, was shared with all participants prior to the beginning of the project.

RESEARCH:

Research can also be used as a performance assessment. It may be completed individually or by a group of students. For example, in Amy Sou's biology class, students complete an individual research project. They self-select their topics, often using either a teacher-provided list or their investigative journals as resources. Again, students are provided with a rubric prior to the start of the research. It focuses on criteria such as the research questions, resources, primary and secondary sources, technology, and quality of presentation. The research occurs over a period of two months, and includes techniques such as investigating related topics on selected websites, interviewing, and surveying. Student–teacher conferences are held periodically. When the research is completed, students self-select the methods they will use to share the results with the class. Dramatizations, demonstrations, PowerPoint presentations, exhibitions, digital movies, and student-authored books are the formats most commonly selected. A rubric, especially designed for the biology research project, is used to evaluate it. Ms. Sou uses the research rubric to evaluate her students' investigations when they are complete. In addition, her students use the rubric to engage in self-evaluation before they present their work, and peers use the rubric to offer feedback after students have presented their work. After they have reviewed the teacher-completed rubric, their self-evaluation, and their peers' comments, students can engage in goal setting for the next time they do research.

EXHIBITIONS:

Exhibitions usually embody multiple performance requirements that extend over a period of time. These are typically multimedia in nature and may involve writing a paper, making an oral presentation, building a model, creating computer graphics, or responding spontaneously to questions from peers. Exhibitions may be individual or collaborative and are often used as culminating activities (Willis, 1996). Exhibitions generally begin with students' self-selected topics and a project plan that includes the rubric that will be used to evaluate student performance. Student–teacher conferencing and cooperative learning play integral roles as students progress with their investigations. To complete the exhibition, its creators present it to an audience. The final step involves reflection on the part of the students creating the exhibition, their peers, and the teacher. Maria Ramirez has used collaborative exhibitions in her ninth-grade science classes for several years. At the outset, Ms. Ramirez provides students with a description of the exhibition and a rubric delineating the evaluation criteria. Students self-select their topics and cooperative groups are structured based on topic interest. For example, one group selected noise pollution as a topic and used multiple resources, including the Internet, to investigate it. They also based their research on primary and secondary sources. One of their primary sources was an interview the students conducted at the local airport with a pilot from US Airways. They had a lengthy discussion with him about what the airlines are doing to minimize noise. They learned that plane manufacturers are working on planes that are as quiet as cars, and that the hours of operation are restricted at some airports so the planes don't interfere with neighbors' sleep. These students also used multimedia to present their exhibition, including a PowerPoint presentation, DVDs, CDs, and interactive charts. At the conclusion of their presentation, students conducted a question-and-answer session with their audience.

PROJECTS:

Projects such as First-Person Experiences (see Chapter 12) and student-authored electronic books (see Chapter 13) are also examples of performance assessments. These projects provide students with opportunities to show what they have learned in richly interactive ways. They require decision making on the part of the students that ranges from topic selection to mode of presentation. The project format also provides students with alternative ways to respond, which may be more suitable to their individual learning styles.

Rubrics based on essential criteria are used to evaluate these projects. For an example of a First Person Experience rubric, see Figure 12.8 in Chapter 12; for an example of a rubric for student-authored electronic books, see Figure 13.5 in Chapter 13.

DEBATES:

Because state standards place great emphasis on developing critical thinking and students' abilities to speak and listen for a variety of purposes, debates appear to be regaining popularity. These performances provide opportunities for students to take positions and express, challenge, and defend ideas orally. When structuring a debate, students select the issue and prepare pro and con arguments to support their thinking. In math class, for example, they may choose to debate the applicability of a particular formula or mathematical concept; in science, they may debate the use of the scientific method or the results of an experiment; in history, they may debate political issues or the decision whether to fund a particular exploration; in literature class, they may debate who deserves the title of greatest American author. Whatever the topic, students have ownership of the debate process from the outset. They select the topic, establish debating teams, raise issues, and conduct the actual debate. As teachers, we serve as facilitators.

Debate provides students with opportunities to focus their thinking, develop persuasive arguments, reflect on the ideas presented, and interact with peers. Criteria such as these would be included in the rubric developed to evaluate this type of performance.

Performance assessments can be used in all content areas, and students may create them independently or in cooperative groups. The performance tasks discussed in this section illustrate the dynamic, multidimensional nature of such assessments and the need to use rubrics to evaluate them. Information about rubrics, including the process of creating them, is featured later in this chapter.

TEACHER-CREATED OR TEXT-RELATED TESTS. Of course, we also use traditional summative assessments such as teacher-created or textbook-related tests. The summative nature of these measures is clear, because students often take them at the conclusion of a chapter or a unit of study. In contrast to the other summative assessment examples, test scores are usually a culmination of points earned by responding correctly to various questions or sections of the test.

Making Connections
TO WRITING

Students often use writing to communicate ideas when engaging in formative and summative assessments. When writing is used in formative assessments, it is draft-stage writing—that is, students do not have opportunities to revise their work. In this case, we should not assess conventions of writing such as sentence structure and spelling. When writing is used in summative assessments, students should have multiple opportunities to revise their writing. Then it is appropriate to include conventions of writing as evaluation criteria. ■

Evaluation (Grading)

As contemporary assessment practices have evolved, methods of evaluating or grading student progress have also changed. For example, rather than rely on the traditional 100-point system or letters (A, B, C, D, F) to grade student work, rubrics are often used to evaluate students' performances.

Rubrics are scoring guides that provide criteria for evaluating performance assessments (Arter, 1996; Goodrich 1996–1997, McLaughlin, 1995; McTighe & O'Connor, 2005). They are designed to accommodate a range of levels; 0–4 and 0–6 are the most common. Rubrics also provide gradations of quality for each criterion. For example, on a 4-point rubric, gradations might include *exceptional, thorough, adequate,* and *inadequate* when describing levels of understanding.

Rubrics clearly delineate the criteria on which the performance assessment will be evaluated. They offer direction to student work, facilitate teacher and student evaluation of performances, provide information for future goal setting, and guide student revision. The completed rubrics also influence instructional planning. The process of creating rubrics for performance assessments is delineated in Figure 14.4.

Student involvement is an important consideration in rubric design. Students may have input into the process either from the beginning or after the teacher has created a draft of the rubric. Taking part in designing rubrics gives students additional confidence in, and ownership of, the assessment process.

Although we use rubrics to evaluate performances, our students should also have the opportunity to work with the rubrics. For example, they can use the rubrics for self- and peer evaluation, and they can use the results to revise their work before it is submitted to the teacher. This affords students additional confidence in the assessment process, an opportunity to examine the criteria by which their work will be evaluated, and a chance to improve their work before it is submitted for teacher evaluation.

Teachers who are just beginning to use rubrics or who are working with students who are not accustomed to using rubrics may want to begin by developing one that addresses a non-academic area. When we first begin creating rubrics, it is helpful to choose a topic with which we are very familiar. For example, creating a restaurant rubric works well because most people— including our students— have prior knowledge of restaurants. Criteria such as quality of food, service, and atmosphere are frequently suggested. Then gradations of quality are discussed. For example, on a 4-point rubric, food might be described as *delicious, tasty, adequate,* or *unpalatable.* Service might be described *exceptional, thorough, adequate,* or *inadequate.* Actually visiting a restaurant allows participants to use the rubric in an appropriate context. As an alternative, participants can use the rubric to evaluate a restaurant with which they are very

FIGURE 14.4
Creating a Rubric for a Performance Assessment

A rubric is a scoring guide that offers a description of student performance. It is used to evaluate a performance and to offer students specific feedback. The following guidelines delineate rubric design.

1. Begin with the state standards the performance task is addressing. Then review several rubric models and consider working with peers to develop the rubric.

2. Think about each standard in terms of performance levels. Decide how many levels of performance the rubric will have. The ranges 0–4 and 0–6 are the most commonly used. Decide which criteria need to be in the rubric. Next, describe each level of performance for each criterion. You may wish to begin by detailing what an exemplary performance is and then moving on to how an unacceptable performance would be described. This approach often makes it easier to describe the middle level or acceptable performance. Make certain there are clear distinctions between levels for each standard. Make the descriptors as detailed as possible.

3. Having a model of the performance at each level facilitates the use of rubrics. For this reason, you may wish to designate "anchor performances" that you feel are truly representative of each level of the rubric.

4. Share the rubrics with students before they begin the performance. This practice enables the students to focus on the criteria they are working to achieve.

5. When the performance is complete, students can use the rubric for self- and peer evaluation. After such evaluation has occurred, be sure to provide an opportunity for students to revise their work before submitting the final version to you.

6. Use the same rubric to evaluate students' performances. When first beginning to use rubrics, you may wish to invite the peers with whom you designed the performance task and rubric to join you in evaluating the performances. This may offer greater reliability to the evaluation process.

7. Return the completed rubrics to the students. They can use the information to set new personal goals and you can use the results to inform future planning.

Criteria	4 (Exceptional)	3 (Very Good)	2 (Acceptable)	1 (Poor)
Food	Delicious food	Tasty, good food	Edible food	Inedible food
Service	Outstanding service	Attentive service	Adequate service	Inadequate service
Cleanliness	**Exceptionally clean**	Very clean	Adequately clean	**Poor**
Atmosphere	Extraordinarily welcoming	Inviting	Acceptable	Uninviting
Location	**Excellent**	**Very good**	Acceptable	Unacceptable
Parking	**Excellent**	**Very good**	Adequate	**Poor**

Comments: _____

_____

FIGURE 14.5
Restaurant Rubric

familiar. Figure 14.5 shows a restaurant rubric that can be used to introduce this type of evaluation to middle school or high school students.

When using rubrics, it is important that we explain the criteria to our students before they begin the performance assessment. A well-designed rubric will delineate all of the requirements of the performance assessment, which helps students understand what needs to be included as well as which levels of proficiency are required to attain a particular level of evaluation (e.g., 4, 3, 2, 1, 0). After the work has been evaluated, the rubric should also provide direction for revision and future goal setting. For example, a student who received the completed research project rubric featured in Figure 14.6 should be able to notice what she did well, such as using quality sources and organizing the project, and understand what she needs to improve, such as formatting the

CATEGORY	4	3	2	1
Sources (quality, current)	Excellent sources	Very good sources	Adequate sources	Inadequate sources
Research	Outstanding research of topic	In-depth research of topic	Adequate research of topic	Inadequate research of topic
Organization (introduction, body, conclusion)	Excellent organization	Very good organization	Adequate organization	Inadequate organization
Style	Information flows perfectly sensibly and smoothly	Information flows very sensibly and smoothly	Information flows sensibly and smoothly	Information does not flow sensibly and smoothly
APA formatting (citations, references)	APA format is consistently applied with no errors	APA format is consistently applied with a few errors	APA format is consistently applied with several errors	APA format is inconsistently or incorrectly applied
Presentation	Excellent presentation	Very good presentation	Good presentation	Poor presentation

Comments: _____

_____

_____

FIGURE 14.6
Rubric for High School Research Project

citations and references. The latter point should lead to the student revising the way she formatted the references and in-text citations in this paper and setting future goals to do the same in the next research paper she writes.

When using rubrics to evaluate students' work, we often use anchor performances. These are examples of projects created by former students that received a 4, 3, 2, 1, or 0 in past classes. Sharing such examples with current students often helps them to understand the criteria and determine why their paper or project might be evaluated as a 2 instead of 3 or a 3 instead of a 4.

How Can We Organize and Manage Student Assessments?

If we use the types of formative and summative assessments we have been discussing, we need to be able to organize them effectively. In many cases, from kindergarten to university admissions to graduate classes, portfolios serve this purpose. Portfolios come in many shapes and sizes and are constructed for a variety of purposes. In this section of the chapter, we focus on portfolios that are standards-based, multidimensional collections of student performance. They demonstrate students' efforts, progress, and achievement and are both descriptive and evaluative in nature. They afford insight into students' engagement in learning and are created through the collaborative efforts of students and teachers. To facilitate the development of portfolios in the content areas, consider the guidelines delineated in Figure 14.7.

Organizing and using portfolio assessment can be demanding. Developing and implementing portfolios is time consuming, as is using portfolios when we are teaching 150-plus students per day. It is also challenging to develop and use innovative assessment practices such as portfolios in districts that continue to use traditional numeric grade report cards and standardized tests (see Chapter 3) to evaluate student progress.

Conversely, numerous benefits are derived from using portfolios in the content areas. They include the following:

- Students, parents, teachers, and administrators are aware from the outset of the standards students are striving to achieve.
- Students, parents, and teachers can see evidence of student growth over time.
- As a collaborative process, portfolios often reinvent the student–teacher relationship.
- Students engage in self-reflection and set personal goals within the framework of course standards.
- Portfolios accommodate students' learning styles.
- Portfolios provide a focus for student–teacher and student–parent–teacher conferencing.
- Portfolios can be directly linked to the reporting system.
- Developing and maintaining portfolios assists students who need to submit portfolios as part of the university admissions process.

Characteristics of Assessment Portfolios

Portfolio assessment can be defined as a purposeful, multifaceted process of collecting documentation of students' growth, progress, and effort over time. The portfolios should meet several criteria. In particular, they should:

- *Be clearly linked to instructional objectives.* If the two are not connected, the portfolio is just an accumulation of work with little assessment value or future instructional value.
- *Be an ongoing assessment system* that allows teachers to observe the continuous, dynamic movement of students' growth. Teachers must avoid discontinuous or static methods of assessing students' skills and abilities.

FIGURE 14.7 Creating Viable Portfolio Assessment Systems

1. Develop in-depth understanding of the concept of portfolio assessment and its related terminology. Share your awareness of these topics with your peers. Be supportive of one another's concerns regarding the assessment process.

2. Think about your reasons for valuing and implementing portfolio assessment and then examine those thoughts from the perspectives of students, teachers, parents, administrators, and community members.

3. Reflect on the national standards developed in your discipline and your state's assessment guidelines. Focus on the descriptions of student standards. Meet with colleagues and administrators to discuss and/or develop your district's standards. Then work with teachers across your grade level or within your department to develop discipline-specific benchmarks to facilitate students' achievement of the standards.

4. Hold a district-wide forum. Share information from grade-level meetings with all district teachers and administrators to assure natural, meaningful development from grade to grade toward achieving the district, state, and national standards.

5. Share plans for curricular and assessment innovations with students, parents, and community members. Invite their input.

6. Identify types of student performances that will support your standards. Remember that assessment is a natural, dynamic, ongoing part of instruction. Assessments should be both informal and formal and may include, but are certainly not limited to, problem solving, concept applications, audiotapes, strategies, videotapes, journal entries, observations, conferences, interest/attitude surveys, exhibitions, projects, research papers, and tests.

7. Design authentic assessment tasks. Create meaningful tasks that require thoughtful application of students' knowledge, relate to their life experiences, and encourage students to demonstrate their knowledge in a variety of ways.

8. If you plan to evaluate a performance, create specifying scoring criteria. It is more beneficial for both teachers and students if the rubrics are shared before the assessment begins.

9. Continue to share news concerning assessment innovations with school district residents. You may wish to create a newsletter or sponsor an open house. Remember to invite parents to take an active role in the assessment process.

10. Introduce the concept of portfolio assessment to your students. Model the process by sharing your portfolio with them. Focus on the collaborative roles of teachers and students as you engage in this process.

11. Encourage administrators to take ownership of the portfolio process. Contributing ideas, facilitating staff development, redeploying time, and sharing portfolios with students are just a few of the many ways in which administrators can facilitate meaningful assessment/evaluation practices.

12. Decide how you will physically structure the portfolios and where they will be stored. Plastic crates of hanging files containing expandable or pocket folders are one possibility; electronic portfolios are another. Remember that students need to experience ownership of their portfolios. Make sure the portfolios are readily accessible to them and encourage them to share their portfolios with their peers.

13. Decide how to effectively manage your classroom assessment system. One management aid that you may wish to employ is the portfolio index, which offers an at-a-glance overview of course standards and portfolio contents.

14. Implement the portfolio process in your classroom by modeling assessment-related techniques such as self-reflection, coordinating performances with standards, and completing entry slips.

15. Establish a baseline measure for each standard when students begin to use their portfolios. These will tell what the students are capable of doing at the start. This information assists in measuring students' progress throughout the academic year.

16. Encourage students to interact with their portfolios on a regular basis. Both you and your students will select items to be included. Parents may also wish to contribute pertinent information.

17. Conference with your students. Invite them to share their portfolios. Reflect on their strengths, versatility, efforts, and progress. Then encourage students to set new goals for themselves that will further their progress toward their course standards.

18. Reflect on the portfolio contents, note how designated entries relate to the rubrics, consider evidence supported by informal assessments, and make the connection between the student's portfolio and your district's reporting system. Utilize the portfolio as the basis for standards-based reports of student progress.

19. Share assessment and evaluation information. Two-way conferences between the student and you, followed by three-way conferencing in which the parent(s) also participate, is one viable plan. Include conference notes and/or parents' written reactions in the portfolio.

20. At the middle and high school levels, encourage students to include an end-of-course reflection that will introduce their work to the teacher of a subsequent course or facilitate their preparation of a portfolio for the university admissions processes.

21. Use the results of portfolio assessment to document student progress, give direction to the curriculum, evaluate your teaching, analyze program effectiveness, and provide information for accountability.

- *Avoid becoming a teacher-manufactured document.* Because students use the portfolios to analyze their growth and development, they should have a voice in selecting which items are included.

- *Be performance based and emphasize purposeful learning.* The portfolios should be ongoing in the cultural contexts of school, home, and community. They should also celebrate, support, and encourage students' development and learning.

As Herman and Winters (1994) have noted, "Well-designed portfolios represent important, contextualized learning that requires complex thinking and expressive skills" (p. 48). Portfolios encourage teachers and schools to focus on important student outcomes, provide parents and the community with the credible evidence of student achievement, and inform policy and practice at every level of the educational system.

Reporting

Unfortunately, advancements in reporting have not kept pace with innovative assessment practices. In some districts, innovative assessments are used, but traditional report cards remain in place. In other districts, the innovative assessment practices are connected to innovative reporting systems. In this section, we describe and discuss some of these reporting innovations.

Because our teaching and assessment of students correlate with educational standards, it is only logical that reporting should also be standards based. The reporting process is greatly facilitated—and much more meaningful—when curriculum, instruction, assessment, and reporting are aligned. The ultimate goal is to provide accurate, meaningful information about student progress.

If the reporting process is standards based, it should follow the same levels of performance as the course rubrics. For example, if the rubrics are based on a 4-point scale, that should also be the basis of the reporting system. Students are then evaluated based on multiple standards, with the final number representing a composite of the scores.

Once the standards and the scale are in place, levels of quality need to be developed. A variety of terms can be used to describe the levels of performance. For example, we might consider using terms such as *advanced* (4), *proficient* (3), *developing* (2), and *emerging* (1).

Using a continuum to record student progress accommodates tensions concerning accurate evaluation. When a student seems to be "more than developing (2)," but "not quite proficient (3)," we can indicate this by marking the continuum in the "developing" section, but appropriately closer to "proficient." These innovations in reporting can also be managed electronically.

Information about the reporting system should be shared with both students and parents at the beginning of the school year. For example, the school district could send a newsletter home or hold an open house at the school to share information and address parents' and students' questions and concerns. Explaining the process early in the school year facilitates students' and parents' understanding, provides an opportunity to demonstrate consistency across grade levels, and helps to create a learning community.

Implementation Considerations

Teachers and administrators consistently identify five topics as facilitating the development of assessment systems.

ADMINISTRATIVE SUPPORT. Teachers have found it essential to have administrators who support, understand, and enable the development of innovative assessment systems. This often involves administrators' full participation in professional development programs focused on designing assessment systems.

ONGOING PROFESSIONAL DEVELOPMENT. Teachers believe that ongoing professional development keeps them in touch with educational advancements.

- *Communication with experts.* Teachers have deemed communication with experts as vital to their knowledge and understanding of contemporary practice.
- *Colleague interaction.* Opportunities for teachers to interact are an often-overlooked professional development resource that is essential to learning and contextualizing contemporary assessment, evaluation, and reporting.
- *Learning opportunities.* Professional conferences, professional publications, university courses, in-district courses, colleague observation, mentoring, and peer coaching are the opportunities that the teachers believe provide connections between what they know and up-to-the-minute educational developments. For more information about professional development, see Chapter 15.

TIME. For most teachers, having enough time to learn about, implement, and reflect on contemporary assessment and evaluation practices tops their list of concerns. We need time to learn about innovative practices, share knowledge with colleagues and students, integrate innovations, confer with students, and explore resulting outcomes. In addition, we need time to analyze and synthesize data provided by school- and state-mandated assessments (Angaran, 1999).

COMMUNICATION WITH PARENTS. Inviting parents to join the conversations about assessment and evaluation practices has been recognized as a critical component of successful implementation. Distributing newsletters and sponsoring community meetings are two effective ways to encourage parents to participate.

TRANSITIONING STUDENTS. Plans for transitioning students to the next grade, to the next school building, or to an institution of higher learning need to be in place before the contemporary assessment practices begin. This will provide continuity for the students and allow teachers to view assessment as a progressive process.

Openly addressing these issues in the early stages of planning greatly facilitates implementation of innovative assessments. Discussions based on these topics also help to establish a sense of trust and confidence among the participants.

FINAL THOUGHTS

Using innovative practices such as performance assessments and portfolios in the content areas helps us to accommodate students' individual learning styles, relate learning to life experiences, and incorporate educational standards. These practices offer windows into students' minds and insights into their thinking processes. Further, in student-centered learning contexts, these types of assessment support students' engagement in inquiry-based learning and alternatives modes of representation, both of which are richly characterized by critical and creative thinking.

Wiggins and McTighe (2008) suggest that we should design curriculum, instruction, and assessment with the knowledge that our ultimate goal is the effective and purposeful use of content. Shephard (2005) concurs, noting that all of our students should strive to extend their knowledge of content and apply it in new situations.

Integrating innovative assessment practices is challenging and time consuming, but the rewards are plentiful. Some will ask if it is worth all the effort. Eisner (1999) offers a simple but eloquent affirmative response: "What's at stake is not only the quality of life our children might enjoy but also the quality of the culture that they will inhabit" (p. 660).

In the next chapter, we focus on professional development and issues, such as content standards and texts, that challenge us in the classroom. Then we discuss our goal of becoming lifelong learners.

Teaching Connections

APPLYING WHAT WE HAVE LEARNED

E-Links

Consider how portfolio assessment could benefit your content area students. (1) Think about how students could use standards-based portfolios to document their progress in attaining state standards. (2) Consider what benefits portfolio assessment might hold for high school juniors and seniors applying to universities. Share your thinking with peers in small-group discussions.

SAMPLE WEBSITES
Use information from websites such as these to support your thinking:

Portfolio Assessment in the Foreign Language Classroom
http://www.nclrc.org/portfolio/2-1.html

TeacherVision: Portfolios
http://www.teachervision.fen.com/assessment/teaching-methods/20153.html

The Use of Portfolios in Evaluation
http://ag.arizona.edu/fcs/cyfernet/cyfar/Portfo~3.htm

Accountable Talk

At the beginning of this chapter, Peter Johnston (1997) was quoted as saying, "Teachers must become assessment experts." Think about what this means to you as a teacher in your content area, and share your thoughts with peers in a small group. Then reflect on how you might become such an expert. Record your thoughts as a reflective entry in your portfolio.

Portfolio/Performance Opportunity

Meet with peers in a small group and create a performance assessment and rubric that you would use in your content area teaching. As you and your colleagues work, notice the collegial nature of your task. Share the outcomes of your work with the class by briefly discussing (1) which state standards the performance addresses, (2) how the performance assessment accommodates students' learning styles, (3) how the rubric informs student planning, and (4) what new goals the students might set based on the completed rubric. Include the performance, the rubric, and your reflection on this task as an entry in your portfolio.

15

Meeting Challenges and Continuing to Learn through Professional Development

While enrolled in this course, we have learned a great deal about teaching reading in the content areas, but our learning does not end here. The next steps are to fully apply what we have learned in our teaching and to continue to discover the latest developments in education and in our content areas. In other words, our next step is to become lifelong learners. Because no one can predict what the next challenge or educational development will be, as teachers, we need to keep our minds open to the many possibilities that lie ahead.

And so, in this final chapter, we discuss three important topics: experiencing success in our teaching, participating in a mentoring program, and engaging in professional development. First, we examine the challenges often encountered during teaching. Next, we focus on the importance of partnering with a knowledgeable, experienced mentor. Finally, we explore the key components of professional development and discuss how to create meaningful professional development plans.

What Challenges Might We Encounter in Our Teaching?

As content area teachers, we face challenges every day. We teach a wide variety of students. We infuse critical and creative thinking, inquiry-based learning, and technology into our work, and we do it all while accommodating federal programs, state standards, and individual students' needs. To become the best content area teachers we can be, we need to be able to meet any challenges that may arise. Ideas about how we might do that follow.

Time

To explore some of the obstacles and opportunities in a new teaching career, go to the Resources tab in the MyEducation-Lab for your course and click on Beginning Your Career

Most of us would agree that there simply is not enough time in the teaching day to do all that needs to be done. We need time to plan and teach, as well as to accommodate students' diverse academic, linguistic, and cultural needs.

Time will always be a concern for teachers, but we can take some steps to ensure that we use time to our best advantage. We might begin by considering how much time we need for planning and teaching. For example, rather than always teaching in a whole-group setting, we can use pairs and small groups when students are preparing presentations, creating projects, or applying what they are learning in other ways (see Chapter 8). This provides us with time to observe students, to interact with them about the projects they are creating, to provide suggestions about their research, or to conference about their progress.

There are many other things we can do to use time more efficiently. Consider the following examples:

- *Pre-assessing students' prior knowledge.* Before teaching a new topic, we can use techniques such as Admit Slips, Tickets Out, Semantic Maps, or Quickwrites for two purposes: to learn what students already know and to determine a starting point for our teaching that will accommodate students' needs.

- *Working with others who teach our content area.* Sharing ideas, resources, and planning with colleagues can help us to gain other perspectives and save time preparing materials and lessons.

- *Collaborating with teachers who do not teach our content area.* Certain skills, such as generating questions and using graphic organizers, benefit students across the curriculum. If we encourage all content teachers to focus on teaching and using such skills, individual teachers will need to spend less time teaching them. Of course, if we can persuade teachers across grade levels to teach and use these skills and strategies, we would only need to review them by the time the students reached the levels at which we teach.

Making Connections
TO ENGLISH LEARNERS

We can also engage the support of ESL teachers. Meeting with these teachers and learning how we can best help our English learners to succeed is often an invaluable experience. We can learn how to use supports such as visuals and a variety of response modes. Knowing how to explain and demonstrate these supports will save time that otherwise might be needed for reteaching. ■

Content Standards

As discussed in Chapter 3, national and state content standards have been developed in virtually every area of the curriculum. Most state assessments are based on those standards, which describe what students know and can do in the content areas. Sometimes we may feel pressure to "teach to the test" to help students perform at acceptable levels on high stakes tests, such as state assessments. This becomes complicated when students lack the prior knowledge and skills needed to successfully learn and apply content concepts.

We may be able to meet this challenge by remembering that our teaching is standards-based. We don't ignore the content when implementing innovative approaches, but rather support and enhance it. For example, we can invite students to engage in Inquiring Minds (see Chapter 12)—a small-group, inquiry-based, and standards-based research project in which students self-select topics—rather than writing individual traditional reports on the same subject. We can also help our students by teaching skills and strategies they may not know (see Chapters 4 through 10).

Texts and Other Resources

Some school districts may provide us with content texts and supplemental materials that are either outdated or overly demanding. Problems associated with this issue include inaccurate information, uninteresting text formats, few opportunities for student interaction, unnecessarily long texts, absence of critical and creative thinking, focus on literal meaning, and lack of strategy integration. As a result, we and our students may be unmotivated—a factor that influences not only the amount of learning that takes place, but also the quality of the experience for everyone involved.

In response to this challenge, we can use multiple types of text in our teaching (see Chapter 8). Informational text from magazines, newspapers, journals, and websites is up-to-date and readily available, so we should never feel limited to using textbooks (see Chapter 8). In addition, appropriate theme-related poetry or novels can significantly enhance students' understanding. For example, if we are teaching English/Spanish translation, we can access the works of poets such as Pablo Neruda in both English and Spanish. An example is Neruda's "Ode to a Chestnut on the Ground," which is entitled "Oda a Una Castaña En el Suelo" in Spanish; this poem is available in English and Spanish on the Internet. Another example would be integrating current information about a topic we are teaching. For example, if we are teaching DNA in biology, we might motivate students by sharing information about how DNA is now used in the search for justice; information about this topic is also available on the Internet. For an example of how to align young adult novels with a historical topic such as World War II, see Figure 2.3, which lists young adult novels about World War II that can be used to teach critical literacy.

Making Connections
TO MULTIPLE LITERACIES

The idea of alternative texts is virtually boundless when we engage in multiple literacies. In critical literacy, the nature of text includes books, articles, and lyrics, but also moves beyond traditional views of text to encompass conditions (e.g., sociocultural influences, state-assessment-driven curriculums funding or lack of it) or relationships and situations in everyday life (e.g., analyzing an occurrence from another person's perspective). Media literacy incorporates texts such as film and photography, and informational literacy provides access to the seemingly endless texts of the virtual world. ■

Creativity

Some content teachers believe that only "creative people" can teach students how to use methods such as inquiry-based learning and alternative representations. However, when creative teaching ideas are explained and demonstrated using classroom examples, these teachers often seem more willing to take the risk. Throughout this text, we have been encouraged to scaffold learning by explaining, demonstrating, guiding, practicing, and reflecting when teaching new methods or strategies to our students. These examples may include sketching or illustrating. Consider how teachers who doubt their creativity might feel after reviewing the rubric for student-authored electronic books (see Chapter 13). They would know that one of the criteria for that project is the relationship of illustrations to text. That might be an issue of concern if the teachers doubt their ability to illustrate the book, but in the case of electronic books we have choices. We—and our students—can download photos from the Internet or use computer clipart to illustrate such books. Utilizing these resources enables us to be creative without requiring us to be artists.

We can also choose to work through our "creative doubts" with colleagues in our content area. In fact, we can even invite them to work with us on examples we can share and use at different points during the school year.

Making Connections | **Thinking about Our Creativity**

■ Think about yourself as a creative person and about the role that creativity plays in teaching. (1) Consider how comfortable you would feel sketching, singing, or writing poetry when teaching through alternative representations. (2) Consider what you could do to help students feel comfortable in such situations.

■ Share your thoughts with others in small-group discussions.

Innovation Versus Reality

Another challenge we may experience is the contrast between what we have learned in our teacher education programs and what we see being practiced in the schools in which we teach. We have learned about new and interesting teaching methods such as student-centered, inquiry-based learning, yet when we go into the field we may see more traditional approaches, such as reading chapters and answering questions or round-robin reading, being used (see Chapter 8).

To meet this type of challenge, we need to consider the nature of each task and develop specific responses. For example, if we see content area teachers still asking students to silently read chapters and respond to questions or to take turns reading the chapter aloud (round-robin reading), we can invite them to consider multiple ways to respond to text (see Chapters 10, 12, and 13) and alternatives to round-robin reading (see Chapter 8). We can probably be most effective in sharing these techniques if we work with one or two teachers who demonstrate interest in engaging in more innovative practices. We can also serve as effective teaching models.

If it is difficult to find other teachers who choose to teach content subjects in creative and innovative ways, we shouldn't be discouraged. While some teachers enthusiastically endorse new approaches, others remain in a fixed position—teaching the way they've always taught. If we find ourselves surrounded by those for whom content teaching simply means lectures and test taking, we will need to act as the trailblazers. Of course, both we and our students will be the winners!

Making Connections | **Thinking about Innovative Practice**

■ Think about how you have integrated innovative practices into your teaching. Imagine that you were hired by a school district that supported very traditional methods of teaching. What would you do to introduce other teachers to alternatives to round-robin reading and other innovative approaches?

■ Share your thoughts with others in small-group discussions.

Student Diversity

Another common concern of content teachers at all levels is the challenge of meeting students' individual needs. Factors such as background knowledge and experience, language proficiency, learning styles, reading abilities, and culture all affect students' access to content. Classroom realities include large class sizes, increasing numbers of English learners, lack of materials to meet students' needs, unmotivated learners, and teachers who may feel unprepared to deal with these challenges.

We need to believe that our teaching methods can bridge these differences and help both teachers and students come together in a learning community. We know that we can differentiate our instruction (see Chapter 8). We also know that teaching that incorporates creative, strategy-based approaches benefits all students, including English learners and students with special needs. If we believe that "thinking" exists regardless of reading or language ability, then we can see that for many students, "other ways of knowing" may include drama, music, technology, hands-on manipulation, art, poetry, and physical movement. We have all taught students who can express their thoughts better in one mode than in others—students whose strength may not be written responses, but who share their thoughts freely through discussion; or students whose strength may not be discussion or writing, but can freely share their ideas through projects or dramatizations. Chapter 13 features information about alternative representations of student thinking, such as transmediations, in which students take content presented in one medium and change it into another, and Rapping for Review, in which students use essential information to create and sing a rap about the current topic of study.

Incorporating these ideas into content teaching provides opportunities for all students to share their thinking. In many ways, it levels the learning playing field.

Making Connections
TO STRUGGLING READERS

Knowing our students' needs helps us to differentiate instruction. For example, when working with struggling students, we can design projects that incorporate alternative modes of representation. Offering students choices about how to represent their thinking has dual benefits: It motivates students, and it provides opportunities for them to use their strength modalities. ■

Classroom Organization and Management

The challenge for today's teachers is to create student-centered classrooms in which students take ownership of learning. When we release some of the responsibility for learning to the students, classroom management issues change. A variety of grouping patterns, multiple texts, daily schedules, and classroom routines become prevalent, and management becomes more of a shared responsibility between teacher and students (see Chapter 8).

Keeping an open mind and being versatile with classroom organization enhances students' experiences in content area learning. We may wish to think about how we might organize our classrooms so that management issues are not paramount. We also need to think about how we might organize groups of students who will work together, plan for a system of accountability for students (such as daily group progress checks), and determine the degree to which we need to monitor each activity. Thinking through these issues carefully before we implement innovative approaches will help ensure success for everyone concerned.

Assessment and Evaluation

Tests, quizzes, and reports are the more traditional means of assessing student knowledge of content material. These methods of assessment are relatively quick to grade, the "correct answers" are easy to determine, and teachers, administrators, parents, and students all understand what the grades have meant.

When integrating creative and innovative teaching ideas, however, we use dynamic measures such as observation, discussion, strategy use, informal writing, and projects to document student progress (see Chapter 14.). In this area, challenges may arise when assessment is viewed as separate from instruction, when the role of informal assessments is not understood, when the measures used do not accommodate students' strength modalities, and when criteria for performance assessments are not provided. As innovative strategies are integrated, assessment becomes a natural part of everyday teaching and learning. In such contexts, informal and formal assessments combine to offer a fuller, more meaningful picture of students' abilities. Another important benefit is that students can become more engaged in self-assessment, reflecting on their roles as active learners as well as their levels of understanding.

Students Working Independently

Because we want to ensure that our students continue to learn when they work independently, we may occasionally be concerned about whether they have the necessary skills and motivation to effectively work on their own. We can meet this challenge by teaching our students how to be active, independent learners who are motivated to engage in a variety of tasks. For example, Bookmark Technique, INSERT Method, Patterned Partner Reading and Say Something (see Chapters 4 through 8) require students to take an active role in learning by commenting on, questioning, making connections to, or summarizing what they are learning. We can also teach our students how to use techniques such as structured note taking and double-entry journals (see Chapter 8), which students can use as supports when working independently. Participating in interactive group tasks, such as Internet Workshops (see Chapter 11) or Discussion Circles (see Chapter 8), also foster student independence.

Making Connections
TO WRITING

Writing plays an important role when students are working independently. Although students also engage in discussion, the responses they write when using ideas such as structured notetaking, journaling, or Bookmark Technique provide informal assessments of student progress that we can read at a later time. Discussion does provide similar information, but we need to be able to observe that as it is occurring. ■

To ensure that our students are well-motivated, we can activate their prior knowledge and provide additional background information if necessary. For example, if we determine that students have little or no prior knowledge of a topic we will be teaching, we can use read-alouds of informational articles and trade books to enhance their knowledge (see Chapter 8). To engage our students in learning, we can also offer them choices, such as self-selecting topics and choosing formats when they are creating projects.

For example, when creating First-Person Experiences (see Chapter 12), students often choose unique ways to present their research. One student researched the Pilgrims' journey to America and presented her findings in a parchment travel journal rolled up and placed inside a bottle. She chose the "message in a bottle format" because the captain of the boat had announced that land had been sighted and, as a passenger approaching a new land, she feared what awaited her and her family. Another student researched Ben Franklin and came to class dressed as the inventor. "Franklin" presented his research by regaling the class with stories about "his" life. Still another student researched Edgar Allen Poe for his American poetry class. He came to class dressed as Poe, shared fascinating information about "his" life, and toward the end of the presentation noted that he was very pleased that he and his poetry remained so popular so long after his death. To support this premise, he shared a brief video clip about "The Raven" from an episode of *The Simpsons* television show. These three students self-selected their topics and chose distinctive presentation modes that embedded both the depth of their understanding and their engagement in learning.

Final Thoughts on Challenges We May Encounter in Our Teaching

Although we may encounter challenges during our teaching careers, we know that if we learn well, plan well, and teach well, we can meet them all. The essence of our success seems to involve our background knowledge: how well we know our students, how well we motivate them, how well we teach them, and how well we encourage them to apply what they learn in innovative and creative ways.

In the next section, we discuss mentoring, another process that can help us become better teachers. Early in our careers, we may be mentees. Later, we may become mentors.

How Can Mentoring Benefit Our Teaching?

As educators, we need to make our teaching all that it can be. We need to reflect on our efforts, and continually strive to enrich our teaching and learn more about our content areas. Mentors can help us achieve these goals.

The term "mentor" has a long-standing history. It dates back to Greek mythology and the story of Odysseus. When he left to fight the Trojan War, Odysseus entrusted his son, Telemachus, to his close friend, Mentor. Mentor was responsible for the protection, guidance, and education of Telemachus. Mentor taught Telemachus to think and to do things for himself with good judgment.

There are numerous definitions of mentoring. The descriptors that follow are drawn from a combination of resources (Allen, Cobb, & Danger, 2003; Holloway, 2001; Mtetwa & Kwari, 2003; Shank, 2005; Trubowitz & Robins, 2003). They agree that mentoring is:

- an active, evolving, one-on-one process.
- a reciprocal relationship in which an experienced, knowledgeable, and caring teacher invests time and knowledge to help a new teacher successfully acclimate to the real-life demands of experiences in the teaching profession.
- a professional partnership that successfully benefits both mentor and mentee.
- situationalized. The environment—which includes the school, the faculty, the administration, and the community—plays an integral role in the mentoring process.

Most novice teachers soon discover that while they are striving to address their goals, their school is focused on student success in federal programs and on state assessments. According to Mandel (2006), while school districts are focusing on state testing, new teachers are focusing on survival. Mentors, who understand the agenda needs to come from the first year teachers, can help those teachers meet the unique challenges they face during their first year. Mandel further notes that the concerns of the new teachers fall into five broad categories:

1. Setting up the classroom and preparing for the first weeks of class (physical arrangement, materials, bulletin boards, discipline problems, what to teach when, homework, and tests).
2. Covering the required curriculum without falling behind or losing student interest.
3. Grading fairly.
4. Dealing with parents. (Always have the student present for parent–teacher conferences.)
5. Maintaining personal sanity.

We may be somewhat surprised that the general category of "continuing professional development" was not included in Mandel's list. It is a topic we will add and explore as we examine the challenges that novice teachers face. First, however, we discuss those experienced educators who are available to guide first-year teachers as they strive to develop meaningful ways to meet the challenges described by Mandel. These teachers are the mentors.

Characteristics of Effective Mentors

Mentors are lifelong learners who understand and respect the mentoring process. They participate in special training and support mentees in all aspects of their teaching.

Mentors have patience, enthusiasm, and respect for their colleagues. They also have the respect of their colleagues. They have demonstrated expertise in their field and are willing to share it. Their goal is to provide less experienced teachers with guidance and support, while encouraging them to make their own decisions (Allen et al., 2003; Holloway, 2001; Mtetwa & Kwari, 2003; Shank, 2005; Trubowitz & Robins, 2003). Although mentors most often assist first-year teachers, they are also called upon to aid experienced teachers who may be beginning a new teaching assignment.

Mentors are dedicated educators who freely give their time to help others. They are respectful and nurturing in their quest to encourage mentees to reach their greatest potentials.

Characteristics of Mentees

Mentees are usually novice teachers who understand and respect the mentoring process. These lifelong learners appreciate their colleagues' willingness to be mentors. Mentees make their own decisions with the advice and encouragement of their mentors (Allen et al., 2003; Holloway, 2001; Mtetwa & Kwari, 2003; Shank, 2005; Trubowitz & Robins, 2003).

As noted earlier, mentees are most often first-year teachers. They are new to the full-time teaching experience, although their teacher education programs likely involved multiple professional experiences in addition to student teaching. Mentees may also be experienced teachers who become involved in mentoring when they begin a new teaching assignment. For example, if a teacher has taught seventh grade for ten years and is transferred to tenth grade, she might be offered the opportunity to work with a mentor from that grade level.

Good mentoring relationships are reciprocal in nature. Both the mentor and the mentee contribute to the relationship's success, which often depends on the context or situation in which the mentoring occurs. For example, when mentoring was introduced in the New York City Schools, the program in general was found to be helpful (Keller, 2006). In fact, mentoring participants were twice as likely to stay on their jobs compared to those who did not have mentors, but the mentors encountered a number of challenges including the number of mentees, the lack of a second year of mentoring, and poor communication between those in the mentoring program and building administrators.

When establishing a mentoring program, Northwest Regional Educational Laboratory (NWREL, 2001) suggests that we follow these general guidelines:

- *Provide support and training for mentors.* This should include program goals and purposes, district philosophies, and observational techniques and feedback methods (Halford, 1999).

- *Reward the mentors.* A reward system engenders positive feelings in both the mentor and the mentee (Halford, 1999).

- *Provide support, funding, and leadership to establish and maintain mentoring programs* (Halford, 1999). Mentors are not administrative representatives. Principals should take an active interest in the mentoring process.

- *Schedule mentor/mentee meetings on a regular basis.* Scheduling mentoring meetings can be a challenge. School districts should consider hiring one person who is a full-time mentor or retired teachers whose schedules may be more flexible.

Figure 15.1 lists selected books about mentoring. For additional resources, see the mentoring websites listed in the E-Links section at the conclusion of this chapter.

Final Thoughts on Mentoring

Mentoring is a valued component of teaching. As Halford (1998) notes, creating successful induction programs for novice teachers is an important goal of educational reform. Most districts that have mentoring partnerships have found that beginning teachers who participate in them are more likely to remain members of the teaching profession (Trubowitz, 2004). "As instructional leaders and master teachers, mentors can be a professional lifeline for their new colleagues" (Halford, 1998, p. 36). From our standpoint it is particularly important to note that mentoring

Breaux, A. L. (2002). *101 "answers" for new teachers & their mentors: Effective teaching tips for daily classroom use.* Larchmont, NY: Eye on Education.

Hicks, C. D., Glasgow, N. A., & McNary, S. J. (2004). *What successful mentors do: 81 research-based strategies for new teacher induction, training, and support.* Thousand Oaks, CA: Corwin.

Jonson, K. F. (2008). *Being an effective mentor: How to help beginning teachers succeed* (2nd ed.). Thousand Oaks, CA: Corwin.

Niday, D., Boreen, J. Potts, J., & Johnson, M. K. (2009). *Mentoring beginning teachers: Guiding, reflecting, coaching* (2nd ed.). Portland, ME: Stenhouse.

Portner, H. (Ed.). (2008). *Mentoring new teachers.* Thousand Oaks, CA: Corwin.

works well in high school settings. Shank (2005, p. 81) draws these conclusions from her work in a secondary setting:

> New and veteran teachers alike can share their expertise and take responsibility for the learning of other teachers. They can develop a broader understanding of teaching approaches that are prevalent in their school. Through collegial support and challenge, novices and experienced teachers can learn to be open about their practices and grapple with the complexities of teaching. Together, teachers can develop and maintain a shared focus and a dynamic culture where collaborative and reciprocal mentoring can take place.

How Can We Make Professional Development a Meaningful Part of Our Teaching?

When thinking about professional development, we must begin by defining the term. Wiggins and McTighe (2006) suggest that four characteristics distinguish professionals in any field:

> Professionals (1) act on the most current knowledge that defines their field; (2) are client-centered and adapt to meet the needs of the individuals whom they serve; (3) are results-oriented; and (4) uphold the standards of the profession in their own practice and through peer review. (p. 27)

Kelleher (2003) extends these ideas to professional development in education, suggesting that the best programs "help teachers to think critically about their practice; to develop new instructional strategies, along with new techniques for creating curriculum and assessments; and to measure how new practices have affected student learning" (p. 754). Duffy (2004) extends the definition of professional development by addressing what kind of knowledge professional developers should be providing:

> As instructional situations change, teachers transform knowledge to fit the situation, often on a case-by-case basis. Consequently, our professional development goal should not be to simply disseminate knowledge to teachers; it should be to teach teachers to make judgments about how to modify or adapt professional knowledge to fit changing situations. (p. 11)

Greenleaf and Schoenbach (2004) classify professional development as high quality if teachers are involved in learning over time, necessary resources are accessible, opportunities for teachers to reflect on teaching and learning are created, and teachers' expertise is increased. Accountability is also a major factor. Because professional development emphasizes student learning, teachers need to be able to demonstrate measurable growth in terms of student learning.

In this section, we explore professional development. We begin by discussing how we can effectively engage in professional development. Then we examine a variety of professional development resources that can help us to reach our goals.

Becoming Lifelong Learners through Professional Development

Because we are lifelong learners, we engage in professional development throughout our teaching careers. Our goal is to increase our students' understanding and performance. Research suggests that professional development can help us to make profound changes in our practice and, consequently, provide learning opportunities that make a difference in student achievement (Greenleaf & Schoenbach, 2004).

The structure of professional development has changed over time. For example, its purpose was once viewed as increasing teachers' knowledge of various educational topics; now, however, its goals have moved beyond teacher knowledge to student learning. The focuses of professional development emerge from student learning, and the outcomes are measured through increased student performance. To ensure that the professional development in which we engage is meaningful, we should consider the following guidelines (Kelleher, 2003):

- Choose a goal that emerges from your students' learning and is related to school and district-wide goals.
- Set specific, measurable targets for student achievement.
- Create study groups, agree on how student work will be evaluated, or otherwise prepare for the professional development experience.
- Engage in a variety of settings and use a range of quality resources.
- Use meaningful measures to determine teacher and student growth.
- Self-reflect and share experiences with peers.
- Determine the changes you will make based on professional development and peer sharing.

Plans are often three years in duration and include learning through technology. Throughout the process, administrators, mentors, or peer coaches serve as guides and provide the participants with regular feedback.

Based on our understanding of professional development and guidelines such as those presented, we can develop an action plan by following these steps:

1. Consider topics such as integrating new literacies, content disciplines, or innovative teaching methods. Ultimately, however, the topic we choose should emerge from the needs of our students.
2. Consider the duration of our professional development and determine how we could measure change in students' performance that occurs as a result.
3. Consider settings, learning at some points in study groups and at other times with a peer.
4. Develop professional development goals based on students' needs.
5. Learn new information and integrate our learning into our teaching.
6. Measure student learning.
7. Reflect and share ideas throughout this process.

Although professional development is tied to district and school practices, we need to remember that it is always personal. Topics emerge from our students' learning, and we develop plans to address those needs. We make choices—the length of the plan, the settings in which we will learn, the formats we will use, and the resources we will integrate—throughout the process. When we engage in meaningful professional development experiences, such as these guidelines would provide, our learning informs students' learning, and we become "designers as well as implementers, informed professionals rather than mere conduits for other people's designs and agendas" (Greenleaf & Schoenbach, 2004, pp. 122–123).

Professional Development Resources

Resources for professional development range from more traditional graduate courses to online offerings. In fact, most resources are now accessible through electronic as well as traditional means. The types of resources we use relate directly to our professional development focus and the contexts in which we choose to learn. All are designed to help us discover new teaching methods, learn more about our content areas and other educational issues, and demonstrate our dedication to teaching.

The following professional development resources are easily accessible.

PROFESSIONAL ORGANIZATIONS. Most disciplines have professional organizations that are designed to help members learn about new advances in teaching and learning. Figure 15.2 lists some of these organizations, along with their website addresses.

PROFESSIONAL EDUCATION JOURNALS. Figure 15.3 features a list of some of the many journals published by professional educational organizations. Subscriptions are often available in hard copy as well as electronic formats. Most of these journals are peer reviewed.

PROFESSIONAL BOOKS. These publications are often available from professional organizations and groups dedicated to education in general. Of course, most titles are available from educational publishers, bookstores, and online booksellers, such as Amazon.com.

PROFESSIONAL STUDY GROUP MODULES/STUDY GROUPS. According to Baker (2004), study groups consist of literacy educators who share professional development interests. These educators meet on a regular basis to read and discuss materials about a topic they wish to study in depth. The composition of the group is determined by the participants; it may be organized formally within a school or school district, or informally by colleagues with comparable job responsibilities. The focus of the study group's work is often a study group module published by a professional organization. For examples of available modules, see the International Reading Association's website http://www.reading.org for literacy-related topics, such as adolescent literacy and reading comprehension, and the Association for Supervision and Curriculum Development's (ASCD) website http://www.ascd.org for general education topics, such as problem-based learning and differentiated instruction.

Making Connections | Thinking about Professional Study Groups

- Reflect on all that you have learned and (1) consider an educational topic that you would like to explore in a professional study group. Justify your choice. (2) Consider the value of such study groups within school districts.
- Share your thoughts with others in small-group discussions.

GRADUATE COURSES. Offered by universities, these courses can be taken individually, based on interest, or as part of graduate degree programs. Many university courses are now offered both in the traditional manner and in electronic format through distance education. When taking distance education courses, we can remain in our homes and participate in class by using the Internet. These courses, which often are discussion and project based, eliminate the expenses associated with traveling to and from classes, as well as the time such a commute requires. Listings of traditional and distance education courses are usually posted on university websites.

IN-DISTRICT COURSES. School districts often offer courses to help teachers fulfill ongoing state certification requirements. These programs, which are usually provided at no cost, are taught by district teachers and administrators. The content focuses on developments in research and practice related to teaching in general or to specific content areas. Announcements about these courses are shared through district email, and the class meetings are generally held after school.

PROFESSIONAL WORKSHOPS, PRESENTATIONS, AND SEMINARS. Offered at the international, national, regional, and state levels, these meetings enable teachers to learn about specific

English

National Council for Teachers of English (NCTE)
http://www.ncte.org/

ESL

National Association for Bilingual Education (NABE)
http://www.nabe.org/

Teachers of English Speakers of Other Languages (TESOL)
http://www.tesol.org/s_tesol/index.asp

Fine Arts

National Art Education Association (NAEA)
http://www.naea-reston.org

MENC: National Association for Music Education
http://www.menc.org

Foreign Language

American Council on the Teaching of Foreign Language (ACTFL)
http://www.actfl.org/i4a/pages/index.cfm?pageid=1

Modern Language Association (MLA)
http://www.mla.org/

Health

American Alliance for Health, Physical Education, Recreation, and Dance (AAHPERD)
http://www.aahperd.org/index.cfm

History

National Council for Social Studies (NCSS)
http://www.ncss.org

Math

National Council for Teachers of Mathematics (NCTM)
http://www.nctm.org/

Reading

International Reading Association (IRA)
http://www.reading.org

Science

American Association of Physics Teachers (AAPT)
http://www.aapt.org/

National Association of Biology Teachers (NABT)
http://www.nabt.org

National Science Teachers Association (NSTA)
http://www.nsta.org/

Special Education

Council for Exceptional Children (CEC)
http://www.cec.sped.org//AM/template.cfm?Section=Home

National Association of Special Education Teachers (NASET)
http://www.naset.org/

Technology

Association for Educational Communication and Technology (AECT)
http://www.aect.org/default.asp

International Society for Technology in Education (ISTE)
http://www.iste.org/

FIGURE 15.2
Professional Organizations for Teachers

FIGURE 15.3
**Educational Journals
that Support
Professional
Development**

English

National Council for Teachers of English (NCTE)
- *Voices from the Middle*
- *English Journal*

ESL

National Association for Bilingual Education (NABE)
- *Bilingual Research Journal NABE Journal of Research and Practice*

Teachers of English Speakers of Other Languages (TESOL)
- *TESOL Quarterly*

Fine Arts

National Art Education Association (NAEA)
- *Studies in Art Education*

MENC: National Association for Music Education
- *Music Educators Journal*
- *Journal of Music Teacher Education*
- *Journal of Research in Music Education*

Foreign Language

American Council on the Teaching of Foreign Language (ACTFL)
- *Foreign Language Annals*

Modern Language Association (MLA)
- *PMLA*

Health

American Alliance for Health, Physical Education, Recreation, and Dance (AAHPERD)
- *Journal of Physical Education, Recreation, & Dance (JOPERD)*
- *American Journal of Health Education (AJHE)*
- *STRATEGIES: A Journal for Physical and Sport Educators*
- *Research Quarterly for Exercise and Sport (RQES)*

History

National Council for Social Studies (NCSS)
- *Social Education*
- *Middle Level Learning*

Mathematics

National Council for Teachers of Mathematics (NCTM)
- *Journal for Research in Mathematics Education*
- *Mathematics Teaching in the Middle School*
- *Mathematics Teacher*
- *ON-Math*

Reading

International Reading Association (IRA)
- *Reading Research Quarterly*
- *Journal of Adolescent and Adult Literature*

Science

American Association of Physics Teachers (AAPT)
- *American Journal of Physics*
- *The Physics Teacher*

National Association of Biology Teachers (NABT)
- *The American Biology Teacher*

National Science Teachers Association (NSTA)
- *Science Scope*
- *The Science Teacher*

(continued)

FIGURE 15.3
(continued)

Special Education

Council for Exceptional Children (CEC)
■ *TEACHING Exceptional Children*
■ *Exceptional Children*

National Association of Special Education Teachers (NASET)
■ *JAASEP: Research Based Journal in Special Education*
■ *The Special Educator e-Journal*

Technology

Association for Educational Communication and Technology (AECT)
■ *Instructional Science*
■ *TechTrends*
■ *Educational Technology Research and Development*

International Society for Technology in Education (ISTE)
■ *Journal of Research on Technology in Education (JRTE)*
■ *Journal of Computing in Teacher Education (JCTE)*

professional development topics by attending or presenting sessions at these meetings. They usually range in duration from one to four days. To learn about conferences offered in particular content areas, visit the websites for the professional organizations listed in Figure 15.2. Professional development workshops are also offered online through various publishers.

Although this list is not exhaustive, it does include the most common sources teachers use during professional development. As we work to attain the goals we set in our professional development plans, we will engage in a variety of professional readings, courses, and conferences.

Final Thoughts about Professional Development

Professional development is an integral part of content area teaching. It emerges from students' needs, is collaborative in nature, and helps us, as teachers, to continue to learn. Wiggins and McTighe (2006) support teachers' ongoing engagement in professional development, and suggest that teachers should be professional learners:

> Teachers should engage in deep, broad study of the learning they are charged to cause. What works? What doesn't? Where is student learning most successful, and why? How can we learn from that success? Where are students struggling to learn, and why? What can we do about it? Effectively tackling these questions is what the "professional" in "professional practice" means. (p. 26)

Professional development provides a means for us to create responses to these queries.

FINAL THOUGHTS

Although education is a social process, it is a unique journey for each of us—one fortified by ever-growing knowledge in an ever-changing world. As Mtetwa and Kwari (2003) note:

> The information age has resulted in a rapid turnover of knowledge, making lifelong learning increasingly important . . . For teachers, this means they have to perceive themselves as learners even after pre-service education and the period of induction into professional practice. The challenge in education . . . is to provide quality opportunities for people to continue learning throughout their professional and everyday lives. (p. 273)

We hope we and our teaching careers will echo their thoughts.

Teaching Connections:

APPLYING WHAT WE HAVE LEARNED

E-Links

Consider how engaging in mentoring could benefit your teaching. (1) Think about the roles of mentor and mentee. (2) Consider how being a mentee could benefit you as a novice teacher. (3) Consider how being a mentor after you have taught for more than five years could enrich your teaching experience. Share your thinking with peers in small-group discussions, and then write a reflective entry in your portfolio.

Use information from websites such as these to support your thinking.

SAMPLE WEBSITES

Resources for Teacher Leadership: Mentoring and Coaching (Center for Science Education)
http://cse.edc.org/products/teacherleadership/mentoring.asp

Some Teacher Mentoring Resources (Middle Web—Exploring Middle School Reform)
http://www.middleweb.com/mentoring.html

Survival Guide for New Teachers
http://www.ed.gov/teachers/become/about/survivalguide/index.html

Accountable Talk

Consider the "new teacher challenges" discussed in the first section of this chapter. Reflect on the three issues that you think may be most challenging for you. Think about how you will prepare to address them, including specific ideas to manage such challenges. Share your thoughts in small-group discussions, and then record your ideas as a reflective entry in your portfolio.

Portfolio/Performance Opportunity

Professional development is an essential component of teaching. For our final performance opportunity, we will engage in a special professional development project. We will complete small-group projects after we have used individual reflection to provide direction for our thinking.

To begin, imagine your first three years of teaching and predict a literacy-related professional development topic that could emerge from your students' learning. Then join a "study group" of people who wish to focus on a similar topic. After we explain and model the project, use the professional development resource, planning, and demonstration project assignment sheet; project outline; and rubric as guides to complete your groupwork. As you will notice, the project culminates in demonstrations that you and your group members will present to the whole class.

PROFESSIONAL DEVELOPMENT RESOURCE, PLANNING, AND DEMONSTRATION PROJECT ASSIGNMENT SHEET

The professional development resource, planning, and demonstration project has three focuses: (1) study-group investigations of current literacy emphases; (2) development of a 3-year professional development plan; and (3) development, presentation, and evaluation of collaborative professional development sessions. Appropriate dispositions related to reading and the teaching of content must be displayed during all stages of this project.

Part 1: Professional Development Study Groups

Begin by brainstorming professional development topics in which you have interest. Collaborative groups will be formed according to topic selection. Then the groups will review a variety of study modules and current articles related to the chosen topics. We will explain the supportive materials and work with a focus group to demonstrate how study groups function successfully. Finally, the study groups will engage in planning and goal setting and will schedule specific electronic meeting times. Throughout this experience, electronic reflective journals will be maintained.

Part 2: Professional Development Plan

Begin by imagining you have completed your degree and are working as a content area teacher serving a particular grade or grade range. Next, consider what your students' needs might be. Contemplate your professional development needs in that context and create a 3-year professional development plan. Your plan should be based on your professional development goals and should feature a variety of types of professional development, including both events in which you are a participant and events in which you are the professional development provider. Examples of the former include, but are not limited to, participating in district study groups, taking additional courses, attending conferences, and reading articles from professional journals. Examples of the latter include teaching in-district professional development courses; presenting at local, state, or national conferences; and writing articles for state, regional, or national journals. Include your Professional Develpoment Plan in your portfolio.

Part 3: Professional Development Presentation and Evaluation

Use a variety of quality resources and technology to collaboratively develop and present a one-hour professional development session. Include appropriate follow-up information about your study group's topic and Professional Development Plans. Provide quality, informative feedback as you observe, participate in, and evaluate each group's professional development presentation.

PROFESSIONAL DEVELOPMENT RESOURCE, PLANNING, AND PRESENTATION
PROJECT OUTLINE

I. Contents Page

List each component of the professional development resource, planning, and presentation project and its corresponding starting page.

II. Reflective Introduction

Express your thoughts about (a) professional development, (b) your personal professional development interests, (c) your study group's investigation, and (d) your personal professional development plan.

III. Part 1: Study Groups

Begin by reflecting on your study group's topic, what you have learned, and how you plan to use that information in your teaching.

Next, detail your review of the resources that your group used.

Finally, include your study group reflective journal entries.

IV. Part 2: Professional Development Plan

Begin by reflecting on your students' needs and your professional development goals. Explain how you determined them and how what you will learn will affect your teaching.

Next, explain how you plan to achieve your professional development goals.

Finally, include your completed three-year professional development plan.

V. Part 3: Professional Development Presentation and Evaluation

Work collaboratively using a variety of quality resources and technology to plan, create, and present a one-hour professional development session. Include appropriate follow-up information about your study group's topic and Professional Development Plans.

OVERVIEW OF SELECTED MATERIALS

Materials we will use to facilitate our study groups will include but not be limited to the following: *IRA Literacy Study Groups*

- Adolescent Literacy Module (2003)
- English Language Learners Module (2004)
- Reading Comprehension (2003)
- Vocabulary (2003)

The IRA Literacy Study Groups modules offer materials that are representative of research and classroom-tested practices. The resources in the module address instructional issues and provide many suggestions for teachers to consider in developing sound pedagogical practices that will lead their students to success in reading. Each module contains an IRA-published text, a facilitator's guide to help candidates organize the study group, a journal for recording ideas and personal reflections, and a discussion guide that offers related journal articles and study group activities.

The *Discussion Guide and Related Journal Articles* includes information on related IRA resources; abstracts of 6 articles from *Reading Online*; abstracts from 4 ReadWriteThink lesson plans; full text of 11 articles from *The Reading Teacher, Journal of Adolescent & Adult Literacy, Reading Research Quarterly, Thinking Classroom,* and *Reading Today;* and one book chapter from *What Research Has to Say about Reading Instruction,* third edition.

The Common Sense of Differentiation: Meeting Specific Learner Needs in the Regular Classroom DVD and *Facilitator's Guide*

This module (ASCD, 2003) is designed to help candidates differentiate instruction to meet the needs of a wide range of exceptionalities—students with one or more learning problems, students with varying degrees of English language proficiency, students with different interests, students who are very advanced, and students without a "label" but whose learning needs are just as unique. The module includes a DVD and an accompanying *Facilitator's Guide* that shows teachers how a differentiated approach helps meet students' needs when they follow these steps:

- Identify the learning needs of their students
- Understand learner needs that affect students' achievement of learning goals
- Adapt instructional plans to maximize success for each learner
- Create classroom routines that support differentiation

PROFESSIONAL DEVELOPMENT RESOURCE, PLANNING, AND PRESENTATION PROJECT RUBRIC

	4	3	2	1
Resource Review				
Display of Dispositions				
Professional Development Plan				
Use of Technology				
Professional Presentation				
Evaluation of Peers				

4 Excellent review of quality resources. Display of advanced dispositions related to reading and the teaching of content during collaborative study groups and peer observation, evaluation, and feedback. Meaningful, detailed, knowledge-based, three-year professional development plan that continues to foster the acquisition of professional knowledge and advanced dispositions. Fully developed and detailed use of numerous types of technology. Totally professional presentation, including knowledge base, appropriate display of advanced dispositions, technology use, and presentation methods. Excellent quality contributions to collaborative study groups and peer observation, evaluation, and feedback.

3 Skillful review of quality resources. Display of proficient dispositions related to reading and the teaching of content during collaborative study groups and peer observation, evaluation, and feedback. Thorough knowledge-based, three-year professional development plan that continues to foster the acquisition of professional knowledge and proficient dispositions. Good use of technology. Very professional presentation, including knowledge base, display of proficient dispositions, technology use, and presentation methods. Quality contributions to collaborative study groups and peer observation, evaluation, and feedback.

2 Adequate review of quality resources. Display of developing dispositions related to reading and the teaching of content during collaborative study groups and peer observation, evaluation, and feedback. Knowledge-based, three-year professional development plan that continues to foster the acquisition of professional knowledge and advanced dispositions in limited ways. Adequate use of technology. Somewhat professional presentation, including limited knowledge base, display of developing dispositions, technology use, and presentation methods. Satisfactory contributions to collaborative study groups and peer observation, evaluation, and feedback.

1 Inadequate review of resources. Display of unacceptable dispositions related to reading and the teaching of content during collaborative study groups and peer observation, evaluation, and feedback. Poorly designed 3-year professional development plan, including insufficient knowledge base, display of unacceptable dispositions, improper technology use, and ineffective presentation methods. Unsatisfactory contributions to collaborative study groups and peer observation, evaluation, and feedback.

Comprehension Strategy-Based Teaching Ideas and Blackline Masters

TEACHING IDEA

Gallery Images

Students use Gallery Images (Ogle, 2000) to represent text information through sketches. Students work in small groups when creating these images. This teaching idea, which is used after reading, supports comprehension strategies such as making connections, visualizing, and summarizing. (See blackline master, page 290.)

To teach your students how to use gallery images, follow these steps:

1 Explain: Gallery Images support multiple comprehension strategies, including making connections, visualizing, and summarizing. Explain that Gallery Images involve sketching ideas to represent text. Remind students that when we sketch we use simple lines and shapes.

2 Demonstrate: Introduce a text and read a segment aloud. Discuss the text with a small group of students. Suggest an image that you think represents the text. Sketch it on the Gallery Images blackline in the section labeled Image One. Discuss your sketch with the students. Then encourage the other members of the group to suggest an image and sketch it as Image Two on the Gallery Images blackline. Discuss how the two images represent the text. Post the Gallery Images in a section of the classroom where the students' images will be displayed.

3 Guide: Organize students into small groups and guide them to engage in Gallery Images. Read a different text aloud and invite students to read along silently. Then encourage them to discuss the text and create an image. Discuss the image.

4 Practice: Invite students to work with group members to create and discuss a second image. When the Gallery Images are

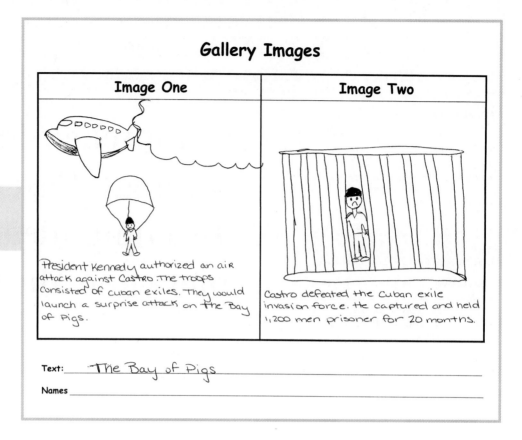

FIGURE A.1
Gallery Images about
the Bay of Pigs

complete, encourage students to post them next to the images your group posted in the class gallery.

5 **Reflect:** Reflect on how we can make connections, visualize, and summarize when we use Gallery Images. Reflect on how using sketching to represent our thinking helps us to understand what we read.

Figure A.1 features an excerpt from Gallery Images about the Bay of Pigs incident. These Gallery Images were completed by students in a history class.

TEACHING IDEA

Genre Pyramids

Students use Genre Pyramids (Waldo, 1991) to summarize what happens in various types of literature, including mysteries. Students work with partners to create Genre Pyramids. This teaching idea, which is similar to the Narrative Pyramid and Bio-Pyramid, provides a structure for students to summarize what they have read. (See blackline master, page 291.)

To teach your students how to use Genre Pyramids, follow these steps:

1 **Explain:** Summarizing is a reading comprehension strategy that helps us to extract essential information from narrative text. When using the Genre Pyramid, we can include elements from a variety of genre. The Pyramid we will be completing today focuses on a mystery.

2 **Demonstrate:** Retell Edgar Allen Poe's "The Tell-Tale Heart." Invite students to contribute to the retelling. Distribute the Genre Pyramid blackline and demonstrate by completing the first two lines. For example, you might say, "The first line asks us to identify the genre. I know that Poe's short story is a mystery, so I will write *mystery* on line 1. The information description for line 2 is 'victim,' so I will write *old man*, because I know he is the one who was murdered." Discuss the first two lines with the students.

3 **Guide:** Encourage students to work with partners to complete lines 3, 4, and 5. Discuss students' responses to each line as they are completed. After the students share their responses, continue to complete the demonstration Genre Pyramid.

4 **Practice:** Invite students to complete lines 6, 7, and 8. Discuss each line as it is completed. Then complete the remaining lines of the demonstration Genre Pyramid. Encourage each pair of students to share their completed Genre Pyramids with another pair of students. Invite a few students to share their pyramids with the class.

5 **Reflect:** Reflect on how we can summarize what we read using Genre Pyramids. Reflect on how completing Genre Pyramids helps us to understand what we read.

Figure A.2 features an example of a Genre Pyramid completed by students in their Short Story class. The genre is mystery and the Pyramid is about "The Tell-Tale Heart."

FIGURE A.2 Genre Pyramid: Mystery "The Tell-Tale Heart"

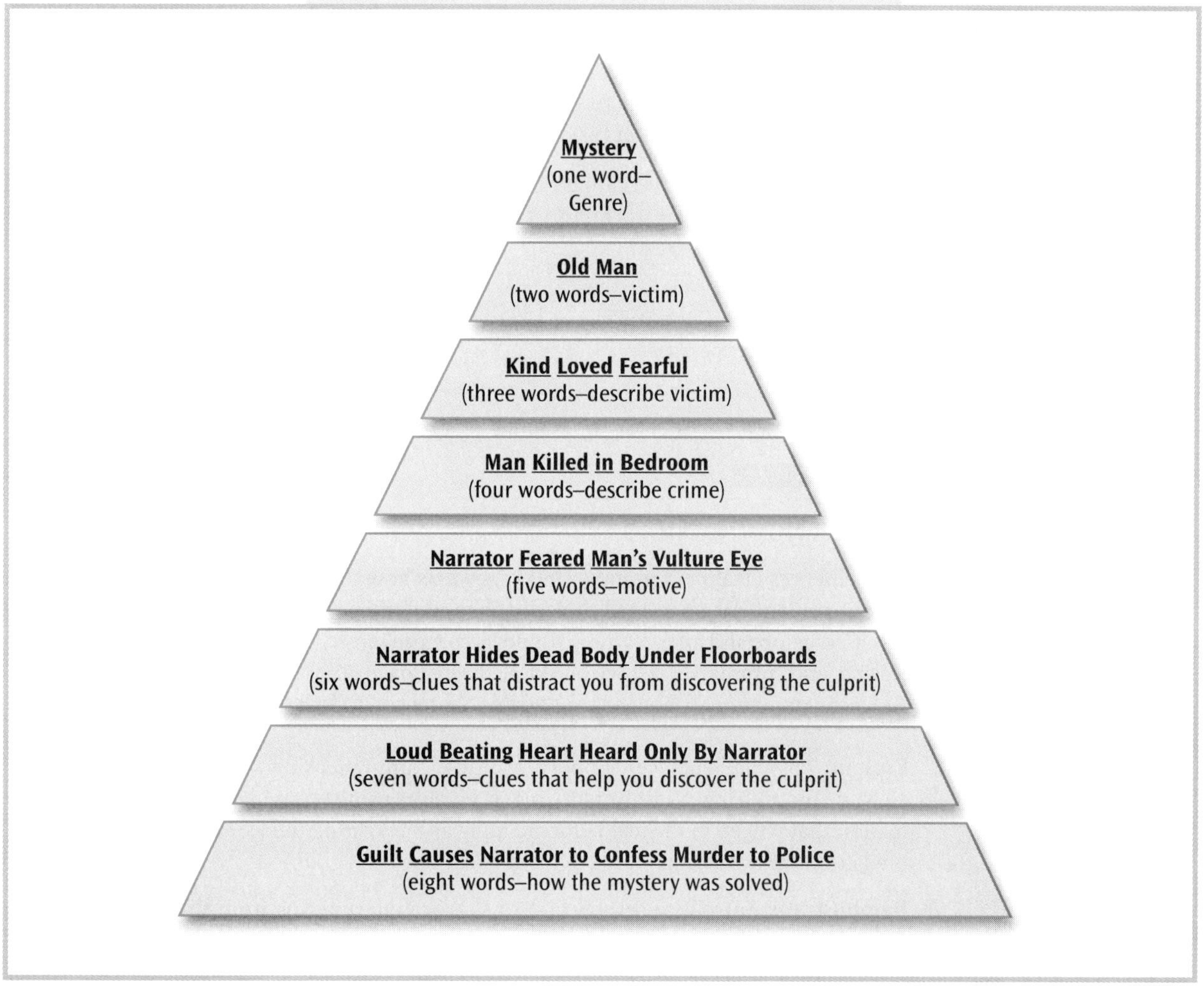

Mystery
(one word–Genre)

Old Man
(two words–victim)

Kind Loved Fearful
(three words–describe victim)

Man Killed in Bedroom
(four words–describe crime)

Narrator Feared Man's Vulture Eye
(five words–motive)

Narrator Hides Dead Body Under Floorboards
(six words–clues that distract you from discovering the culprit)

Loud Beating Heart Heard Only By Narrator
(seven words–clues that help you discover the culprit)

Guilt Causes Narrator to Confess Murder to Police
(eight words–how the mystery was solved)

TEACHING IDEA

List–Group–Label

Students use List–Group–Label (Maring, Furman, & Blum-Anderson, 1985) to preview and monitor information presented in informational text. This teaching idea is used before and after reading to activate background knowledge and to help students become familiar with how selected words relate to a concept and to other words.

To teach your students how to use List–Group–Label, follow these steps:

1 Explain: Explain that List–Group–Label relates to reading comprehension strategies, such as previewing and monitoring. Explain that List–Group–Label helps us refine our understanding of terms and their relation to other words.

2 Demonstrate: Provide a cue word or term and brainstorm examples of related words. Write your brainstormed examples on the chalkboard or overhead transparency. Think aloud about whether any of the brainstormed words should be deleted. Justify your changes. For example, if the cue term was *solar system*, you might brainstorm *Earth*, *Jupiter*, and *Sun*. You might decide the terms were appropriate and choose not to eliminate any of them.

3 Guide: Invite students to work with a partner to brainstorm additional words for the list. Add their responses to the master list. Then invite students to discuss whether any of the responses should be eliminated. Ask them to justify their thinking. Next, encourage the students to meet in groups of four to create clusters of words that relate to one another, and label each category with a descriptive term. Invite students to share their clusters and explain their thinking.

4 Practice: Invite students to read the text. Discuss the text and encourage students to revisit and revise their clusters as necessary. Discuss the final clusters with the students.

5 Reflect: Reflect on how we can use List–Group–Label to preview and monitor information. Reflect on how brainstorming, working with partners, and List–Group–Label help us to understand what we read.

Figure A.3 on page 275 features a List–Group–Label about the solar system that was completed in an earth science class.

TEACHING IDEA

Possible Sentences

Possible Sentences (Stahl & Kapinus, 1991) shows us how to use vocabulary to make predictions about content and then read to verify or modify those predictions. This teaching idea, which is used before and after reading, supports comprehension strategies such as previewing, monitoring, and summarizing. (See blackline master, page 305.)

To teach your students how to use Possible Sentences, follow these steps:

1 Explain: Possible Sentences supports multiple comprehension strategies, including previewing, monitoring, and summarizing. It involves using vocabulary to predict the information that will be in the text before reading and revisiting the words to verify or modify predictions after reading.

2 Demonstrate: Introduce several (6–8) new vocabulary terms from the text and several (4–6) words with which you think the students are already familiar. Think aloud as you discuss and define one word from each list. Then write a sentence using those two words.

Cue term: Solar system		
Before reading: Brainstormed words and clusters		
Stars	**Planets**	**Dwarf Planets**
Sun	Mercury Venus Earth Mars Jupiter Saturn Uranus Neptune	Pluto
After reading: Revised class List–Group–Label		
Stars	**Planets**	**Dwarf Planets**
Sun (Closest star to Earth)	Mercury Venus Earth Mars Jupiter Saturn Uranus Neptune	Pluto Ceres Eris Haumea Makemake

FIGURE A.3
List–Group–Label about the Solar System

3 **Guide:** Invite students to work with partners to discuss and define the remaining words. Encourage students to work on their own to write sentences, using two vocabulary words in each sentence. Discuss their sentences.

4 **Practice:** Distribute a text and read it aloud to students. Invite them to read along silently. Then revisit the text, the definitions, and the sentences to verify that the words are defined and used correctly.

5 **Reflect:** Reflect on how we can preview, monitor, and summarize when we use Possible Sentences. Reflect on how predicting, verifying, and summarizing the information that will appear in text helps us understand what we read.

Figure A.4 on page 276 features Possible Sentences related to the Seneca Falls Convention about Women's Rights of 1848.

TEACHING IDEA

Story Impressions

In Story Impressions (McGinley & Denner, 1987), students use vocabulary to predict the content of a story and make connections between vocabulary and story structure. Story Impressions, which are usually used before reading, also provide a framework for narrative writing. They support reading comprehension strategies such as previewing and making connections. Each impression includes a maximum of ten clues, and each clue can be a maximum of five words. The clues are based on an existing story. As the teacher, it is your decision whether to share the title of the original story before reading the story later in the process. When using this teaching idea, students work in small groups and use a series of sequential clues based on the narrative elements to write a Story Impression—their prediction of the original story's content. (See blackline master, page 314.)

FIGURE A.4

Possible Sentences

> **The Seneca Falls Convention about Women's Rights, 1848**
>
> **I. New Words and Proposed Definitions**
>
> Convention: the summoning or convening of an assembly
> Delegates: a representative to a convention or conference
> Quakers: member of the Society of Friends
> Legislation: the exercise of the power and function of making rules
> Sentiments: attitudes, thoughts, or judgments prompted by feeling
> Usurp: to seize without right
>
> **II. Familiar Words and Proposed Definitions**
>
> Antislavery: opposition to slavery
> Equality: the state or quality of being equal
> Declaration of Independence: the public act by which the Second Continental Congress, on July 4, 1776, declared the Colonies to be free and independent of England
> Resolution: a formal expression of opinion or intention
>
> **III. Possible Sentences** (Use two vocabulary words in each sentence.)
>
> 1. The **delegates** discussed a **resolution** that had been introduced.
> 2. Those who attended the **convention** approved new **legislation**.
> 3. Many people believe in Martin Luther King, Jr.'s **antislavery sentiments**.
> 4. The **Quakers** supported **equality** for all.
> 5. We issued the **Declaration** of **Independence** so England could not usurp our rights.

To teach your students how to use Story Impressions, follow these steps:

1 Explain: Story Impressions support previewing and making connections. In this small-group activity, we use a list of sequential clues to write our impression of a story. Explain that it is important to use the clues in the order in which they appear and that after we write our impressions, we read them to the class and then listen to or read the original story. Later, we compare and contrast our story with the original.

2 Demonstrate: Share a sequential list of clues connected by downward arrows. Note that many of the clues represent narrative elements: characters, setting, problem, attempts to resolve, resolution. Remind students that these elements are present in every story. Then think aloud about how to include the first four clues in your Story Impression. For example, you might write, "A plane crashed, but Jack and Ralph survived."

3 Guide: Invite students to work in small groups as they continue to use the sequential clues to create their Story Impressions. Encourage them to use the next three clues to write the next part of the Story Impression.

4 Practice: Encourage students to use the remaining clues to write the rest of the story. Encourage them to share their completed Story Impressions with the class. Read the original story aloud, and ask students to compare and contrast their story with the original story.

5 Reflect: Reflect on how Story Impressions help us to predict text and make connections between the narrative elements and the story. Discuss how the sequential clues help to guide our writing.

Figure A.5 on page 277 features a Story Impression about *Lord of the Flies* that students completed in English class.

TEACHING IDEA

Summary Cubes

Students use Summary Cubes (McLaughlin & Allen, 2002b) to represent important information in text. Summary Cubes can easily be adapted for biography, mystery, or other genres.

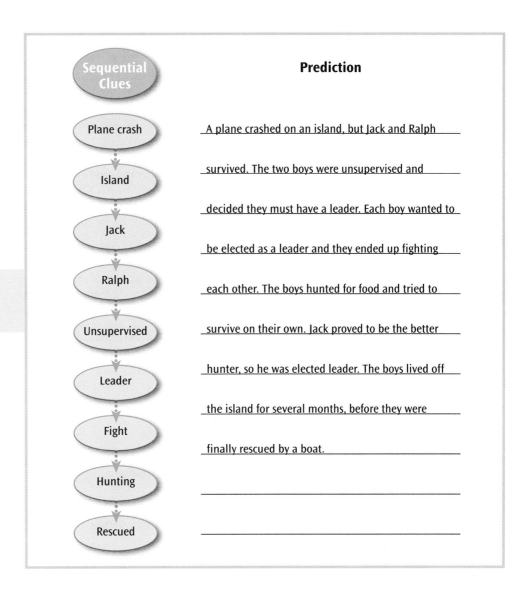

FIGURE A.5
Story Impression for
Lord of the Flies

Sequential Clues:
- Plane crash
- Island
- Jack
- Ralph
- Unsupervised
- Leader
- Fight
- Hunting
- Rescued

Prediction

A plane crashed on an island, but Jack and Ralph survived. The two boys were unsupervised and decided they must have a leader. Each boy wanted to be elected as a leader and they ended up fighting each other. The boys hunted for food and tried to survive on their own. Jack proved to be the better hunter, so he was elected leader. The boys lived off the island for several months, before they were finally rescued by a boat.

Students select a topic and complete the cubes after reading by providing the information required on each side of the cube. They can use websites that you have bookmarked to confirm or gather further information. (See blackline master, page 315, or the electronic graphic found at www.readwritethink.org.)

To teach your students how to use Summary Cubes, follow these steps:

1. **Explain:** Summary Cubes help us to extract important information from narrative and informational text. The cubes can be adapted for use with a variety of genres, including biography (Bio-Cubes) and mystery (Mystery Cubes). Explain that today we will be completing a Bio-Cube and show the students one that has been completed. Explain that we will use the electronic graphic for Bio-Cubes and briefly explain how to complete it online.

2. **Demonstrate:** Read aloud a brief biography and think aloud about the information required for the Bio-Cube. For example, if you are creating a Bio-Cube about Dr. Martin Luther King, Jr., you might think aloud about Dr. King's name and note the years he lived and his place of birth as they were presented in the biography you read. Next, you might write, "M. L. King, Jr., 1929–1968, and Atlanta, Georgia," on the side labeled *Person's Name,*

Time Period, and Place of Birth. Then on the side labeled *Obstacle*, you might think of an obstacle Dr. King needed to overcome. For example, you might write "a segregated society."

3 **Guide:** Invite students to work with partners to complete the next side of the Bio-Cube. This side asks for information about Dr. King's background, so you would guide the students to locate background information in the biography. For example, they might suggest that Dr. King grew up during a time of segregation and his father taught him to stand up for what he believes. They might also suggest that Dr. King became a great speaker and civil rights leader. After a discussion, they could write their ideas on that section of the Bio-Cube. The next side requires information about Dr. King's personality. Invite the students to review the article and share words to describe Dr. King's personality. For example, they might say, "Dr. King was determined, passionate, kind, intelligent, and brave." Encourage students to write their responses on that side of the cube.

4 **Practice:** Encourage students to complete the remaining sides of the Bio-Cube, which include *Quotation* and *Significance*. When the students complete the Bio-Cube, invite them to construct their cube, glue it, and share it with another pair of students. Encourage students to discuss how their Bio-Cubes summarize the person's life. Display the completed cubes.

5 **Reflect:** Reflect on how extracting important information helps us understand what we read. Reflect on how Bio-Cubes help us understand biographies.

Figure A.6 features an example of a completed Bio-Cube about President Barack Obama that students completed in history class. They used the electronic organizer to complete their cube.

FIGURE A.6 **Bio-Cube about Barack Obama**

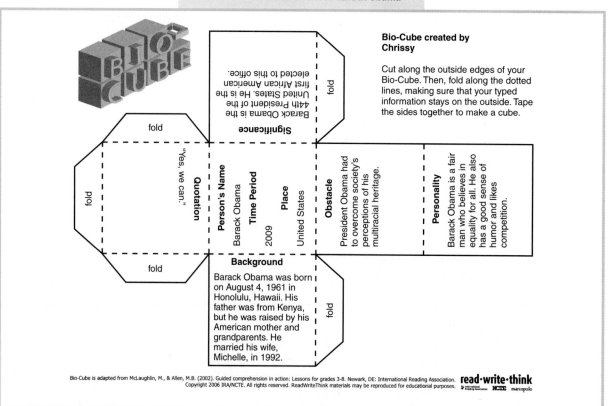

That Was Then . . . This Is Now

That Was Then . . . This Is Now (McLaughlin & Allen, 2002b) provides a format for students to record their thinking before and after reading and compare and contrast their ideas. We can also use this teaching idea to activate background knowledge, create mental images before and after reading, and write summary statements. That Was Then . . . This Is Now can be used with narrative and informational text and supports comprehension strategies such as previewing, visualizing, and summarizing. (See blackline master, page 316.)

To teach your students how to use That Was Then . . . This Is Now, follow these steps:

1 **Explain:** Explain that when we use That Was Then . . . This Is Now, we sketch our thoughts about a specific topic prior to reading and write a summary statement. Next, explain that we read a text and then sketch our thoughts about what we have read and write a summary statement. Finally, we compare and contrast our thinking before and after reading.

2 **Demonstrate:** Self-select a topic related to the class's current studies. Think aloud as you sketch what you currently know about the topic. Create a sketch and write a summary statement. Discuss the sketch and the statement. Then introduce a brief new text, read it, and discuss it with the students. Next, create a sketch representative of your thoughts after reading and write a summary statement about it. Discuss it with the students, focusing on comparisons (similarities) and contrasts (differences) concerning your thoughts before and after reading.

3 **Guide:** Guide students to engage in That Was Then . . . This Is Now by self-selecting a current topic of study. Encourage them to create a sketch about what they know and write a summary statement. Invite them to share their sketches and statements with a peer. Then provide a brief new text for each student to read silently.

4 **Practice:** Encourage students to complete the This Is Now portion of the blackline by creating a sketch and writing a summary statement. Invite them to share their sketches and thoughts with a peer. Engage the students in discussion about comparisons and contrasts concerning their before and after reading sketches and summary statements.

5 **Reflect:** Encourage students to think about what they learned from their reading. Invite them to share their ideas about how That Was Then . . . This Is Now helps us to understand what we read.

Figure A.7 on page 280 features That Was Then . . . This Is Now about cloning completed by a student in science class.

Thinking Hats

Thinking Hats (DeBono, 1985) is a teaching idea that supports summarizing and evaluating. Students use Thinking Hats to represent multiple perspectives about a topic. Small groups of students engage in this teaching idea, which is completed after reading. (See blackline master, page 318.)

To teach your students how to use Thinking Hats, follow these steps:

1 **Explain:** Thinking Hats supports reading comprehension strategies such as summarizing and evaluating. It involves determining different perspectives that exist within a content area event, such as the Revolutionary War, the debate about whether the world was flat in the time of Columbus, the pursuit of flight by scientists such as DaVinci and the Wright brothers, or characters from a short story, novel, or play. Explain that once the event has been determined, we must select five roles that were meaningful in terms of the event.

FIGURE A.7 That Was Then . . . This Is Now about Cloning

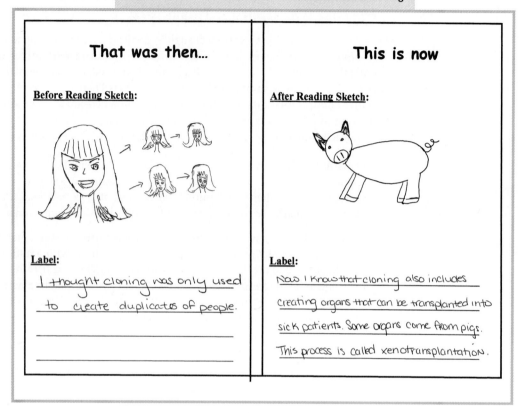

FIGURE A.7 That Was Then . . . This Is Now about Cloning

Finally, explain that this is a small-group activity and that each student is responsible for sharing a perspective.

2 **Demonstrate:** Model Thinking Hats with four students whom you have preselected. Discuss possible topics with the students and select one. Then brainstorm different perspectives that are associated with that topic. Record the different perspectives and indicate what each might say on the Thinking Hats graphic organizer. Provide sufficient time for each group member to choose a perspective and investigate it briefly to expand the knowledge she already has about the topic and the perspective. When the students are ready, gather them in a circle and engage in Thinking Hats by conducting a discussion in which each group member takes on the identity and perspective of one of the individuals associated with this topic.

3 **Guide:** Invite students to engage in Thinking Hats by choosing a topic and brainstorming perspectives. Encourage them to record their thoughts on the Thinking Hats graphic organizer. Invite each student to choose a perspective to represent and read additional information from that point of view. Then guide students to meet in small groups to discuss the event or work from multiple perspectives. The rest of the class should observe while one group is sharing ideas.

4 **Practice:** Encourage other groups to share their versions of Thinking Hats, while class members observe. Discuss Thinking Hats and the value of viewing events from multiple perspectives.

5 **Reflect:** Reflect on how we can engage in summarizing and evaluating when we use Thinking Hats. Discuss how viewing events from multiple perspectives helps us to understand what we read at deeper levels.

Figure A.8 features the Thinking Hats planner developed by a group of students who presented multiple perspectives from Shakespeare's *Romeo and Juliet*.

FIGURE A.8 Excerpt from Thinking Hats about *Romeo and Juliet*

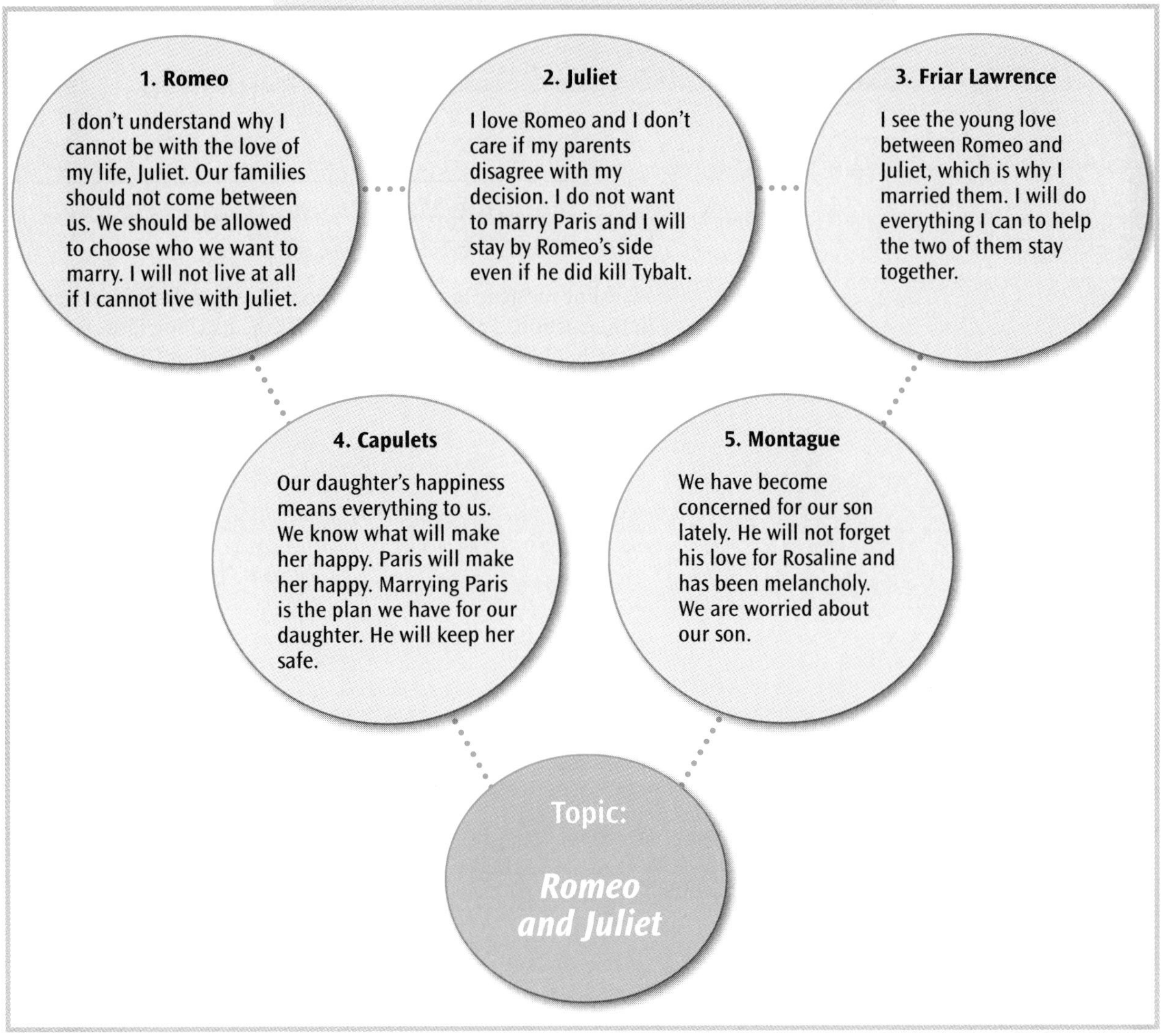

1. Romeo

I don't understand why I cannot be with the love of my life, Juliet. Our families should not come between us. We should be allowed to choose who we want to marry. I will not live at all if I cannot live with Juliet.

2. Juliet

I love Romeo and I don't care if my parents disagree with my decision. I do not want to marry Paris and I will stay by Romeo's side even if he did kill Tybalt.

3. Friar Lawrence

I see the young love between Romeo and Juliet, which is why I married them. I will do everything I can to help the two of them stay together.

4. Capulets

Our daughter's happiness means everything to us. We know what will make her happy. Paris will make her happy. Marrying Paris is the plan we have for our daughter. He will keep her safe.

5. Montague

We have become concerned for our son lately. He will not forget his love for Rosaline and has been melancholy. We are worried about our son.

Topic:

Romeo and Juliet

Blackline Masters for Comprehension-Based Teaching Ideas

Blackline masters for comprehension-based teaching ideas appear in this section. The blacklines support the teaching ideas featured in the book chapters, as well as those included at the start of this Appendix. These forms may be copied for classroom use.

Bio Pyramid

1. Person's name

2. Two words describing the person

3. Three words describing the person's childhood

4. Four words indicating a problem the person had to overcome

5. Five words stating one of his/her accomplishments

6. Six words stating a second accomplishment

7. Seven words stating a third accomplishment

8. Eight words stating how mankind benefited from his/her accomplishments

Bookmark Technique

Bookmark One

Name _____

The part I found most interesting was

I thought it was interesting because

Page _____

Paragraph _____

Bookmark Two

Name _____

Something that confused me was

It confused me because

Page _____

Paragraph _____

Name _____

Bookmark Three

A word I think the whole class needs to talk about is

I think it means

Page _____

Paragraph _____

Name _____

Bookmark Four

The illustration, chart, map, or graph that helped me understand what I was reading was

It helped me to understand because

Page _____

Paragraph _____

Concept of Definition Map

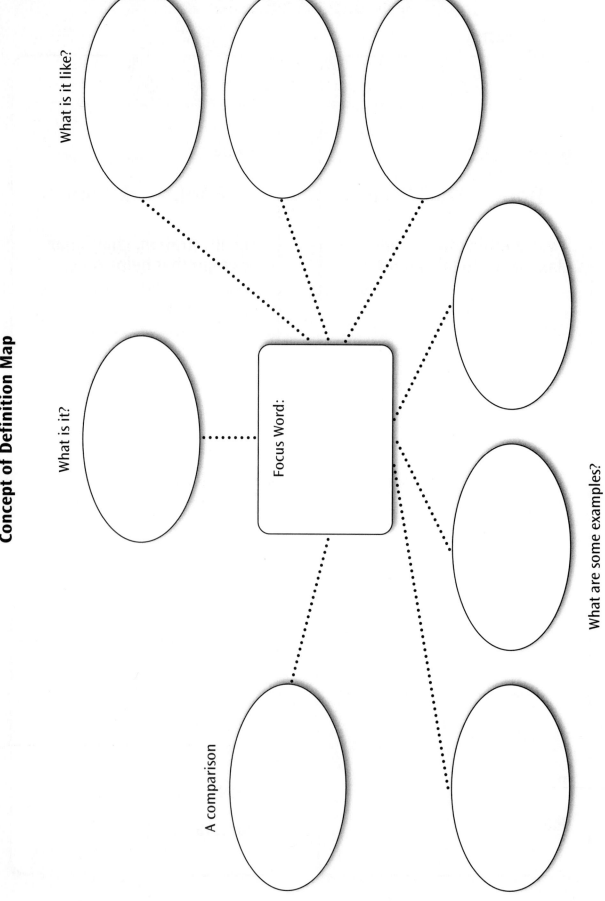

What is it like?

What is it?

Focus Word:

What are some examples?

A comparison

Concept of Definition Map Split Page with Summary Space
Concept of Definition Map

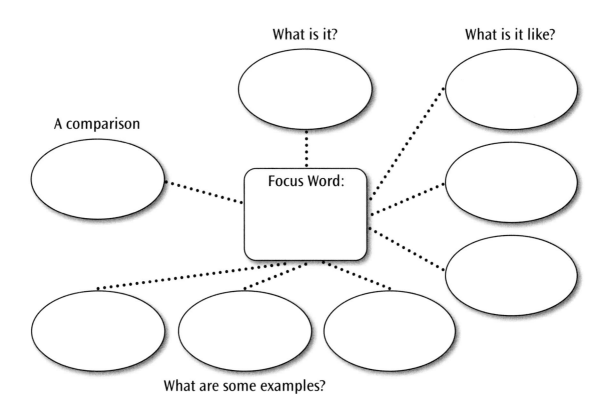

What is it?

What is it like?

A comparison

Focus Word:

What are some examples?

Concept of Definition Map Summary

_____

_____

_____

_____

_____

_____

_____

Contrast Chart

1.

2.

3.

4.

5.

1.

2.

3.

4.

5.

Discussion Web

Yes		

Reasons

Discussion Topic/Question

Conclusion

Reason

No

Gallery Images

Image One	Image Two

Text: _____

Name: _____

Genre Pyramid–Mystery

_____ (one word–Genre)

_____ _____ (two words–victim)

_____ _____ _____ (three words–describe victim)

_____ _____ _____ _____ (four words–describe crime)

_____ _____ _____ _____ _____ (five words–motive)

_____ _____ _____ _____ _____ _____ (six words–clues that distract you from discovering the culprit)

_____ _____ _____ _____ _____ _____ _____ (seven words–clues that help you discover the culprit)

_____ _____ _____ _____ _____ _____ _____ _____ (eight words–how the mystery was solved)

Guided Imagery

Name _____   **Date** _____

Describe image 1:

_____

_____

_____

_____

_____

_____

Describe image 2:

_____

_____

_____

_____

_____

_____

"I Wonder" Bookmark

Page: _____

I wonder . . .

_____

_____

_____

because . . .

_____

_____

_____

Page: _____

I wonder . . .

_____

_____

_____

because . . .

_____

_____

_____

"I Wonder" Bookmark

Page: _____

I wonder . . .

_____

_____

_____

because . . .

_____

_____

_____

Page: _____

I wonder . . .

_____

_____

_____

because . . .

_____

_____

_____

INSERT (Interactive Notation System to Effective Reading and Thinking) (Bookmarks)

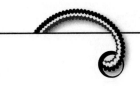

INSERT Bookmark I

✓ = I knew that!

+ = I didn't know that!

− = I thought differently.

? = What does this mean?

_____

Page: _____

I knew that!

Page: _____

I knew that!

INSERT Bookmark II

✓ = I knew that!

+ = I didn't know that!

− = I thought differently.

? = What does this mean?

_____

Page: _____

I didn't know that!

Page: _____

I didn't know that!

INSERT Bookmark III

✓ = I knew that!

+ = I didn't know that!

– = I thought differently.

? = What does this mean?

_____

Page: _____

I thought differently.

Page: _____

I thought differently.

INSERT Bookmark IV

✓ = I knew that!

+ = I didn't know that!

– = I thought differently.

? = What does this mean?

_____

Page: _____

What does this mean?

Page: _____

What does this mean?

KWDL

Topic: _____

K (What I know)	**W** (What I want to know)	**D** (What I did)	**L** (What I learned)

KWL

Topic: _____

K (What I know or think I know)	**W** (What I want to know)	**L** (What I learned)

KWLS

Topic: _____

K (What I know or think I know)	W (What I want to know)	L (What I learned)	S (What I still want to know)

Mind and Alternative Mind Portraits

Alternative Mind Portrait

Reasoning:

Mind Portrait

Reasoning:

Narrative Pyramid

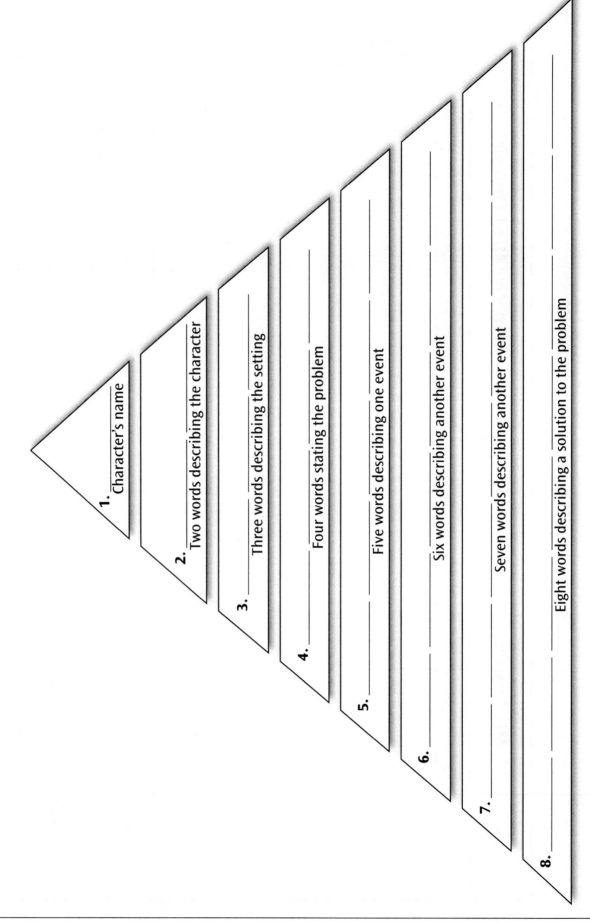

1. Character's name

2. Two words describing the character

3. Three words describing the setting

4. Four words stating the problem

5. Five words describing one event

6. Six words describing another event

7. Seven words describing another event

8. Eight words describing a solution to the problem

Narrative Pyramid: Adapted

Character

Two words to describe the character

Three words to describe the setting

Four words to describe the problem in the story

Five words to describe the solution

Paired Questioning

Name: _____   **Date:** _____

Question 1: _____

Question 2: _____

Question 3: _____

Question 4: _____

Question 5: _____

Question 6: _____

Important Ideas	**Partner's Reasoning**
_____	_____
_____	_____
_____	_____
_____	

Paired Summarizing

Name: _____   **Date:** _____

My Summary	Summary of My Partner's Work
_____	_____
_____	_____
_____	_____
_____	_____
_____	_____
_____	_____
_____	_____
_____	_____
_____	_____
_____	_____
_____	_____
_____	_____

Photographs of the Mind

1	2

3	4

Possible Sentences

Name _____

Date _____

New Words	Proposed Definitions		Familiar Words	Proposed Definitions
1. _____	_____		1. _____	_____
2. _____	_____		2. _____	_____
3. _____	_____		3. _____	_____
4. _____	_____		4. _____	_____
5. _____	_____		5. _____	_____
6. _____	_____		6. _____	_____

Sentences (Use two vocabulary words—one from each list—in each sentence.)

1. _____

2. _____

3. _____

4. _____

5. _____

6. _____

Prereading Plan (PreP)

Name: _____   **Date:** _____

Cue Word(s): _____

Brainstormed Words/Concepts	Reasons for Choosing Words/Concepts
1. _____	1. _____ _____
2. _____	2. _____ _____
3. _____	3. _____ _____
4. _____	4. _____ _____
5. _____	5. _____ _____

Question-Answer Relationships (QAR)

- **In the text**

Right There: The answer is within one sentence in the text.

Example: _____

Think and Search: The answer is contained in more than one sentence in the text.

Example: _____

- **In my head**

Author and You: The answer is information from your background knowledge and the text.

Example: _____

On Your Own: The answer is information from only your background knowledge.

Example: _____

QuIP Research Grid

Topic: _____

Questions	Answers	
	Source 1:	**Source 2:**
A.		
B.		
C.		

QuIP (Split Page with Paragraph Space)

QuIP Research Grid

Topic: _____

Questions	Answers	
	Source 1:	Source 2:
A.		
B.		
C.		

QuIP Paragraph

_____
_____
_____
_____
_____
_____
_____

Save the Last Word for Me

Side 1: Choose an idea, phrase, quote, concept, word, or fact from the text that interests or intrigues you and write it below.

Name: _____   Date: _____

Side 2: Explain why you chose what you wrote on side 1 or share your reaction to it.

Name: _____   Date: _____

Semantic Feature Analysis

Characteristics

Categories							

Semantic Question Map

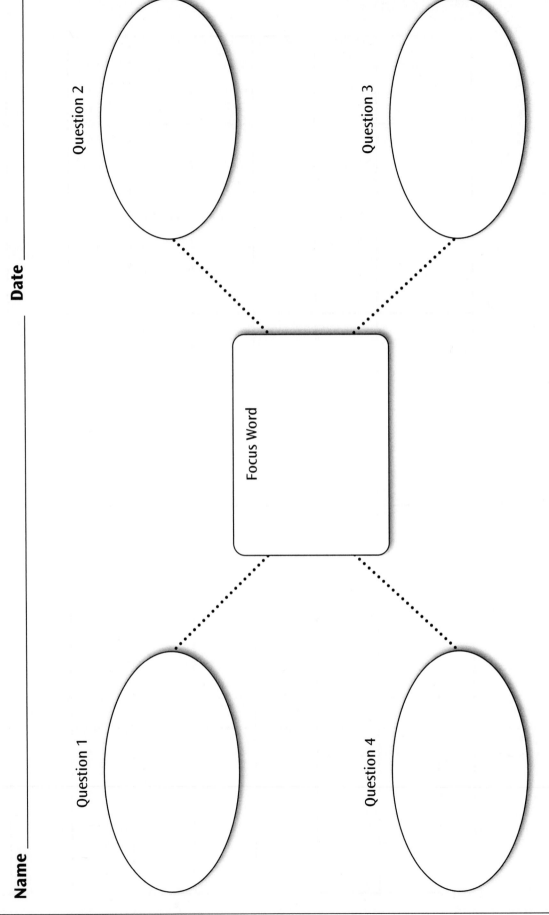

Question 2

Question 3

Focus Word

Question 1

Question 4

Sketch and Label Connections

Name: _____   **Date:** _____

Sketch

Label

_____

_____

_____

_____

Story Impression

Sequential Clues

Prediction

_____

_____

_____

_____

_____

_____

_____

_____

_____

_____

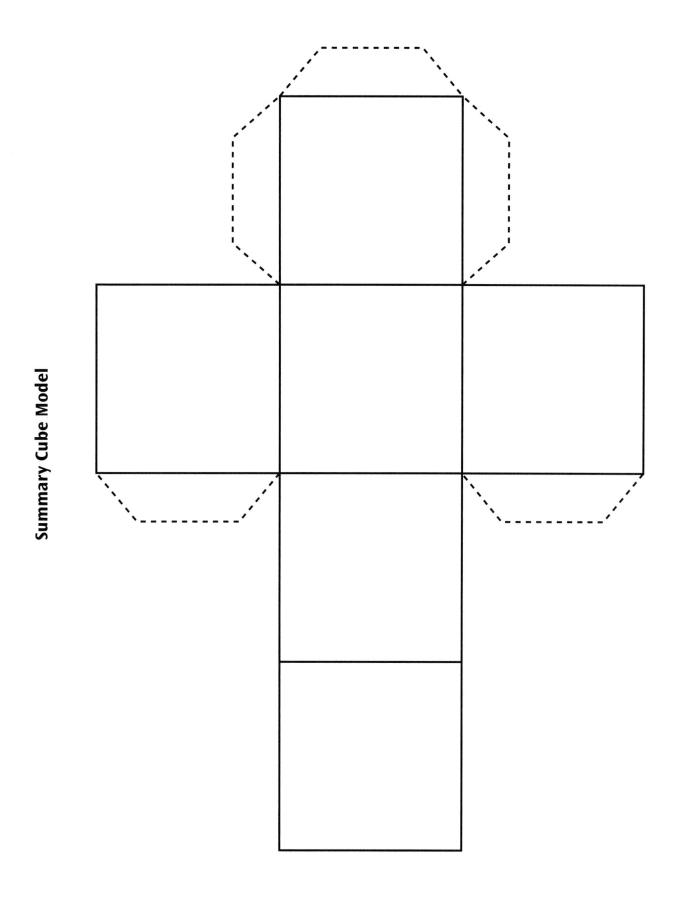

Summary Cube Model

This Is Now . . .

After Reading Sketch:

Label: _____ _____ _____ _____

That Was Then . . .

Before Reading Sketch:

Label: _____ _____ _____ _____

Thick and Thin Questions

Text: _____

Page	Thin Questions	**Thick Questions**

Thinking Hats

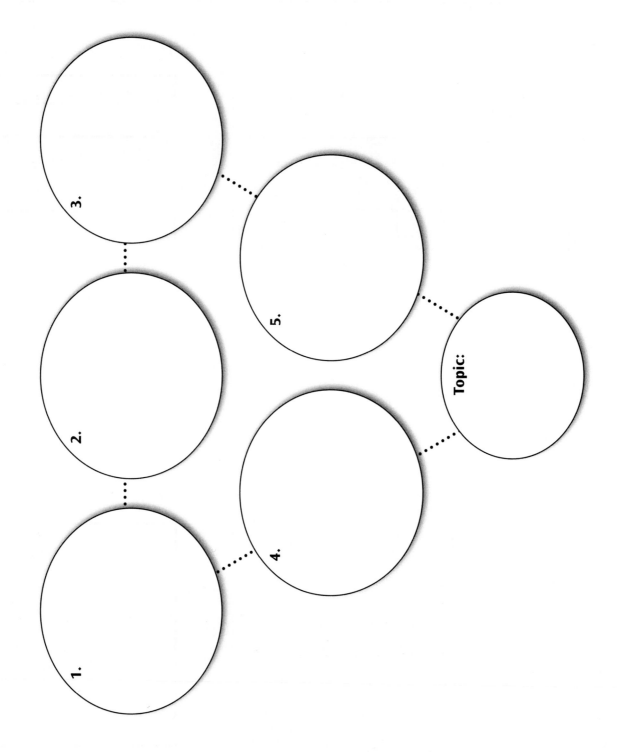

3.

2.

1.

5.

4.

Topic:

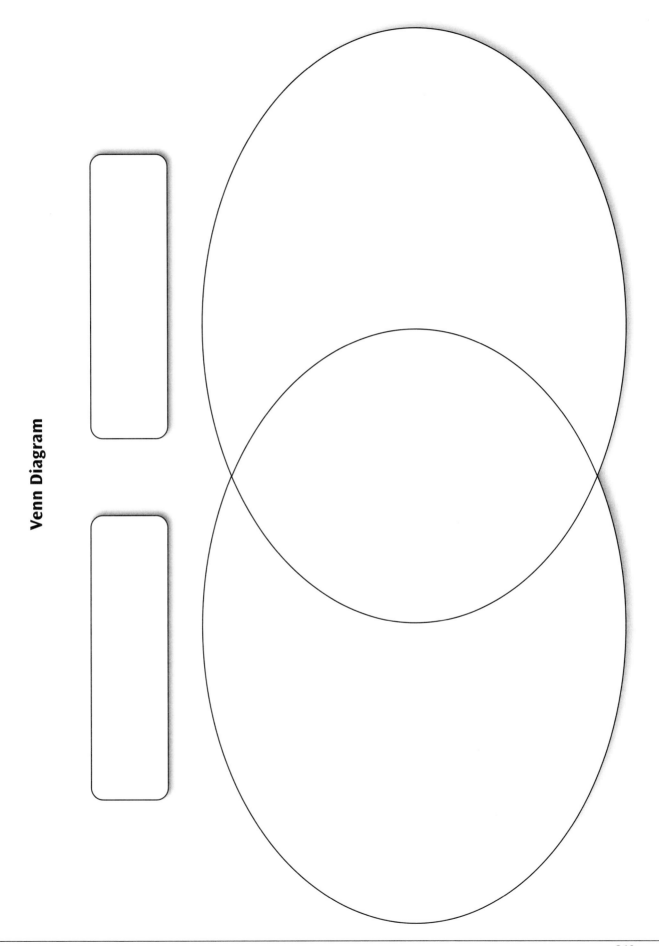

Venn Diagram

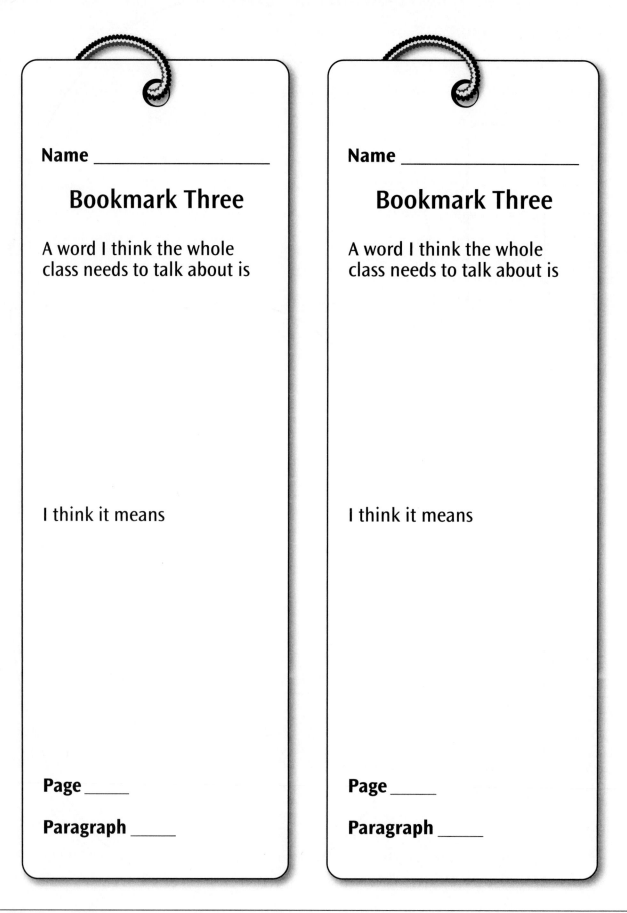

Name _____

Bookmark Three

A word I think the whole class needs to talk about is

I think it means

Page _____

Paragraph _____

Name _____

Bookmark Three

A word I think the whole class needs to talk about is

I think it means

Page _____

Paragraph _____

Skills

Discussion Circle Role Bookmarks

Discussion Director

- Choose topics for discussion.
- Ask questions.
- Convene the group meeting.
- Ensure that all members contribute.

Discussion Questions:

1. _____

   _____

   _____

2. _____

   _____

   _____

3. _____

   _____

   _____

4. _____

   _____

   _____

Passage Selector

- Select memorable or important sections of the text.
- Read them aloud for group.

Memorable Passages:

1. Page _____

   It is about _____

   _____

   _____

2. Page _____

   It is about _____

   _____

   _____

3. Page _____

   It is about _____

   _____

   _____

Connector

- Share text-self, text-text, and text-world connections.

- Encourage other group members to make connections.

Text-Self Connections:

Text-Text Connections:

Text-World Connections:

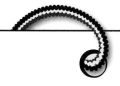

Illustrator

- Sketch visual response

- Use it to encourage others to contribute to the conversation.

Share Sketch

Explain how it relates to the text.

Invite group members to discuss it.

Word Finder

- Locate interesting words.

- Note where they are located in the text.

- Invite group to turn to the page where each word appears.

- Propose definitions based on their use in context.

Word: _____

Page: _____ Paragraph: _____

Proposed Definition: _____

_____

_____

Word: _____

Page: _____ Paragraph: _____

Proposed Definition: _____

_____

_____

Word: _____

Page: _____ Paragraph: _____

Proposed Definition: _____

_____

_____

Generating Questions

Directions: Revisit our text and create one question for each of Ciardiello's four levels:

Memory: Who, what, where, when?
Convergent: Why, how, in what ways?
Divergent: Imagine, suppose, predict, if/then
Evaluative: Defend, judge, justify/what do you think?

Memory Level

_____

_____

Convergent Level

_____

_____

Divergent Level

_____

_____

Evaluative Level

_____

_____

Standards-Based Lesson Plan:
Engaging, Guiding, and Extending Student Thinking

I.   Goals and Related State Standards

II. Bibliographic Information for Text(s) and Additional Materials

III. Engaging Students' Thinking (Before Reading)

IV. Guiding Students' Thinking (During Reading)

V.   Extending Students' Thinking (After Reading)

VI. Assessments

Roots

Root	Meaning	Example
anthropo	man	anthropology
astro	star	astronaut
bio	life	biology
cardio	heart	cardiac
cede	go	precede
chromo	color	chromatology
demos	people	democracy
derma	skin	epidermis
dyna	power	dynamic
geo	earth	geology
helio	sun	heliocentric
hydro	water	hydroponics
hypno	sleep	hypnosis
ject	throw	eject
magni	great, big	magnify
man(u)	hand	manuscript
mono	one	monoplane
ortho	straight	orthodox
pod	foot	podiatrist
psycho	mind	psychology
pyro	fire	pyromania
script	write	manuscript
terra	earth	terrace
thermo	heat	thermometer
zoo	animal	zoology

Prefixes

Prefix	Meaning(s)	Example
ab-, abs-, a-	from, away	abstain
ad-	to, toward	addict
ambi-	both	ambidextrous
ante-	before	antecedent
anti-	against	antifreeze
auto-	self	autobiography
be-	near, about	beside
bene-	well, good	benefactor
bi-	two	bimonthly
cata-	below	catacomb
centi-	hundred	centimeter
circum-	around	circumnavigate
con-	with	concert
contra-	against	contraband
de-	from, down	depress
deci-	ten	decimeter
di-	two	diameter
dia-	through	diagram
dis-	opposite	disrespect
dys-	bad	dysfunctional
en-, em-	cause to	encode
epi-	upon	epidermis
ex-	out, from	excavate
extra-	beyond	extracurricular
for-	off, to the utmost	forward
fore-	before	forecast
hetero-	different	heterogeneous
hyper-	beyond, excess	hyperactive
hypo-	too little, under	hypoactive
in-, il-, im-, ir-	not	immature
in-, im-	in	infringe
inter-	between	interstate
intra-	within	intramurals

intro-	within	introspection
juxta-	near	juxtapose
macro-	large	macrobiology
meta-	beyond, denoting change	metamorphosis
micro-	small	microbiology
mid-	middle	midway
milli-	thousand	millipede
mis-	bad	misbehave
mono-	single	monotone
nano-	billion	nanosecond
neo-	new	neoclassical
non-	not, opposite from	nonviolent
omni-	all	omnipotent
out-	beyond, more than	outlaw
over-	too much	overcompensate
pan-	all	panoramic
para-	side by side, near	paraphrase
per-	throughout	pervade
peri-	all around	periscope
poly-	many	polygon
post-	after	postpone
pre-	before	predetermine
pro-	forward	progress
prot-	first	prototype
re-	again	reappear
retro-	back	retrospect
semi-	half, partly	semicircle
sub-	under	submarine
super-	more than	supermarket
syn-, sym-	together	symbol
trans-	across	transatlantic
ultra-	beyond, extremely	ultraconservative
un-	not	unwilling
with-	against	withhold

Suffixes

Suffix	Meaning(s)	Example
-able, -ible	can be done	comfortable
-al, -ial	relating to	personal
-arium	place of	solarium
-ation, -ition, -ion, -tion	act, process of	animation
-dom	quality/state	freedom
-ed	past tense for verbs	voted
-en	made of	wooden
-er, -est	comparative	harder
-er	one who	dancer
-ful	full of	hopeful
-ic	relating to	characteristic
-ile	quality/state	juvenile
-ing	present participle	hopping
-ism	quality/state	pauperism
-ist	one who practices	zoologist
-ity, -ty	state of	infinity
-ive, -itive, -ative	adjective form of a noun	quantitative
-less	without	homeless
-ly	characteristic of	happily
-ment	action or process	excitement
-ness	condition of	sadness
-ology	study of	biology
-ous, -eous, -ious	quality, state	joyous
-s, -es	more than one	desks
-tion	quality, state	preservation
-ular	relating to	cellular
-y	characterized by	jumpy

Study Guide

I. Making Connections to What We Know (Activating Background Knowledge):

_____

_____

_____

_____

_____

II. Overview of Content

_____

_____

_____

_____

_____

III. Key Vocabulary

    <u>Word</u>   <u>Page</u>   <u>Predicted Meaning</u>

1. _____ _____ _____

                          _____

2. _____ _____ _____

                          _____

3. _____ _____ _____

_____

IV. Sketch and Label Key Ideas.

Sketch	Sketch

Label **Label**

V. Summary Statement

_____

_____

_____

VI. Questions about the Text

_____

_____

_____

Evaluation of a Content Area Textbook

Directions: 1. Please work with a partner to evaluate a content area textbook.

2. Both of you should record your responses on separate copies of the Evaluation of a Content Area Textbook form.

3. When you and your partner have finished completing your forms and you have shared what you have learned with others, please work on your own to write a summary of the information you recorded on your form and, based on what you have learned, explain whether you would use this textbook in your teaching. Justify your thinking.

4. When you have completed this project, remember to put your completed form and your "Summary and Explanation" into your portfolio.

Text Title: _____

Text Series: _____

Publisher: _____

Copyright Year: _____

Cost: _____

Authors: _____

_____

_____

In reviewing the textbook, your question is this: **Are the following qualities present in the text you are examining?** If your answer is "yes," provide an example of it from the text along with the page number on which the example is located. If your answer is "no," explain whether you would be able to teach effectively if this quality were not present in the textbook.

Evaluation of a Content Area Textbook (Continued)

1. Is the text well-organized (contents, glossary, index, chapter structures)?

2. Is the text factually correct? (Review pages at the beginning, middle, and end of the text to determine if they are factually correct. Include examples of factual text from each page you review.)

3. Is the text motivational? (Is it the kind of text that you think would motivate students at that grade level to learn? Is it colorful? Does it have pictures? Does it include graphics? If you were a student, would you want to use this book?)

4. What is the readability level of the text? For which grade was the textbook developed?

5. Does the textbook support state content standards? Is there evidence of standards-based learning? (Does the text include state standards? Does the textbook indicate which standards the content addresses? What are three examples of standards that are included?)

6. Does the teacher's edition support teachers' use of a strategy-based lesson plan? (Does the text promote using a lesson format similar to the one we have learned—engaging, guiding, and extending student thinking? If so, provide examples.)

7. Is the content diverse? (Is there evidence of multiculturalism in the text? Are people with special needs represented? Are genders treated equally in the text?)

8. Does the text require students to use skills and strategies? (Skill examples would include generating questions and recognizing text patterns. Strategy examples would include previewing—such as the Semantic Map; monitoring—such as Bookmark Technique and Patterned Partner Reading; making connections—such as Connection Stems; knowing how words work—such as the Concept of Definition Map; summarizing—such as the Lyric Summary, Concept of Definition Map Summary, and Bio-Pyramid; and evaluating—such as the Discussion Web.)

9. Does the text integrate content literacy? (Using reading, writing, speaking, listening, and viewing across the curriculum?)

10. Does the text focus on meeting the needs of individual learners? (English language learners, struggling readers, special needs students?)

11. Are multiple types of assessment used throughout the text? (Chapter questions, projects, research, tests, teacher observation?)

12. Are students asked to engage in higher-order thinking throughout the text?

Evaluation of a Content Area Textbook (Continued)

13. How is technology represented throughout the text? How are the students asked to use technology? Teachers?

14. Is a teacher's edition available? Are there special resources for English learners, struggling learners, special needs students?

15. Are the charts, maps, graphs, tables, and illustrations accurate? Do they help to support students' thinking?

16. Are supplementary materials available (text on CD, leveled texts, videos)?

Appendix C

Writing

Admit Slip

What I already know about this topic:

_____

_____

_____

_____

_____

_____

_____

Questions I have about this topic:

1. _____

_____

2. _____

_____

3. _____

_____

4. _____

_____

Content Literacies History Prompts

These prompts have been developed to guide you in creating a history of your content literacies. This is not a definitive list of questions to which you should respond, but rather a sequence of ideas intended to stimulate your thinking about the development of your content literacies, starting with your earliest memories. As you listen to your professor's content literacies history, notice that while he or she may have chosen to include many of the ideas expressed in the prompts, they were not used to restrict your professor's thinking. Use the same creative freedom as you write about your experiences.

Early Memories

1. What are your earliest recollections of reading and writing?

2. Were you read to as a child?

3. Before you were able to read, did you pretend to read books? Can you remember the first time you read a book?

4. As a child, did you read and/or write with your siblings or friends?

5. Can you recall your early writing attempts (scribbling, labeling drawings, and so on)?

6. Was a newspaper delivered to your home? Do you recall seeing others read the newspaper? Did you read the newspaper?

7. Did you subscribe to children's magazines? Did your parents or siblings have magazine subscriptions?

8. Did your parents belong to a book club? Did they maintain a personal library? Did they read for pleasure?

9. Can you recall seeing family members making lists and receiving/sending mail?

10. Did you receive and send mail (such as birthday cards, thank-you notes, and letters) when you were a child?

11. Can you remember any other indications that reading and writing were valued in the environment in which you grew up?

12. What are your early memories of math?

13. What do you recall about using math while playing?

14. What do you remember about using money or seeing money used at this age?

15. What do you recall about historic events that may have occurred early in your life?

16. Do you remember how science may have impacted your life when you were very young?

Content Literacy Prompts (Continued)

School Memories

17. What can you recall about your first memories of reading/writing instruction? Materials used? Methods of teaching? Content?

18. What can you recall about reading for pleasure in elementary school?

19. What can you recall about writing for pleasure in elementary school?

20. What can you recall about the first book you chose to read in elementary school?

21. What can you recall about your first writing assignment in elementary school?

22. Did you write a report in elementary school? What do you remember about this experience?

23. Do you remember the purposes for your reading and writing in elementary school? Do you recall any particular type of instruction you received? Can you describe any instructional materials that were used?

24. What memories do you have of learning vocabulary?

25. When you were in school, what would you have described as the three most important things you learned in content area classes?

26. What do you remember about how you were taught in content area subjects?

27. What do you recall about how you used math and other subjects outside of school?

28. What specific experiences do you recall from your content area classes (math, science, history, English, foreign language) in elementary school? Middle school? High school?

29. Describe people or activities that helped you learn in the content areas.

30. Did you enjoy math class at any particular grade level? Why? Why not?

31. Do you feel comfortable using math now? Why? Why not?

32. If you could change one thing about your experiences in learning in the content areas, what would it be? How would you change it?

33. Did you have a library card when you were in elementary school? Did you use it then? In later school years?

34. Did you consider yourself to be a reader when you were in middle school?

35. Were you required to read certain books when you were in high school? How did you feel about that?

Content Literacy Prompts (Continued)

Reading for Pleasure and Social Purposes

36. Can you recall the first book you "couldn't put down"?

37. Have you ever read a book that has made a difference in your life?

38. Have you ever read a book that you knew had been challenged or censored? How did you feel about reading it?

39. Can you recall pleasurably sharing books with friends?

40. Did you read a certain type of book such as mysteries or biographies) at a particular age? Why do you think you made such choices?

41. When did you first visit a bookstore? What was it like?

42. What is your all-time favorite children's book? Novel? Nonfiction work?

43. Have you ever seen a book you've read turned into a film? Describe that experience.

44. Have there been times in your life when you have viewed reading as a pleasurable activity?

45. Have there been times in your life when you have not viewed reading as a pleasurable activity?

46. What contributions have your reading and writing abilities made to your life?

47. Are you a reader now?

48. Are you a writer now?

49. Do you feel comfortable modeling reading and writing in your content areas for your students?

50. What are you currently reading? Writing?

Information Literacy

51. How would you describe your first experience using a computer?

52. How do you use the Internet in your academic work?

53. How do you use a computer in your everyday life?

54. Why do you communicate through e-mail?

55. Which aspects of technology are you comfortable using?

Critical and Media Literacy

56. What can you recall about questioning the veracity of an information source?

57. Do you question an author's intent or a text's purpose? Provide an example.

58. When you are reading and writing, do you consider multiple perspectives? Provide an example.

59. What memories do you have of reading from a critical perspective?

60. What memories do you have of critically reading/listening to/viewing media?

Content Area Inventory

1. The best thing about the subject I am studying is _____

_____

2. The worst thing about the subject I am studying is _____

_____

3. One way that I use this subject outside of school is _____

_____

4. My favorite part of this class is _____

_____

5. In this class, I like to work in groups to _____

_____

6. In this class, I like to work alone to _____

_____

7. When I use what I am learning, I feel _____

_____

8. My class helps me to _____

_____

9. When I think about this class, I am really proud of _____

_____

10. One thing about this subject I wish I knew more about is _____

_____

Content Area Inventory: Language

1. The best thing about the language I am studying is _____

_____

2. The worst thing about the language I am studying is _____

_____

3. One way that I use this language outside of school is _____

_____

4. My favorite part of language class is _____

_____

5. In language class, I like to work in groups to _____

_____

6. In language class, I like to work alone to _____

_____

7. When I speak the language I am studying, I feel _____

_____

8. My language journal helps me to _____

_____

9. When I am using this language, I am really proud of _____

_____

10. One thing about this language I wish I knew more about is _____

_____

Double-Entry Journal

Name: _____   **Date:** _____

Quotes/Ideas from the Text	Reflections/Questions

Double-Entry Journal

Name: _____   **Date:** _____

Summary

Reflection

Editing Checklist

1. Did the writer use complete sentences?

2. Do the sentences begin with capital letters and end with periods?

3. Is the other punctuation appropriate—apostrophe use, comma use?

4. Is the paper written in the active voice?

5. Is there subject–verb agreement?

6. Did the writer use correct verb tenses?

7. Are the paragraphs indented?

8. Are there simple, compound, and complex sentences?

9. Are tired words used—said, nice, good?

10. Do the pronouns correctly reference the people or items to which they refer?

Journal Prompts

When students are creating journal responses, they may self-select a topic to write about or they may respond to a prompt. Prompts may be particularly effective when introducing the concept of content journals or if you need specific feedback from the students. The following example prompts may be used as presented or adapted to promote journal responses.

1. Explain what you know about _____ (a particular course concept).

2. Describe how you can use technology to facilitate your work in this course.

3. Explain how you can use what you learned in this course this week in another class or in your life outside of school.

4. Use the newspaper or news websites to find examples of how a business in our community uses the subject we are studying. Reflect in your journal about which concepts the business uses and how you think the company might benefit from using our subject in additional ways.

5. Create an acrostic poem or definition poem about a particular concept in our subject area.

6. What is/are_____ (include a particular concept taught in subject area)?

7. Write questions about something in our subject area you are having difficulty understanding or write questions about something we haven't studied yet that you would like to know about.

8. Sketch a _____ (person representing our subject area— mathematician, scientist, historian, writer). How might he or she be employed in our community?

9. Describe a _____ (mathematically, scientifically, historically, literarily) talented character from a book or television series.

10. Create a problem based on a concept we are studying and explain how you would solve it.

Paragraph Frame: Cause/Effect

Cause/Effect Paragraph Frame

As a result of the _____, several agencies took action. Because the

_____, federal agencies

responded. As a result of the _____, the

governor of the state directed the _____

_____. In order to

_____,

local authorities also took action.

Paragraph Frame: Comparison/Contrast

Comparison/Contrast Paragraph Frame

_____ and _____ agree on some topics and disagree

on others. They both support _____

_____ (comparison/similarities),

but they differ on _____

_____ (contrast/differences).

Paragraph Frame: Sequence

Sequence Paragraph Frame

When completing the science experiment, it is important to follow the steps. First,

I will _____. Next, I will _____.

Then I will _____. Following that, I will

_____. Finally, I will _____

_____.

Structured Note Taking

Directions:
1. Sketch the general shape of the sections that appear on the page.
2. Write a subheading and relevant notes in each section.
3. Sketch and describe illustrations that appear on the page.
4. Share and discuss with a partner.

Overview of Text Page: _____

Text Boxes

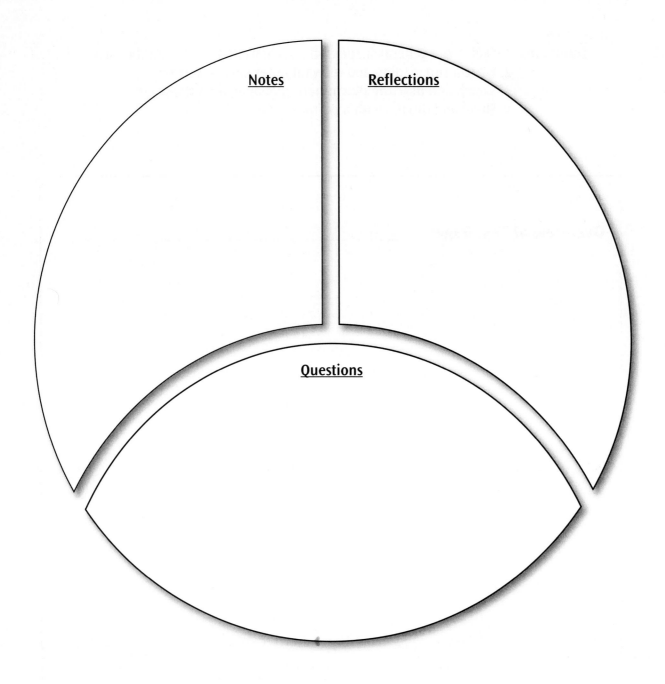

Tickets Out

Ticket Out

The most important thing I learned today is

_____

_____

_____

_____

Ticket Out

One question I have about what I learned today is

_____

_____

_____

_____

Write and Sketch in Math and Science

Write

Sketch

Be a Math or Science Author

Choose a math or science concept and (1) create and solve a problem, (2) design an experiment, or (3) build on the existing concept to create a new math or science concept.

Topic: _____

Checklists and Rubrics

Group Checklist for Rapping for Review

The group

_____ 1. Selected a recently studied content topic to review.

_____ 2. Determined what information they would need.

_____ 3. Used multiple sources to learn essential facts about the topic.

_____ 4. Collaborated well.

_____ 5. Used feedback to revise the rap.

_____ 6. Effectively shared the rap.

Group Comments

_____

_____

_____

_____

Teacher Comments

_____

_____

_____

Names: _____

Date: _____

Internet Inquiry Student Checklist

Directions: Work individually or in small groups organized by interest. Check off each task as you complete it.

_____ 1. Generate research questions about a theme or topics being studied.

_____ 2. Search for responses to the research questions on the Internet.

_____ 3. Analyze the information found online.

_____ 4. Choose a mode to present the findings.

_____ 5. Share the results with the whole class.

Student Comments: _____

_____

_____

Teacher Comments: _____

_____

_____

Observation Checklist: First-Person Experience

The student

_____ 1. Self-selected content-related topic to research.

_____ 2. Determined which person to become.

_____ 3. Selected, accessed, and used relevant information sources.

_____ 4. Sought feedback from several peers during workshop sessions.

_____ 5. Used feedback to revise the project.

_____ 6. Chose a meaningful format for presenting the information.

Comments on Student Performance

_____

_____

_____

_____

_____

Name: _____

Date: _____

Press Conference Student Checklist

_____   1. I chose a topic.

_____   2. I conferenced with the teacher.

_____   3. I used the Questions into Paragraphs (QuIP) organizer.

_____   4. I developed at least three quality research questions.

_____   5. I conducted a viable search for sources.

_____   6. I used at least two quality sources.

_____   7. I demonstrated knowledge of the topic.

_____   8. I presented the Press Conference effectively.

Student's Comments

_____

_____

_____

Teacher's Comments

_____

_____

_____

Name:_____ **Date:**_____

Repeated-Phrase Collaborative Poem Checklist

Group Members

_____ 1. Selected a topic to address in the poem.

_____ 2. Discussed the quotations from which selections would be made.

_____ 3. Brainstormed, discussed, and chose a repeated phrase.

_____ 4. Selected the quotations to include in the poem.

_____ 5. Created a reference list.

_____ 6. Formatted the poem correctly.

_____ 7. Worked well together.

_____ 8. Respected one another's ideas.

Group Comments

_____

_____

_____

Teacher Comments

_____

_____

_____

_____

Names: _____

Date: _____

RUBRICS
Content Area Resource Anthology (CARA) Rubric

Reflection	4_____	3_____	2_____	1
Connections to topic	4_____	3_____	2_____	1
Teaching ideas	4_____	3_____	2_____	1
Differentiated instruction	4_____	3_____	2_____	1
Display of dispositions	4_____	3_____	2_____	1
Use of technology	4_____	3_____	2_____	1
Professional appearance	4_____	3_____	2_____	1

4. Excellent reflection demonstrating depth of reasoning. Outstanding connections to the CARA topic. In-depth, resourceful use of a wide range of creative and innovative teaching ideas, methods, instructional grouping practices (whole-class, small-group, pairs, individual, and computer-based practices), and curriculum materials, including types and levels of text, technology-based information, and nonprint materials for students at differing stages of development and cultural and linguistic backgrounds. Differentiated instruction demonstrates exceptional knowledge of students' abilities, interests, and cultural and linguistic backgrounds. A wide variety of texts (books, articles, technology-based, and nonprint) reflecting students' interests, cultures, and linguistic backgrounds are selected, reviewed, and used. Risk taking is evident. Advanced dispositions related to content area reading are displayed. Fully developed and detailed use of technology. Totally professional in appearance (design, presentation, APA format).

3. Thorough reflection demonstrating sound reasoning. Detailed connections to the CARA topic. Integration of a variety of creative and innovative teaching ideas, methods, grouping practices (whole-class, small-group, pairs, individual, and computer-based), and curriculum materials, including types and levels of text, technology-based information, and nonprint materials for learners at different stages of development and cultural and linguistic backgrounds. Differentiated instruction demonstrates thorough understanding of students' abilities, interests, and cultural and linguistic backgrounds. A variety of texts (books, articles, technology-based, and nonprint) reflecting students' interests, cultures, and linguistic backgrounds are selected, reviewed, and used. Proficient dispositions related to content area reading are displayed. Appropriate use of technology. The paper is professional in appearance (design, presentation, APA format).

2. Adequate reflection demonstrates reasoning. Connections to the CARA topic are somewhat consistent. Teaching ideas, methods, grouping practices (whole-class, small-group, pairs, individual, and computer-based), curriculum materials, including types and levels of text, technology-based information, and non-print materials for learners at different stages of development and cultural and linguistic backgrounds lack variety and creative and innovative perspectives. Differentiated instruction demonstrates adequate knowledge of students' abilities, interests, and cultural and linguistic backgrounds. A limited variety of texts (books, articles, technology-based, and nonprint) reflecting students' interests, cultures, and linguistic backgrounds are selected, reviewed, and used. Developing dispositions related to content area reading are displayed, Limited use of technology. Lacking elements of professional appearance (design, presentation, use of APA format).

1. Inadequate reflection; lacks depth and logical reasoning. Connections to the CARA topic are nonexistent or illogical. Teaching ideas, methods, grouping practices (whole-class, small-group, pairs, individual, and computer-based), curriculum materials, including types and levels of text, technology-based information, and nonprint materials for learners at different stages of development and cultural and linguistic backgrounds are not creative or innovative. Differentiated instruction demonstrates insufficient knowledge of students' abilities, interests, and cultural and linguistic backgrounds. Texts (books, articles, technology-based, and nonprint) have little or no variety and do not reflect students' interests, cultures, and linguistic backgrounds are selected, reviewed, and used. Unacceptable dispositions related to content area reading are displayed. Inadequate use of technology. Less than professional in appearance (design, presentation, APA format).

First-Person Experience Rubric

4.0 Made excellent decisions concerning topic selection. Used outstanding sources. Demonstrated exceptional knowledge of information literacy. Included excellent information. Demonstrated outstanding critical and creative thinking. Chose a superb presentation format. Used workshop format to greatest benefit. Collaborated extremely well with others. Excellent reference list. Outstanding presentation.

3.0 Made very good decisions about topic selection. Used high-quality sources. Demonstrated proficient knowledge of information literacy. Included in-depth information. Demonstrated high levels of critical and creative thinking. Chose a very good presentation format. Used workshop format to great benefit. Collaborated very well with others. Detailed reference list. Skillful presentation.

2.0 Made appropriate decisions concerning topic selection. Used satisfactory sources. Demonstrated adequate knowledge of information literacy. Included essential information. Demonstrated critical and creative thinking. Chose a viable presentation format. Used workshop format to benefit. Collaborated with others. Sufficient reference list. Adequate presentation.

1.0 Made poor decisions about topic selection. Used inadequate sources. Demonstrated insufficient knowledge of information literacy. Included too little information. Demonstrated little critical and creative thinking. Chose a poor presentation format. Used workshop format to little benefit. Did not collaborate well with others. Inadequate reference list. Poor presentation.

Comments:_____

_____

_____

Name:_____**Date:**_____

Oral History Presentation Rubric

4 Distinguished Project: The portrait is thoughtfully selected. Thorough research is evident after reading the news article and viewing the artifacts. Artifacts are present that directly relate to the person's life. The memoir* includes an anecdote. The news article shows a complete understanding of the news article format and is in published form with no major errors. The presenter demonstrates outstanding speaking skills (eye contact, volume, and clarity). Practice for the presentation is clearly evident. The triptych board shows effort and creativity, and the board goes beyond expectations. The board is handed in on time.

3 Proficient Project: The portrait is well chosen. Research is evident after reading the news article and viewing the artifacts. Artifacts relate to the person's life. The memoir* includes an anecdote. The news article shows an understanding of the news article format and has very few editing errors. The presenter demonstrates appropriate speaking skills (eye contact, volume, and clarity). Practice for the presentation is evident. The triptych board shows effort and some creativity. The board follows all guidelines given. The board is handed in on time:

2 Apprentice Project: The portrait shows some thought and planning and is mounted on the board. Only minimal research is evident after reading the news article and viewing the artifacts. Artifacts are present on the board that directly relate to the person's life. The memoir* is mounted on the board and is a narrative timeline. The news article does not demonstrate an understanding of the news article format and needs editing. The presenter needs to improve one or more of the following skills: eye contact, volume, or clarity. More practice is needed in preparing for the oral presentation. The triptych board shows some effort. The board does not follow all of the guidelines given. The board is handed in on time.

1 Novice Project: The portrait shows very little thought and planning. There is very little evidence of research after reading the news article and viewing the artifacts. It is not readily apparent how the artifacts on the board relate to the person's life. The memoir does not include an anecdote. The news article shows a limited understanding of the news article format and many editing errors are present. The presenter needs to improve two or more of the following skills: eye contact, volume, or clarity. Practice is needed in preparing for the oral presentation. The triptych board shows minimal effort and lacks creativity. The board does not follow the guidelines given. The board is not handed in on time.

Source: Diesinger & Kayser, 2000.

Professional Development Resource, Planning, and Presentation Project Rubric

Resource Review	4_____	3_____	2_____	1
Display of Dispositions	4_____	3_____	2_____	1
Professional Development Plan	4_____	3_____	2_____	1
Use of Technology	4_____	3_____	2_____	1
Professional Presentation	4_____	3_____	2_____	1
Evaluation of Peers	4_____	3_____	2_____	1

4 Excellent review of quality resources. Display of advanced dispositions related to reading and the teaching of content during collaborative study groups and peer observation, evaluation, and feedback. Meaningful, detailed, knowledge-based, three-year professional development plan that continues to foster the acquisition of professional knowledge and advanced dispositions. Fully developed and detailed use of numerous types of technology. Totally professional presentation, including knowledge base, appropriate display of advanced dispositions, technology use, and presentation methods. Excellent-quality contributions to collaborative study groups and peer observation, evaluation, and feedback.

3 Skillful review of quality resources. Display of proficient dispositions related to reading and the teaching of content during collaborative study groups and peer observation, evaluation, and feedback. Thorough knowledge-based, three-year professional development plan that continues to foster the acquisition of professional knowledge and proficient dispositions. Good use of technology. Very professional presentation, including knowledge base, display of proficient dispositions, technology use, and presentation methods. Quality contributions to collaborative study groups and peer observation, evaluation, and feedback.

2 Adequate review of quality resources. Display of developing dispositions related to reading and the teaching of content during collaborative study groups and peer observation, evaluation, and feedback. Knowledge-based, three-year professional development plan that continues to foster the acquisition of professional knowledge and advanced dispositions in limited ways. Adequate use of technology. Somewhat professional presentation, including limited knowledge base, display of developing dispositions, technology use, and presentation methods. Satisfactory contributions to collaborative study groups and peer observation, evaluation, and feedback.

1 Inadequate review of resources. Display of unacceptable dispositions related to reading and the teaching of content during collaborative study groups and peer observation, evaluation, and feedback. Poorly designed three-year professional development plan, including insufficient knowledge base, display of unacceptable dispositions, improper technology use, and ineffective presentation methods. Unsatisfactory contributions to collaborative study groups and peer observation, evaluation, and feedback.

Name:_____ Date:_____

Research Project Rubric

CATEGORY	4	3	2	1
Sources (quality, current)	Excellent sources	Very good sources	Adequate sources	Inadequate sources
Research	Outstanding research of topic	In-depth research of topic	Adequate research of topic	Inadequate research of topic
Organization (introduction, body, conclusion)	Excellent organization	Very good organization	Adequate organization	Inadequate organization
Style	Information flows perfectly sensibly and smoothly	Information flows sensibly and smoothly	Information flows somewhat sensibly and smoothly	Information does not flow sensibly and smoothly
APA formatting (citations, references)	APA format is consistently applied with no errors	APA format is consistently applied with a few errors	APA format is consistently applied with several errors	APA format is inconsistently or incorrectly applied
Presentation	Excellent presentation	Very good presentation	Good presentation	Poor presentation

Comments: _____

_____

_____

Name:_____ Date:_____

Restaurant Rubric

Criteria	4 (exceptional)	3 (very good)	2 (acceptable)	1 (poor)
Food	Delicious food	Tasty good food	Edible food	Inedible food
Service	Outstanding service	Attentive service	Adequate service	Inadequate service
Cleanliness	Exceptionally clean	Very clean	Adequately clean	Poor
Atmosphere	Extraordinarily welcoming	Inviting	Acceptable	Uninviting
Location	Excellent	Very good	Acceptable	Unacceptable
Parking	Excellent	Very good	Adequate	Poor

Comments: _____

_____

_____

Student-Authored Electronic Books Rubric

Creativity	4_____3_____2_____1
Quality of information	4_____3_____2_____1
Content area connections	4_____3_____2_____1
Relation of illustrations to text	4_____3_____2_____1
Use of technology	4_____3_____2_____1
Professional appearance	4_____3_____2_____1

4 Outstanding creativity is evident. Excellent-quality information. Exceptional content area connections. Excellent relation of illustrations to text. Fully developed use of technology, Totally professional in appearance (format, conventions of writing, design, text, illustrations, and references).

3 In-depth creativity is evident. High-quality information is consistently used. Proficient content area connections, Skillful relation of illustrations to text. Consistent use of various types of technology. Very professional in appearance (format, conventions of writing, design, text, illustrations, and references).

2 Creativity is evident. Quality of information is adequate. Consistent connections to the content areas. Illustrations and text are related. Use of technology is evident. Professional appearance (format, conventions of writing, design, text, illustrations, and references).

1 Creativity is lacking. Quality of information is inadequate. Inconsistent connections to the content. Illustration and text relations are inappropriate. Poor use of technology. Less than professional in appearance (format, conventions of writing, design, text, illustrations, and references).

Student Comments: _____

_____

_____

Teacher Comments: _____

_____

_____

Name: _____ **Date:** _____

Appendix

E

Appendix Overview

BLACKLINE MASTERS

Alternative Modes of Representation

Bio-Poem

First name

Noun

Four adjectives

Lover of . . . three things

Who enjoys . . . three things

Who believes in . . .

Who wanted to . . . three things

Who uses . . . three things

Who gave us . . . three things

Who said . . .

Last name

Cinquain

_____
One word—noun

_____ _____
Two adjectives describing line one

_____ _____ _____
"ing" words telling actions of line one

_____ _____ _____ _____
Four-word phrase describing a feeling related to line one

_____
**One word—synonym
or reference to line one**

Definition Poem

What is _____ **?**

_____

_____

_____

_____

_____

_____

_____

_____

_____

_____

_____

That is _____ **!**

Diamante

_____
Subject—one noun

_____ _____
Two adjectives describing the subject

_____ _____ _____
Three participles ("ing" words) telling about the subject

_____ _____ _____ _____
Four nouns—first two relate to the first noun, last two to opposite

_____ _____ _____
Three participles ("ing" words) telling about the opposite

_____ _____
Two adjectives describing the opposite

_____
Opposite of subject—one noun

Repeated-Phrase Collaborative Poem Group Planning Sheet

Names: _____

Topic: _____

Repeated Phrase: _____

_____

Three Passages

    Source: _____

Passage 1

Passage 2

Passage 3

Lyric Summary

Directions

- Engage in small-group brainstorming of ideas about the topic or theme.
- Choose a song everyone knows.
- Work together as a group to write your summary as lyrics to the song.
- Sing the Lyric Summary for the whole class.

Brainstormed Ideas

Song Title: _____

Lyric Summary

_____

_____

_____

_____

_____

_____

_____

_____

_____

_____

Project Examples

Content Area Resource Anthology Example

Reflective Introduction Example

Geometry is often thought of as the least-liked class among high school students. It has many abstract concepts that can be difficult to understand for students who are often used to concrete thinking. Until geometry is introduced, students have rarely been exposed to abstract thinking. Often students struggle with abstract thinking because it's a new concept, but sometimes students haven't developed cognitively enough to process abstract thought. Because it's often a difficult concept for students to understand, I chose geometry for my Content Area Resource Anthology (CARA). I believe that the more resources I have to help students comprehend, the more likely they are to understand what they are reading.

I wanted to find resources and innovative techniques for geometry. Using picture books, poems, informational articles, websites, and DVDs is a perfect way to help students grasp very abstract concepts. All students have different learning styles and, therefore, need teachers who use varied teaching styles. This CARA provides a broad range of resources that can be used during lessons to reach different learning styles. These resources also appeal to different intelligences. For example, students who have artistic intelligence will find that poetry helps them become comfortable with the concept.

This collection of resources is a starting point for me to build upon in the future. This anthology guides me in thinking outside the box when designing lesson plans. It serves as a reminder that utilizing resources can help me develop creative, innovative lessons that can intrigue and appeal to students who may have previously been bored with the topic.

Picture Book Example
Source: Micklethwait, L. (2004). *I spy shapes in art.* New York: Greenwillow.

Summary: In this seek-and-find book, students are asked to discover geometric shapes in famous paintings. This book depicts the work of many famous artists, including O'Keeffe, Matisse, Escher, and Warhol.

Teaching Idea: The Rest of the Story. I would incorporate The Rest of the Story teaching idea with *I Spy Shapes in Art*. The students would pick one of the artists whose work is featured in the book and research the artist and the specific piece that incorporated shapes. They would use technology such as a webpage, power point presentation, or exhibition to present their research findings to the class. The students could also present their research findings by creating their own artwork relevant to the era and genre of their artist. They would describe why their art depicts the genre of their artist, why (if known) the artist used those shapes, and the five most interesting facts they learned about the author.

Informational Article Example

Source: Hodara, S. (2007, March 4). From nature's geometry, healing art. *The New York Times*. Retrieved February 25, 2008, from nytimes.com.

Summary: This article, about an artist who paints using geometric shapes, tells of her experience with art and her inspiration from shapes in nature. Geometric shapes such as arcs, circles, and triangles are dominant in her work.

Teaching Idea: Press Conference. I would use this article to stimulate interest in discovering newspaper and magazine articles that relate to geometry. The class will discuss, analyze main points, and share our opinions of this article. I will encourage students to share their views on such issues as whether using shapes is really art. After our discussion, students will search online databases using the library's resources to find an article related to math that interests them. They will read the article using Bookmark Technique. Then they will analyze and critique the article. Finally, they will present Press Conferences in small groups. Group members will ask questions and offer comments regarding the article.

**Student-Authored Electronic
Alphabet Book Example**

H is for...Hieroglyphics

The Ancient Egyptians developed their own form of writing called hieroglyphics. Ancient Egyptian writing uses more than 2,000 hieroglyphic characters. Each hieroglyph represents a common object in ancient Egypt. Hieroglyphs could represent the sound of the object or they could represent an idea associated with the object.

T is for...Tutankhamun

Tutankhamun was only eight or nine years old when he became pharaoh, and he ruled for approximately ten years. Due to his young age, he had a lot of help from advisors when making decisions. He was not a well-liked king and some scientists think that he was murdered. King Tutankhamun is the most famous king found in the Valley of the Kings because his tomb was in almost perfect condition when it was found. The mummy of King Tut was found in 1922 by Howard Carter and Lord Carnarvon.

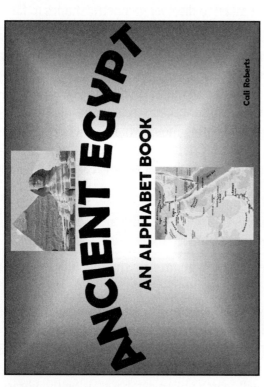

ANCIENT EGYPT

AN ALPHABET BOOK

Cali Roberts

M is for... Mummification

The process of mummification was a method developed by the ancient Egyptians. They preserved the bodies of the dead in order for them to remain lifelike. The process included embalming the bodies and wrapping them in strips of linen and oils.

**Student-Authored Electronic
Informational Book Example**

REAL WORLD MATH

A Comprehensive
Look at the Modern
Day World and the
Jobs That Need Math
to Function.

Joshua C. Miller

Industrial Engineer

◆ Industrial Engineers are extremely important to the industrial world because they use math to help increase the productivity and efficiency of companies. These engineers use math to analyze data to make managerial decisions, design effective work environments, and solve any industrial problems that may arise.

Astronomers and Astrophysicists

◆ Astronomers and astrophysicists use math in their daily findings. These are men and women who study the stars, planets and galaxies that exist in our universe. These men and women often work in places such as NASA. Their discoveries help us to understand the worlds outside of our own.

Architects

◆ Architects are the men and women behind the scenes of all buildings. These men and women use their knowledge of math to create scale model drawings of buildings and people's dream houses. They use math to help calculate the most efficient way to use the space provided and to create the illusion of buildings being bigger than they actually are.

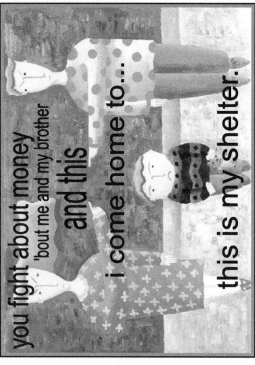

you fight about money
'bout me and my brother
and this
i come home to...
this is my shelter.

in our family portrait
we look pretty happy
let's play pretend, act
like it goes naturally

in our family portrait
we look pretty happy
we look pretty normal
let's go back to that

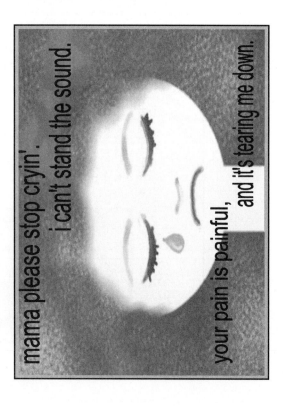

mama please stop cryin'.
i can't stand the sound.

your pain is painful,
and it's tearing me down.

can we work it out?
can we be a family?

i promise i'll be better.
mommy i'll do anything,
daddy please don't leave.

REFERENCES

Abilock, D. (2007). *Building blocks of research: Overview of design, process, and outcomes.* Retrieved May 15, 2009 http://www.noodletools.com/debbie/literacies/information/1over/infolit1.htm/

Afflerbach, P. (2002). Authentic assessment. In B. Guzzetti (Ed.), *Literacy in America: An encyclopedia of history, theory, and practice*, pp. 36–39 Santa Barbara, CA: ABC Publishing.

Aguilar, C. M., Fu, D., & Jabo, C. (2007). English language learners in the classroom. In K. Beers, R. E. Probst, & L. Reif (Eds.), *Adolescent literacy: Turning practice into promise* (pp. 105–125). Portsmouth, NH: Heinemann.

Albright, L. K. (2002). Bringing the Ice Maiden to life: Engaging adolescents in learning through picture book read-alouds in content areas. *Journal of Adolescent & Adult Literacy, 45*(5), 418–429.

Allen, D.D., Cobb, & Danger, S. (2003). Inservice teachers mentoring aspiring teachers. *Mentoring & Tutoring, 11*(2), 177 – 182.

Allington, R. L. (2002). You can't learn much from books you can't read. *Educational Leadership, 60*(3), 16–19.

Almasi, J. F. (1996). A new view of discussion. In L. B. Gambrell & J. F. Almasi (Eds.), *Lively discussions! Fostering engaged reading* (pp. 2–24). Newark, DE: International Reading Association.

Alvermann, D. (1991). The discussion web: A graphic aid for learning across the curriculum. *The Reading Teacher, 45,* 92–99.

Alvermann, D.E., & Nealy, A. (2004). Professional development content for reading educators at the middle and high school levels. In D. Strickland, & M. Kamil (Eds.) *Improving reading achievement through professional development* (pp. 85–94). Norwood, MA: Christopher Gordon.

Anderson, R. C. (1994). Role of reader's schema in comprehension, learning, and memory. In R. B. Ruddell, M. R. Ruddell, & H. Singer (Eds.), *Theoretical models and processes of reading* (4th ed., pp. 469–482). Newark, DE: International Reading Association.

Angaran, J. (1999). Reflection in an age of assessment. *Educational Leadership, 56*(6), 71–72.

Angelou, M. (1993). *Life doesn't frighten me.* New York: Stewart, Tabori, & Chang.

Arter, J. (1996). *Assessing student performance: A professional inquiry kit.* Alexandria, VA: Association for Supervision and Curriculum Development.

Baker, L., & Wigfield, A. (1999). Dimensions of children's motivation for reading and their relations to reading activity and reading achievement. *Reading Research Quarterly, 34*(4), 452–481.

Baker, L., Afflerbach, P., & Reinking, D. (1996). Developing engaged readers in school and home communities: An overview. In L. Baker, P. Afflerbach, & D. Reinking (Eds.), *Developing engaged readers in school and home communities* (pp. xiii–xxvii). Hillsdale, NJ: Lawrence Erlbaum Associates.

Baker, M. (2004). The International Reading Association's literacy study group initiative. In D. Strickland, & M. Kamil (Eds.) *Improving reading achievement through professional development* (pp. 236–237). Norwood, MA: Christopher Gordon.

Banks, J. A., Cookson, P., Gay, G., Hawley, W.D., Irvine, J. J., Nieto, S., Schofield, J. W., & Stephan, W. G. (2001). Diversity within unity: Essential principles for teaching and learning in a multicultural society. *Phi Delta Kappan, 82,* 196–203.

Barton, P. E. (2002). *Staying on course in education reform.* Princeton, NJ: Statistics & Research Division, Policy Information Center, Educational Testing Service.

Beck, I. L., McKeown, M. G., & Kucan, L. (2002). *Bringing words to life: Robust vocabulary instruction.* New York: Guilford Press.

Bell, R. (2001). Implicit instruction in technology integration and the nature of science: There's no such thing as a free lunch. *Contemporary Issues in Technology and Teacher Education,* 1(4), *Contemporary Issues in Technology and Teacher Education* [Online serial], *1*(4). Available: http://www.citejournal.org/vol1/iss4/currentissues/science/article1.htm

Biancarosa, G., & Snow, C. E. (2006). *Reading next—A vision for action and research in middle and high school literacy: A report from the Carnegie Corporation of New York* (2nd ed.). Washington, DC: Alliance for Excellent Education.

Blachowicz, C. L. (2007). *Vocabulary across the curriculum.* Paper presented at the Alaska State Literacy Conference, Anchorage, AK.

Blachowicz, C. L., & Fisher, P. (2000). Vocabulary instruction. In M. Kamil, P. D. Pearson, & R. Barr (Eds.), *Handbook of reading research* (Vol.3, pp. 503–523). Mahwah, NJ: Lawrence Erlbaum Associates.

Blachowicz, C. L., Fisher, P., Ogle, D. M., & Watts-Taffe, S. (2006). Vocabulary: Questions from the classroom. *Reading Research Quarterly, 41*(4), 524–539.

Blessing, C. (2005). Reading to kids who are old enough to shave. *School Library Journal, 51*(4), 44–45.

Block, C. C., Schaller, J. L., Joy, J. A., & Gaine, P. (2002). Process-based comprehension instruction. In C. C. Block & M. Pressley (Eds.), *Comprehension instruction: Research-based best practices* (pp. 42–61). New York: Guilford.

Boise State University. *A guide for mentor teachers, supervisors, and liaisons: Mentoring.* Available at: http://education.boisestate.edu/mentorteacher/Mentoring.htm

Boling, E., Castek, J., Zawilinski, L., Barton, K. & Nierlich, T. (2008). Collaborative literacy: Blogs and Internet projects. *The Reading Teacher, 61*(6), 504–506.

Brabham, E. G., & Villaume, S. K. (2002). Vocabulary instruction: Concerns and visions. *The Reading Teacher, 56*(3), 264–269.

Brandenburg, M.L. (2002). Advanced math? Write! *Educational Leadership, 30*(3), 67–68.

Brandt, R. (1991). Time for reflection. *Educational Leadership, 48*(6), 3.

Brass, J.J. (2008). Local knowledge and digital movie composing in an after-school literacy program. *Journal of Adolescent & Adult Literacy, 51*(6), 464–473.

Brooks, J. G., & Brooks, M. G. (1993). *In search of understanding: The case for constructivist classrooms.* Alexandria, VA: Association for Supervision and Curriculum Development.

Brown, J. A. (1998). Media literacy perspectives. *Journal of Communications, 48*(1), 44–57.

Bruce, B.C., & Bishop, A.P. (2002). Using the Web to support inquiry-based literacy development. *Journal of Adolescent & Adult Literacy, 45*(8), Reading Online, 5*(7). Available: http://www.readingonline.org.

Burke, J. (2002). The Internet reader. *Educational Leadership, 60*(3), 38–42.

Burke, K., & Dunn, R. (2003). Learning style-based teaching to raise minority student test scores. *The Social Studies, 94,* 167–170.

Busching, B. A., & Slesinger, B. A. (1995). Authentic questions: What do they look like? Where do they lead? *Language Arts, 72*(5), 341–351.

California State Board of Education. (n.d.). *History–Social Science Content Standards—Grade 10.* Sacramento, CA: Author.

Cambourne, B. (1995). Toward an educationally relevant theory of literacy learning: Twenty years of inquiry. *The Reading Teacher, 49,* 182–192.

Cambourne, B. (2002). Holistic, integrated approaches to reading and language arts instruction: The constructivist framework on an instructional theory. In A.E. Farstrup & S.J. Samuels (Eds.), *What research has to say about reading instruction* (pp. 25–47). Newark, DE: International Reading Association.

Carlo, M. S., August, D., McLaughlin, B., Snow, C. E., Dressler, C., Lippman, D. N., Lively, T. J., & White, C. E. (2004). Closing the gap: Addressing the vocabulary need of English-language learners in bilingual and mainstream classrooms. *Reading Research Quarterly, 39*(2), 188–215.

Carrier, K. A., & Tatum, A. W. (2006). Creating sentence walls to help English-language learners develop content literacy. *The Reading Teacher, 60*(3), 285–288.

Carroll, A. (Ed.). (2001). *War letters: Extraordinary correspondence from American wars.* New York: Scribner.

Castek, J. Bevans-Mangelson, J, & Goldstone, B. (2006). Reading adventures online: Five ways to introduce the new literacies of the Internet through children's literature. *The Reading Teacher, 59*(7), 714–728.

Checkley, K. (1997). Problem-based learning: The search for solutions to life's messy problems. *ASCD Curriculum Update,* 1–8.

Ciardiello, A. V. (1998). Did you ask a good question today? Alternative cognitive and metacognitive strategies. *Journal of Adolescent and Adult Literacy, 42*(3), 210–219.

Ciardiello, A. V. (2003). "To wander and wonder": Pathways to literacy and inquiry through question-finding. *Journal of Adolescent and Adult Literacy, 47*(3), 228–239.

Ciardiello, A. V. (2007). *Puzzle them first: Motivating adolescent readers with question-finding.* Newark, DE: International Reading Association.

Clinchy, E. (1995). Learning in and about the real world: Recontextualizing public schooling. *Phi Delta Kappan, 76* (5), 400–404.

Coiro, J. (2007). *Exploring changes to reading comprehension on the Internet: Paradoxes and possibilities for diverse adolescent readers.* Unpublished doctoral dissertation, University of Connecticut, Storrs. Available online at http://www.newliteracies.uconn.edu/coirodissertation/

Coiro, J., & Dobler, E. (2007). Exploring the online reading comprehension strategies used by sixth-grade skilled readers to search for and locate information on the Internet. *Reading Research Quarterly, 42,* 214–57.

Coiro, J., Knobel, M., Lankshear, C., & Leu, D.J. (2008). *Handbook of research on new literacies.* Mahwah, NJ: Erlbaum.

Comber, B. (2001). Critical literacies and local action: Teacher knowledge and a "new" research agenda. In B. Comber & A. Simpson (Eds.), *Negotiating critical literacies in classrooms* (pp. 271–282). Mahwah, NJ: Lawrence Erlbaum Associates.

Considine, D. (1995). An introduction to media literacy: The what, why, and how tos. Retrieved May 15, 2009. http://www.ced.Appstate.edu/departments/ci/programs/edmedia/media/it/article/htm/.

Daniels, H. (1994). *Literature circles: Voice and choice in the student-centered classroom.* York, ME: Stenhouse.

Darling-Hammond, L., & Falk, B. (1997). Using standards and assessments to support student learning. *Phi Delta Kappan, 79*(3), 190–199.

Davey, B. (1983). Think-aloud—modeling the cognitive processes of reading comprehension. *Journal of Reading, 27,* 44–47.

Davis, S.J.H. (1997). How mastering technology can transform math class. *Educational Leadership, 55*(3), 49–51.

de Argaez, E. (2006, January). One billion Internet users. *Internet world stats news, 14.* Retrieved February 1, 2006, from http://www.internetworldstats.com/pr/edi014.htm#3

DeBono, E. (1985). *Six thinking hats.* Boston: Little, Brown.

Dickinson, D., Hyler, D., Reilly, L., & Romano, S. (2006). *The oral history project: Connecting students to their community, grades 4–8* Portsmouth, NH: Heinemann.

Diesinger, J., & Kayser, A. (2000). *Oral history project CD-ROM.* BCD Interactive Productions.

Dixon-Krauss, L. (2001/2002). Using literature as a context for teaching vocabulary. *Journal of Adolescent & Adult Literacy, 45*(4), 310–318.

Dodge, B. (1995). *Meet Bernie Dodge: The Frank Lloyd Wright of learning environments.* Retrieved March 2, 2008 from http://www.educationworld.com

Dong, Y. R. (2004/2005). Getting at the content. *Educational Leadership, 62*(4), 14–19.

Douillard, K. (2002). Going past done: Creating time for reflection in the classroom. *Language Arts, 80,* 92–99.

Draper, R. J. (2002). School mathematics reform, constructivism, and literacy: A case for literacy instruction in the reform-oriented math classroom. *Journal of Adolescent and Adult Literacy, 45*(6), 520–529.

Drucker, M. J. (2003). What reading teachers should know about ESL learners. *The Reading Teacher, 57*(1), 22–29.

Duffy, G. (2004). Teachers who improve reading achievement: What research says about what they do and how to develop them. In D. Strickland, & M. Kamil (Eds.) *Improving reading achievement through professional development* (pp. 3–22). Norwood, MA: Christopher Gordon.

Duke, N. (2001). *A new generation of researchers looks at comprehension.* Paper presented at the 51st Annual Meeting of the National Reading Conference, San Antonio, TX.

Duke, N. (2007). *Comprehension throughout the day.* Paper presented at the Alaska State Literacy Conference, Anchorage, AK.

Duke, N., & Pearson, P. D. (2002). Effective practices for developing comprehension. In A. Farstrup & J. Samuels (Eds.), *What research has to say about reading instruction* (3rd ed., pp. 205–242). Newark, DE: International Reading Association.

Duke, N.K., & Pearson, P.D. (2002). Effective practices for developing reading comprehension. In A.E. Farstup & S.J. Samuels (Eds.), *What research has to say about reading instruction* (2nd ed., pp. 205–242). Newark, DE: International Reading Association.

Dunn, R., & Dunn, J. (1993). *Teaching secondary students through their individual learning styles: Practical approach for grades 7–12.* Boston: Allyn and Bacon.

Durkin, D. (1978–1979). What classroom observations reveal about reading comprehension instruction. *Reading Research Quarterly, 14,* 481–533.

Dymock, S. J., & Nicholson, T. (1999) *Reading comprehension: What is it? How do you teach it?* Wellington, New Zealand: New Zealand Council for Educational Research.

Echevarria, J., & Graves, A. (1998). *Sheltered content instruction: Teaching English language learners with diverse abilities.* Boston: Allyn & Bacon.

Echevarria, J., Vogt, M. E., & Short, D. J. (2008). *Making content comprehensible for English learners.* Boston: Allyn and Bacon.

Eick, C.J., & Reed, C.J. (2002). What makes an inquiry oriented science teacher? The influence of learning histories on student teacher role identity and practice. *Science Teacher Education, 86,* 401–416.

Eisner, E. (1999). The uses and limits of performance assessment. *Phi Delta Kappan, 80*(9), 658–660.

Eisner, E. (2006). The satisfactions of teaching. *Educational Leadership, 63*(6), 43–46.

Eisner, E.W. (1993). Forms of understanding and the future of educational research. *Educational Researcher, 22*(7), 5–11.

Eisner, E.W. (1997). Cognition and representation: A way to pursue the American dream? *Phi Delta Kappan, 78*(5), 348–353.

El-Hindi, A. E. (1998). Beyond classroom boundaries: Constructivist teaching with the Internet. *The Reading Teacher, 51*(8), 694–700.

Falk, B. (2002). Standards-based reforms: Problems and possibilities. *Phi Delta Kappan, 83*(8), 612–620.

Ferrara, S., & McTighe, J. (1992). A process for planning: More thoughtful classroom assessment. In A. Costa, J. Bellanca, & R. Fogarty (Eds.), *If minds matter: A forward to the future* (Vol. 2). Palantine, IL: Skylight.

Fisher, D., Flood, J., Lapp, D., & Frey, N. (2004). Interactive read-alouds: Is there a common set of implementation practices? *The Reading Teacher, 58*(1), 8–17.

Fitzgerald, J., & Graves, M. (2004/2005). Reading supports for all. *Educational Leadership, 62*(4), 68–71.

Flint, A. S., & Bomer, R. (2002). Inquiry-based instruction. In B. Guzzetti, Ed. *Literacy in America: An encyclopedia of history, theory, and practice,* (Vol . I, pp. 249–251. Santa Barbara, California: ABC-CLIO.

Flood, J., Lapp, D., Flood, S., & Nagel, G. (1992). Am I allowed to group? Using flexible patterns for effective instruction. *The Reading Teacher, 45*(8), 608–616.

Forbes, L. S. (2004). Using web-based bookmarks in K-8 settings: Linking the Internet to instruction. *The Reading Teacher, 58*(2), 148–153.

Frand, J. (2000). The information age mindset: Changes in students and implications for higher education. *EDUCAUSE Review, 35*(5), 15–24.

Freeman, E. B., & Person, D. G. (1998). *Connecting informational children's books with content area learning.* Boston, MA: Allyn and Bacon.

Freire, P. (1970). *Pedagogy of the oppressed.* New York: Continuum.

Freire, P. (1983). The importance of the act of reading. *Journal of Education, 165,* 5–11.

Freire, P. (1998). *Teachers as cultural workers: Letters to those who dare to teach.* Boulder, CO: Westview.

Fry, E. (1977). Fry's readability graph: Clarifications, validity, and extension to level 17. *Journal of Reading, 21,* 242 – 252.

Fulton, K., Burns, M., & Goldenberg, L. (2005). Teachers Learning in Networked Communities: The TLINC Strategy. *Phi Delta Kappan, 87*(4), 298–305.

Gambrell, L. B. (1996). Creating classroom cultures that foster reading motivation. *The Reading Teacher, 50*(1), 14–25.

Gambrell, L. B. (1996). What research reveals about discussion. In L. B. Gambrell & J. F. Almasi, *Lively discussions! Fostering engaged reading* (pp. 25–38). Newark, DE: International Reading Association.

Gambrell, L. B., Palmer, B. M., Codling, R. M., Mazzoni, S. A. (1996). Assessing motivation to read. *The Reading Teacher, 49(7),* 518–533.

Gamill, D. M. (2006). Learning the write way. *The Reading Teacher, 59(8),* 754–762.

Genesee, F. (Ed.). (1999). Program alternatives for linguistically diverse students. (Educational Practice Report I). Washington, DC: Center for Research on Education, Diversity & Excellence.

Gersten, R., & Baker, S. (2002). What we know effective instructional practices for English-language learners. *Exceptional Children, 55,* 451–471.

Gibson, V., & Hasbrouck, J. (2008). Differentiated instruction. New York: McGraw-Hill.

Gilster, P. (1997). Digital literacy. New York: John Wiley & Sons.

Goldman, S. R., & Rakestraw, J. A. (2000). Structural aspects of constructing meaning from text. In M. Kamil, P. D. Pearson, & R. Barr (Eds.), *Handbook of reading research* (Vol. 3, pp. 311–335). Mahwah, NJ: Lawrence Erlbaum Associates.

Goodrich, H. (1996–1997). Understanding rubrics. *Educational Leadership, 54*(4), 14–17.

Gordon, C. J., & Macinnis, D. (1993). Using journals as a window on students' thinking in mathematics. *Language Arts, 70*, 37–43.

Gratz, D. B. (2000). High standards for whom? *Phi Delta Kappan, 81*, 681–687.

Graves, M. F., & Watts-Taffe, S. M. (2002). The place of word consciousness in a research-based vocabulary program. In A. E. Farstrup & S. J. Samuels (Eds.), *What research has to say about reading instruction* (pp. 140–165). Newark, DE: International Reading Association.

Greene, M. (1997). Metphors and multiples: Representation, the arts, and history. *Phi Delta Kappan, 78*(5), 387–394.

Greenleaf, C.L., & Schoenbach, R. (2004). Building capacity for the responsive teaching of reading in the academic disciplines: Strategic inquiry designs for middle and high school teachers' professional development. In D. Strickland, & M. Kamil (Eds.) *Improving reading achievement through professional development* (pp. 97–128). Norwood, MA: Christopher Gordon.

Guskey, T. (2003). What makes professional development effective? *Phi Delta Kappan, 84*(10), 748–750.

Guthrie, J. (2005). Preparing students for high-stakes test taking in reading. In Z. Fang (Ed.), *Literacy teaching and learning: Current issues and trends* (pp. 285–295). Boston: Allyn and Bacon.

Guthrie, J. T., & Alvermann, D. (Eds.). (1999). *Engagement in reading: Processes, practices, and policy implications.* New York: Teachers College Press.

Guthrie, J. T., & Wigfield, A. (1997). *Reading engagement: Motivating readers through integrated curriculum.* Newark, DE: International Reading Association.

Guthrie, J. T., Wigfield, A., Metsala, J. L., & Cox, K. E. (1999). Motivational and cognitive predictors of text comprehension and reading amount. *Scientific Studies of Reading, 3*(3), 231–256.

Haag, C. C., & Williams, J. (2004). Classroom language: Inviting all students to participate. In F. B. Boyd, C. H. Brock, & M. S. Rozendal (Eds.), *Multicultural and multilingual literacy and language* (pp. 54–74). New York: Guilford.

Hadaway, N. L., & Young, T. (2006). Changing classrooms: Transforming instruction. In T. Young & N. L. Hadaway (Eds.), *Supporting the literacy development of English learners* (pp. 6–21). Newark, DE: International Reading Association.

Haertel, E. H. (1999). Performance assessment and educational reform. *Phi Delta Kappan, 80*(9), 662–666.

Haggard, M. R. (1986). The vocabulary self-collection strategy: Using student interest and world knowledge to enhance vocabulary growth. *Journal of Reading, 29*(7), 634–642.

Halford, J.M. (1998). Easing the way for new teachers. *Educational Leadership, 55*, 33–36.

Halford, J.M. (1999). Policies to support new teachers. *Educational Leadership, 56*(8), 85. Retrieved March 26, 2001, from the World Wide Web: http://www.ascd.org/

Harris, T. L., & Hodges, R. E. (Eds.). (1995). *The literacy dictionary: The vocabulary of reading and writing.* Newark, DE: International Reading Association.

Harste, J., Burke, C., & Short, K. (1988). *Creating classrooms for authors.* Portsmouth, NH: Heinemann.

Harvey, S., & Goudvis, A. (2000). *Strategies that work: Teaching comprehension to enhance understanding.* York, ME: Stenhouse.

Herman, J. L., & Winters, L. (1994). Portfolio research: A slim collection. *Educational Leadership, 52*(2), 48–55.

Herman, J. L., Ashbacher, P. R. & Winters, L. (1992). A practical guide to alternative assessment. Alexandria, VA: Association for Supervision and Curriculum Development.

Hiebert, E. (1994). Becoming literate through authentic tasks: Evidence and adaptations. In R. B. Ruddell, M. R. Ruddell, H. Singer (Eds.), *Theoretical models and processes of reading (4th ed.).* Newark, DE: International Reading Association.

Hiebert, E. H., Pearson, P. D., Taylor, B. M., Richardson, V., & Paris, S. G. (1998). *Every child a reader.* Ann Arbor, MI: Center for the Improvement of Early Reading Achievement.

Hoffman, J. V., Assaf, L. C., & Paris, S. G. (2001). High-stakes assessments in reading: Today in Texas, tomorrow? *The Reading Teacher 54*(5), 482–492.

Holloway, B. (2001). The benefits of mentoring. *Educational Leadership, 58*(8), 85–86.

Holmes, K., Powell, S., Holmes, S., & Witt, E. (2007). Readers and book characters: Does race matter? *The Journal of Educational Research, 100*(5), 276–282.

Hosking, N. J. (2000). *Student-centered literacy instruction in the middle years.* Dubuque, IA: Kendall/Hunt Publishing Company.

Howe, N. (2005). Harnessing the power of millennials: New education strategies for a confident, achieving youth generation. *School Administrator, 62*(8).

Howe, N., & Strauss, W. (2000). *Millennials rising: The next great generation.* New York: Vantage Books.

Howe, N., & Strauss, W. (2001). The rise of the millennials. *The Futurist,* 7.

Hoyt, L. (1992). Many ways of knowing: Using drama, oral interactions, and the visual arts to enhance reading comprehension. *The Reading Teacher, 45* (8), 580–584.

International Reading Association & National Council Teachers of English. (1996). *Standards for the English language arts.* Newark, DE: Authors.

International Reading Association, Commission on Adolescent Literacy. (August/September 2001). Adolescent literacy: Seven principles. *Reading Today, 18*(7), 23.

International Reading Association. (2000). *Excellent reading teachers: A position statement of the International Reading Association.* Newark, DE : IRA.

International Reading Association. (2007). IRA Standards for Reading Professionals – Excerpts from the Revised Role Definitions. Newark, DE: International Reading Association.

Isaacson, W. (2007). *Einstein: His life and universe.* New York: Simon & Schuster.

Ivey, G. (2000). Redesigning reading instruction *Educational Leadership, 58*(1), 42 – 45.

Jennings, P., & Brewster, T. (1998). *The century.* NewYork: Doubleday.

Johnson, C. C. (2006). Effective professional development and change in practice: Barriers science teachers encounter and implications for reform. *School Science & Mathematics, 106*(3), 150–161.

Johnson, D. D., & Pearson, P. D. (1984). *Teaching reading vocabulary* (2nd ed.). New York: Holt, Rinehart and Winston.

Johnson, D., & Zufall, L. (2004). Web watch not just for kids anymore: Webquests for professional development. *Reading Online*, 26–30.

Johnston, P. (1997). *Knowing literacy: Constructive literacy assessment.* York, Maine: Stenhouse Publishers.

Kadjer, S. B. (2007). Unleashing potential with emerging technologies. In K. Beers. R.E. Probst, & L. Reif (Eds.), *Adolescent reading: Turning promise into practice* (pp. 213 – 229). Portsmouth, NH: Heinemann.

Kamil, M., & Lane, D. (1998). Researching the relation between technology and literacy: An agenda for the 21st century. In D. Reinking, M.C. McKenna, L.D. Labbo, & R.D. Keiffer (Eds.), *Handbook of literacy and technology: Transformations in a post-typographic world* (pp. 323 – 341). Mahwah, NJ: Erlbaum.

Keene, E., & Zimmermann, S. (1997). *Mosaic of thought: Teaching comprehension in a reader's workshop.* Portsmouth, NH: Heinemann.

Kelleher, J. (2003). A model of assessment-driven professional development. *Phi Delta Kappan, 84*(10), 751–756.

Keller, B. (2003). Teachers travel the globe for professional development. *Education Week, 23*(14), 8. (12/3/2003)

Keller, B. (2006). New mentoring program found helpful for novice teachers in NYC. *Education Week, 25*(36), 7. (5/10/2006)

Kifer, E. (2001). *Large-scale assessment: Dimensions, dilemmas, and policies.* Thousand Oaks, CA: Corwin Press.

Kist, W. (2000). Beginning to create the new literacy classroom: What does the new literacy look like? *Journal of Adolescent & Adult Literacy, 43*(8), 710–718.

Kist, W. (2002). Finding 'new literacy' in action: An interdisciplinary high school western civilization class. *Journal of Adolescent & Adult Literacy, 45*(5), 368–377.

Knipper, K. J., & Duggan, T. J. (2006). Writing to learn across the curriculum: Tools for comprehension in content area classes. *The Reading Teacher, 59(5),* 462–470.

Koskinen, P., Blum, I., Bisson, S., Phillips, S., Creamer, T., & Baker, T. (1999). Shared reading, books, and audiotapes: Supporting diverse students in school and at home. *The Reading Teacher, 52*(5), 430–444.

Kramer, M. C. (2001). Triumph out of the wilderness: A reflection on the importance of mentoring. *Phi Delta Kappan, 82*(5), 411–412.

Krashen, S. (1982). *Principles and practice in second language acquisition.* Oxford, UK: Pergamon.

Langer, J. & Applebee, A. (1985). Learning to write: Learning to think, *Educational Horizons, 64,* 1, 36–39.

Langer, J. (1981). From theory to practice: A prereading plan. *Journal of Reading, 25,* 152–156.

Lasear, D. (1991). *Seven ways of teaching: The artistry of teaching with multiple intelligences.* Palatine, IL: Skylight Publishing, Inc.

Leahy, S., Lyon, C., Thompson, M., & Wiliam, D. (2005). Classroom assessment: Minute by minute, day by day. *Educational Leadership, 63*(3), 19–24.

Lefkowits, L., & Miller, K. (2006). Fulfilling the promise of the standards movement. *Phi Delta Kappan, 87*(5), 403–407.

Lester, J. H. (2003). Planning effective secondary professional development programs. *American Secondary Educations, 32*(1), 49–61.

Leu, D. J. (2000). Our children's future: Changing the focus of literacy and literacy instruction. *The Reading Teacher, 53*(5), 424–429.

Leu, D. J. (2001). Internet project: Preparing students for new literacies in a global village. *The Reading Teacher, 54,* 568–572.

Leu, D. J. (2002). Internet workshop: Making time for literacy. *The Reading Teacher, 55,* 466–472.

Leu, D. J. (2002). The new literacies: Research on reading instruction with the Internet. In A. E. Farstrup & S. J. Samuels (Eds.), *What research has to say about reading* (3rd ed., pp. 310–336). Newark, DE: International Reading Association.

Leu, D. J., Coiro, J., Castek, J., Hartman, D. K., Henry, L. A., & Reinking, D. (2008). Research on instruction and assessment in the new literacies of online reading Comprehension. In C. C. Block and S. Parris (Eds.) (pp. 321–347). *Comprehension instruction: Research-based best practices.* New York: Guilford Press.

Leu, D. J., Jr., & Kinzer, C. K. (1999). Effective reading instruction K-8 (4th ed.). Englewood Cliffs, NJ: Merrill.

Leu, D.J., Jr., & Kinzer, C.K. (2000). The convergence of literacy instruction and networked technologies for information and communication. *Reading Research Quarterly, 35,* 108–127.

Leu, D. J., Kinzer, C. K., Coiro, J. L., & Cammack, D. W. (2004). Toward a theory of new literacies emerging from the Internet and other information and communication technologies. In R. B. Ruddell & N. J. Unrau (Eds.), *Theoretical Models and Processes of Reading* (5th ed., pp. 1570–1613). Newark, DE: International Reading Association.

Leu, D.J., & Leu, D.D. (1999). *Teaching with the Internet: Lessons from the classroom* (2nd ed.) Norwood MA: Christopher-Gordon Publishers.

Leu, D.J., Zawilinski, L., Castek, J., Banerjee, M., Housand, B.C., Liu, Y., & O'Neil, M. (2007). What is new about the new literacies of online reading comprehension? In L. S. Rush, A. J. Eakle, & A. Berger (Eds.) (pp. 37–68). *Secondary School Literacy: What Research Reveals for Classroom Practice.* Urbana, IL: National Council Teachers of English.

Lewin, L. (1998). *Great performances: Creating classroom-based assessment tasks.* Alexandria, VA: ASCD.

Lewis, J., & Day, G. (2004). Continuing professional development for teachers. *Journal of Biological Education, 38*(3), 144–146.

Lidz, C. S. (1995). Dynamic assessment and the legacy of L. S. Vygotsky. *School Psychology International, 16,* 143–153.

Lipson, M. Y. (2001). A fresh look at comprehension. Paper presented at the Reading Language Arts Symposium, Chicago, Illinois.

Lipson, M. Y., & Wixson, K. (2009). *Assessment and instruction of reading and writing difficulties: An interactive approach* (4th ed.). Boston: Allyn & Bacon.

Littman, C. B., & Stodolsky, S. S. (1998). The professional reading of high school academic teachers. *Journal of Educational Research, 92*(2), 75–85.

Lonergan, D. (1997). Network science: Bats, birds, and trees. *Educational Leadership, 55*(3), 34–36.

Long, S. A., Winograd, P. N., & Bridge, C. A. (1989). The effects of reader and text characteristics on imagery reported during and after reading. *Reading Research Quarterly, 24*(3), 353–372.

Long, S.A., Winograd, P.A., & Bridge, C.A. (1989). The effects of reader and text characteristics on reports of imagery during and after reading. *Reading Research Quarterly, 24,* 353–372.

Lonsdale, M., & McCurry, D. (2004). *Literacy in the new millennium.* Formal report: National Centre for Vocational Education Research. Retrieved May 15, 2009. http://www.ncver.edu.au./research/proj/nr2.pdf

Luke, A., & Freebody, P. (1999). Further notes on the four resources model. *Reading Online.* Retrieved May 15, 2009, from http://www.reading.org/publications/ROL/.

Macon, J.M. (1991). Bio-Pyramid. In J.M. Macon, D. Bewell, & M.E.Vogt (Eds). *Responses to literature: Grades K-8.* Newark, DE: International Reading Association.

Madaus, G. F., & Kellaghan, T. (1993). Testing as a mechanism of public policy: A brief history and description. *Measurement and Evaluation in Counseling and Development, 26,* 6–10.

Madaus, G. F., & O'Dwyer, L. M. (1999). A short history of performance assessment. *Phi Delta Kappan, 80*(9), 688–695.

Mandel, S. (2006). What new teachers really need. *Educational Leadership, 63*(6), 66–69.

Mansilla, V.B., & Gardner, H. (1997). Of kinds of disciplines and kinds of understanding. *Phi Delta Kappan, 78*(5), 381–386.

Manzo, A. V. (1969). The ReQuest procedure. *The Journal of Reading, 13*(2), 123–126.

March, T. (2003/2004). The learning power of WebQuests. *Educational Leadership, 61*(4), 42–46.

Maring, G., Furman, G., & Blum-Anderson, J. (1985). Five cooperative learning strategies for mainstreamed youngsters in content area classrooms. *The Reading Teacher, 39*(3), 310–313.

Marsalis, W. (2005). *Jazz A-B-Z: An ABC collection of jazz portraits.* Cambridge, MA: Candlewick Press.

McCullough, D. (2001). *John Adams.* New York: Simon & Schuster.

McGinley, W. & Denner, P. (1987). Story impressions: A prereading/prewriting activity. *Journal of Reading, 31,* 248–253.

McKeown, M. G., & Beck, I. L. (1993). Grappling with text ideas: Questioning the author. *The Reading Teacher, 46*(7), 16–21.

McLaughlin, E.M. (1987). QuIP: A writing strategy to improve comprehension of expository structure. *The Reading Teacher, 40*(7), 650–654.

McLaughlin, M. (1995). *Performance assessment: A practical guide to implementation.* Boston, MA: Houghton Mifflin.

McLaughlin, M. (2001). Sociocultural influences on content literacy teachers' beliefs and innovative practices. Paper presented at the 51st Annual Meeting of the National Reading Conference, San Antonio, TX.

McLaughlin, M. (2003). *Guided Comprehension in the primary grades.* Newark, DE: International Reading Association.

McLaughlin, M., & Allen, M. B. (2002a). *Guided Comprehension: A teaching model for grades 3–8.* Newark, DE: International Reading Association.

McLaughlin, M., & Allen, M. B. (2002b). Guided Comprehension in action. Newark, DE: International Reading Association.

McLaughlin, M., & Allen, M. B. (2009). *Guided Comprehension in grades 3–8* (2nd ed.). Newark, DE: International Reading Association.

McLaughlin, M., & DeVoogd, G. (2004a). Critical literacy as comprehension: Expanding reader response. *Journal of Adolescent and Adult Literacy, 48*(1), 42–52.

McLaughlin, M., & DeVoogd, G. (2004b). *Critical literacy: Enhancing students' comprehension of text.* New York: Scholastic.

McLaughlin, M., & Kennedy, A. (1993). A classroom guide to performance-based assessment. Princeton, NJ: Houghton Mifflin.

McLaughlin, M., & Vogt, M. E. (1996). *Portfolios in teacher education.* Newark, DE: International Reading Association.

McLaughlin, M., & Vogt, M.E. (1998) Portfolio assessment for inservice teachers: A collaborative model. In M. McLaughlin, M. E. Vogt, J. Anderson, J. Dumez, M. G. Peter, & A. Hunter *Professional portfolio models: Applications in education,* (pp. 1–70) Norwood, MA: Christopher-Gordon.

McNergney, R. F., & Herbert, J. M. (1998). *Foundations of education: The challenge of professional practice* (2nd ed.). Boston, MA: Allyn and Bacon.

McPherson, J.M. (2002). *Field of Fury: The American Civil War.* New York: Atheneum.

McTighe, J., & O'Connor, J. (2005). Seven keys to effective learning. *Educational Leadership, 63*(3), 10–17.

Means, B. (2000/2001). Technology use in tomorrow's schools. *Educational Leadership, 58*(4), 57–61.

Mike, D. G. (1996). Internet in the schools: A literacy perspective. *Journal of Adolescent and Adult Literacy, 40*(1), 4–13.

Miller, K.R. & Levine, S.J. (2008). *Biology.* Upper Saddle River, NJ: Prentice Hall.

Minick, N. (1987). Implications of Vygotsky's theories for dynamic assessment. In C. S. Lidz (Ed.) *Dynamic assessment: An interactional approach for evaluating learning potential* (pp. 116–140). New York: Guilford.

Moje, E. B. (1996). "I teach students, not subjects": Teacher–student relationships as contexts for secondary literacy. *Reading Research Quarterly, 31*(2), 172–195.

Moorman, G., & Horton, J. (2007). Millennials and how to teach them. In J. Lewis & G. Moorman (Eds.), *Adolescent literacy instruction: Policies and promising practices* (pp. 263–285). Newark, DE: International Reading Association.

Morrison, T.G., & Chilcoat, G.W. (1998). The "Living Newspaper Theatre" in the language arts classroom. *Journal of Adolescent and Adult Literacy, 42* (2), 104–115.

Morrow, L. M., Cunningham, K., & Murray-Olsen, M. (1994). *Current strategies for literacy development in early childhood science texts* (Reading Research Report, No. 11). College Park, MD: Reading Research Center.

Mtetwa, D. K. J., & Kwari, R. (2003). Peer mentoring by resource teachers in Zimbabwean schools. *Mentoring & Tutoring: Partnership in Learning, 11*(3), 273–283.

Murray, D. M. (2007). Teach writing your way. In K. Beers, R . E. Probst, & L. Reif (Eds.), *Adolescent reading: Turning promise into practice* (pp. 179–187). Portsmouth, NH: Heinemann.

Nagy, W. (1988). *Teaching vocabulary to improve reading comprehension.* Newark, DE: International Reading Association.

National Commission on Excellence in Education. (1983). *A nation at risk: The imperative for educational reform.* Washington, DC: U.S. Department of Education.

National Commission on Teaching and America's Future. (1997). *Doing what matters most: Investing in quality teaching.* Available at http://www.tc.columbia.edu/-teachingcomm.

National Council of Teachers of Mathematics. (1989). *Curriculum and evaluation standards for school mathematics.* Reston, VA: Author.

National Reading Panel. (2000). *Teaching children to read: An evidence-based assessment of the scientific research literature on reading and its implications for reading instruction.* Washington, DC: National Institutes of Health.

Noddings, N. (1997). Thinking about standards. *Phi Delta Kappan, 79*(3), 184–189.

Northwest Central Regional Educational Laboratory (NCREL) & Metiri Group. (2003). *21st century skills: Literacy in the digital age.* http://www.metiri.com/features.html Downloaded May 15, 2009.

Northwest Regional Educational Laboratory (NWREL). (2001). Teacher Mentoring Programs. Available at http://www.nwrel.org/request/may01/mentoring.html

Oblinger, D. (2003). Boomers, Gen-Xers & Millennials: Understanding the new students. Educase Review, 37–47.

Ogle, D. (1986). K-W-L: A teaching model that develops active reading of expository text. *The Reading Teacher, 39,* 564–570.

Ogle, D. (2000). Making it visual: A picture is worth a thousand words. In M. McLaughlin & M.E. Vogt (Eds.), *Creativity and innovation in content area teaching* (pp. 55–71). Norwood, MA: Christopher-Gordon.

Opitz, M. F., & Harding-DeKam, J. L. (2007). Understanding and teaching English-language learners. *The Reading Teacher, 60*(6), 590–593.

Oravec, J. A. (2002). Bookmarking the world: Weblog applications in education. *Journal of Adolescent & Adult Literacy, 45*(7), 616–621.

Pallotta, J. (2004). *The battle alphabet book.* Watertown, MA: Charlesbbridge Publishing.

Palmer, R. G., & Stewart, R. A. (1997). Nonfiction trade books in content area instruction. *Journal of Adolescent and Adult Literacy, 40,* 630–641.

Patrick, H., & Yoon, C. (2004) Early adolescents' motivation during science investigation. *Journal of Educational Research, 97*(6), 319–328.

Pearson, P. D. (2001). What we have learned in 30 years. Paper presented at the 51st Annual Meeting of the National Reading Conference, San Antonio, TX.

Pearson, P. D., Hiebert, E. H., & Kamil, M. L. (2007). Vocabulary assessment: What we know and what we need to learn. *Reading Research Quarterly, 42*(2), 282–296.

Peregoy, S. F., & Boyle, O. F. (2005). English learners reading English: What we know, what we need to know. In Z. Fang (Ed.), *Literacy teaching and learning: Current issues and trends* (pp. 18–27). Upper Saddle River, NJ: Pearson/Merrill/Prentice Hall.

Perkins-Gough, D. (2007). Focus on adolescent English language learners. *Educational Leadership, 64*(6), 90–91.

Pew Internet & American Life Project (2001). The Internet and education: Findings of the Pew Internet & American Life Project. Retrieved May 15, 2009 from http://www.pewInternet.org/reports <http://www.pewinternet.org/reports>.

Pilgreen, J. (2006). Supporting English learners: Developing academic language in the content area classroom. In T. Young & N. L. Hadaway (Eds.), *Supporting the literacy development of English learners* (pp. 41–60). Newark, DE: International Reading Association.

Pressley, M. (2000). What should comprehension instruction be the instruction of? In M. Kamil, P. Mosenthal, P. D. Pearson, & R. Barr (Eds.), *Handbook of reading research* (Vol. 3, pp. 545–561). Mahwah, NJ: Lawrence Erlbaum Associates.

Pressley, M. (2002). *Reading instruction that works: The case for balanced teaching* (2nd ed.). New York: Guilford.

Pressley, M., & Afflerbach, P. (1995). *Verbal protocols of reading: The nature of constructively responsive reading.* Hillsdale, NJ: Lawrence Erlbaum Associates.

Raphael, T. (1986). Teaching children question–answer relationships, revisited. *The Reading Teacher, 39,* 516–522.

Ravitch, D. (1995). *National standards in American education.* Washington, DC: Brookings Institute.

Readence, J., Bean, T., & Baldwin, R. (2000). *Content area reading: An integrated approach* (7th ed.). Dubuque, IA: Kendall Hunt.

Reif, L. (2007). Writing: Commonsense matters. In K. Beers, R.E. Probst, & L. Reif (Eds.), *Adolescent reading: Turning promise into practice* (pp. 189–208). Portsmouth, NH: Heinemann.

Reigeluth, C. M. (1997). Educational standards: To standardize or to customize learning? *Phi Delta Kappan, 79*(3), 202–206.

Reinking, D. (1998). Introduction: Synthesizing technological transformations of literacy in a post-typographic world. In D. Reinking, M. McKenna, L. Labbo, & R. Kieffer (Eds.), *Handbook of literacy and technology* (pp. xi–xxx). Mahwah, NJ: Lawrence Erlbaum Associates.

Richard-Amato, P.A. (1988). *Making it happen: Interaction in the second language classroom.* New York: Longman.

Richardson, J. (2004). Content area literacy lessons go high tech. *Reading Online, 8*(1), 6–16.

Richek, M. A. (2005). Words are wonderful: Interactive, time-efficient strategies to teach meaning vocabulary. *The Reading Teacher, 58*(5), 414–423.

Robinson, F. P. (1946). *Effective study* (2nd ed.). New York: Harper & Row.

Roit, M. L. (2006). Essential comprehension strategies for English learners. In T. Young & N. L. Hadaway (Eds.), *Supporting the literacy development of English learners* (pp. 80–95). Newark, DE: International Reading Association.

Romano, T. (2007). Teaching writing from the inside. In K. Beers. R.E. Probst, & L. Reif (Eds.), *Adolescent reading: Turning promise into practice* (pp. 167–178). Portsmouth, NH: Heinemann.

Rosenblatt, L. (2002, December). *A pragmatist theoretician looks at research: Implications and questions calling for answers.* Paper presented at the 52nd annual meeting of the National Reading Conference, Miami, Florida.

Rosenblatt, L. M. (1978). *The reader, the text, and the poem: The transactional theory of the literary work.* Carbondale, IL: Southern Illinois University Press.

Ruddell, R. B. (1995). Those influential reading teachers: Meaning negotiators and motivation builders. *The Reading Teacher, 48,* 454–463.

Ruddell, R. B. (2004). Researching the influential literacy teacher: Characteristics, beliefs, strategies, and new research directions. In R. B. Ruddell & N. J. Unrau (Eds.), *Theoretical models and processes of reading* (5th ed., pp. 979–997). Newark, DE: International Reading Association.

Rupley, W. H., Logan, J. W., & Nicholas, W. D. (1998/1999). Vocabulary instruction in a balanced reading program. *The Reading Teacher, 52*(4), 336–346.

Salomon, G. (1997). Of mind and media: How culture's symbolic forms affect learning and thinking. *Phi Delta Kappan, 78*(5), 375–380.

Santa, C. M. (2006). A vision for adolescent literacy: Ours or theirs? *Journal of Adolescent and Adult Literacy, 49*(6), 466–476.

Santoro, L. E., Chard, D. J., Howard, L., & Baker, S. K. (2008). Making the very most of classroom read-alouds to promote comprehension and vocabulary. *The Reading Teacher, 61*(5), 396–408.

Savage, J. (1998). *Teaching reading and writing: Combining skills, strategies, and literature* (2nd ed.). Boston, MA: McGraw-Hill.

Savery, J. R., & Duffy., T. M. (1995). Problem-based learning: An instructional model and its constructivist framework. *Educational Technology, 35,* 31–38.

Scharrer, E. (2002–2003). Making a case for media literacy in the curriculum: Outcomes and assessment. *Journal of Adolescent & Adult Literacy, 46*(4), 354–358.

Schmar-Dobler, E. (2003). Reading on the Internet: The link between literacy and technology. *Journal of Adolescent and Adult Literacy, 47*(1), 80–85.

Schmitt, N., & Carter, R. (2000). The lexical advantages of narrow reading for second language learners. *TESOL Journal, 9*(1), 4–9.

Schmoker, M., & Marzano, R. J. (1999) Realizing the promise of standards-based education. *Educational Leadership, 56*(6), 17–21.

Schoenbach, R., Greenleaf, C., Cziko, C., & Hurwitz, L. (1999). *Reading for understanding.* San Francisco: Jossey-Bass.

Schon, D. (1987). *Educating the reflective practitioner.* San Francisco, CA: Jossey-Bass.

Schwartz, D. M. (2001). *Q is for quark: A science alphabet book.* Berkeley, California: Tricycle Press.

Schwartz, R., & Raphael, T. (1985). Concept of definition: A key to improving students' vocabulary. *The Reading Teacher, 39*(2), 198–205.

Scribner, S., & Cole, M. (1981). *The psychology of literacy.* Cambridge, MA: Harvard University Press.

Serafini, F. (2003, February). Informing our practice: Modernist, transactional, and critical perspectives on children's literature and reading instruction. *Reading Online, 6*(6). Available: http://www.readingonline.org/articles/art_index.asp?HREF=serafini/index.html. Downloaded May 15, 2009.

Shank, M.J. (2005). Mentoring among high school teachers: A dynamic and reciprocal group process. *Mentoring and Tutoring, 13*(1) 73–82.

Shepard, L.A. (2005). Linking formative assessment to scaffolding. *Educational Leadership, 63*(3), 66–70.

Short, D., & Echevarria, J. (2004/2005). Teacher skills to support English language learners. *Educational Leadership, 62*(4), 8–13.

Short, K. G., & Burke, C. (1996). Examining our beliefs and practices through inquiry. *Language Arts, 73,* 97–103.

Short, K., Harste, J., & Burke, C. (1996). *Creating classrooms for authors and inquirers.* Portsmouth, NH: Heinemann.

Shurtz, J. (November, 1998). *. . . and YOU are there! Helping your students write about history.* Unpublished workshop handout. Springfield, MO: Drury College Reading Conference.

Silverblatt, A. (2000, September). Media literacy in the digital age. *Reading Online, 4*(3). http://www.readingonline.org/newliteracies/lit_index.asp?HREF=/newliteracies/silverblatt/index.html.

Singer, D. G., & Singer, J. L. (1998). Developing critical viewing skills and media literacy in children. *Annals of the American Academy of Political and Social Science, 557,* 164–180.

Sippola, A. E. (1995). K-W-L-S. *The Reading Teacher, 48*(6), 542–543.

Sippola, A. E. (1995). K-W-L-S. *The Reading Teacher, 48,* 542–543.

Smith, F. (1997). *Reading without nonsense.* New York: Teachers College Press.

Stahl, S., & Kapinus, B. (1991). Possible sentences: Predicting word meaning to teach content area vocabulary. *The Reading Teacher, 45,* 36–43.

Stepien, B. & Gallagher, S. A. (1993). Problem-based learning: As authentic as it gets. *Educational Leadership, 50*(7), 25–28.

Stepien, B., & Gallagher, S. A. (1997). Infusing critical thinking skills into the problem-based learning process. A paper presented at the Assessment-Instruction Connection: ASCD Conference on Teaching and Learning, Orlando, Florida.

Stiggins, R., & DuFour, R. (2009) Maximizing the power of formative assessments. *Phi Delta Kappan, 90*(9), 640–644.

Strickland, D., & Kamil, M. (2004). *Improving reading achievement through professional development.* Norwood, MA: Christopher Gordon.

Summers, S. L. (2000, October). Get 'em thinking! Using the "3 Rs" of media literacy. *Reading Online, 4*(4). http://www.readingonline.org/newliteracies/lit_index.asp?HREF=/newlitera-cies/summers/index.html.

Teachers of English to Speakers of Other Languages (TESOL). (2006). *PreK – 12 English Language Proficiency Standards in the core content areas.* http://dcsd.k12.nv.us/pdc/2006_ tesol_proficiency_stds.htm Downloaded May 15, 2009.

Thompson, S. (2001). The authentic standards movement and its evil twin. *Phi Delta Kappan, 82,* 358–362.

Tierney, R. (1998). Literacy assessment reform: Shifting beliefs, principled possibilities, and emerging practices. *The Reading Teacher, 51*(5), 374–389.

Tierney, R. (2008). The agency and artistry of meaning makers within and across digital spaces. In S.E. Israel, & G.G. Duffy (Eds.) (pp. 261–288) *Handbook of Research on Reading Comprehension.* Lawrence Erlbaum Associates.

Tierney, R.J., & Pearson, P.D. (1983). Toward a composing model of reading. *Language Arts, 60,* 569–580.

Tomlinson, C. A. (2000). Reconcilable differences? Standards-based teaching and differentiation. *Educational Leadership, 58*(1), 6–11.

Tomlinson, C.A. (1999). *The differentiated classroom: Responding to the needs of all learners.* Alexandria, VA: Association for Supervision and Curriculum Development

Tomlinson, C.A., & Doubet, K. (2005). Reach them to teach them. *Educational Leadership, 62*(7), 8–15.

Topping, D.H., & McManus, R.A. (2002). A culture of literacy in science. *Educational Leadership, 60*(3), 30–33.

Trubowitz, S. (2004). The why, how, and what of mentoring. *Phi Delta Kappan, 85*(1), 59–62.

Trubowitz, S., & Robins, M. (2003). *The good teacher mentor: Setting the standard for support and* success. New York: Teachers College Press.

Tyner, B., & Green, S. E. (2005). *Small-group reading instruction: A differentiated model for intermediate readers, grades 3–8.* Newark, DE: International Reading Association.

Tyson, H., & Woodward, A. (1989). Why students aren't learning very much from textbooks. *Educational Leadership, 47*(3), 14–17.

Valencia, S. W. (1998). *Literacy portfolios in action.* Fort Worth, Texas: Harcourt Brace.

Vardell, S. M., Hadaway, N. L., & Young, T. A. (2006). Matching books and readers: Selecting literature for English learners. *The Reading Teacher, 59*(8), 734–741.

Vaughn, J., & Estes, T. (1986). *Reading and reasoning beyond the primary grades.* Boston: Allyn and Bacon.

Villegas, A. M., & Lucas, T. (2007). The culturally responsive teacher. *Educational Leadership, 64*(6), 28–33.

Vogt, M.E. (2000). Active learning: Dramatic play in the content areas. In M. McLaughlin and M.E. Vogt (Eds.), *Creativity and innovation in content area teaching* (pp. 73–90). Norwood, MA: Christopher Gordon Publishers.

Vogt, M. E., & McLaughlin, M. (2004). Teaching and learning in a global society: Examining changing definitions of literacy. In M. Pandis, A. Ward, & S. R. Mathews (Eds.), *Reading, writing, thinking: Proceedings of the 13th European Conference on Reading.* Newark, DE: International Reading Association.

Vygotsky, L. (1978). *Mind in society.* Cambridge, MA: Harvard University Press.

Vygotsky, L. S. (1987). The development of scientific concepts in childhood. In R. W. Rieber & A. S. Carton (Eds.) *The collected works of L. S. Vygotsky. Vol.1.* New York: Plenum.

Wagner, B.J., & Barnett, L.A. (1998). *Educational drama and language arts: What research shows.* Portsmouth, NH: Heinemann.

Waldo, B. (1991). Story pyramid. In J.M. Macon, D. Bewell, & M.E.Vogt (Eds). *Responses to literature: Grades K-8* (pp. 23–24). Newark, DE: International Reading Association.

Weber, E. (1999). *Student assessment that works. A practical approach.* Boston: Allyn Bacon.

Wiggins, G., & McTighe, J. (1998). *Understanding by design.* Alexandria, VA: Association for Supervision and Curriculum Development.

Wiggins, G., & McTighe, J. (2006). Examining the teaching life. *Educational Leadership, 63*(6), 26–29.

Wiggins, G., & McTighe, J. (2008). Put understanding first. *Educational Leadership, 65*(8), 36–41.

Willis, S. (1996). Student exhibitions put higher-order skills to the test. *Education Update, 38* (2), 1, 3. Alexandria, VA: Association for Supervision and Curriculum Development.

Young, T. A., & Hadaway, N. L. (2006). *Supporting the literacy development of English learners.* Newark, DE: International Reading Association.

Zemelman, S., Daniels, H., & Hyde, A. (2005). *Best practice: New standards for teaching and learning in America's schools,* (3rd ed.). Portsmouth, NH: Heinemann.

NAME INDEX

Abilock, D., 14, 23
Afflerbach, P., 9, 46, 235
Aguilar, C. M., 139–140, 151
Albright, L. K., 132
Allen, D. D., 113, 126, 259, 260
Allen, M. B., 4, 20, 48, 59, 66–67, 72, 94, 222, 226
Allington, R. L., 15
Almasi, J. F., 8, 43
Alvermann, D., 9, 85–86
Anderson, R. C., 8, 43, 232
Angaran, J., 251
Angelou, M., 75, 226
Apfel, M., 86
Applebee, A., 158
Arter, J., 243, 245
Ashbacher, P. R., 238
Assaf, L. C., 39
August, D., 155

Baker, C., 240–241
Baker, L., 9
Baker, M., 263
Baker, S. K., 132, 153
Baker, T., 143
Baldwin, R., 49, 113
Banerjee, M., 182–184
Banks, J. A., 25
Barnett, L. A., 219, 226
Barton, K., 189
Barton, P. E., 39
Basquiat, J-M., 226
Bean, T., 49, 113
Beck, I. L., 118, 154
Bell, A. G., 202
Bell, R., 182
Bevans-Mangelson, J. 179
Biancarosa, G., 7, 15–17, 26, 90, 91
Bishop, A. P., 194
Bishop, D., 72, 130
Bisson, S., 143
Blachowicz, C. L., 94–96
Blake, G., 35
Blessing, C., 134
Block, C. C., 46
Blum, I., 143
Boling, E., 189
Bomer, R., 195
Booth, J. W., 83
Boyle, O. F., 139, 144
Brabham, E. G., 94
Bradbury, R., 65
Brandenburg, M. L., 157
Brandt, R., 235

Brass, J.J., 178
Brewster, T., 172
Bridge, C. A., 73
Brooks, J. G., 7, 226, 234, 235
Brooks, M. G., 7, 226, 234, 235
Brown, J. A., 24
Bruce, B. C., 194
Burke, C., 7, 56, 67, 82, 154, 226
Burke, E., 55
Burke, J., 182
Burke, K., 5
Busching, B. A., 119

Cambourne, B., 2, 7, 8, 9, 43, 232
Cammack, D. W., 14, 23, 43, 151, 180, 182
Carlo, M. S., 155
Carrier, K. A., 154
Carter, R., 154
Castek, J., 178, 179, 182–184, 189
Chard, D. J., 132
Checkley, K., 196
Chilcoat, G.W., 221
Ciardiello, A. V., 65, 88, 119, 120, 122, 123
Clinchy, E., 235
Cobb, J. B., 259, 260
Codling, R. M., 9
Coiro, J. L., 14, 23, 43, 151, 178, 180, 181, 182, 184
Cole, M., 15
Columbus, C., 17–18
Comber, B., 19, 20
Considine, D., 24
Cookson, P., 25
Cox, K. E., 9
Creamer, T., 143
Cunningham, K., 118
Cziko, C., 15

Danger, S., 259, 260
Daniels, H., 33, 131
Darling-Hammond, L., 33, 37–38
Davey, B., 143
Davis, S. J. H., 178
DeArgaez, E., 178
Denner, P., 53
DeVoogd, G., 18–20, 45
Dickinson, D., 173
Dickinson, E., 60
Dixon-Krauss, L., 94
Dobler, E., 181
Dodge, B., 188
Dong, Y. R., 139, 153, 155, 156
Doubet, K. 34
Douillard, K., 235

Draper, R. J., 8
Dressler, C., 155
Drucker, M. J., 138
Duffy, G., 261
Duffy, T. M., 7, 43
DuFour, R., 239
Duggan, T. J., 158
Duke, N. K., 2, 43, 44, 46, 94, 157
Dunn, J., 5
Dunn, R., 5
Dupuis, P., 35
Durkin, D., 43
Dymock, S. J., 124

Echevarria, J., 139, 140, 144, 147, 153
Eick, C. J., 195
Einstein, A., 202
Eisner, E. W., 211, 212, 229, 251
El-Hindi, A. E., 180
Engle, M., 73
Estes, T., 66, 82, 113, 122

Falk, B., 31, 33, 37–38
Fernandez, M., 65
Ferrara, S., 231
Fisher, D., 132
Fisher, P., 95–96
Fitzgerald, J., 138
Fitzpatrick, D., 34
Flint, A. S., 195
Flood, J., 115, 132
Flood, S., 115
Forbes, L. S., 190
Frand, J., 6
Freebody, P., 19, 45
Freeman, E. B., 132
Freire, P., 18, 19, 232
Frey, N., 132
Fu, D., 139–140, 151

Gaine, P., 46
Gallagher, K. M., 206
Gallagher, S. A., 197, 198
Galler, E., 75
Gambrell, L. B., 9, 43
Gamill, D. M., 157–158
Gardner, H., 212
Gay, G., 25
Genesee, F. 144
Gersten, R., 153
Gibson, V., 113, 114
Gilster, P., 181
Goldman, S. R., 45, 124
Goldstone, B., 179

SUBJECT INDEX

Academic standards. *See* Standards-based teaching
Academic vocabulary development, 153–154
Accessible texts, 145–147
Accommodations, in assessment process, 237
Accountability, standards-based teaching and, 31, 33
Acrostic Poems, 213–214
Adapted text, 144
Admit Slips, 161, 337
Adolescent literacy
    nature of, 15
    teacher knowledge of, 16–17
Aesthetic stance, 45
After-reading activities, for English language learners
    (ELL), 150–152
Alliance for Excellent Education, 26
Alphabet Books, 173, 225–226, 227–228
Alternative modes of representation, 370–375
Anticipation/Reaction Guide, 49–50, 113
Art, 223–229
    instructional strategies based on, 223–229
    nature of, 223
Articles, as content area texts, 133–134
Assessment. *See also* Course-based assessment; High-stakes
    assessments
    authentic, 235
    classroom assessment plan, 237–238
    current thinking about, 232–237
    defined, 231
    dynamic nature of, 234–235
    of formal writing, 174
    glossary of terms, 233
    of informal writing, 171
    of inquiry-based learning (IBL), 207–209
    multiple response formats, 237
    portfolios in, 248–251
    professional development and, 257–258
    reflective, 232–233, 235–236
    standards in, 236, 250
Authentic assessment, 235

Background knowledge, 8, 139–140, 158–161, 254
Backward mapping, 28–29, 33
Be a Math or Science Author, 166, 355
Before-reading activities, for English language learners
    (ELL), 148–159
Being literate, 15
"Big picture," 10
Bio-Impressions, 53–55
Bio-Poem, 370
Bio-Pyramids, 79, 113, 283
Blackline masters, 283–320, 322–335, 337–355, 376–380
Blogs, 189
Bookmark Technique, 66–67, 106–107, 113, 127, 149, 284–285
Boolean searching, 183

Cause and effect
    cause/effect clues, 97
    text pattern, 125
Checklists, 357–361
    editing, 346
    First-Person Experience, 359
    Internet Inquiry 358
    Press Conference, 360
    Rapping for Review, 357
    Repeated-Phrase Collaborative Poem, 361
Cinquains, 214–215, 371
Classroom assessment plan, 237–238
Classroom organization and management. *See also* Instructional
    strategies; Lesson plans
    professional development and, 112–136, 257
Coding the Text, 57–59
Collaborative learning, 16
    professional development and, 254, 263
    to support English language learners (ELL), 142
Communicating information, 184, 241, 251
Compact discs (CDs), 131–132, 144, 146, 255
Comparison and contrast, text pattern, 124
Comparison/contrast clues, 96–97
Comprehension. *See* Reading comprehension
Concept of Definition Maps, 100–101, 113, 150, 168–170,
    242, 286, 287
Connections in comprehension. *See* Making connections
Connection Stems, 55–56, 149
Connection role in Discussion Circles, 131
Constructivism
    assessment and, 232
    collaborative learning and, 16, 142
    in formative assessment, 241
    nature of, 7–9, 43
    student construction of meaning, 8, 139–140
    writing and, 157–158
Content Area Inventory, 158–159
Content Area Resource Anthology (CARA), 191–193, 362
Content areas, 15–17
    standards-based teaching in, 28–31
    texts in. *See* Content area texts
    writing in, 174–176. *See also* Writing
Content area texts
    accessible, 145–147
    adapted for English language learners, 144
    on compact disc or tape, 131–132, 144, 146, 255
    critical literacy and, 18–19, 22, 180
    diversity of, 17
    expanded notion of, 18–19, 22, 132–134
    methods of class-based reading, 126–134
    nature of, 10
    professional development and, 255
    questions to evaluate, 119
    in reading comprehension, 46–47